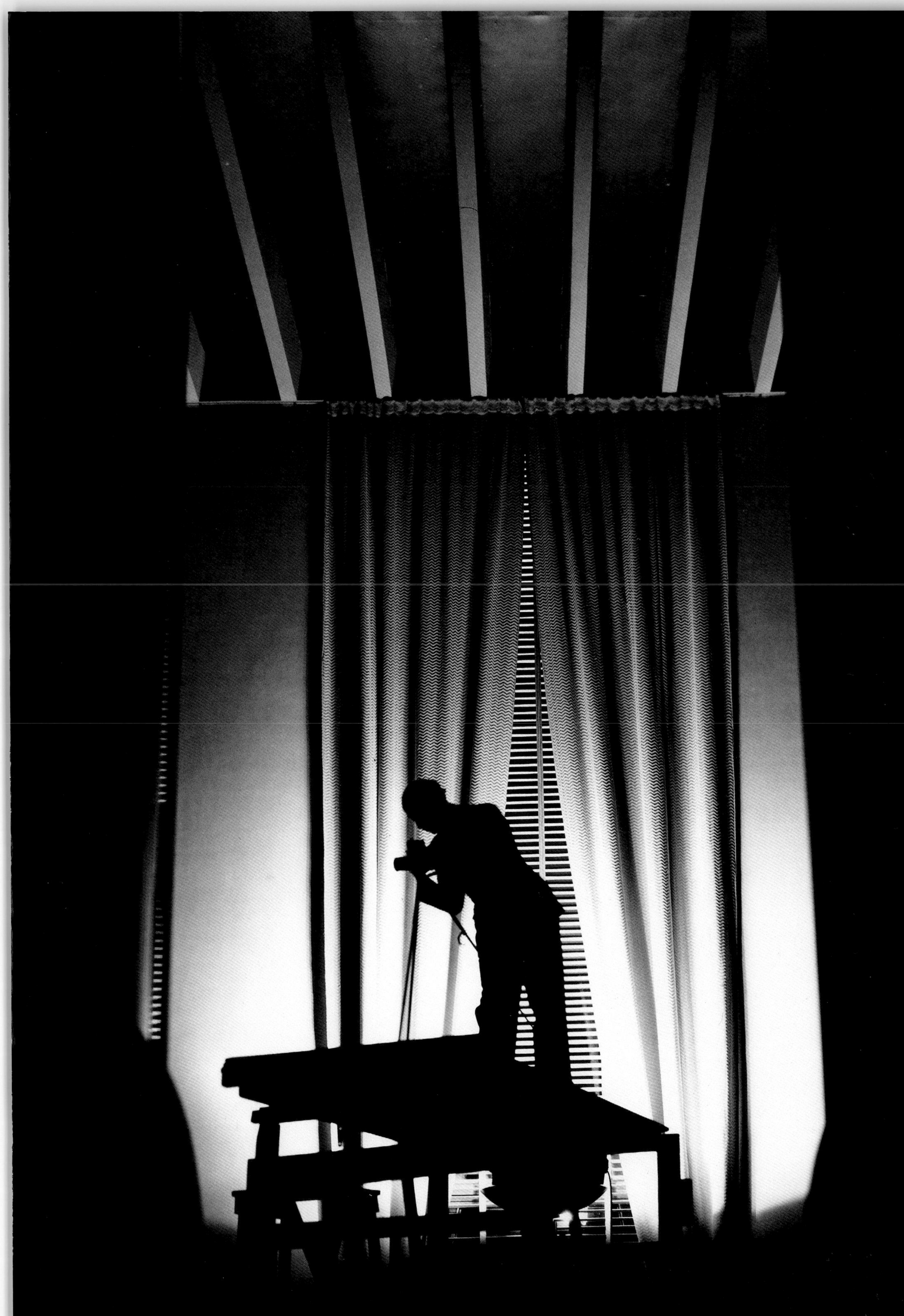

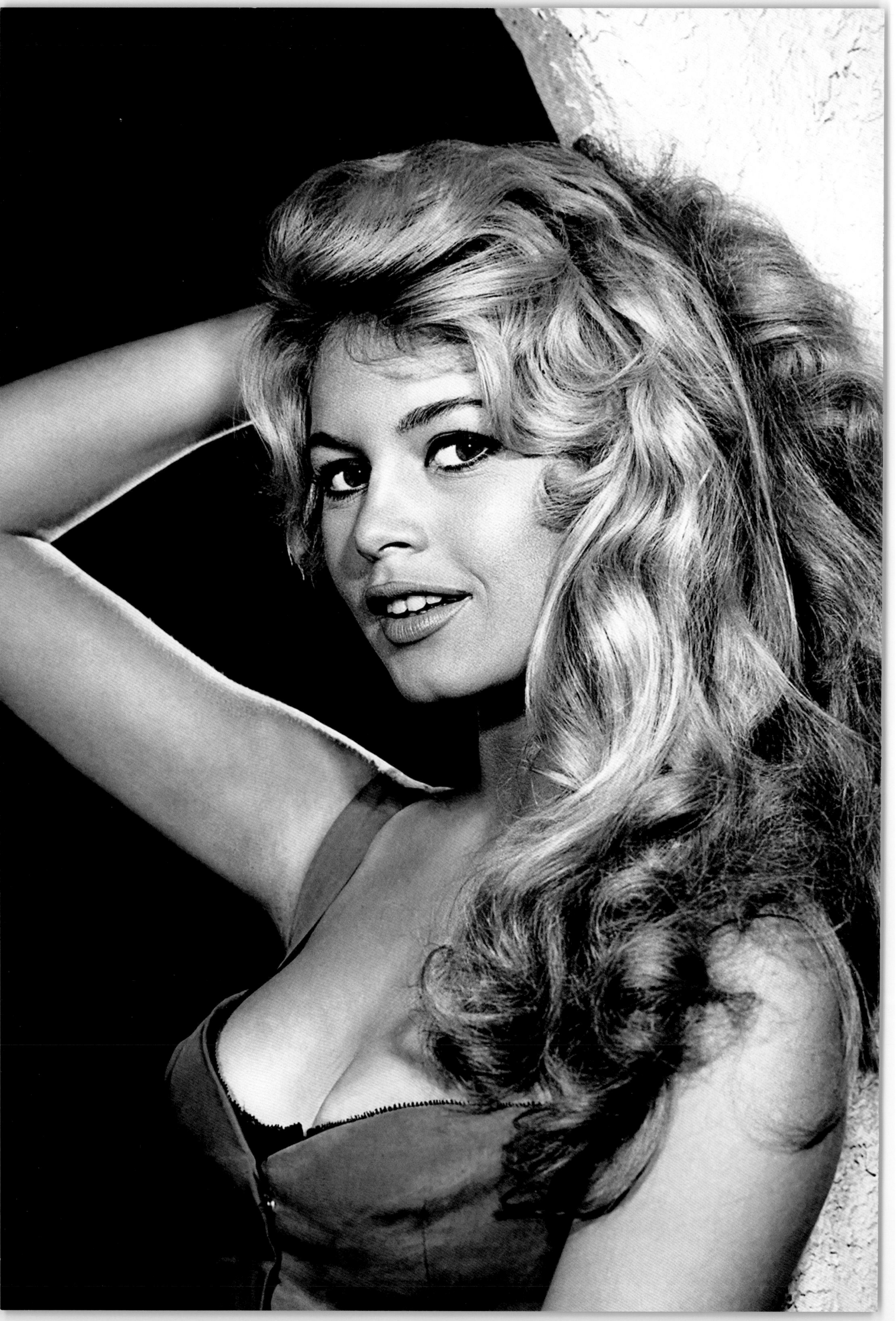

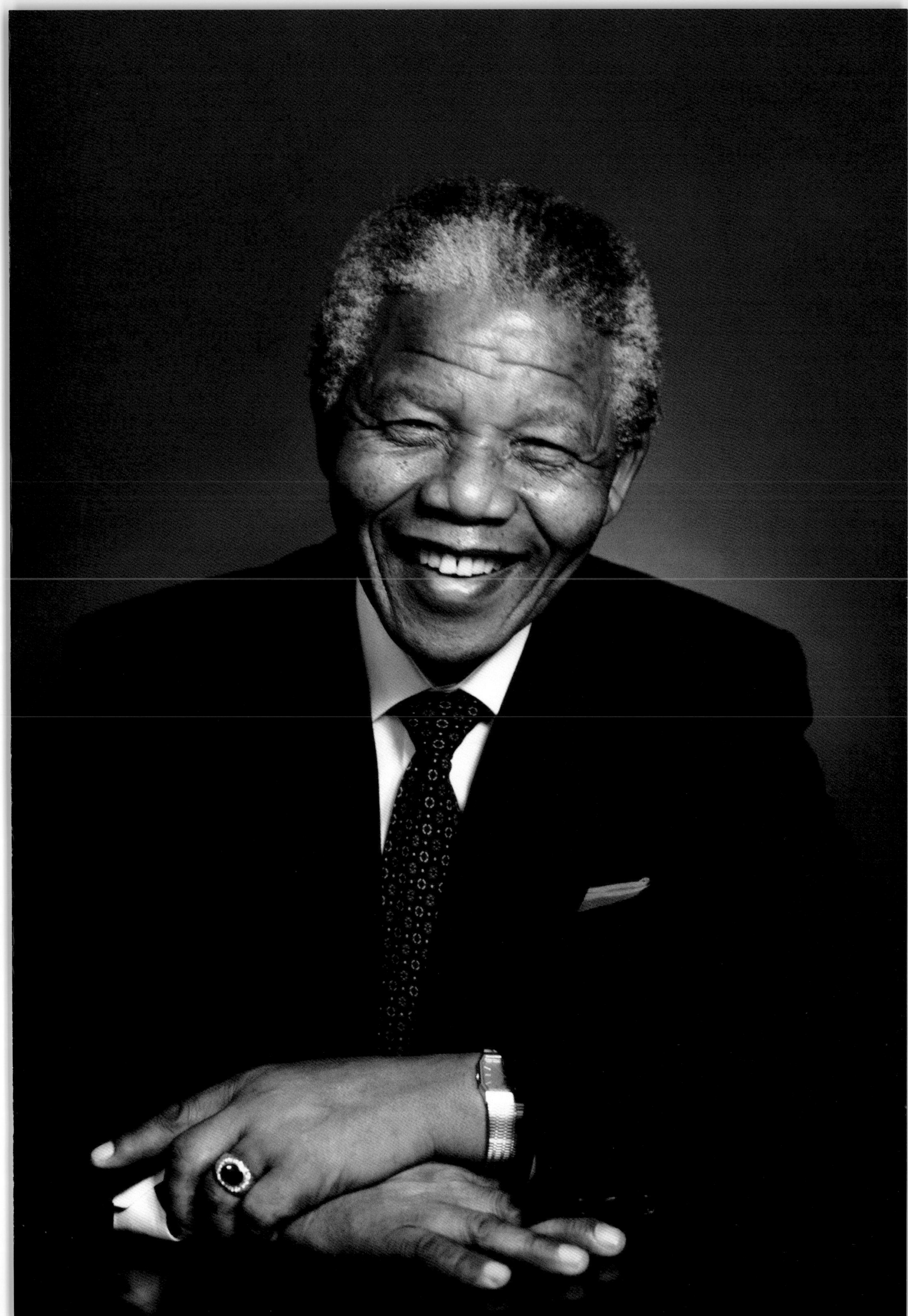

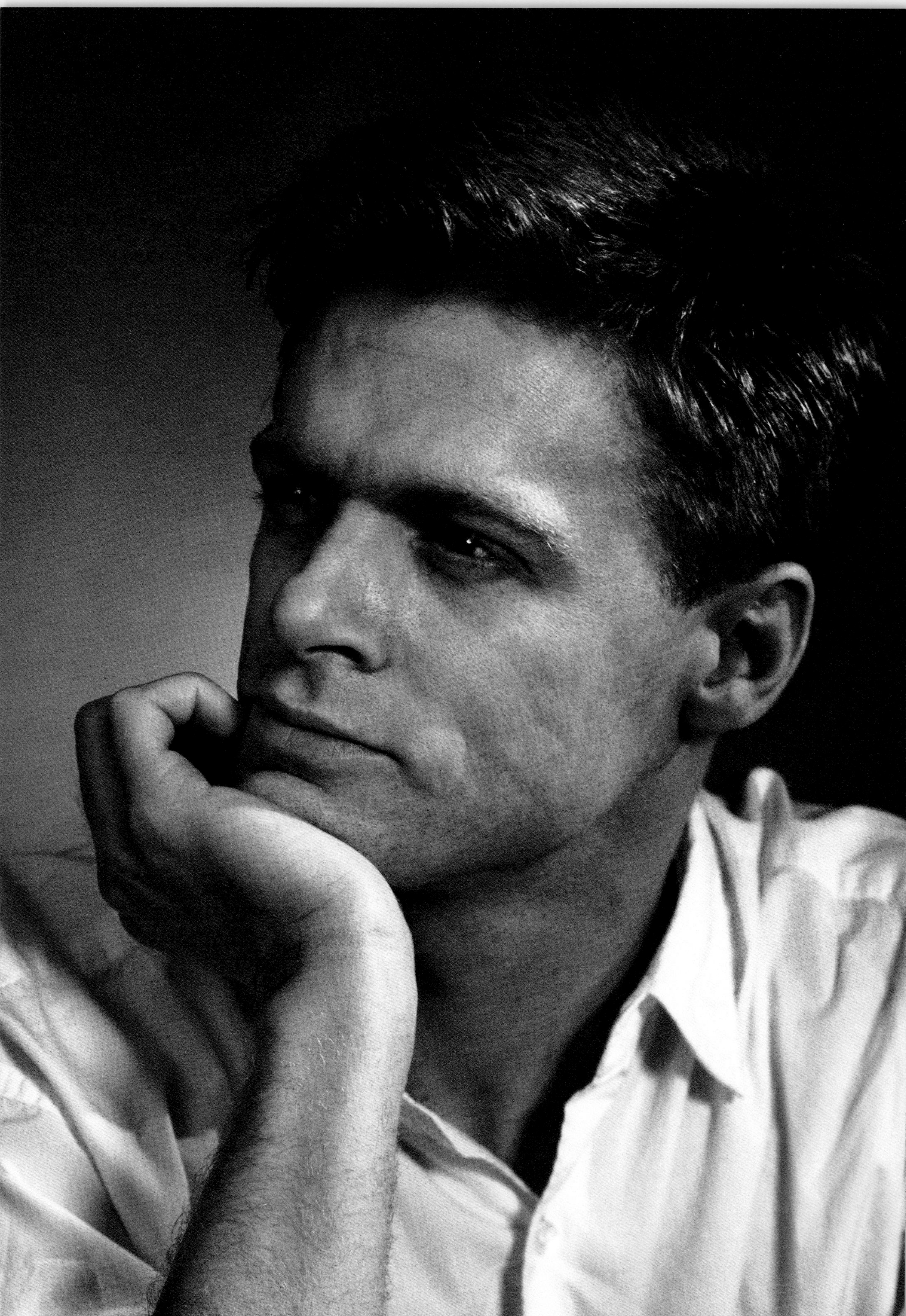

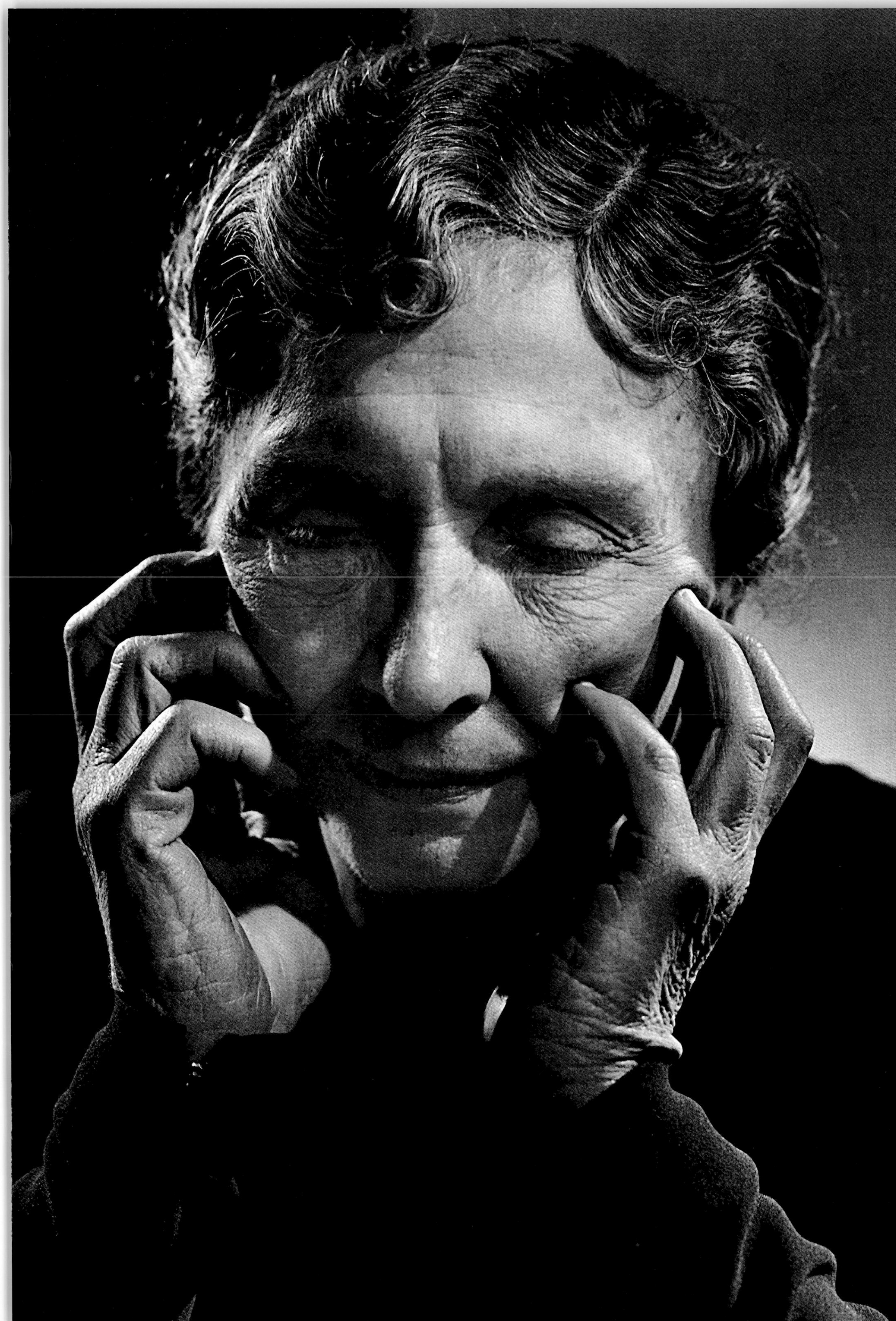

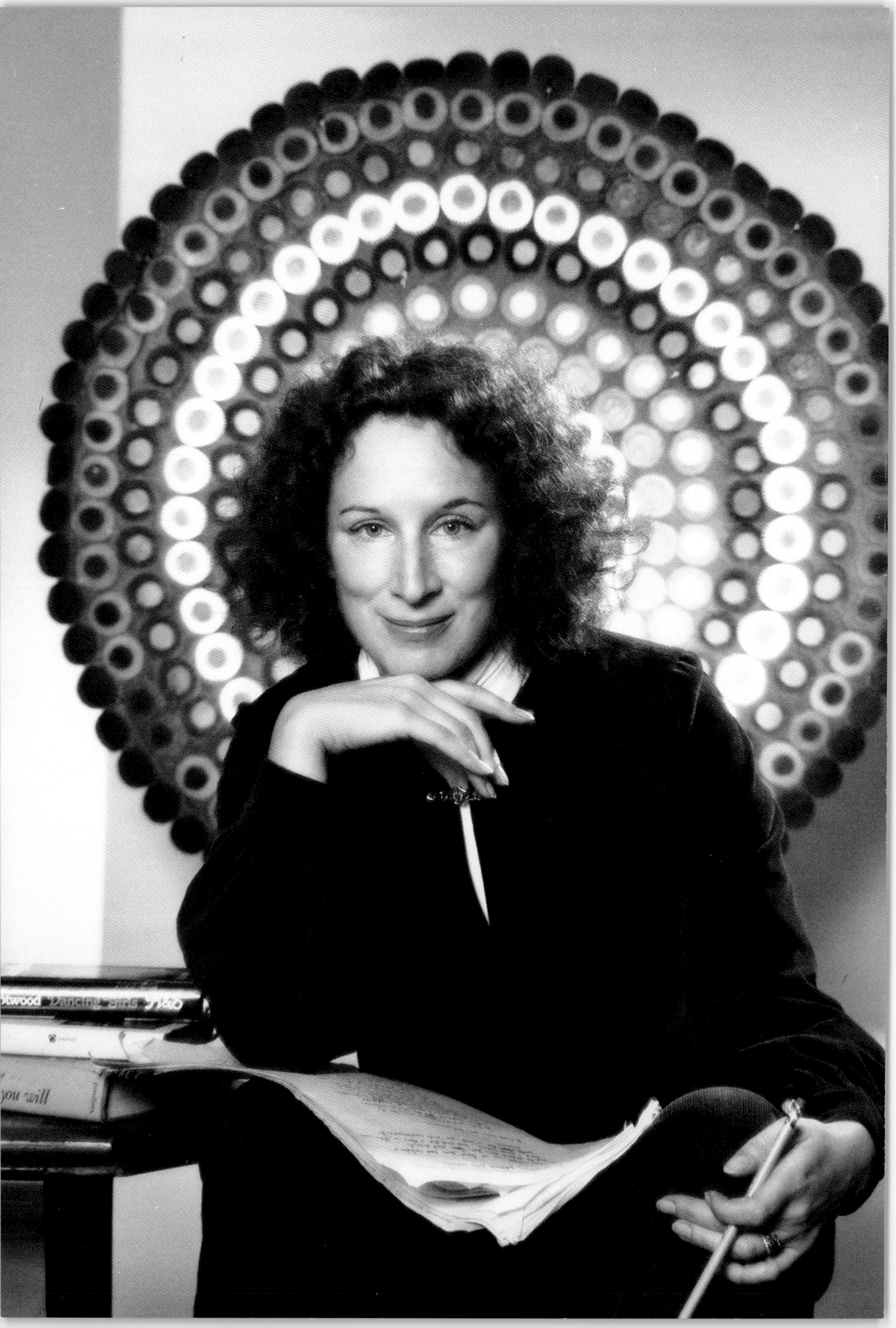
Dancing Girls
you will

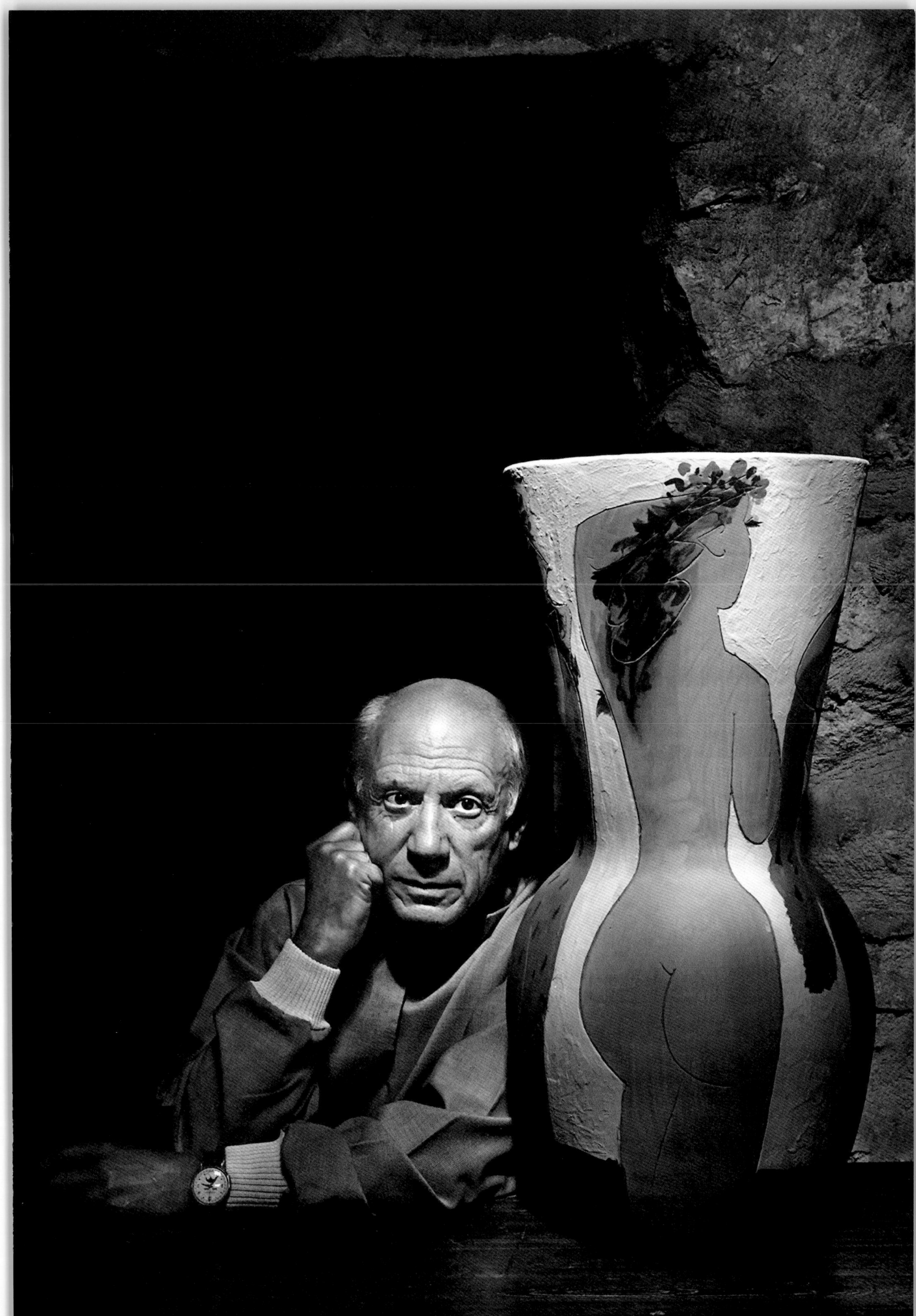

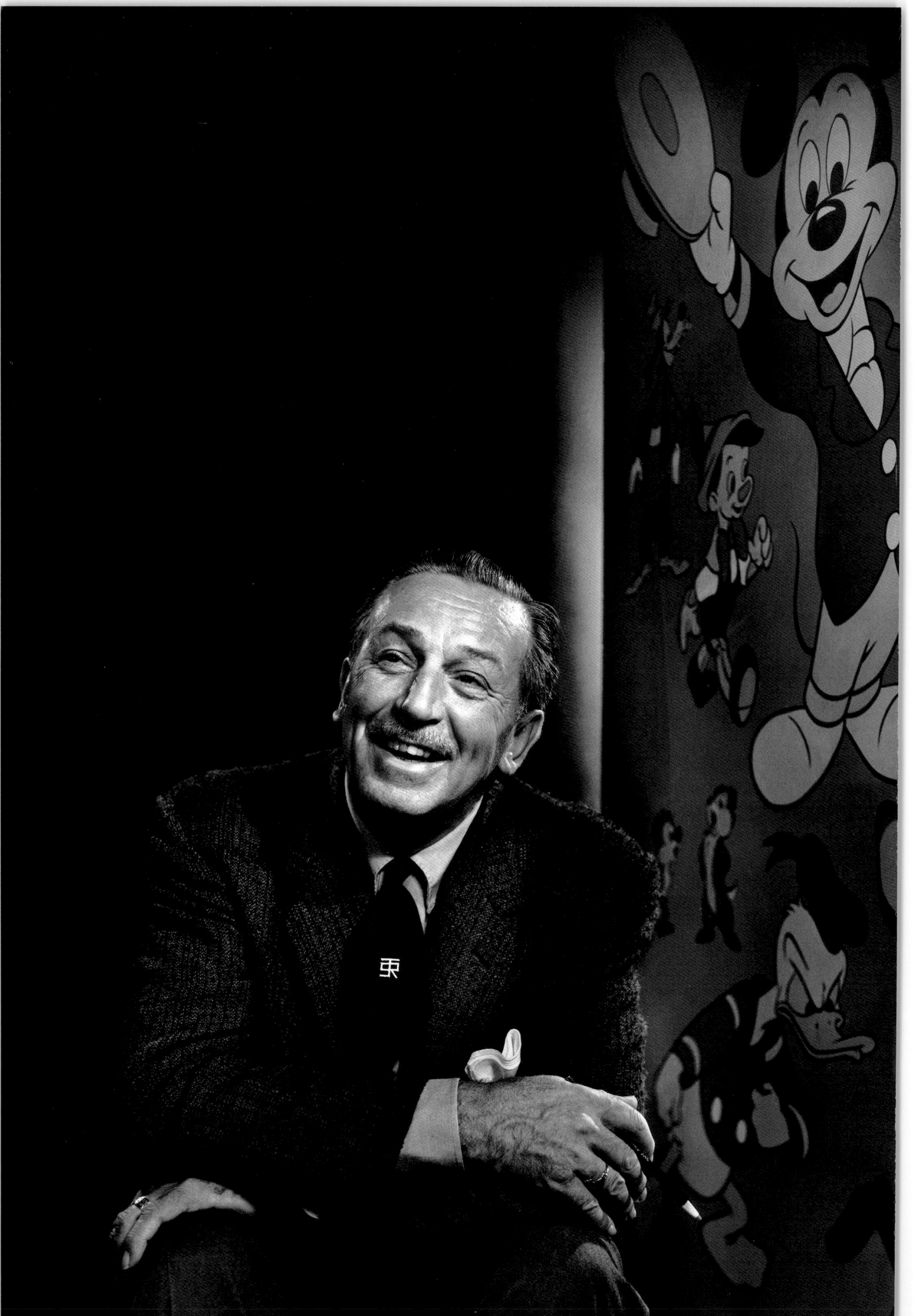

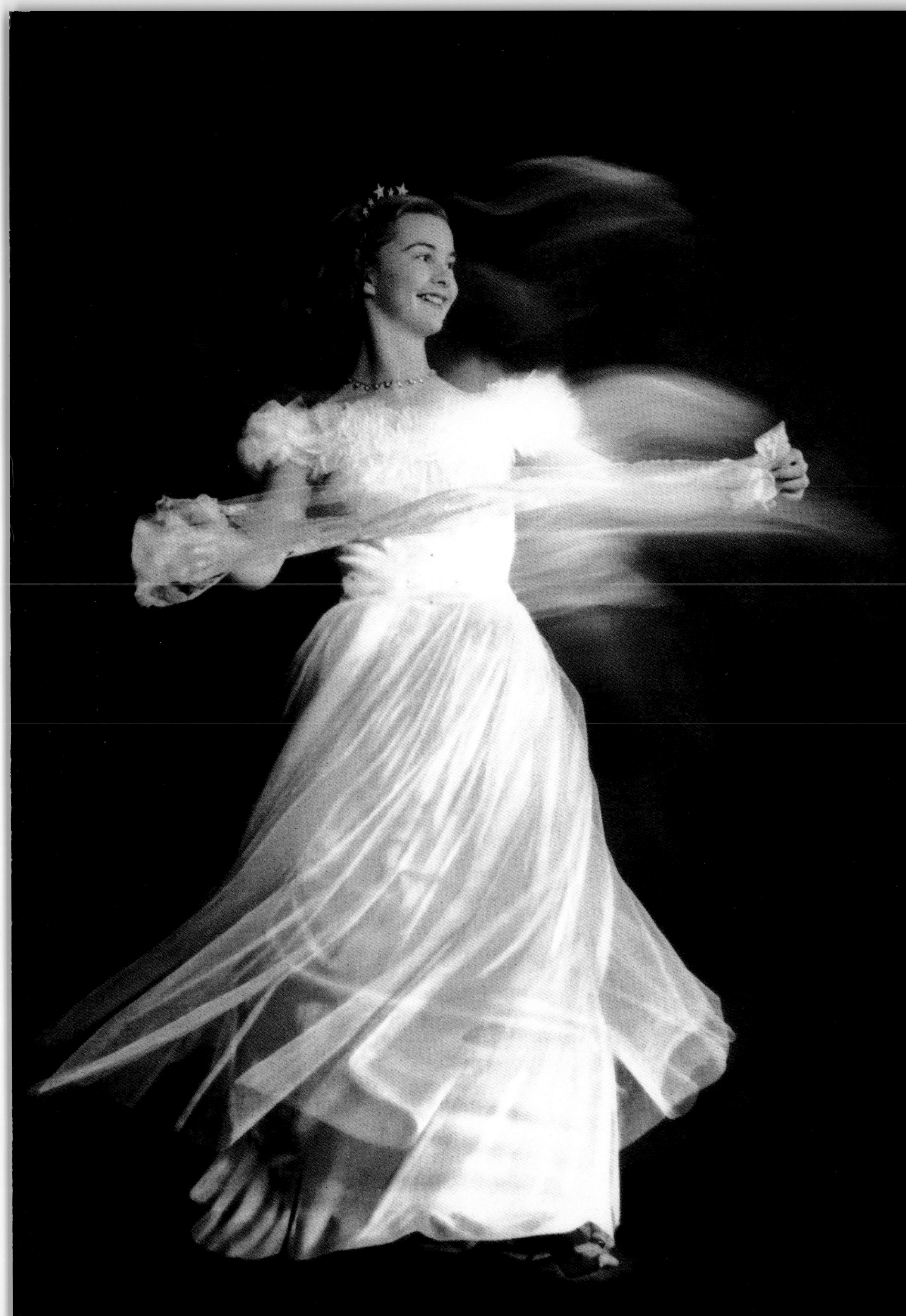

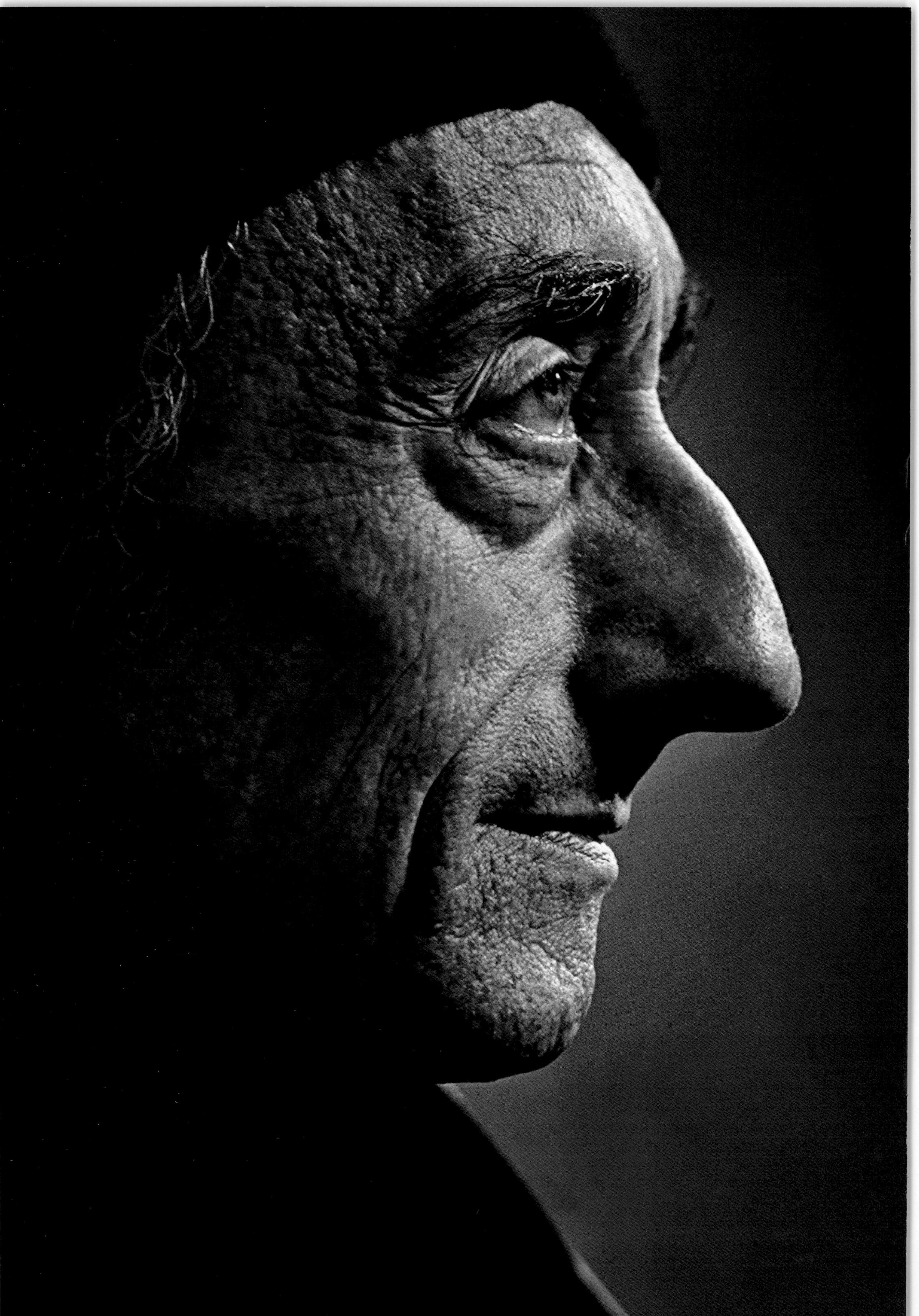

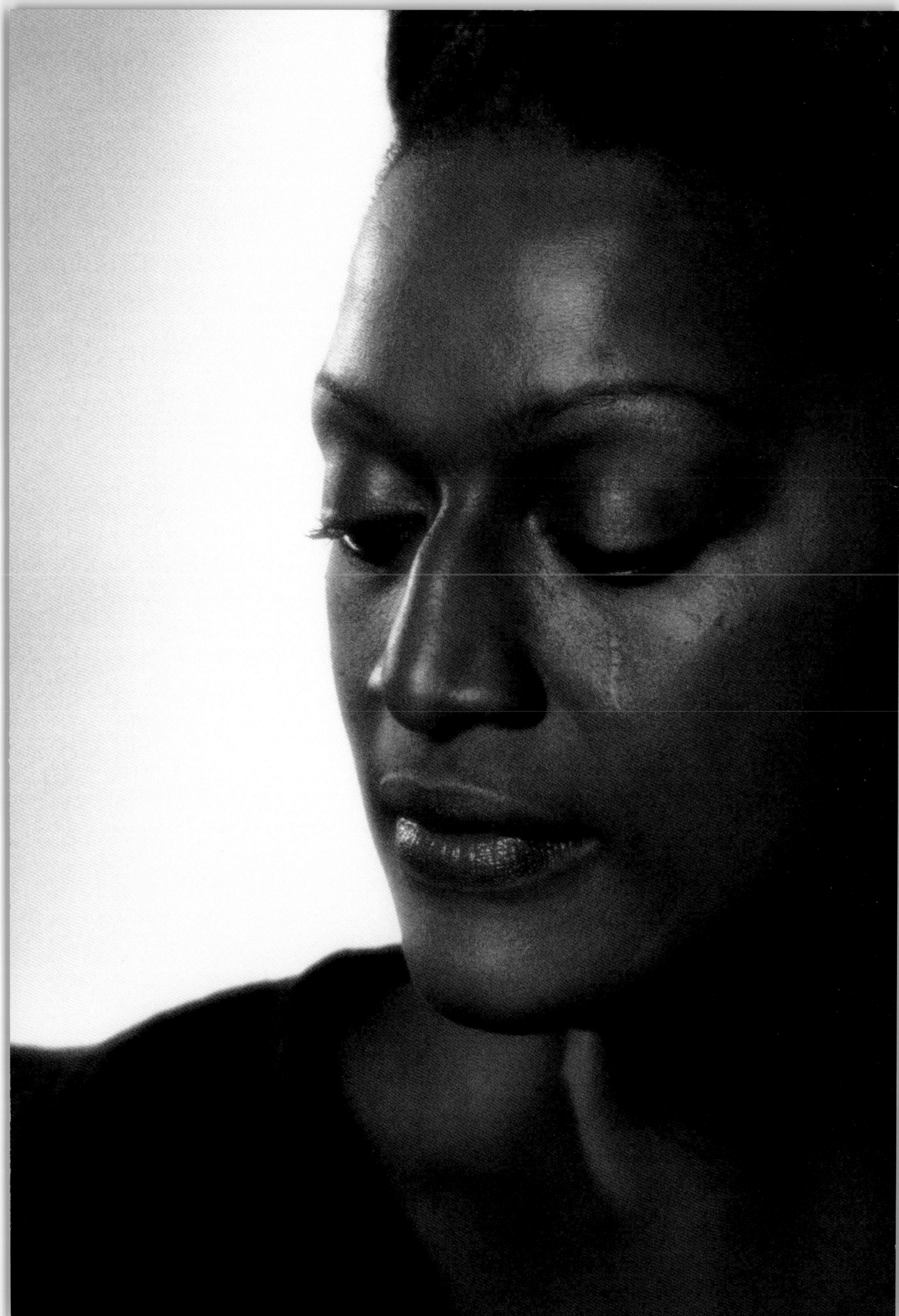

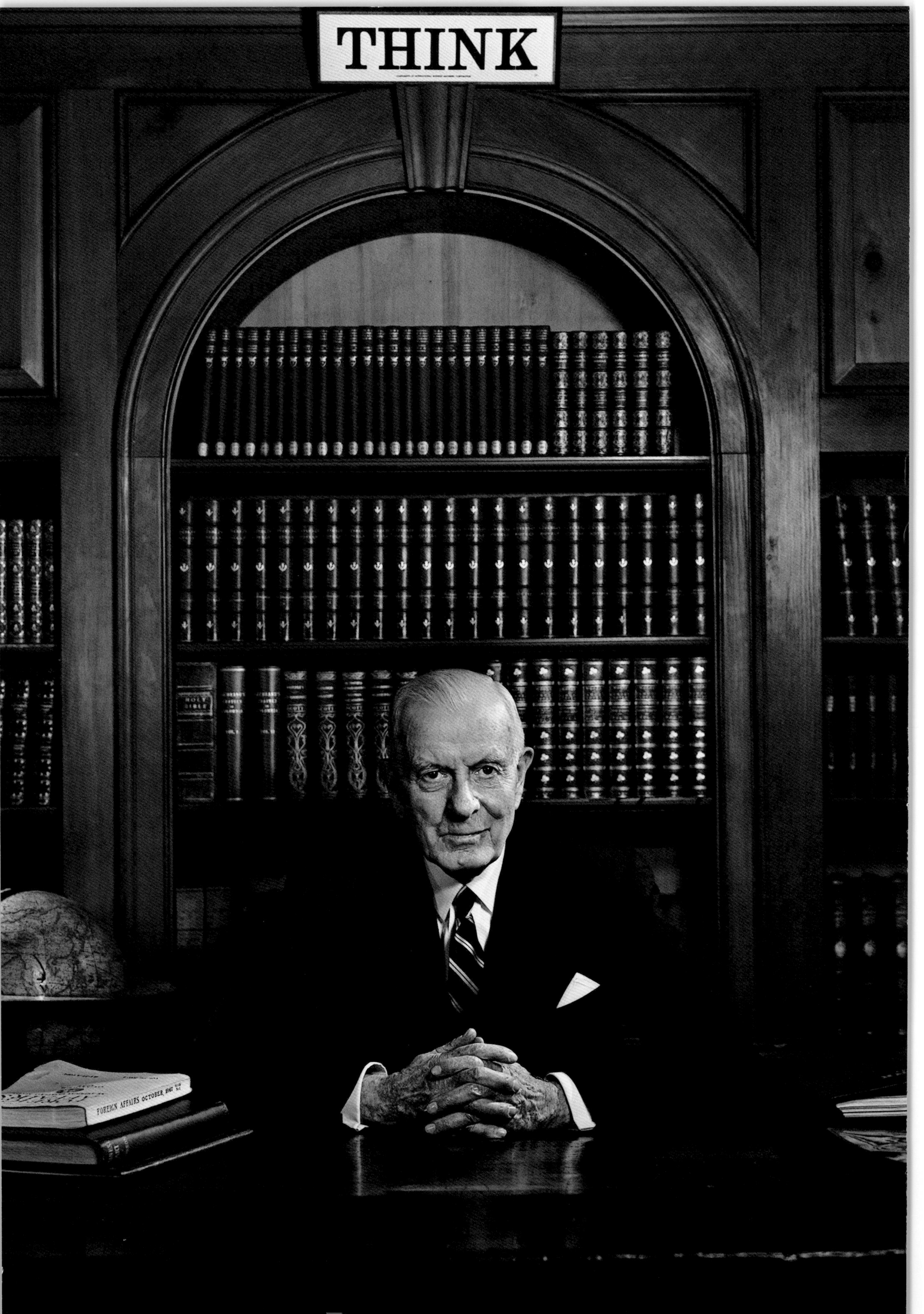
THINK
FOREIGN AFFAIRS OCTOBER, 1947

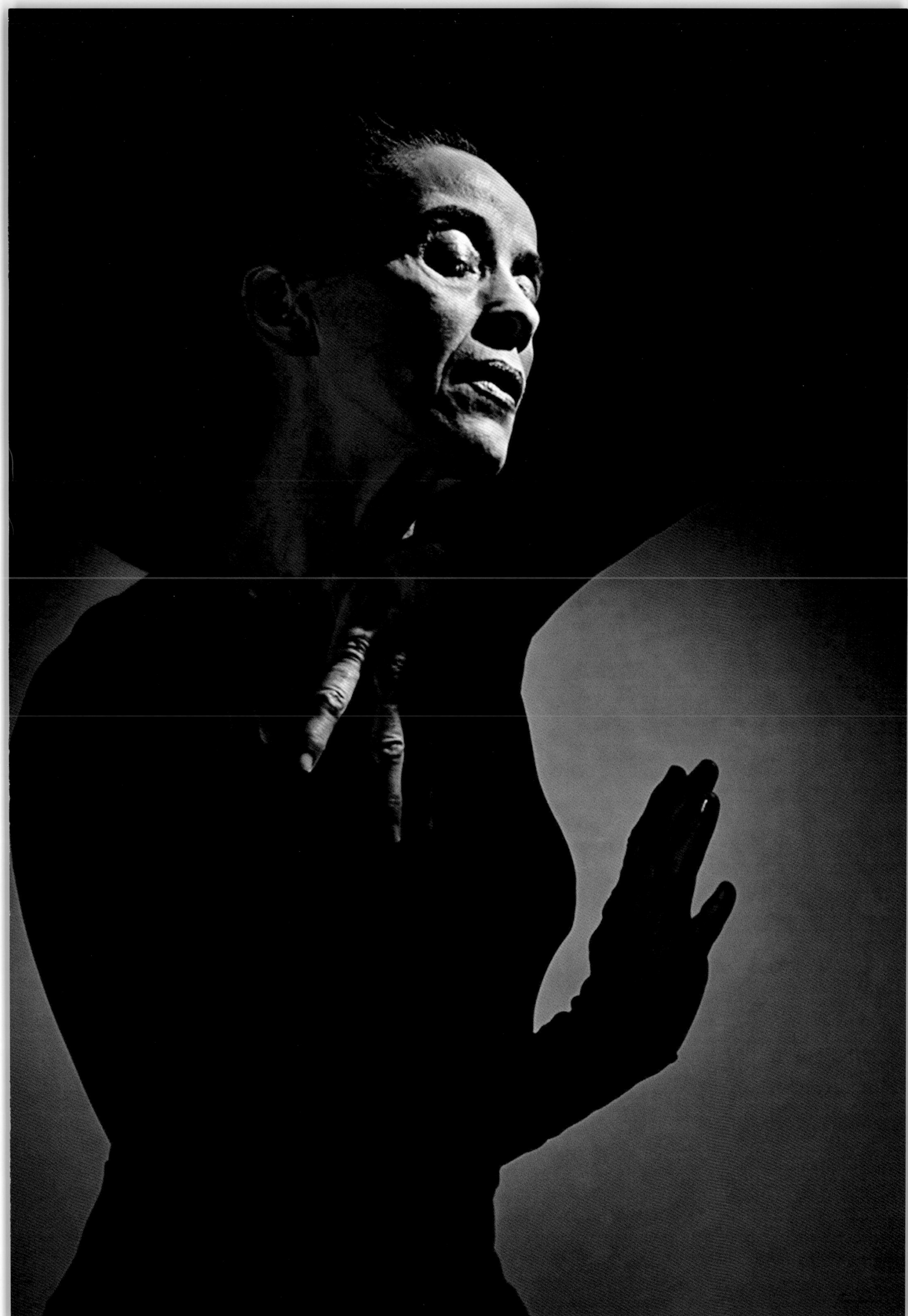

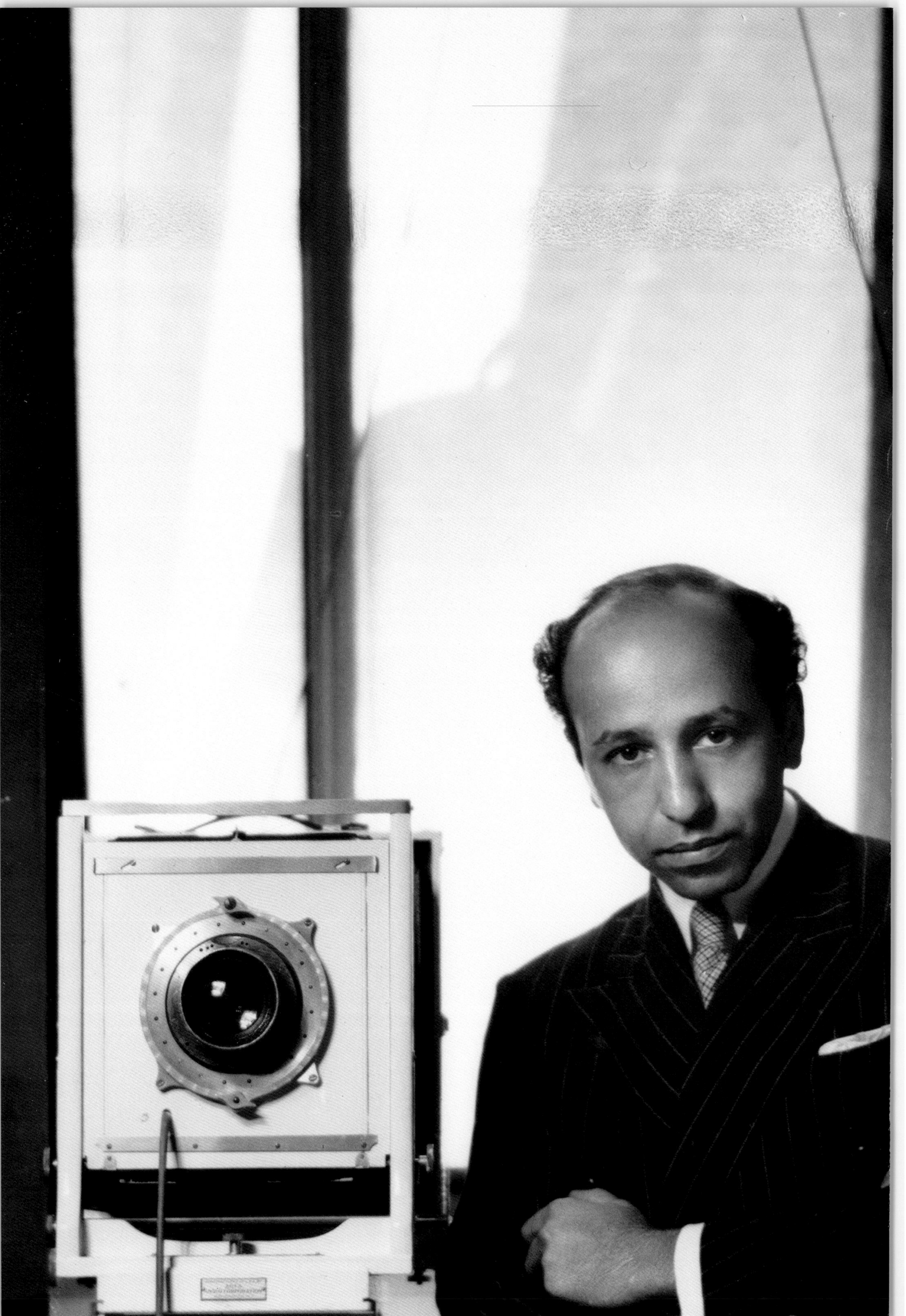

THE CANADIAN ART LIBRARY

Yousuf Karsh

LIFE & WORK

By Melissa Rombout

This book was made possible thanks to the generous support of its benefactors

SEASON SPONSOR, 2025–2026 PUBLICATIONS
POWER CORPORATION OF CANADA

TITLE SPONSOR
TIM AND FRANCES PRICE

GOLD SPONSOR
DAVID BINET

BRONZE SPONSOR
JASON DONVILLE

PRINT BOOK SPONSOR
THE KARSH CENTER AT THE MUSEUM OF FINE ARTS, BOSTON

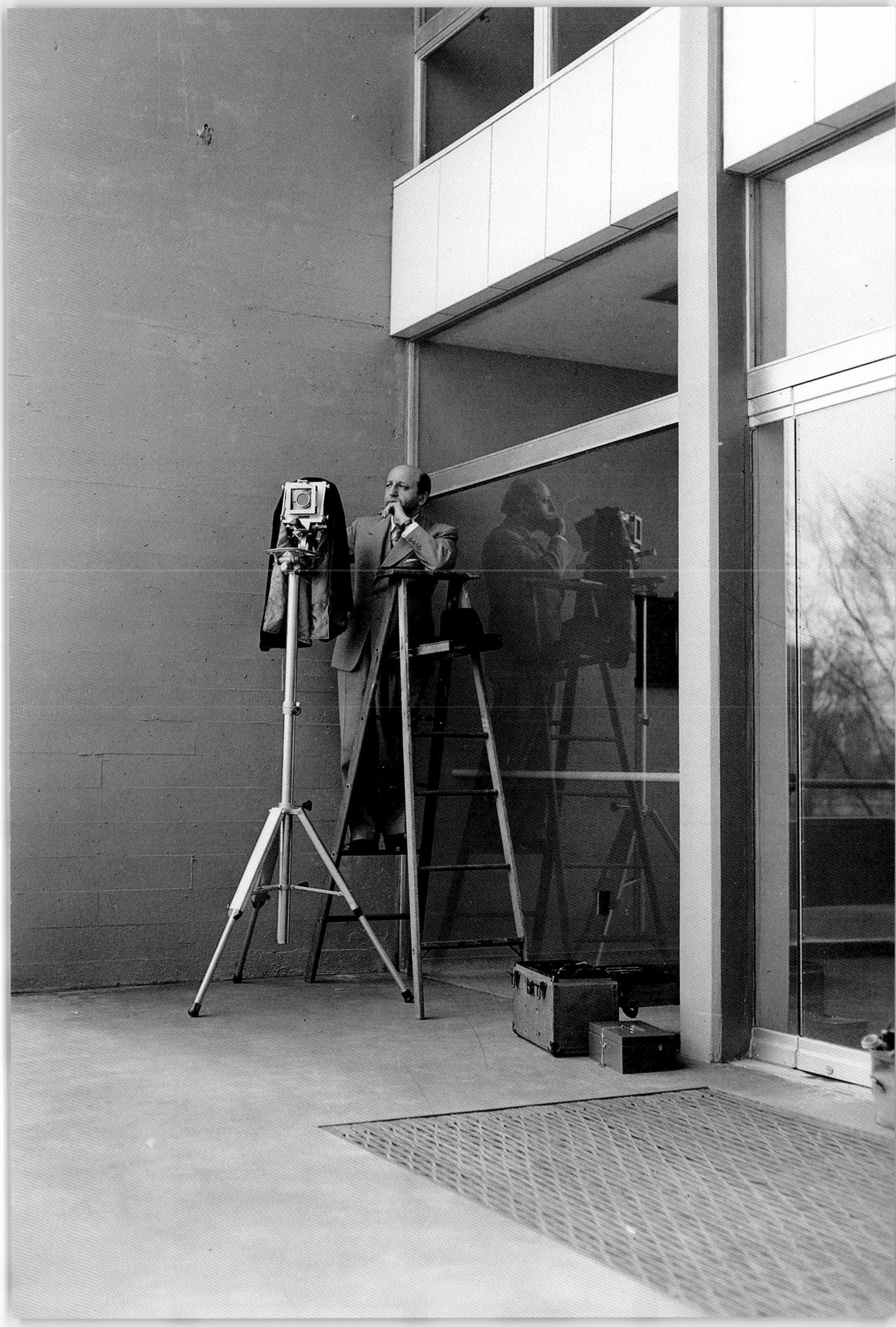

Contents

21 Introduction

25 Biography

25 A Refugee Arrives
27 "My University"
30 Mastering Light and Shadow
34 A Widening Sphere
44 Chronicler of His Time
48 On Assignment
50 In Search of Greatness
60 New Perspectives
64 Later Years

66 Key Works

68 *Woman in a Turban (Betty Low)*, 1936
70 *Sir Winston Churchill*, 1941
74 *Princess Elizabeth*, 1951
76 *Daniel Makokis*, 1952
80 *Jawaharlal Nehru*, 1956
84 *Anna Magnani*, 1958
86 *Jean-Paul Riopelle*, 1965
88 *Roppeita Kita, with Grandson Nagayo Kita*, 1969
92 *Andy Warhol*, 1979
94 *Lilly Koltun*, 1987
96 *Jessye Norman*, 1990

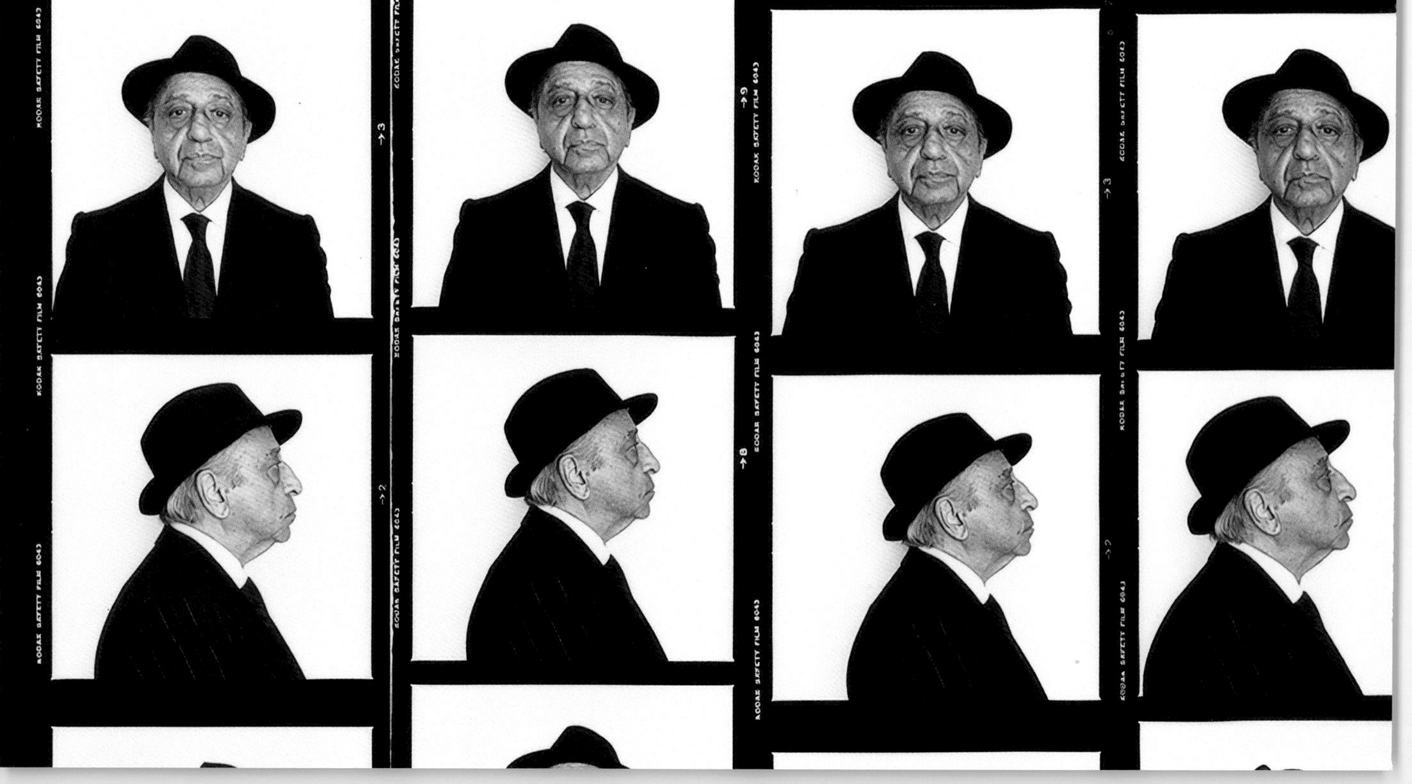

99 **Significance & Critical Issues**

99 Karsh the Storyteller
103 A Courtly Tradition
105 Framing the Hero
111 Picturing Indigeneity
119 Hope and Catharsis

123 **Style & Technique**

123 The Portrait Sitting
128 Setting and Symbolism
132 In the Darkroom
138 Karsh in Colour
142 Experimentation
149 After Karsh

153 **Sources & Resources**

153 Key Exhibitions
155 Posthumous Exhibitions
156 Archival Collections
157 Museum Collections
157 Selected Publications by Yousuf Karsh
158 Selected Writings on Yousuf Karsh
159 Audio and Video about the Artist
159 Further Reading

161 **Where to See**

167 NOTES
174 CREDITS
181 ACKNOWLEDGEMENTS
183 ABOUT THE AUTHOR

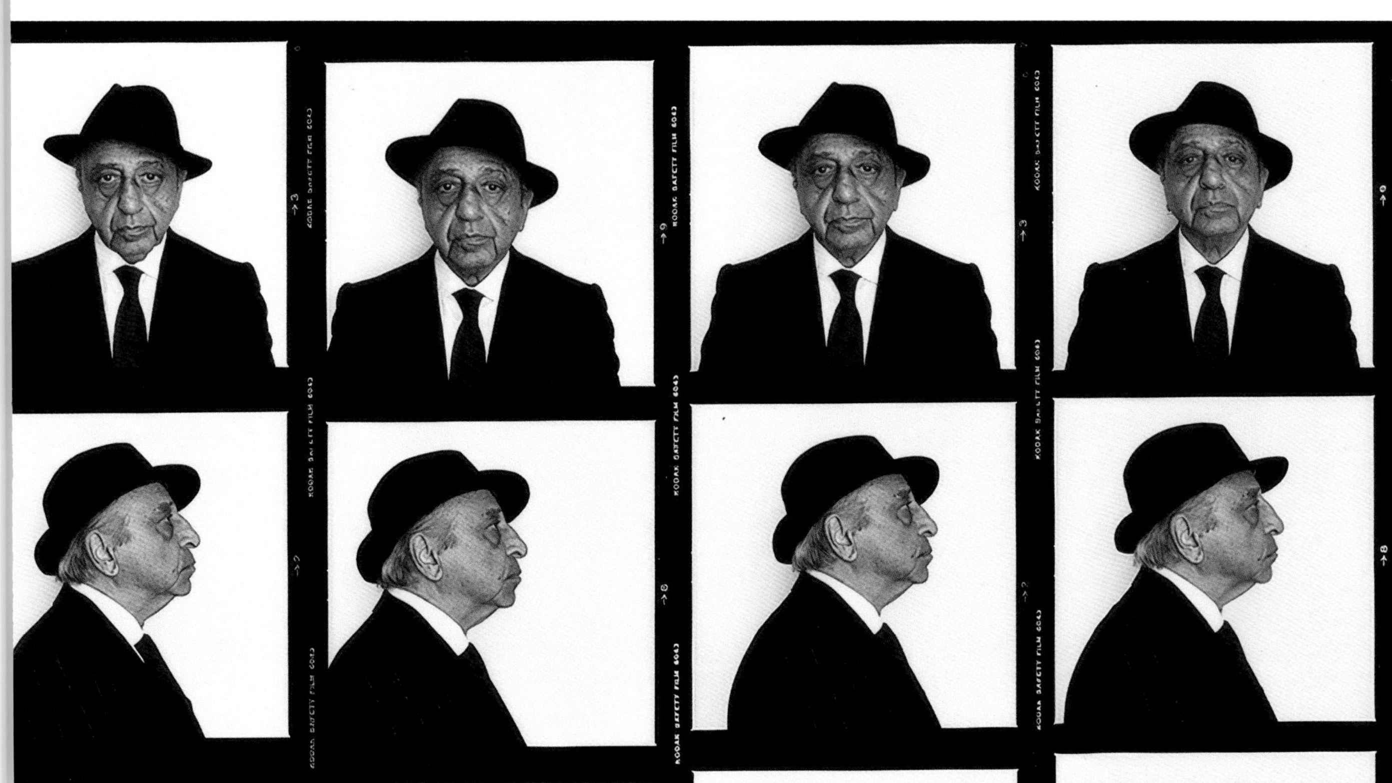

S.S. CANADA **(ORIGINAL)** Alexandria Nov 30 1924

FORM 30A.

S.S. Canada Class 2nd Date of Sailing

1924

DECLARATION OF PASSENGER TO CANADA.

1. NAME KERCH YOUSSEF Age 15
(PRINT IN BLOCK LETTERS, FAMILY NAME FIRST)

2. Sex M. Are you married, single, widowed or divorced? Single
If married, are you accompanied by husband or wife? If so, give name of husband or wife —

3. Present occupation Scholar Intended occupation Scholar

4. Birthplace Djyardeil Race or people Syrian

5. Citizenship Syrian Religion Roman Catholic
(IF PROTESTANT, STATE DENOMINATION)

6. Object in going to Canada to join his uncle

7. Do you intend to remain permanently in Canada? yes

8. Have you ever lived in Canada? no If you have, give Canadian address —
Port of first arrival in Canada Date
Port of last departure from Canada Date

9. Why did you leave Canada?

10. Money in possession belonging to passenger $ 15
(I am aware that I must have on my arrival in Canada the sum of $

11. Can you read? Yes What language? French & Arabic

12. By whom was your passage paid? my uncle

13. Ever refused entry to, or deported from Canada? no

14. Destined to A. Z. Nakash uncle
25a. Wellington St., Sherbrooke. Que.

(IF JOINING RELATIVE, FRIEND OR EMPLOYER (1) STATE WHICH AND IF RELATIVE GIVE RELATIONSHIP; (2) GIVE HIS OR HER NAME AND CANADIAN ADDRESS; (3) IF NOT JOINING ANY PERSON IN CANADA, GIVE YOUR OWN CANADIAN ADDRESS.)

16. Nearest relative in country from which you came
Jean Hallak,
(NAME) (RELATIONSHIP)
Djeide Aly Syria
(GIVE FULL ADDRESS OF SUCH RELATIVE)

17. Are you or any of your family mentally defective? no
Tubercular? no Physically defective? no
Otherwise debarred under Canadian Immigration Law? no

(Before answering question 17 see the prohibited classes named in Immigration Booklet 30A which will be handed to you by Booking Agent.)

I declare the above statements are true: I am aware that an inaccurate statement constitutes misrepresentation and that the penalty is a fine, imprisonment or deportation.

Signature of passenger Youseph Karch

I hereby declare that the above is the signature of passenger and that I have handed passenger a copy of Immigration Booklet 30A.

Sig. of Booking Agent P.P. at Montreal

Introduction

On December 30, 1941, Yousuf Karsh photographed Winston Churchill following a wartime speech that the British prime minister had given in Canada's Parliament. Just before taking the shot, in a career-defining moment of bravado and genius, the thirty-three-year-old portraitist defiantly removed the elder statesman's cigar from his mouth and captured a fierce expression of determination and strength. Known today as *Roaring Lion*, the portrait became iconic, epitomizing Allied resolve and appearing on magazine covers. The picture's celebrated reception catapulted the young photographer to fame, transforming his status from a promising talent to an internationally revered figure sought after by leaders and luminaries. It also established what would become Karsh's defining artistic skill: in his hands, the camera could reveal a person's true self in a single frame.

Known simply by his surname, Karsh built a remarkable career spanning the next five decades, during which he documented the life and times of the twentieth century. His portraits defined the public image of some of the most influential figures in modern history. From Pierre Elliott Trudeau, John F. Kennedy, and Nelson Mandela to Georgia O'Keeffe, Glenn Gould, and Andy Warhol, his sitters formed a pantheon of world-changing politicians, artists, scientists, actors, and writers. In the process, Karsh became one of the nation's most celebrated cultural exports: an immigrant whose artistry, perseverance, and vision helped secure Canada's place in the international story of modern photography.

Born in Mardin (now in Turkey) in 1908, Karsh grew up amid the turmoil of the Armenian Genocide. At the age of fifteen, he arrived in Canada as a displaced refugee, and he settled in Sherbrooke, Quebec, where he was taken under the wing of his uncle, photographer Aziz George Nakash. This apprenticeship introduced Karsh to the camera, but it was his subsequent training under Boston portrait photographer John H. Garo that proved decisive. From Garo, Karsh absorbed not only technical skills but also an appreciation for the artistry and power of photography. Returning to Canada in the 1930s, he would use these lessons to document history. Wisely, Karsh chose the nation's capital as the location for his studio, knowing that a proximity to Parliament would provide a steady stream of visiting dignitaries and national leaders.

Before long, Karsh's name became a verb. To have your portrait taken by him was *to be Karshed*, which also meant becoming part of an enduring record of history. As Melissa Rombout explains in this book's pages, "What made Karsh's approach distinct was the connection between the allure of the portrait and the photographer's own narrative of the sitting." Storytelling became key to his remarkable success, and his detailed accounts of his experiences photographing his sitters serve as anecdotes in his published portfolios, including *Faces of Destiny: Portraits by Karsh* (1946), *Portraits of Greatness* (1959), and *Karsh: American Legends* (1992). In each of these volumes, Karsh elevates portraiture into

Opposite: Declaration of Passenger to Canada, December 31, 1924. This official document records the arrival and record of immigration of Yousuf Karsh (spelled here as "Youssef Kerch"). The form notes that he departed from Alexandria on November 30, intends to study, was born in Mardin(e), holds Syrian citizenship, is Roman Catholic, can read French and Arabic, and will live with his sponsor, George Nakash.

something akin to stagecraft. He is not simply documenting appearances; he is distilling character, ambition, and power into an image.

Though he is known primarily for his portraits of famed personalities, as we learn in this book, an equally significant part of Karsh's body of work is his portraits of lesser-known subjects, including those taken as part of a major commission from *Maclean's* magazine. Between 1952 and 1954, Karsh's Canadian Cities project resulted in the creation of an estimated eight thousand photographs depicting the country's increasingly multicultural population at a time when few Canadian media outlets were concerned with diversity.

Throughout the second half of the twentieth century, Karsh's adopted country continued to provide both a stage and a context for his work into the later decades of his career. In 1973, he relocated his studio to a suite of rooms on the sixth floor of the Château Laurier hotel, where he welcomed artists, writers, and performers whose works would help shape Canadian identity. In 1978, Karsh published *Karsh Canadians*, a volume that gathers portraits of more than seventy of the nation's distinguished figures, including Margaret Atwood, Jean Paul Riopelle, and Karen Kain.

With *Yousuf Karsh: Life & Work*, Rombout has created a text that is about not only the famed photographer's art but also the remarkable story of what his body of work means to a twenty-first-century audience. At a time when selfies have become ubiquitous and portrait-making rests in the palm of our hands, Rombout invites readers to closely explore an artist who laid a historic foundation for how the camera is used. Taking an in-depth look at his acclaimed oeuvre, she traces the trajectory of Karsh's career from apprentice to master, outlining the artistic choices that defined his style and detailing the cultural impact of his work across six decades up to today.

In doing so, Rombout reveals how, in the decades following Karsh's passing, his legacy endures. It is one that reminds us how photography, when guided by vision, empathy, and great artistry, is much more than representation. It is history itself, and it is a testimony to the fact that a masterfully composed portrait conveys not only the likeness of one person but the very essence of the human spirit.

Sara Angel, CM, PhD
Founder and Executive Director, Art Canada Institute
September 2025

Opposite: Covers of Karsh's books. Top row, left to right: *Portraits of Greatness* (Toronto: University of Toronto Press, 1959); *Faces of Destiny* (Chicago: Ziff-Davis Publishing Company, 1946); and *Karsh Canadians* (Toronto: University of Toronto Press, 1978). Middle row, left to right: *Karsh Portraits* (Toronto: University of Toronto Press, 1976); *Karsh: American Legends* (Boston: Bulfinch Press, 1992); and *Faces of Our Time* (Toronto and Buffalo: University of Toronto Press, 1971). Bottom row, left to right: *Karsh Portfolio* (Toronto: University of Toronto Press, 1967); *This Is Newfoundland*, edited by Ewart Young with portraits by Yousuf Karsh (Toronto, Halifax, and Vancouver: The Ryerson Press, 1949); and *Yousuf Karsh & John Fisher See Canada*, written by John Fisher, illustrated by Yousuf Karsh (Toronto: Thomas Allen, 1960).

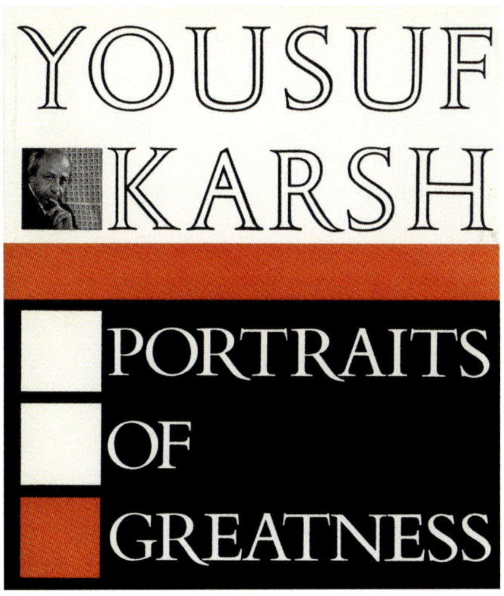
YOUSUF
KARSH
PORTRAITS
OF
GREATNESS

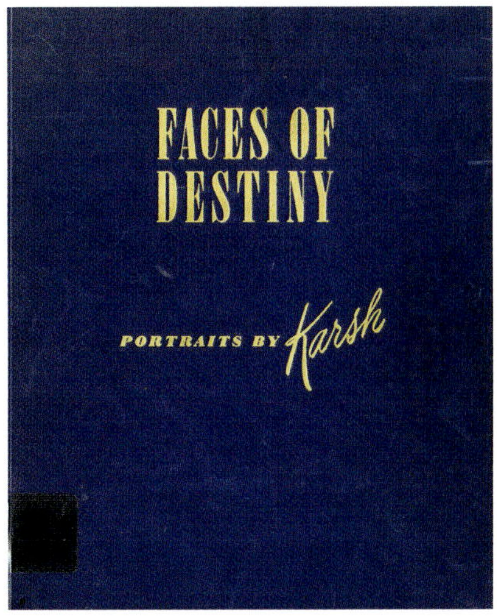
FACES OF
DESTINY
PORTRAITS BY Karsh

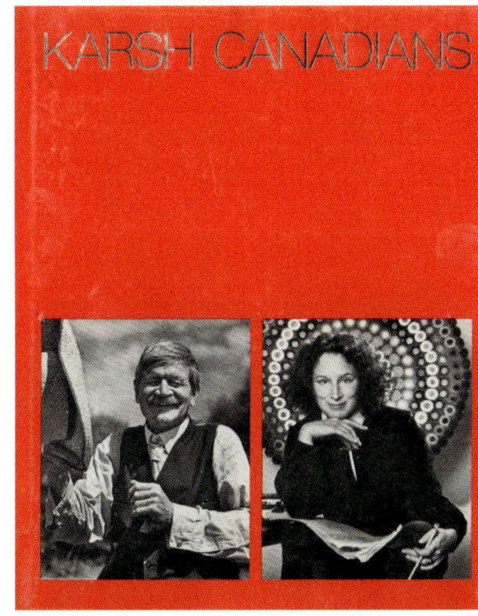
KARSH CANADIANS

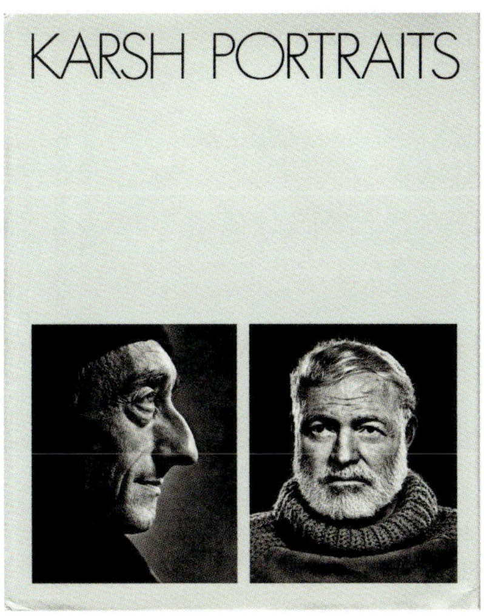
KARSH PORTRAITS

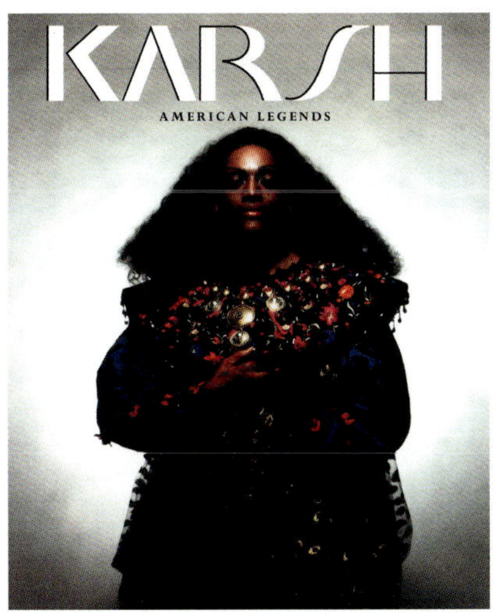
KARSH
AMERICAN LEGENDS

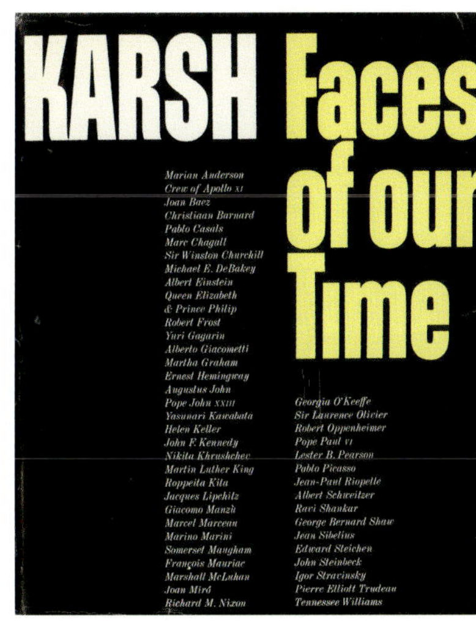
KARSH
Faces
of our
Time
Marian Anderson
Crew of Apollo XI
Joan Baez
Christiaan Barnard
Pablo Casals
Marc Chagall
Sir Winston Churchill
Michael E. DeBakey
Albert Einstein
Queen Elizabeth
& Prince Philip
Robert Frost
Yuri Gagarin
Alberto Giacometti
Martha Graham
Ernest Hemingway
Augustus John
Pope John XXIII
Yasunari Kawabata
Helen Keller
John F. Kennedy
Nikita Khrushchev
Martin Luther King
Roppeita Kita
Jacques Lipchitz
Giacomo Manzù
Marcel Marceau
Marino Marini
Somerset Maugham
François Mauriac
Marshall McLuhan
Joan Miró
Richard M. Nixon
Georgia O'Keeffe
Sir Laurence Olivier
Robert Oppenheimer
Pope Paul VI
Lester B. Pearson
Pablo Picasso
Jean-Paul Riopelle
Albert Schweitzer
Ravi Shankar
George Bernard Shaw
Jean Sibelius
Edward Steichen
John Steinbeck
Igor Stravinsky
Pierre Elliott Trudeau
Tennessee Williams

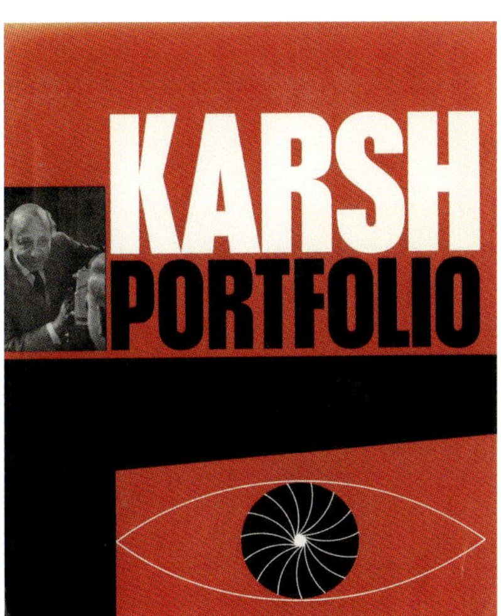
KARSH
PORTFOLIO

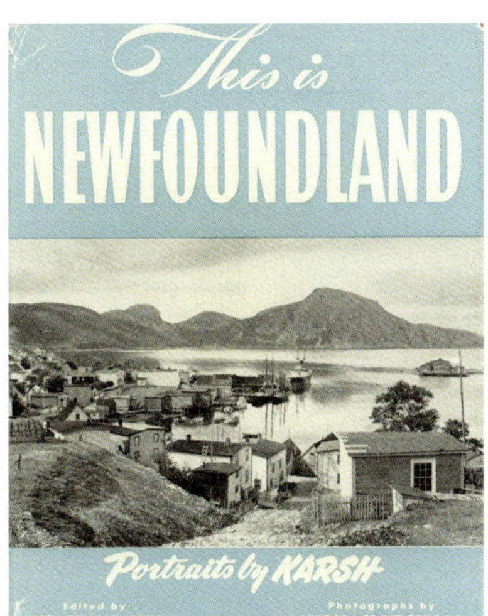
This is
NEWFOUNDLAND
Portraits by KARSH
Edited by
EWART YOUNG
Photographs by
CYRIL MARSHALL

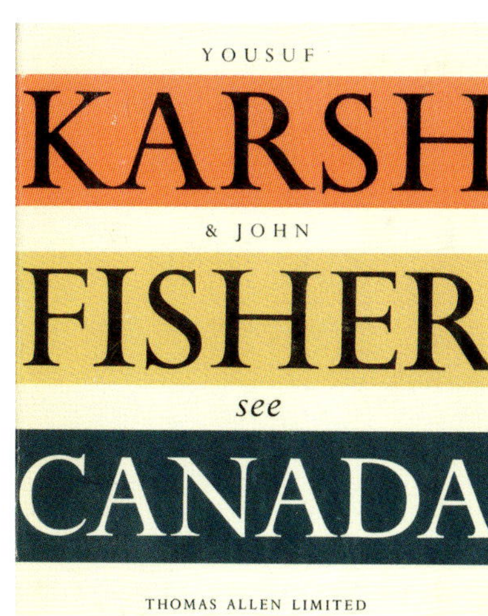
YOUSUF
KARSH
& JOHN
FISHER
see
CANADA
THOMAS ALLEN LIMITED

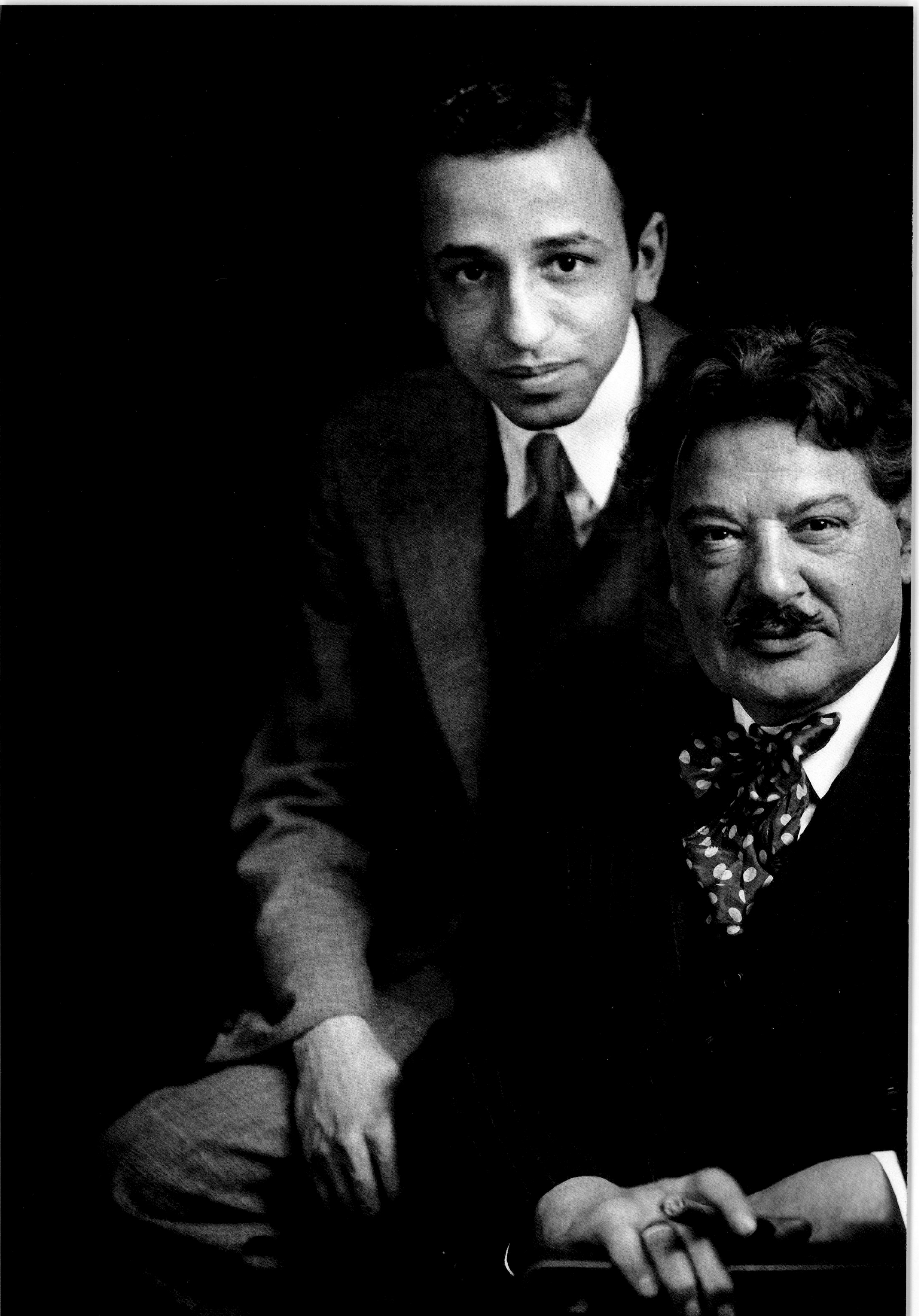

Biography

Yousuf Karsh (1908–2002) is recognized as one of the leading photographers of the twentieth century. Arriving in Canada in 1924 as an Armenian refugee, Karsh eventually settled in Ottawa. Over six decades, he mastered the art of portraiture and created a unique chronicle of his time through images of celebrated legends. To achieve both creative and commercial success, Karsh immersed himself in technical codes related to photographic technology, aesthetic codes from painting and art photography, and social codes to access elite society. A celebrity in his own right, he was an elegant and charming public figure, captivating audiences with compelling stories told in images and words. Karsh sought to capture, as he put it, the "elusive moment of truth," revealing the essential nature of his subjects as reflected in their eyes, hands, and attitudes.

A Refugee Arrives

Yousuf (né Hovsep) Karsh was born on December 23, 1908, the eldest child of a middle-class Armenian family in Mardin, in what is now Turkey. Descendants of an ancient civilization, Western Armenians were ruled by the Ottoman Empire in the early twentieth century. Karsh's mother, Bahiyah Nakash, was the daughter of an engraver and had been educated at the Protestant-sponsored American Mission School.[1] His father, Abel al-Massih Karsh, was a successful weaver and importer of specialty artisanal goods,

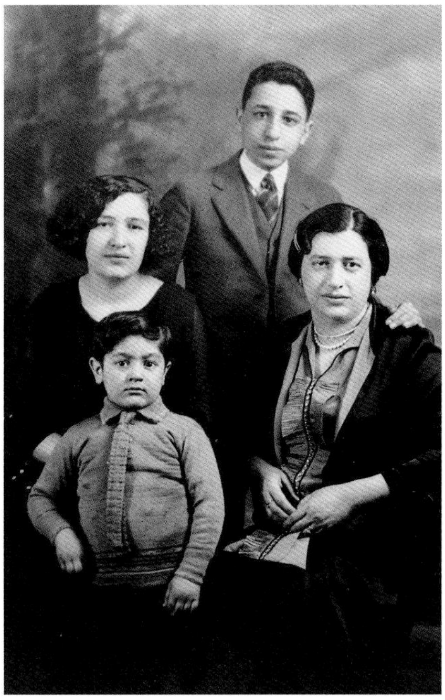

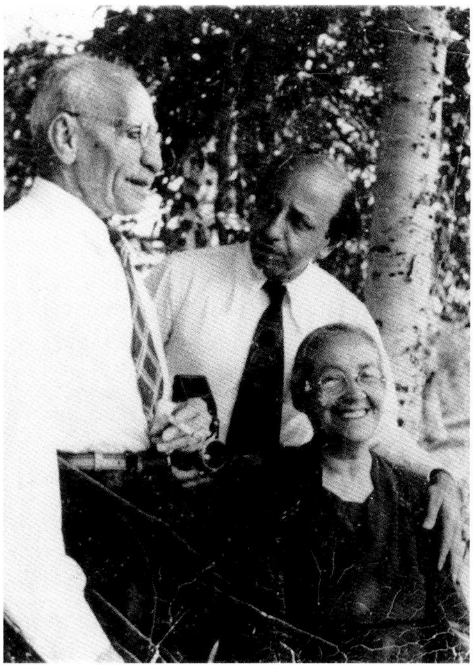

Opposite: Portrait of Yousuf Karsh (*back*) at age twenty-two with John Garo, 1930 (detail), photographer unknown. Above left: Yousuf Karsh (*back*) at age eighteen in a family portrait, c.1926, photograph by George Nakash. Above right: Yousuf Karsh with his parents, Abel al-Massih and Bahiyah Karsh, c.1948, photographer unknown.

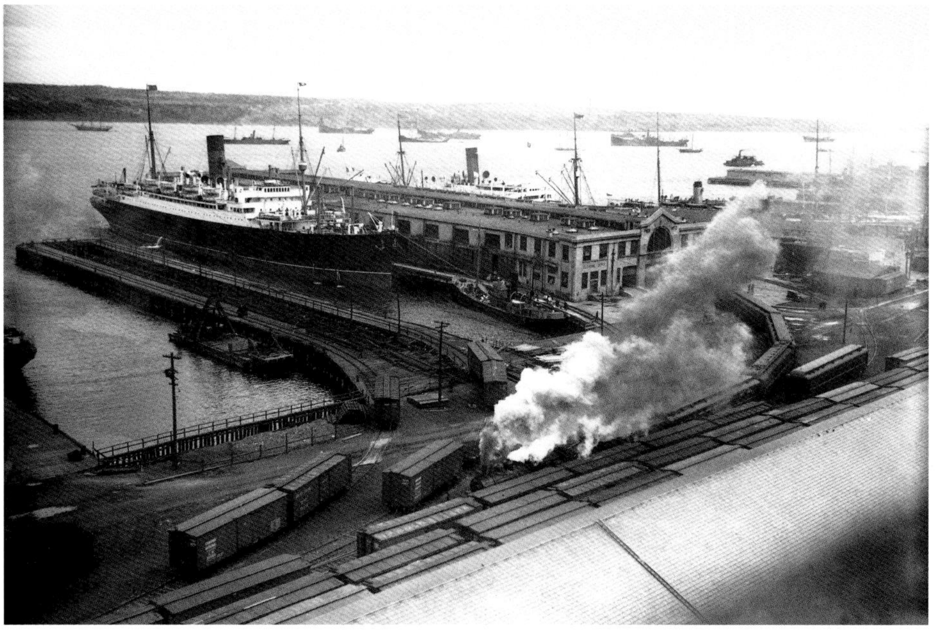

such as spices, indigo, silks, and textiles acquired in markets on the Persian Gulf.[2] Karsh and his siblings were raised speaking Arabic and confirmed in the Roman Catholic faith.

In 1915, when Karsh was seven years old, his family was entrapped by what is now known as the Armenian Genocide. As a largely Christian minority, Armenians were systemically targeted by the Ottoman government for starvation, persecution, forced deportation, or massacre, ultimately resulting in the deaths of over a million people. As a child, Karsh endured starvation and displacement and witnessed acts of violence, including against members of his own family.[3] His father's diverse heritage and Arabic speaking ability played a key role in the family's survival. In 1922, authorities allowed the Karshes to flee by caravan to Syria, where they eventually settled in Aleppo, trying to rebuild their lives as displaced refugees.[4]

As a measure to safeguard his future, in 1924, Karsh's parents arranged for their son, then just fifteen, to move to Sherbrooke, Quebec, to live with his mother's brother, Aziz George Nakash (1892–1976), a portrait photographer. Karsh was permitted to enter the country as part of a humanitarian initiative to reunite displaced Armenians with family members already in Canada.

Karsh departed from Beirut, Lebanon, crossing the Atlantic on the *SS Versailles*, and later quipped that he carried with him "only his good manners."[5] He arrived in Halifax, Nova Scotia, four weeks later, docking during a New Year's Eve snowstorm. He could speak Armenian and Arabic fluently but knew little French and no English when he was interviewed by Canadian immigration officials. Karsh had never met his uncle, a thirty-two-year-old bachelor, who had travelled there to escort him to Sherbrooke. Leaving Halifax in early 1925, they set off together by train, a journey of nearly one thousand kilometres through severe winter conditions.

After his arrival in Sherbrooke, Karsh enrolled in the local English-language high school, anglicizing his name to "Joe." Despite the challenge of learning English—his fourth language after Armenian, Arabic, and French—he quickly formed friendships, including with the daughters of the mayor, who had been photographed by his uncle and who introduced Karsh to Canadian pastimes like ice skating.

Pier 2, the Deep Water Terminals, Halifax, c.1928, photograph by W.R. MacAskill.

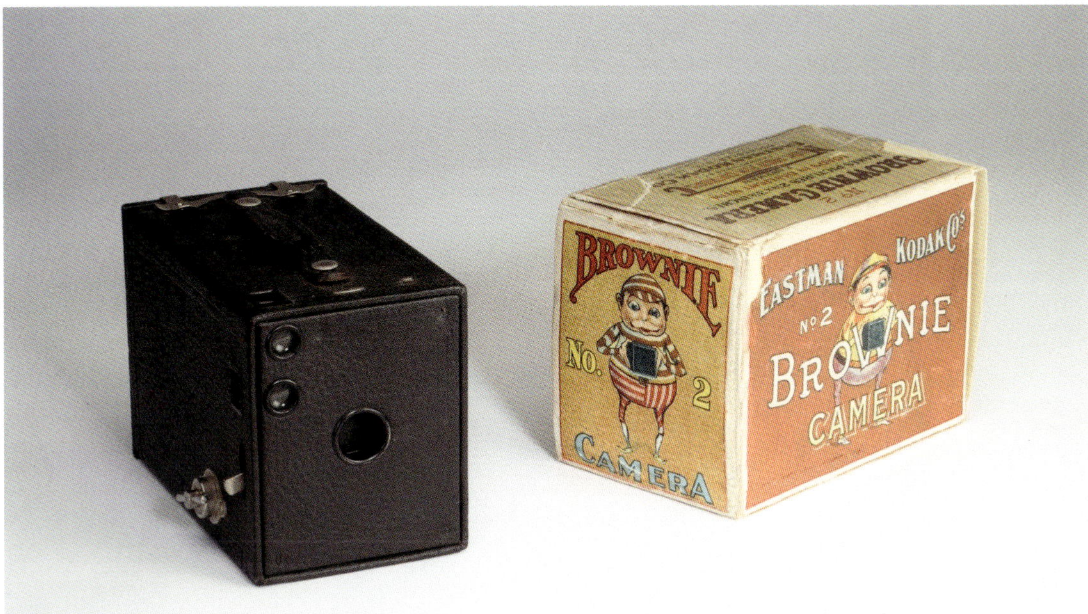

"My University"

At the end of his first semester in Sherbrooke, Karsh began working in his uncle Nakash's portrait studio, learning to use a large-format camera on a tripod, developing photographs exposed on glass-plate negatives, and printing in the darkroom. He also began taking his own photographs using the first portable camera: a Kodak Brownie. As Karsh later recalled, "I began to roam the countryside about Sherbrooke every weekend, developing the pictures I took myself. It was an excellent experience, and Uncle Nakash was a valuable and patient critic."[6]

Karsh's earliest extant work is a picturesque landscape featuring children playing along a riverbank. The soft focus and atmospheric quality of this gentle scene exemplify the art photography style of the period, Pictorialism, which emulated classical genres and the painterly expression of fine art.[7] Karsh gave this print to a classmate, who, without Karsh's knowledge, entered it in a photo contest sponsored by the T. Eaton Company. The photograph won first prize and a sizable fifty dollars. Karsh "gave ten dollars to my friend and happily sent the rest to my parents in Aleppo, the first money I could send to them from Canada."[8]

With artistic encouragement and technical experience, Karsh committed to pursuing his passion for photography as a profession. In 1928, his uncle Nakash arranged for Karsh, now twenty, to further his studies as an assistant to John H. Garo (1870–1939), a distinguished portrait photographer based in Boston, Massachusetts, who was also part of the Armenian diaspora. Garo operated an elegant portrait studio by day and hosted a lively salon attended by leading cultural figures at night.

Garo had left Armenia at a young age and settled in Worcester, Massachusetts, in 1885, before becoming a professional photographer. Widely known for his studio portraits and art photography, Garo was also a painter and actively participated in Pictorialist networks in the Boston region. He was familiar with the salon exhibition circuits both as an artist and as a jury member, and he closely studied other photographers, including members of the Photo-Secession movement whose pieces were published in the art photography journal *Camera Work*.[9]

Eastman Kodak Company's No. 2 Brownie Model D camera with Brownie character box, 1914.

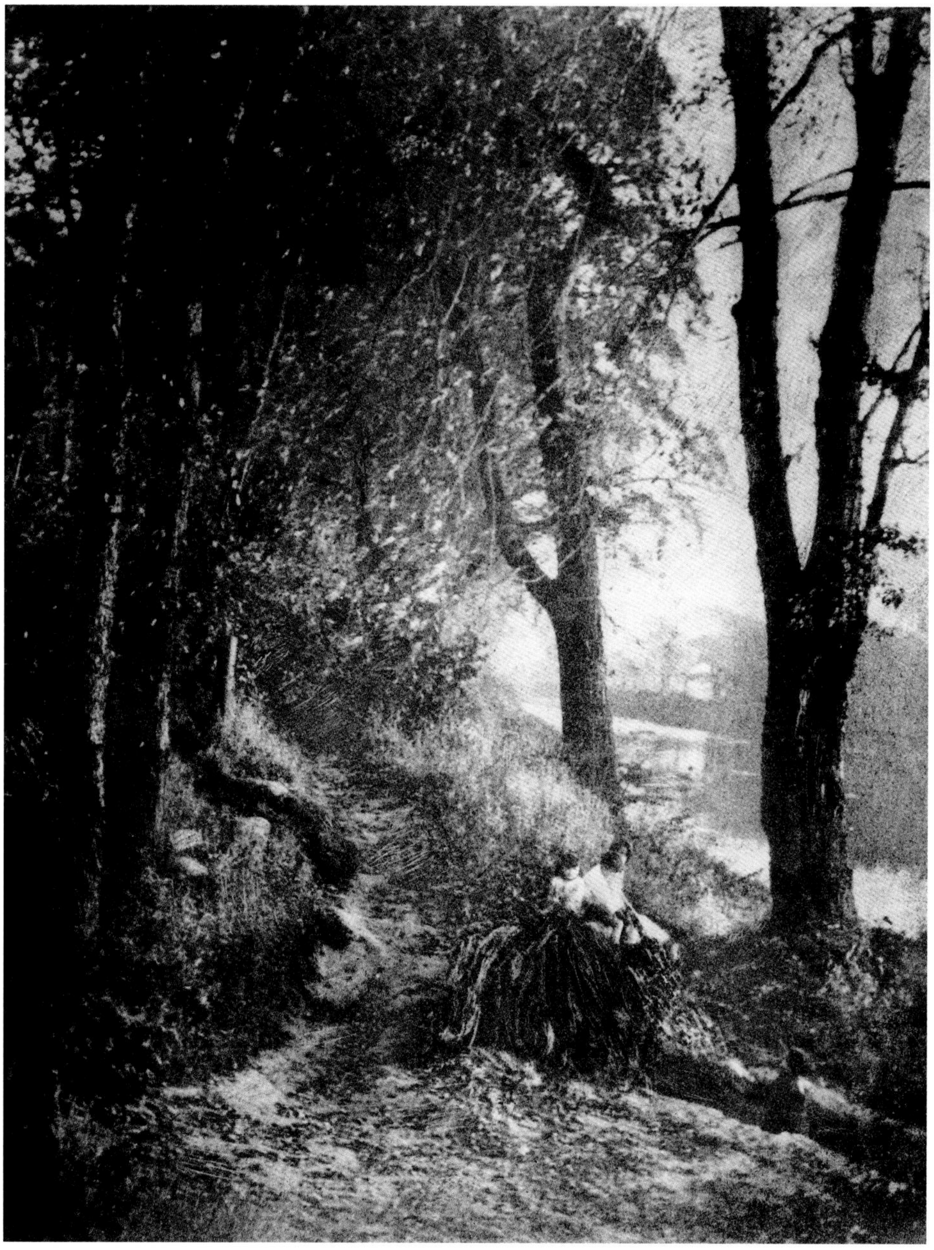

Under Garo's tutelage, Karsh expanded his camera skills, took classes at the Boston Museum of Fine Arts, and studied great masterworks of portraiture during visits to Boston's museums and great libraries. Karsh also had the opportunity to study first-hand many painted portraits by classical masters, laying a foundation for his signature aesthetic choices: a perceptive psychological portrayal featuring a half-length format, prominent placement of the sitter's hands, and objects symbolizing the sitter's status, profession, or talent.

In addition to closely studying paintings and carefully mixing chemicals in the darkroom, Karsh learned an essential skill during his apprenticeship with Garo: how to photograph and socially interact with prominent people.[10] Karsh observed how Garo received his subjects at the studio, relaxing and directing them during portrait sittings. It

Yousuf Karsh, *Early Landscape*, 1926, gelatin silver print, 24 x 18.3 cm, Yousuf Karsh Fonds, Library and Archives Canada, Ottawa. Opposite: Yousuf Karsh, *Early Portrait*, 1929, Estate of Yousuf Karsh.

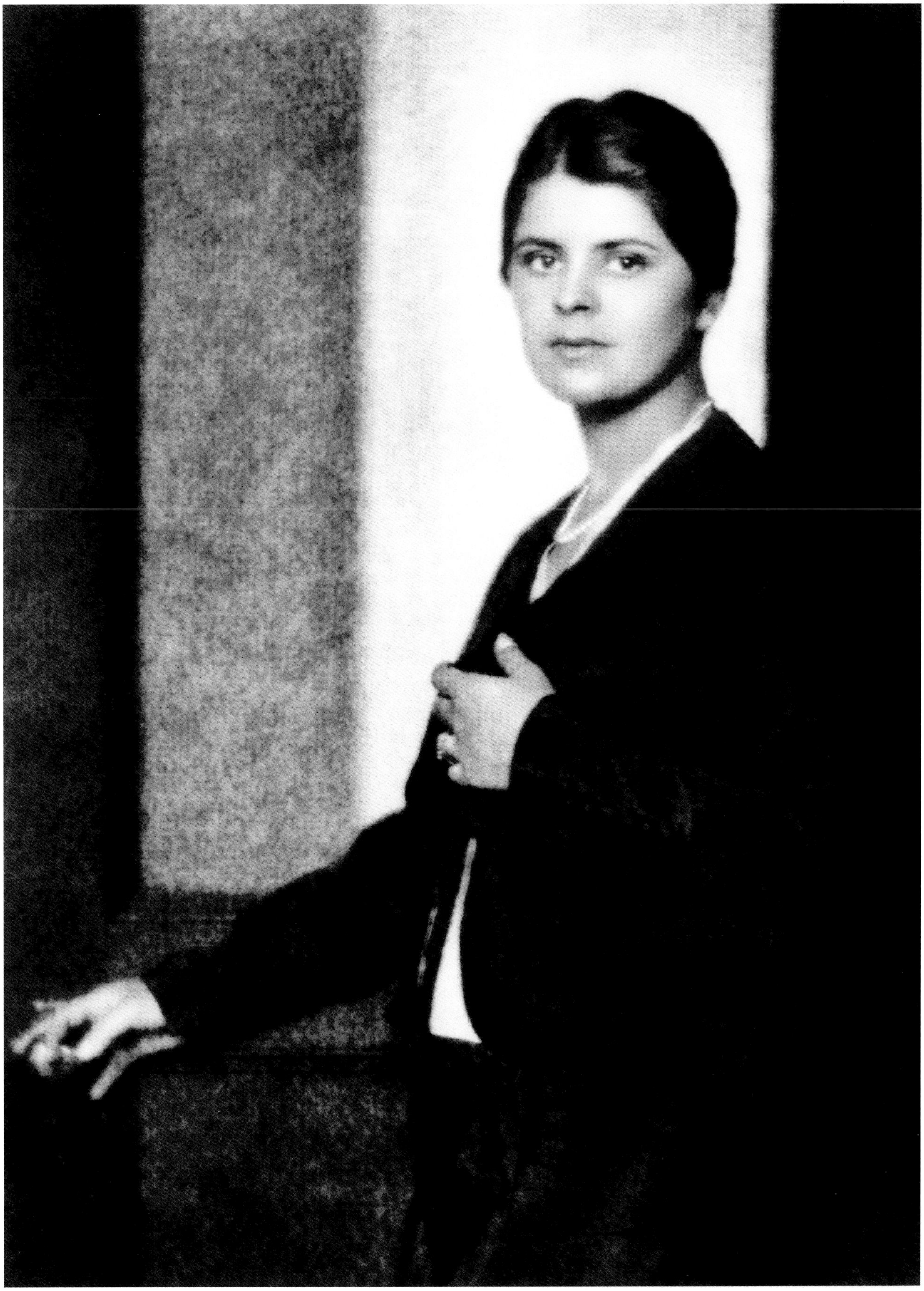

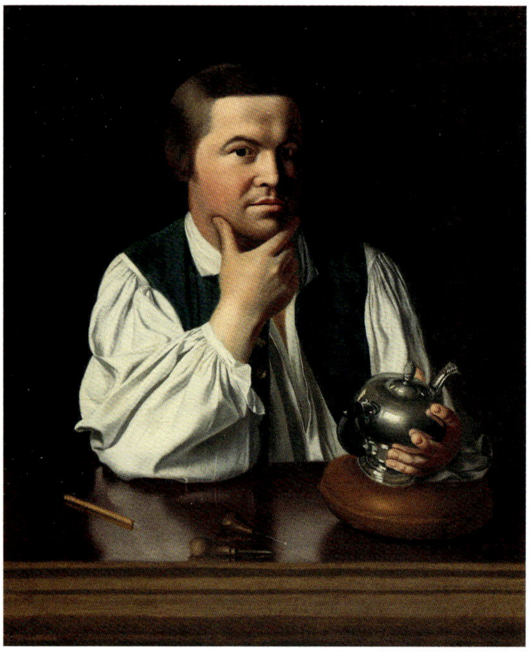
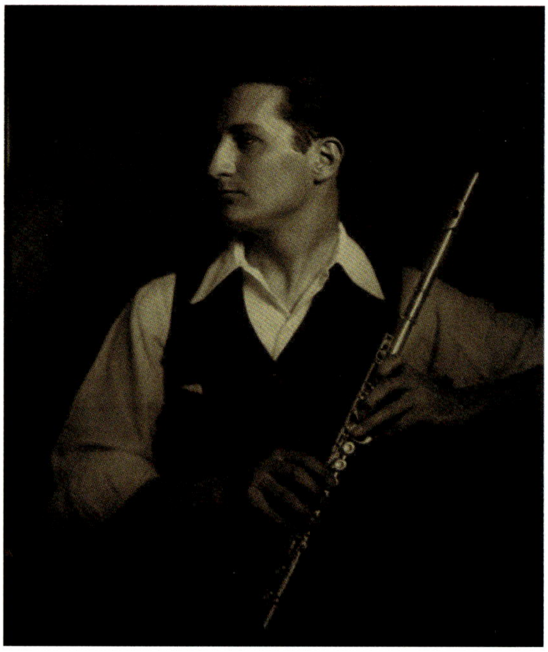

was also Karsh's responsibility to assist with the smooth operation of the animated salon sessions in the evenings as bartender.[11] This social environment significantly shaped the direction of Karsh's work, fostering his ease around famous personalities and his confidence in directing them.

Garo opened Karsh's artistic world and taught him advanced photographic processes. Karsh later reflected, "Garo taught me something more important than technique alone—he taught me to see, and to remember what I saw. He also prepared me to think for myself and evolve my own distinctive interpretations."[12] Karsh's mentorship with Garo ended in 1931 when his temporary work papers expired, requiring him to return to Canada. What had been intended to be a six-month apprenticeship had lasted three years: "Garo's salon was my university, a noble institution at which to have been permitted to study."[13]

Mastering Light and Shadow

After three years apprenticing with John H. Garo in Boston and a brief stint working at his uncle Nakash's Sherbrooke studio, Karsh chose Ottawa for his portrait practice. As the seat of government, Ottawa promised a steady stream of clients from diplomatic, societal, and cultural circles. Initially, Karsh worked for established local portrait photographer John Powis. In 1933, despite the worsening economic conditions of the Great Depression, Karsh took over Powis's Sparks Street lease to launch his own stylish but fledgling studio.

Less than ten years after arriving in Canada as a young refugee fleeing the Armenian Genocide, Karsh was proficient at the pictorial, technical, and social codes needed to become a portrait master. Several key factors contributed to his success during these early years: foremost was his exposure to dramatic lighting techniques and his new understanding of the photographer's role as director of scenes through his work with Ottawa's amateur theatre community.

Left: John Singleton Copley, *Paul Revere*, 1768, oil on canvas, 89.2 x 72.4 cm, Museum of Fine Arts, Boston. Copley presents an idealized image of the artisan at work, portraying the American revolutionary and silversmith pausing to gaze pensively at the viewer, cradling one of his own teapots with one hand. This work was acquired and newly on display during Karsh's apprenticeship to Garo. Right: John H. Garo, *Laurente Torno*, 1927, gelatin silver print, 43 x 35.3 cm, Harvard Art Museums / Fogg Museum, Cambridge, Massachusetts.

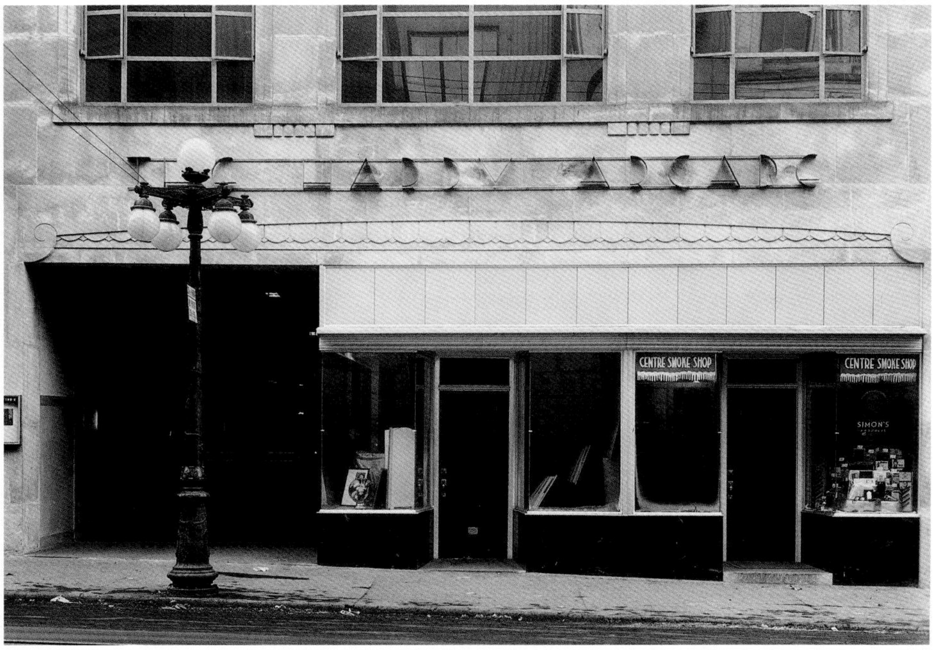

Rather than use natural light and large-format glass negatives, as Garo had done, Karsh adopted a more modern approach: he worked with nitrate film negatives and used the artificial lighting favoured in fashion and film photography, such as the portraits published in *Vanity Fair* magazine. In 1933, Karsh—who may have been introduced to artificial studio lighting by his uncle Nakash or John Powis—began volunteering to photograph productions at the Ottawa Little Theatre. This admission into the world of theatre was both strategic and significant, providing him with the opportunity to study the performances' dramatic lighting and complex compositions.[14]

In contrast to Garo's soft modulations of light and shadow in the Pictorialist tradition, Karsh's photographs of the 1930s began to feature a theatricality, with sharper definitions and stronger contrasts.[15] Karsh befriended Madge Macbeth, author and founding member of the Ottawa Little Theatre. In a 1936 portrait, Karsh demonstrates his mastery of theatrical light and shadow by posing Macbeth as a silhouette enveloped in the filigree pattern cast by backlit ironwork. This work exemplifies Karsh's early commissions and his signature approach to portraying mature women as consequential agents of change.

In his first season photographing the productions of the Ottawa Little Theatre, Karsh also formed a friendship with one of its leading ladies, Solange Gauthier. "Something more important than my introduction to incandescent lighting came out of the Little Theatre," Karsh later reflected regarding his meeting with Solange. "My first night there I was ushered into the dressing room of the leading lady, the spirited and independent Solange Gauthier.... From our marriage some years later, to her death in 1961, she was a source of encouragement, understanding, and inspiration."[16]

Solange left her job as secretary to a member of Parliament from Quebec to become Karsh's studio manager in 1936 and his wife in 1939. Born in France in 1900, Solange had immigrated to Canada with her mother. Eight years older than Karsh and previously married, the gregarious and free-spirited Solange was a well-connected and creative individual in her own right. She was an important muse and a keen business manager, focused on

Exterior view of 130 Sparks Street, renovated in 1936 into the Hardy Arcade, featuring Karsh's studio on the upper level, Ottawa, December 11, 1936, photograph by Yousuf Karsh.

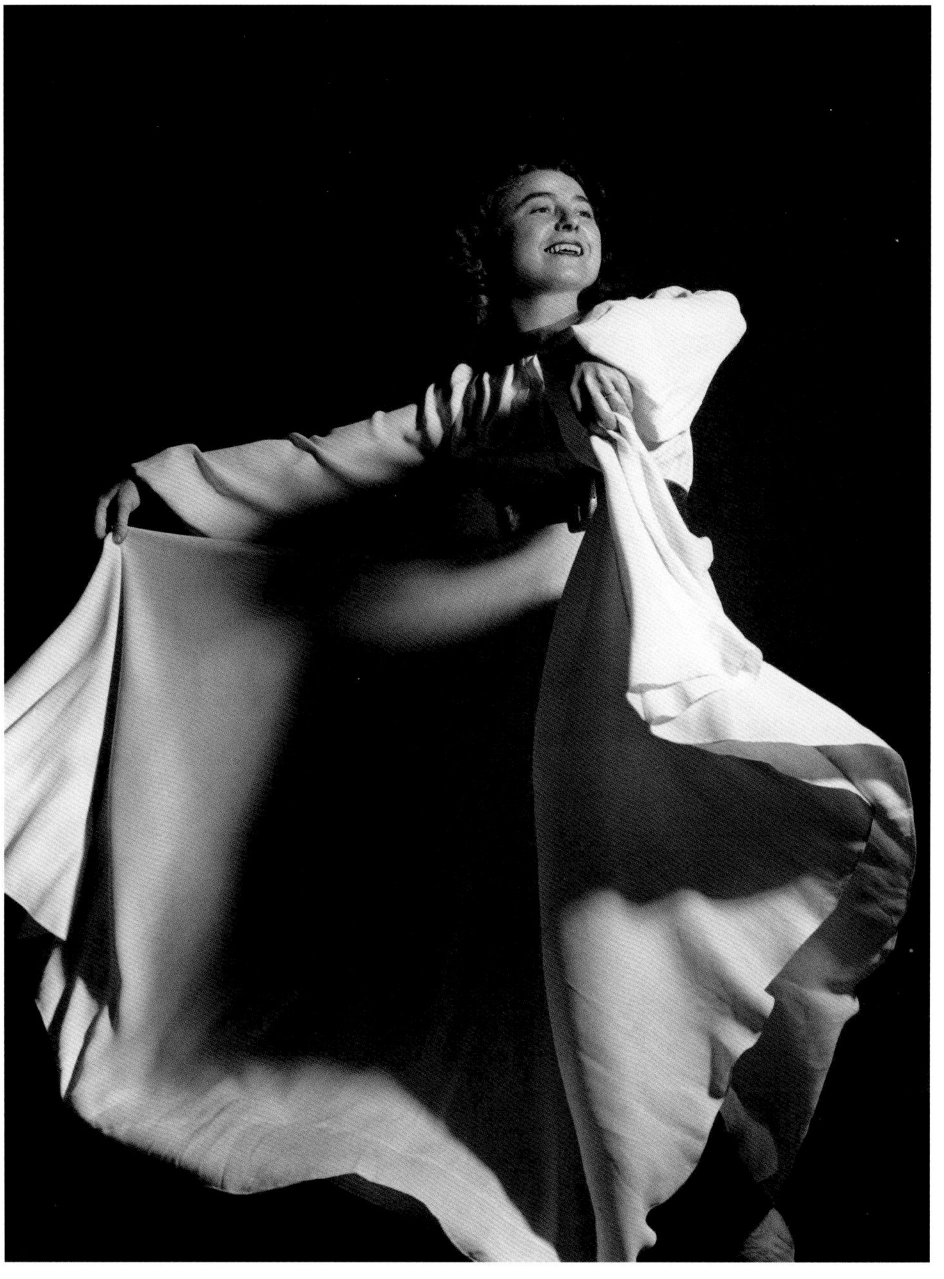

all aspects of promotion and publication, as well as the efficient running of Karsh's studio. Although she said that it was her job to see that the bills went out and the money came in,[17] she also employed her considerable skills in social charm, prepared textual narratives recounting Karsh's important portrait sittings, and generated promotion and publicity. She was also an invaluable counterpoint to Karsh's sometimes anxious perfectionism.

As an immigrant and visible minority who spoke English with a heavy accent, Karsh valued the opportunity to form social connections within the welcoming and socially fluid creative community of the Ottawa Little Theatre. His connection to one of the company's leading players, the young Viscount Duncannon, Frederick Ponsonby, led to an introduction to Ponsonby's parents, Governor General Vere Ponsonby, Earl of

Yousuf Karsh, *Solange Gauthier*, June 14, 1935, Estate of Yousuf Karsh. Opposite: Yousuf Karsh, *Madge Macbeth*, August 3, 1936, gelatin silver print, 33 x 26.7 cm (image), 50.8 x 40.6 cm (mount), Estate of Yousuf Karsh.

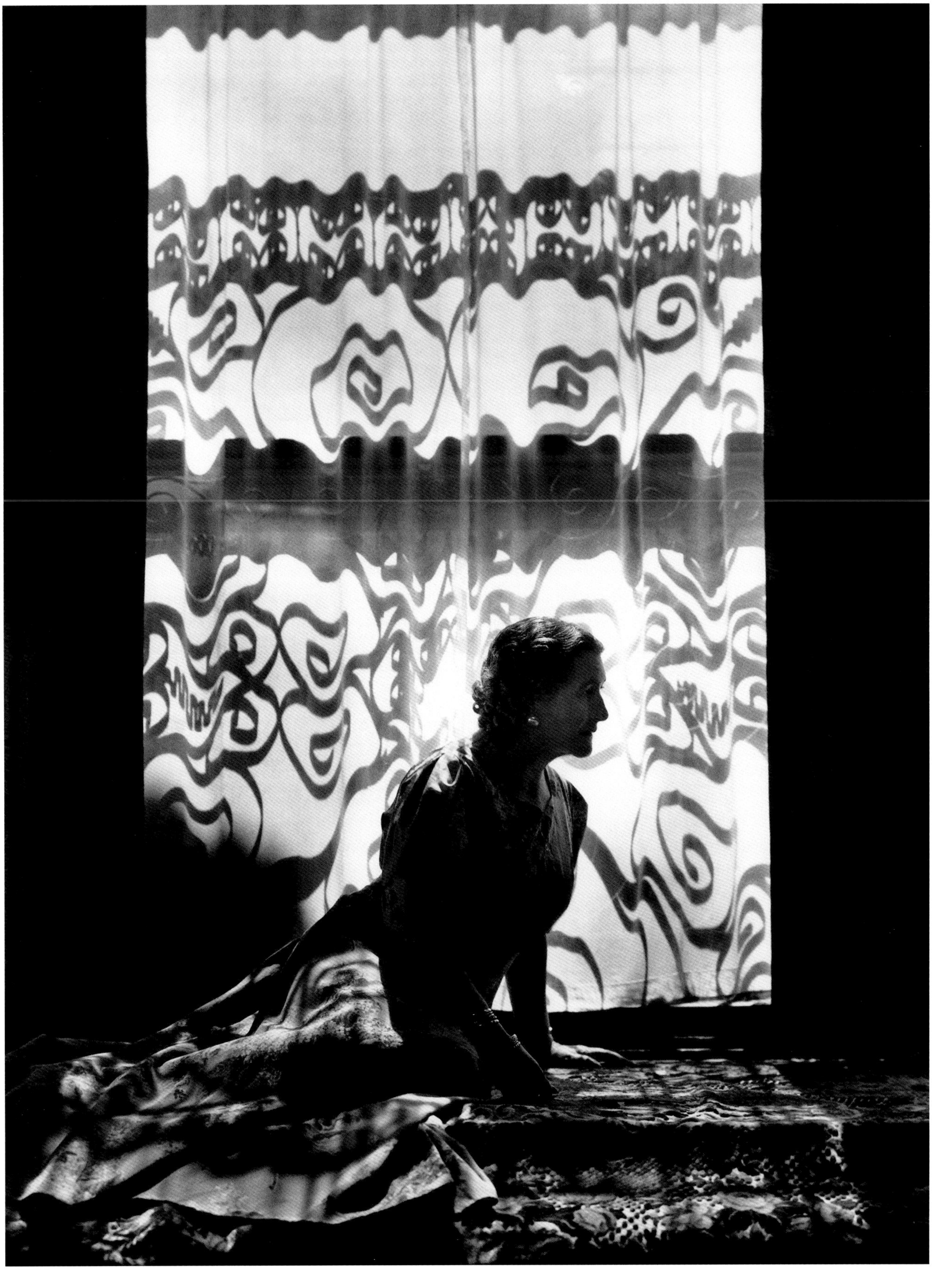

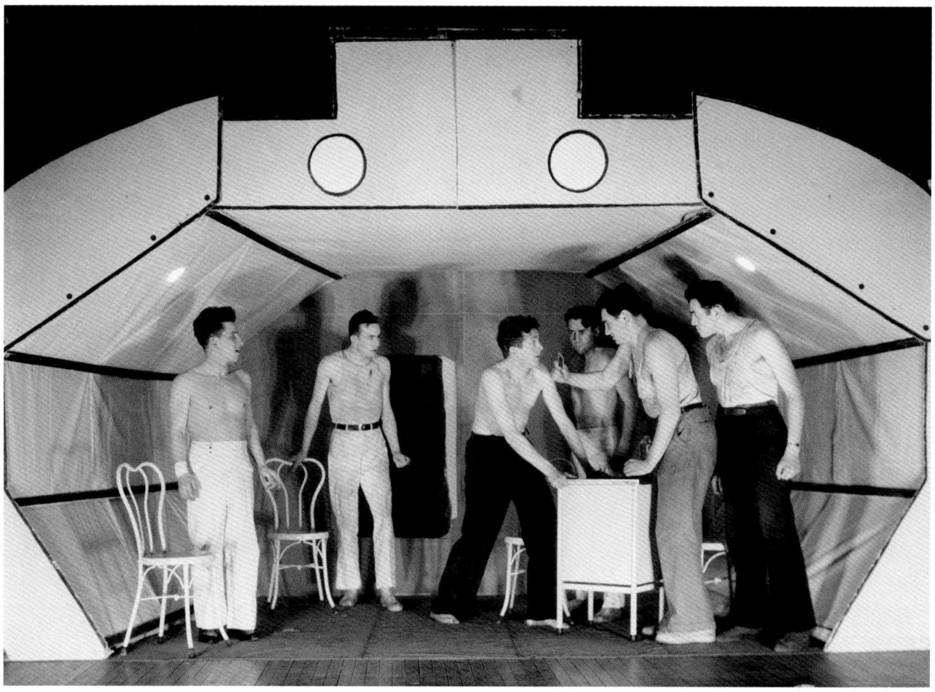

Bessborough, and his wife, Roberte Ponsonby, Countess of Bessborough. Lord and Lady Bessborough were the founders and honorary patrons of the Dominion Drama Festival, an annual spring competition featuring performances from regional theatre companies across Canada. Karsh's charismatic personality and impeccable manners accelerated his promotion to official photographer of the festival's productions, and he was soon asked to produce the couple's official portrait.

A Widening Sphere

Karsh's connection to the creative circle of Ottawa's theatre productions provided him with more than a life partner and an opportunity to master dramatic lighting. It also opened important channels to circulate his work to a national audience. In early 1933, while Karsh was photographing productions of the Dominion Drama Festival, he was introduced to Adele M. Gianelli, social editor of Canada's weekly illustrated magazine, *Saturday Night*. Founded in Toronto in 1897, *Saturday Night* had become, under the direction of its editor, B.K. Sandwell, a leading journal of writings on politics, literature, and the arts, with a strong emphasis on Canada's distinct cultural perspective. Gianelli advocated for Karsh's work to be featured in the magazine, garnering the support of Sandwell.

For Karsh, *Saturday Night* was an ideal venue for both his artistic and his business objectives. The journal's large, luxurious format, printed on coated paper, introduced his work to a national audience, increasing portrait bookings at his studio. From that point onward, he worked closely with Sandwell to coordinate the publication of his best work.

By the mid-1930s, Karsh was rapidly becoming Ottawa's leading photographer, building important connections within the city's creative community. With patience and promotion, he took on more commissions for various purposes, from passport photos and business headshots to portraits commemorating special events, including key moments in the social calendars of the city's elite.

Production image from *Submerged*, Dominion Drama Festival, Ottawa, April 27, 1934, photograph by Yousuf Karsh, Yousuf Karsh Fonds, Library and Archives Canada, Ottawa.

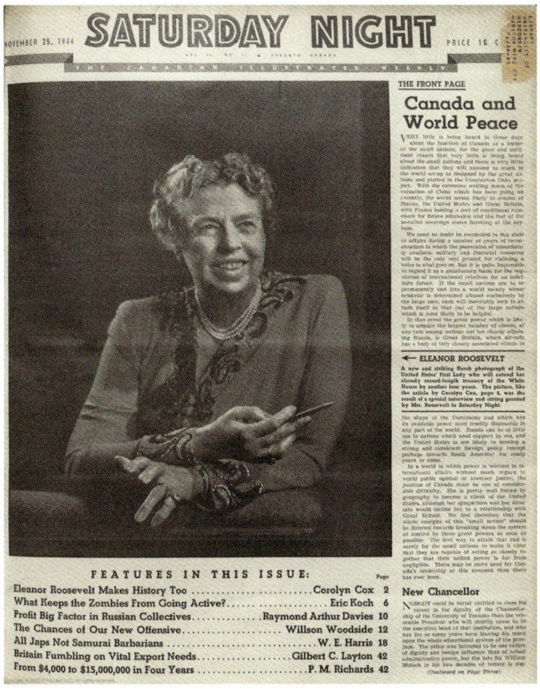

NOVEMBER 25, 1944 **SATURDAY NIGHT** PRICE 10 C

THE CANADIAN ILLUSTRATED WEEKLY

THE FRONT PAGE

Canada and World Peace

VERY little is being heard in these days about the function of Canada as a leader of the small nations, for the good and sufficient reason that very little is being heard about the small nations and there is very little indication that they will amount to much in the world set-up as designed by the great nations and plotted in the Dumbarton Oaks project. With the extensive writing down of the valuation of China which has been going on recently, the world seems likely to consist of Russia, the United States and Great Britain, with France holding a sort of conditional raincheck for future admission and the rest of the so-called sovereign states listening at the keyhole.

We must no doubt be reconciled to this state of affairs during a number of years of reconstruction in which the possession of immediately available military and financial resources will be the only real ground for claiming a voice in what goes on. But it is quite impossible to regard it as a satisfactory basis for the regulation of international relations for an indefinite future. If the small nations are to be permanently tied into a world society whose behavior is determined almost exclusively by the large ones, each will inevitably seek to attach itself to that one of the large nations which is most likely to be helpful.

In that event the great power which is likely to acquire the largest number of clients, at any rate among nations not too closely adjoining Russia, is Great Britain, which already has a body of very closely associated clients in

← ELEANOR ROOSEVELT

A new and striking Karsh photograph of the United States' First Lady who will extend her already record-length tenancy of the White House by another four years. The picture, like the article by Corolyn Cox, page 2, was the result of a special interview and sitting granted by Mrs. Roosevelt to Saturday Night.

the shape of the Dominions and which has its available power most readily disposable in any part of the world. Russia can be of little use to nations which need support by sea, and the United States is not likely to develop a strong and consistent foreign policy except perhaps towards South America for many years to come.

In a world in which power is wielded in international affairs without much regard to world public opinion or abstract justice, the position of Canada must be one of considerable difficulty. She is pretty well forced by geography to become a client of the United States, although her sympathies and her interests would incline her to a relationship with Great Britain. We feel therefore that the whole energies of this "small nation" should be directed towards breaking down the system of control by three great powers as soon as possible. The best way to attain that end is surely for the small nations to make it clear that they are capable of acting so closely together that their united power is far from negligible. There may be more need for Canada's leadership at this moment than there has ever been.

New Chancellor

NOBODY could be better entitled to close his career in the dignity of the Chancellorship of the University of Toronto than the venerable President who will shortly cease to be the executive head of that institution, and who has for so many years been leaving his mark upon the whole educational system of the province. The office was intended to be one rather of dignity and benign influence than of actual administrative power, but the late Sir William Mulock in his two decades of tenure is sup-

(Continued on Page Three)

FEATURES IN THIS ISSUE:

		Page
Eleanor Roosevelt Makes History Too	Corolyn Cox	2
What Keeps the Zombies From Going Active?	Eric Koch	6
Profit Big Factor in Russian Collectives	Raymond Arthur Davies	10
The Chances of Our New Offensive	Willson Woodside	12
All Japs Not Samurai Barbarians	W. E. Harris	18
Britain Fumbling on Vital Export Needs	Gilbert C. Layton	42
From $4,000 to $15,000,000 in Four Years	P. M. Richards	42

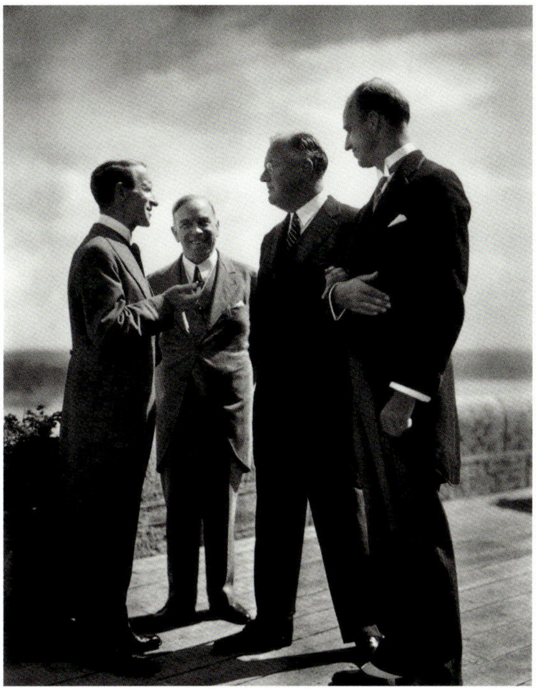

Karsh's studio, which he had taken over after John Powis's retirement in 1933, was located on the top floor of 130 Sparks Street, later named the Hardy Arcade. The fashionable Art Deco–style building provided ample natural light and was situated along one of Ottawa's busiest streets, one block from Parliament Hill. Karsh's work attracted high-profile patrons, notably Prime Minister William Lyon Mackenzie King, who was photographed by Karsh at his office and home multiple times. King also commissioned Karsh to create portraits of visiting dignitaries as part of Canada's historical record on the world stage.

In August 1936, King arranged for Karsh to photograph the visit of Franklin Delano Roosevelt, the first American president to come to Canada, and his son James Roosevelt. Karsh later recounted how a fortunate blend of skill and luck allowed him the opportunity to secure his desired portrait during a crowded press conference: "Later in the afternoon, President Roosevelt appeared with his son James, Lord Tweedsmuir and the Canadian Prime Minister. They consented to be photographed and posed very stiffly and militarily for me. I pretended to take the picture, and thanked them, whereupon they relaxed, and Lord Tweedsmuir began to tell one of the Scottish stories for which he was famous. As they listened, at ease, I took the picture."[18]

In addition to portraits commissioned for official government business and the historical record, Karsh attracted important patrons, including members of Parliament, ambassadors, and touring performers. Among them were Myra Armour, wife of American diplomat Norman Armour, and Paul Robeson, an actor and bass-baritone concert artist. After the onset of the Second World War in 1939, the regular appearance of Karsh's portraits of political leaders, socialites, and theatrical stars in the pages of *Saturday Night* was enhanced with an expanding gallery of wartime bureaucrats accompanied by text that outlined their roles in wartime operations.[19] Sandwell was

Left: Cover of *Saturday Night*, November 25, 1944. Right: Yousuf Karsh, *Canada's Governor General Lord Tweedsmuir and Prime Minister William Lyon Mackenzie King with American President Franklin Roosevelt and his son, James Roosevelt*, August 14, 1936, 35 x 71 cm, gelatin silver print, Estate of Yousuf Karsh.

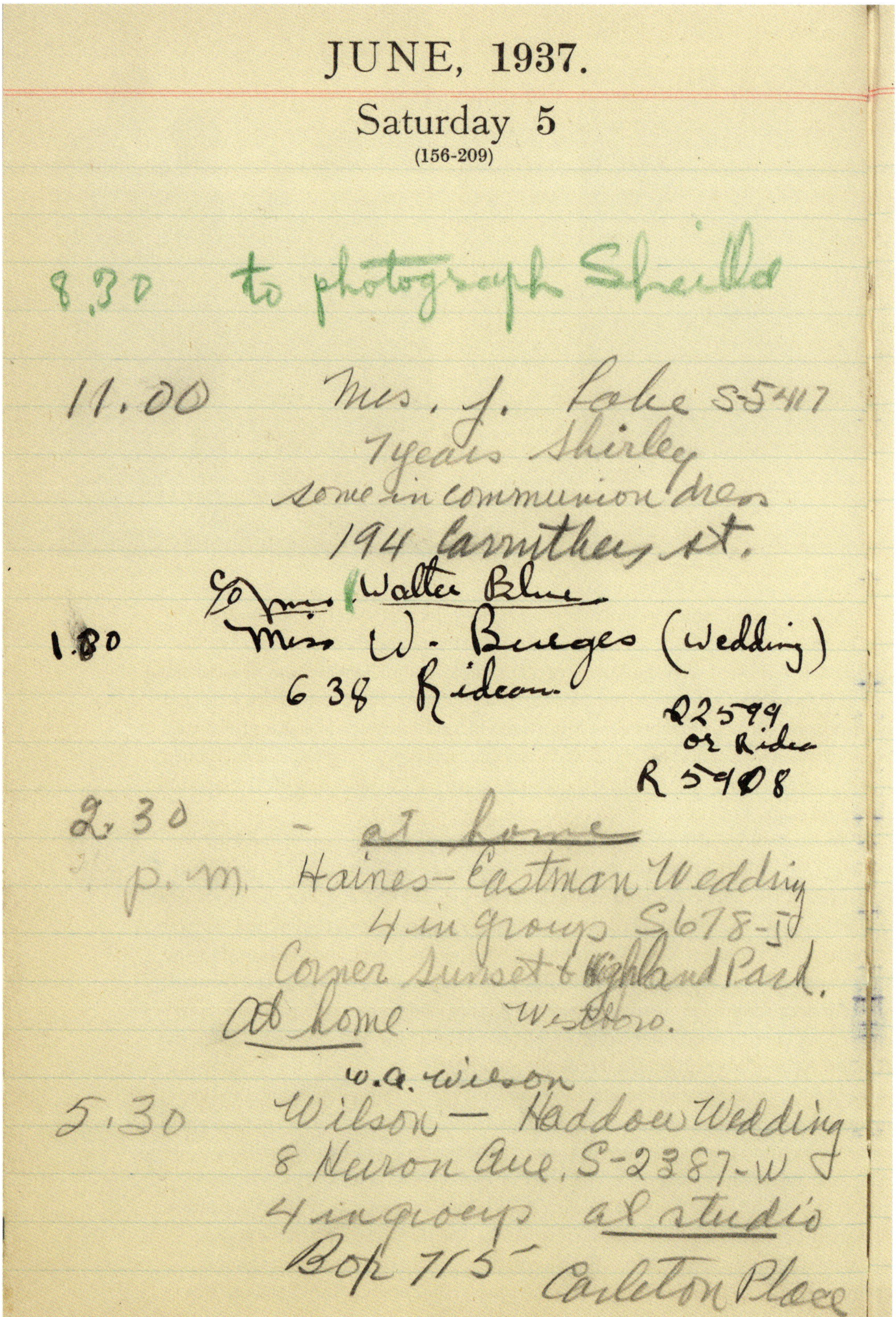

JUNE, 1937.

Saturday 5
(156-209)

8.30 to photograph Shields

11.00 Mrs. J. Lake S-5417
7 years Shirley
some in communion dress
194 Carruthers St.

Mrs. Walter Blue
1.30 Miss W. Burges (Wedding)
638 Rideau
R2599 or Rideau R5908

2.30 – at home
p.m. Haines-Eastman Wedding
4 in groups S678-J
Corner Sunset & Highland Park.
At home Westboro.

W. A. Wilson
5.30 Wilson – Haddow Wedding
8 Heron Ave. S-2387-W J
4 in groups at studio
Box 715 Carleton Place

Yousuf Karsh's appointment calendar noting Shirley Lake's eleven o'clock sitting on Saturday, June 5, 1937.

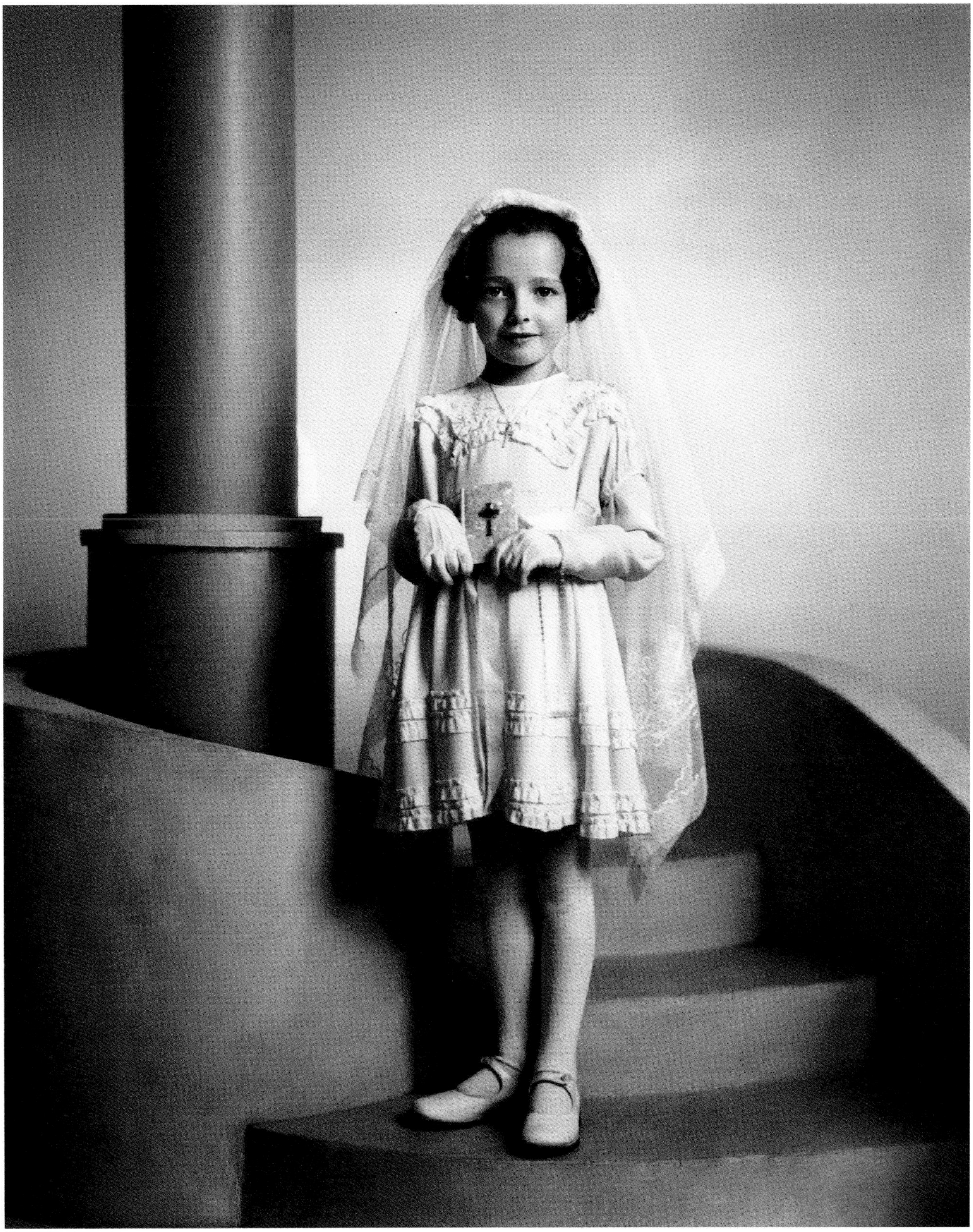

Yousuf Karsh, *Shirley Lake*, June 5, 1937, gelatin silver print, 1937, 24.1 x 19 cm (image), 35 x 27.7 (sheet), Yousuf Karsh Fonds, Library and Archives Canada, Ottawa.

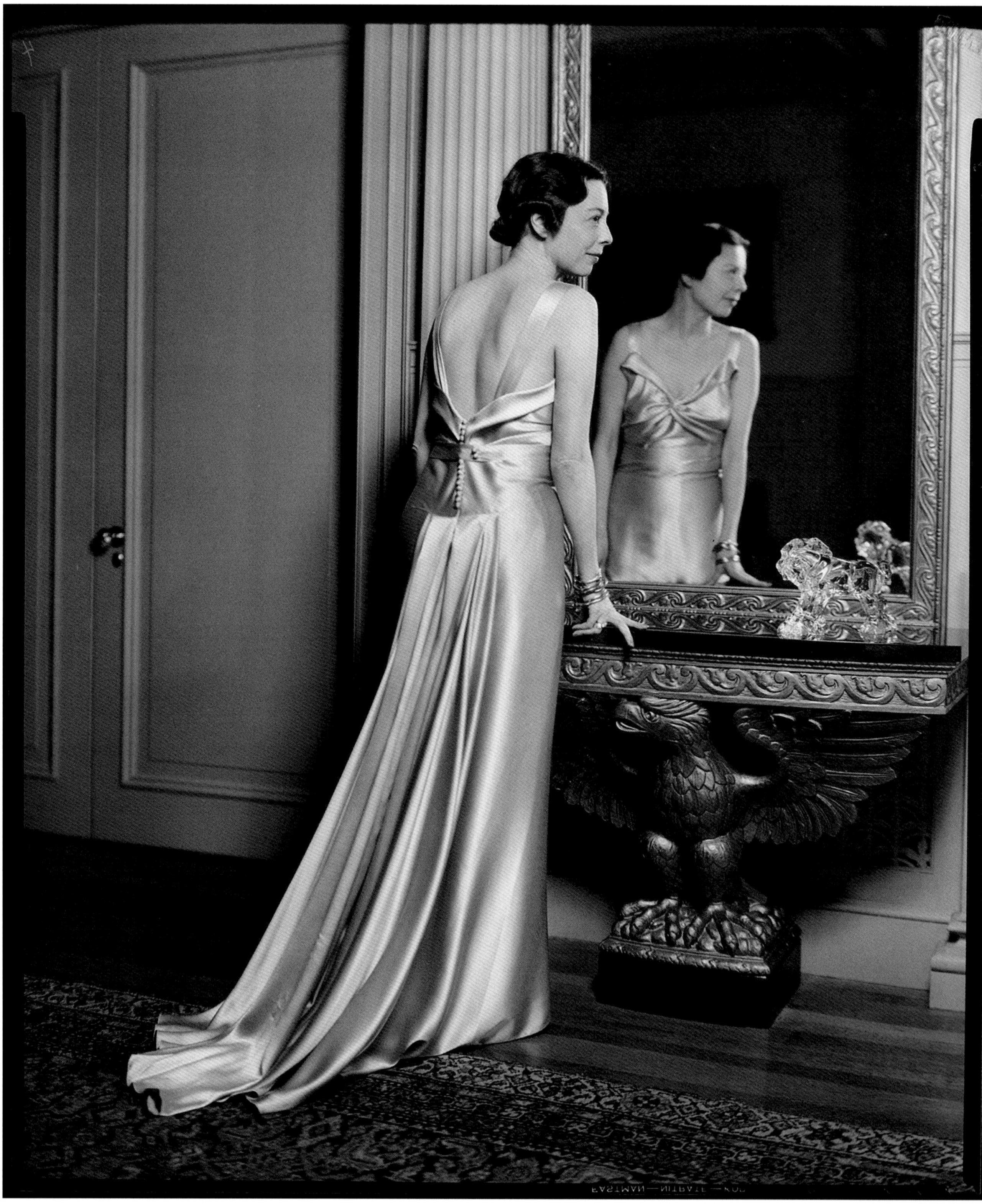

Yousuf Karsh, *Mrs. Norman Armour*, March 18, 1937, interpositive made from original nitrate negative, 25 x 19.9 cm, Yousuf Karsh Fonds, Library and Archives Canada, Ottawa.

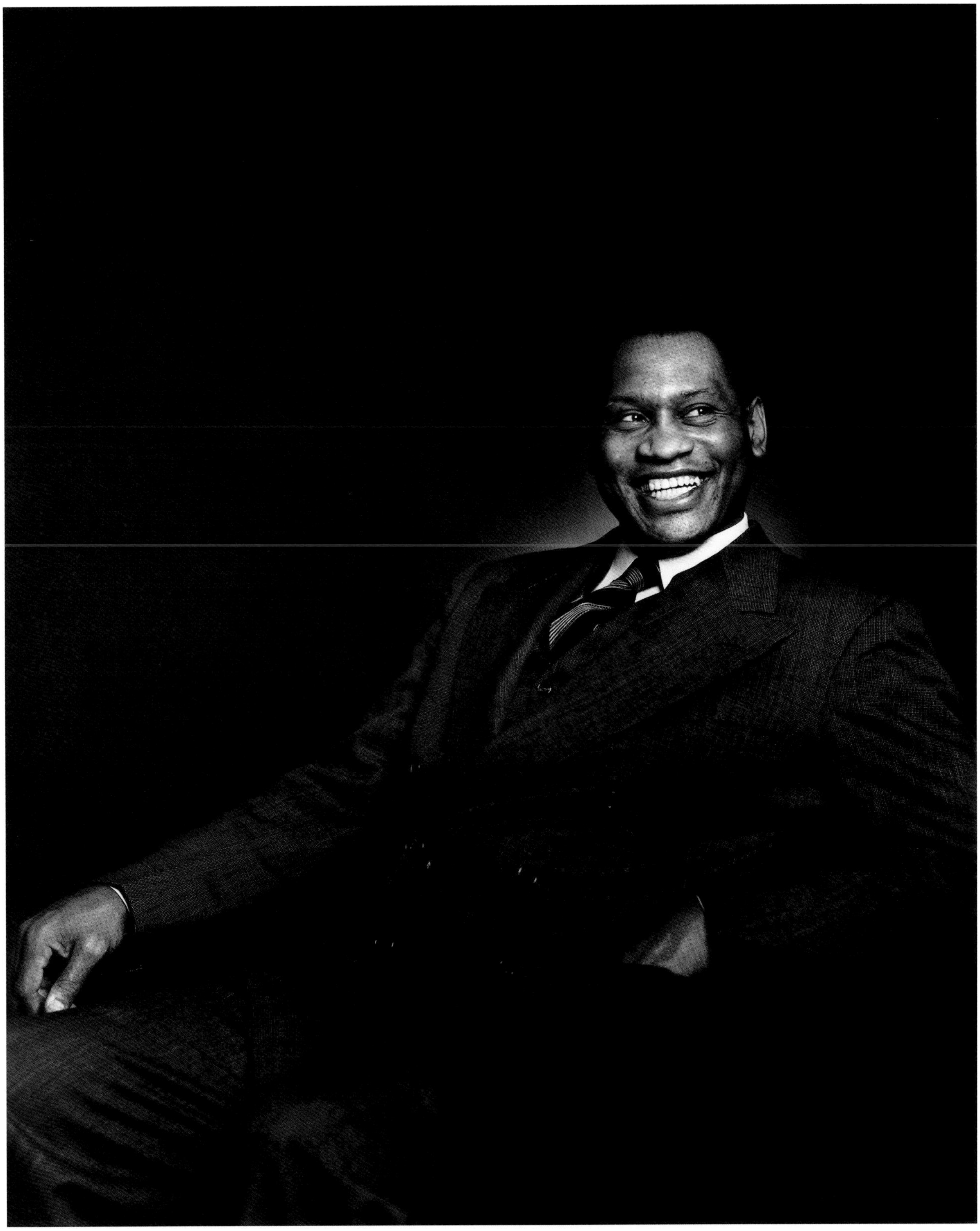

Yousuf Karsh, *Paul Robeson*, October 30, 1941, gelatin silver print, 48.9 x 39.1 cm (image), 71.1 x 55.9 cm (mount), Estate of Yousuf Karsh. Paul Robeson achieved acclaim as a scholar, actor, concert singer, and political activist. At the time of this sitting with Karsh, he was noted for his performances in London's Savoy Theatre production of *Othello* (1930) and the films *The Emperor Jones* (1933) and *Show Boat* (1936).

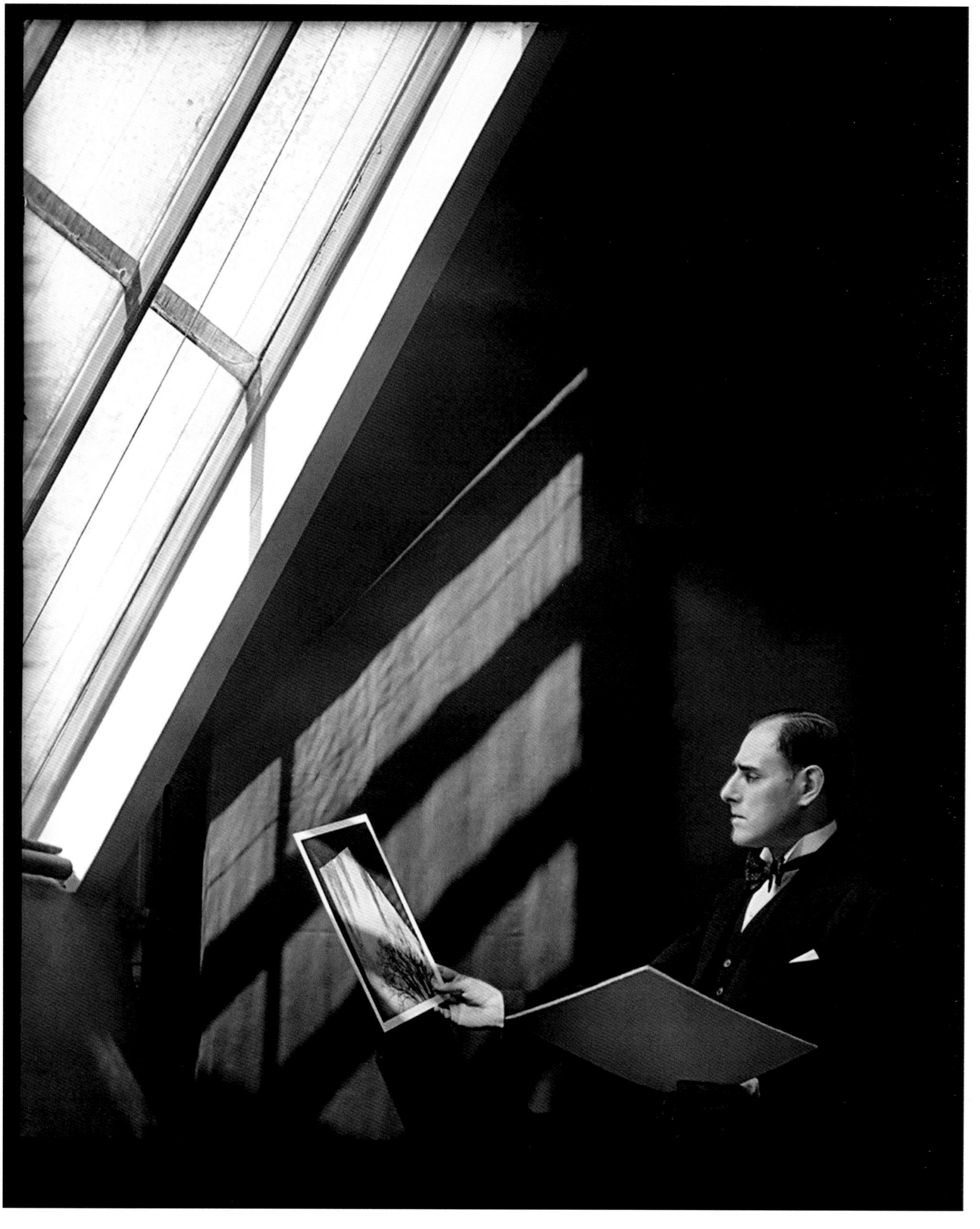

Yousuf Karsh, *Johan Helders*, August 12, 1936, gelatin silver print, 44.6 x 36.8 cm, Montreal Museum of Fine Arts.

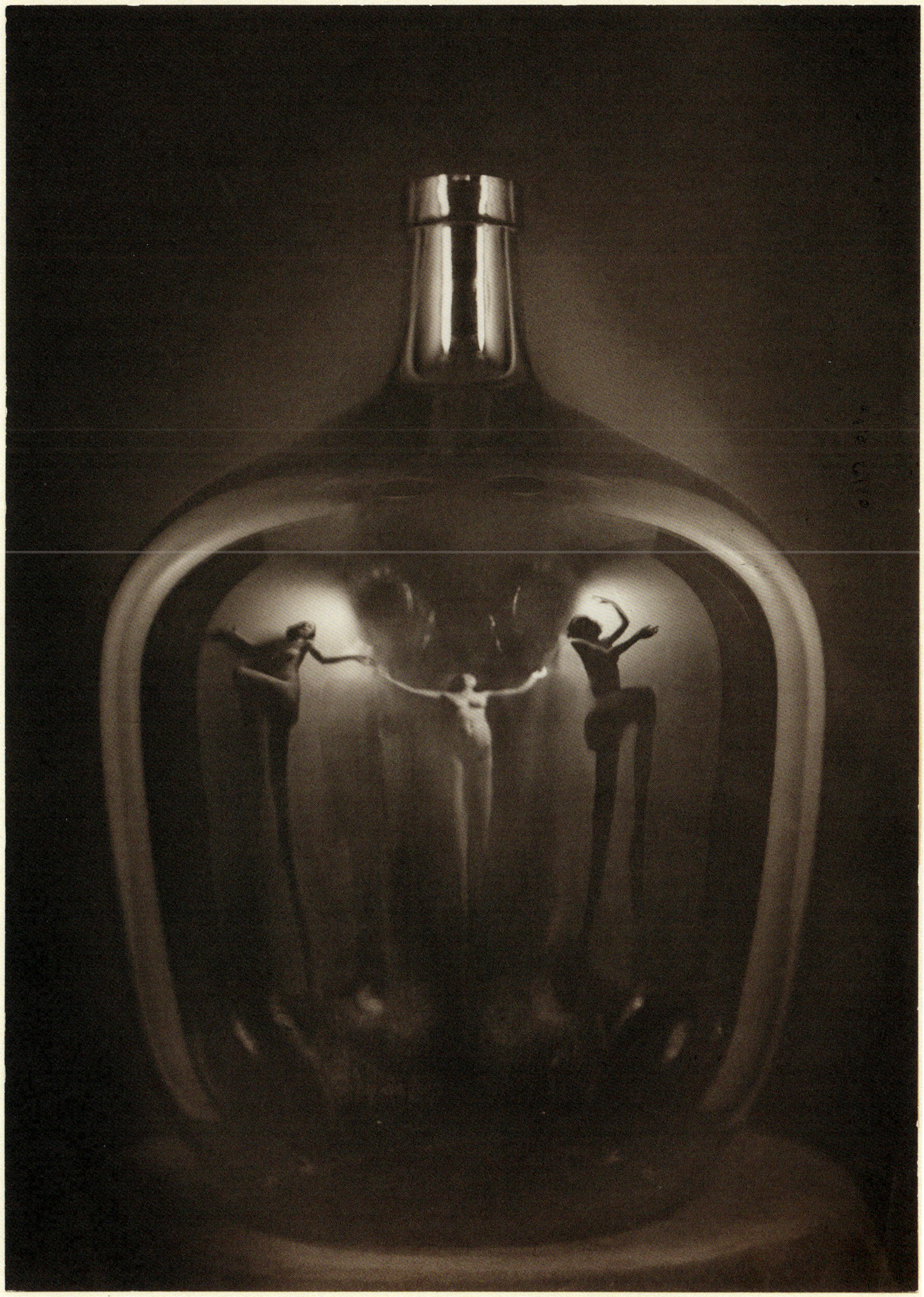

Yousuf Karsh, *Elixir*, September 1938, chlorobromide print, 44 x 31.7 cm, Yousuf Karsh Fonds, Library and Archives Canada, Ottawa.

also instrumental in arranging Karsh's first solo exhibition, which was presented at the flagship Simpson's department store in Toronto in June 1938.

Karsh also fostered opportunities to exhibit his prints through the prestigious art photography salon circuit. He was keenly aware of his mentor Garo's energetic participation in the salon movement as a way of accruing credibility as a photographic artist. Separate from the commercial photographic realm, the salon movement was composed of dedicated and talented amateur photographers who shared, critiqued, and displayed their works in meetings, lectures, and competitive salons. Importantly for Karsh, participating members featured art photographs reflective of their modern machine-age world, preferring sharp-focus images over soft-focus romanticism.

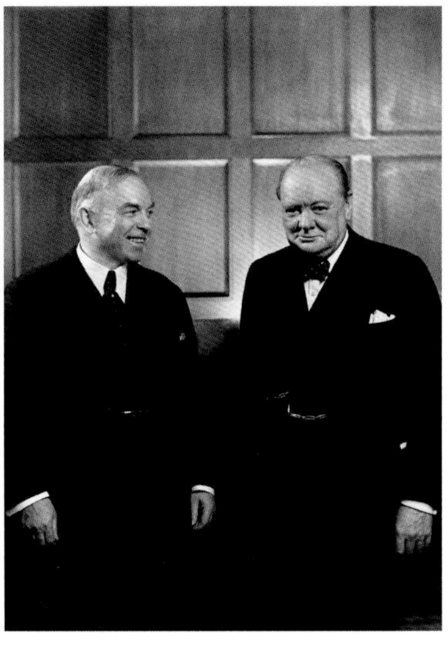

Karsh's avid study of leading photographers such as Edward Steichen (1879–1973) and his exposure to contemporary art movements permeated his self-directed salon work. Some of his salon entries represented his portraiture with an emphasis on sharply delineated contrasts, such as the 1938 portrait of fellow photographer Johan Helders (1888–1956) studying a print in natural light. Other works were experimental and reflected Karsh's awareness of and interest in surrealist currents and combination printing. *Elixir*, 1938, features nude studies of Solange seemingly trapped within a bottle.[20] Although he had limited time to step away from paid portrait sittings, he submitted artistic photographs to national and international salons, earning him membership as an associate of the Royal Photographic Society in 1938.

On December 30, 1941, Karsh made a portrait that would launch him toward international fame. King arranged for Karsh to photograph British Prime Minister Winston Churchill in the Speaker's chamber moments after his historic wartime speech to members of the Canadian Senate and House of Commons. As he prepared his large camera and lights, Karsh requested that Churchill remove his cigar from his lips. He refused, and Karsh took the famous exposure just after snatching the cigar away, capturing the prime minister's indignant and belligerent facial expression.

Karsh later remarked, "The world's reception of that photograph—which it was said epitomized the indomitable spirit of the British people—changed my life."[21] The iconic portrait was immediately published widely: it came to define the face of the Allied effort during the Second World War and became one of Karsh's most reproduced works almost overnight.

Yousuf Karsh, *William Lyon Mackenzie King and Winston Churchill*, December 30, 1941, Estate of Yousuf Karsh.

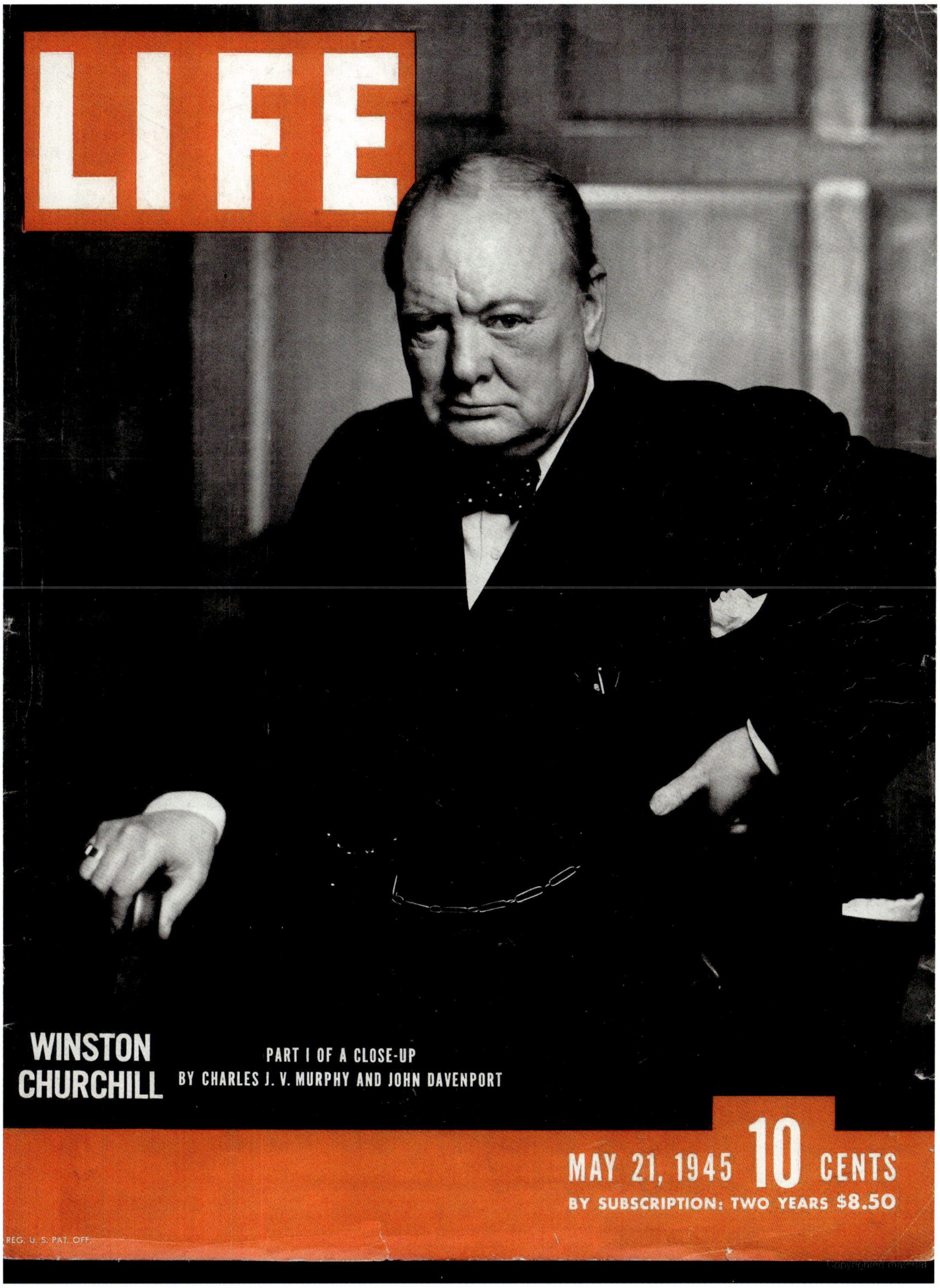

Cover of *LIFE*, May 21, 1945. Published shortly after Victory in Europe Day (May 8, 1945) marking Germany's surrender, this issue of *LIFE* magazine featured Karsh's definitive portrait of the wartime leader. It remained the most requested portrait throughout Karsh's career. His business papers show that requests for copies came from private citizens, shop owners, military personnel, clergy, artists, and photographers.

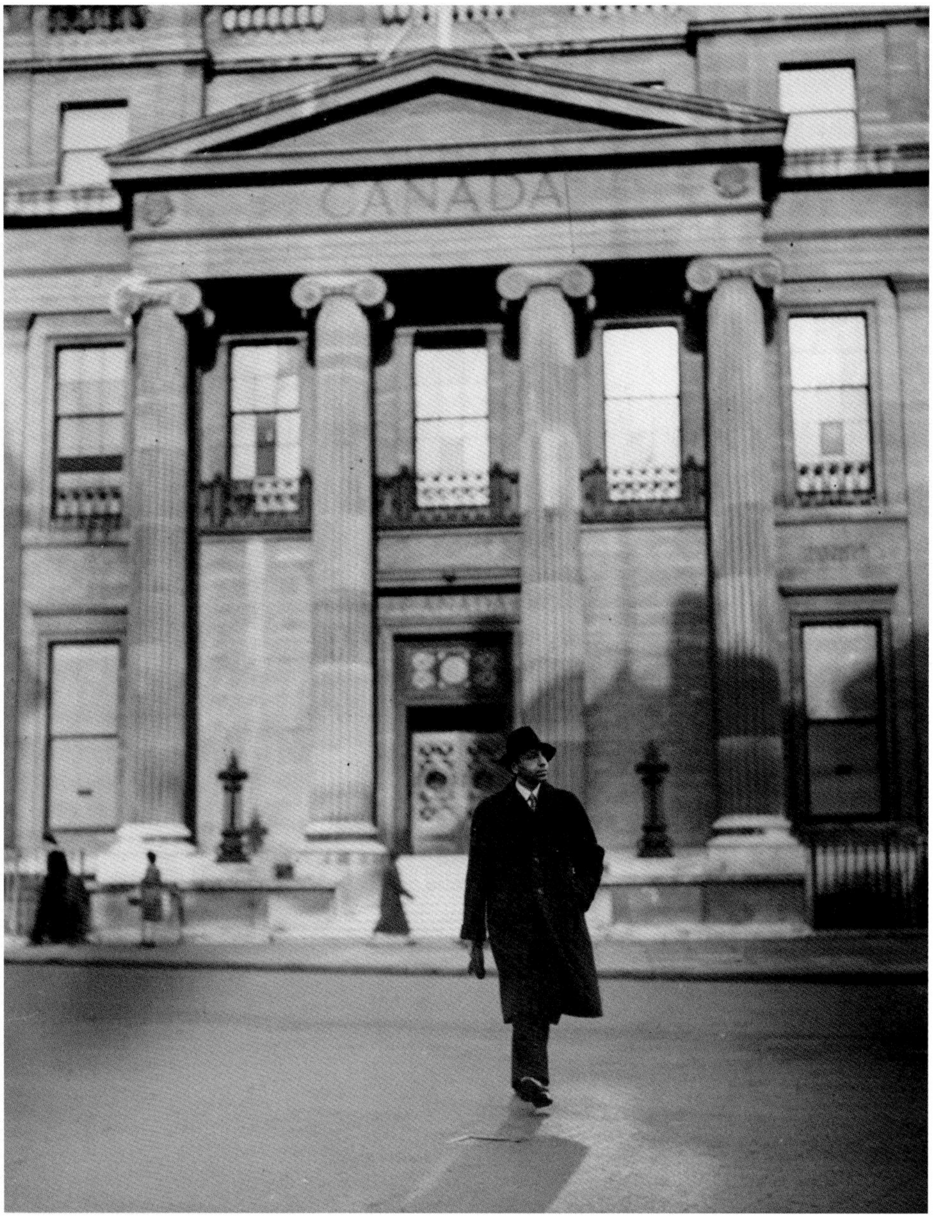

Chronicler of His Time

Karsh's sudden celebrity following the publication of the 1941 Churchill portrait launched a remarkable career spanning the next five decades. He began to see his work as an evolving collective portrait of his time. From 1942 until the close of his studio in 1992, Karsh photographed leading figures of the twentieth century, including heads of state, royalty, film stars, authors, artists, and scientists.

His name even became a verb when Field Marshal Bernard Law Montgomery (commander of the Allied ground forces during the D-Day invasion of German-occupied Western Europe) remarked after his 1946 portrait session that he had been "Karshed." Montgomery's turn of phrase implied that being photographed by Karsh was akin to joining a pantheon of significant figures, all immortalized by his signature elegant and elevating style.

Yousuf Karsh leaving Canada House, London, 1943, photograph by Pictorial Press.

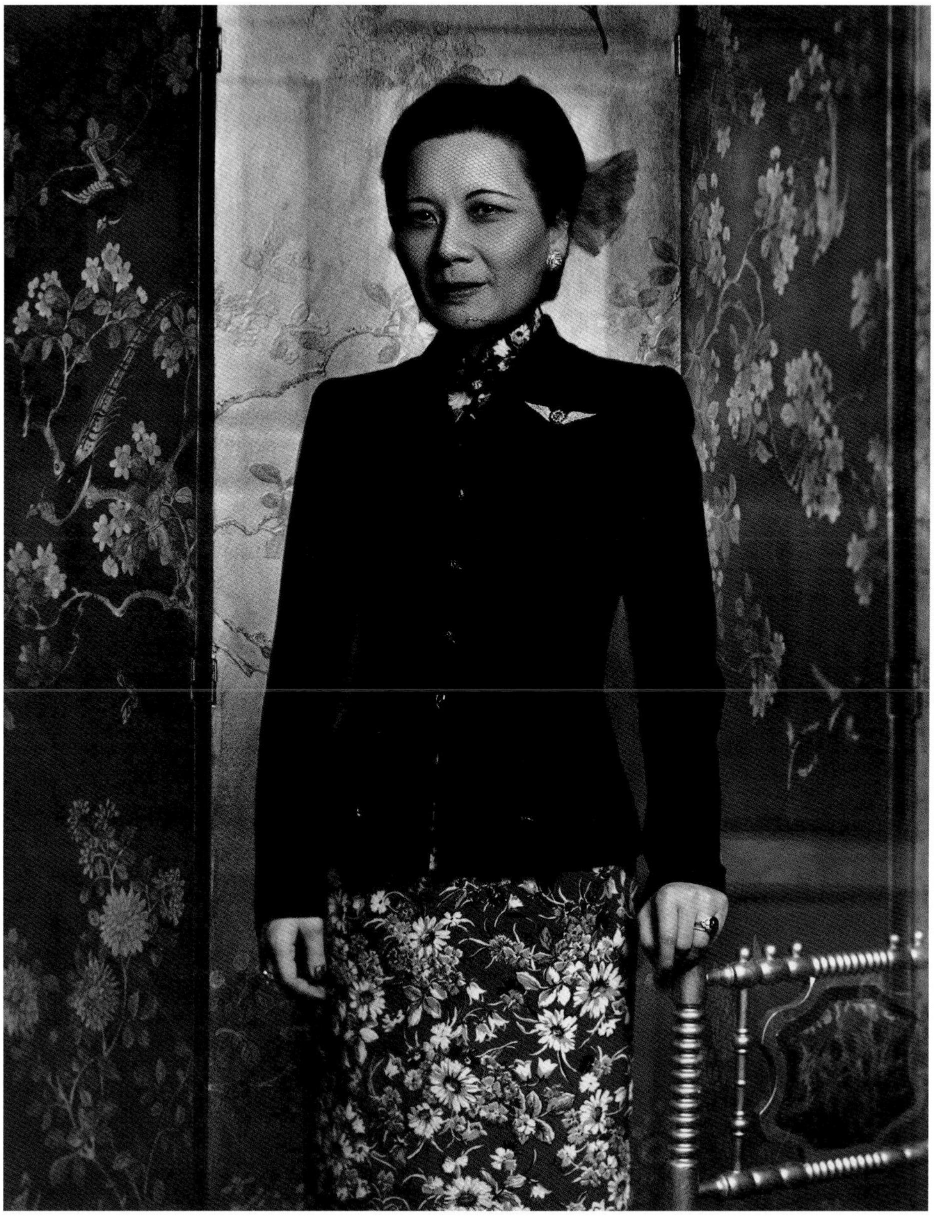

Karsh considered his work to be a collective portrait, a historical chronicle of his time. The idea of creating an enduring record of important personalities was popularized by nineteenth-century French photographer Gaspard-Félix Tournachon (1820–1910), known as Nadar, who conceived of a *galerie contemporaine* featuring leading figures as a portrait of one's own time. Curator David Travis further cites such examples as *The Gallery of Illustrious Americans* (1850) by Mathew Brady (c.1823–1896) and *Men of Mark* (1913) by Alvin Langdon Coburn (1882–1966).[22] While Karsh's concept of assembling a collective portrait in photographs was not unique, the mass circulation of his images through books, magazines, and exhibitions over the next fifty years surpassed any precedent.

What made Karsh's approach distinctive and set a template for his later work was the connection between the allure of the portrait and the photographer's own narrative of the sitting. By linking Winston Churchill's portrait to the story of Karsh's own act

Yousuf Karsh, *Madame Chiang Kai-Shek*, June 15, 1943, gelatin silver print, 49.5 x 38.3 cm (image), 71.2 x 55.8 cm (mount), Estate of Yousuf Karsh.

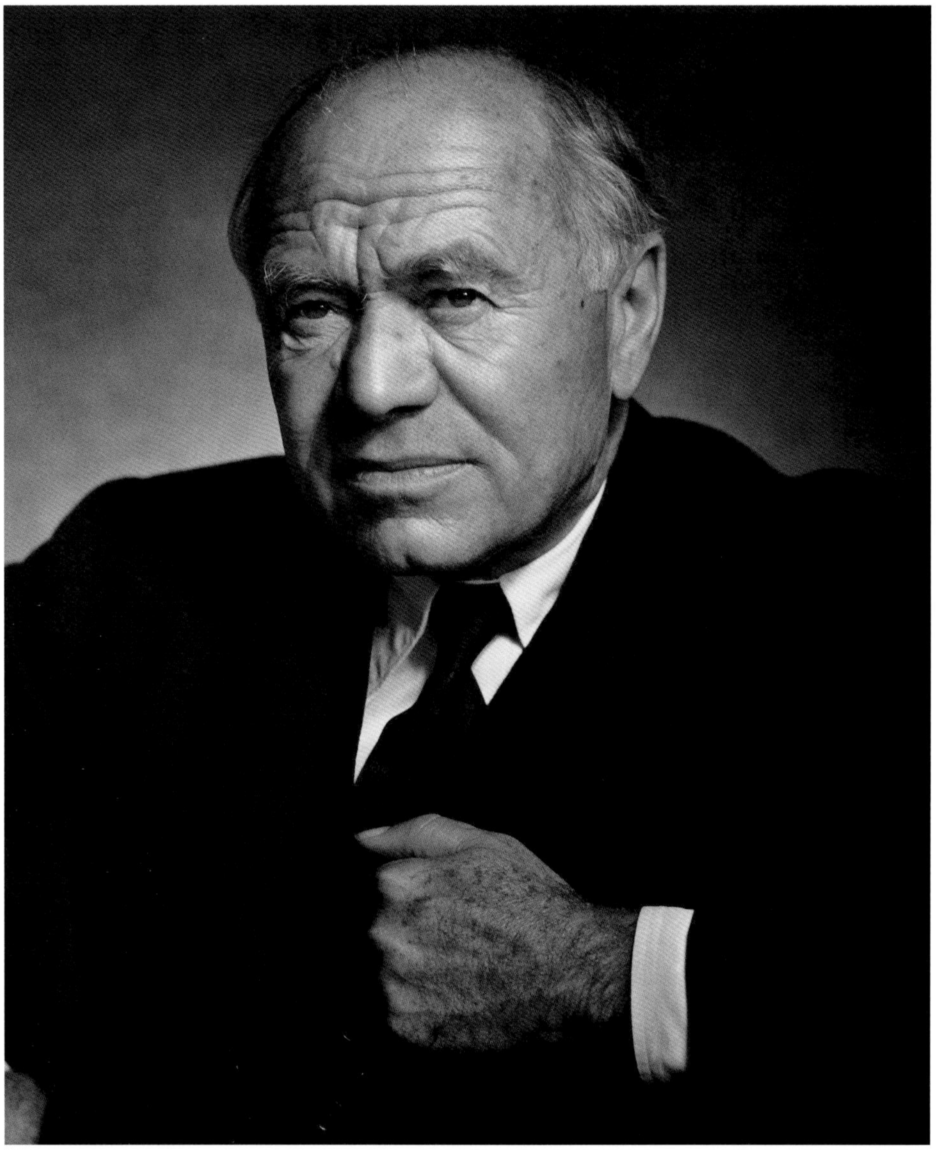

of removing the cigar, image and text worked together to amplify the viewer's sense of proximity to greatness. Karsh himself became a celebrity through the publication of sumptuous galleries of his famous sitters, which included biographical notes and his own engaging anecdotes about the portrait sessions.

Karsh's first portfolio, *Faces of Destiny*, was published in 1946, just after the Second World War. It featured seventy-three full-page portraits, each accompanied by Karsh's narrative detailing the sitter's position and role in contemporary life. The edition included recent portraits taken during Karsh's international travels. In 1943, following Prime Minister King's instruction to the Canadian embassy in London, and supplied with an advance from *Saturday Night* editor B.K. Sandwell, Karsh secured passage by convoy across the perilous Atlantic waters. As he explained, "It was in London that I started the practice which I continue to this day of 'doing my homework,' of finding out as much as I can about each person I am to photograph."[23]

Yousuf Karsh, *Lord Beaverbrook*, September 12, 1943, Estate of Yousuf Karsh.

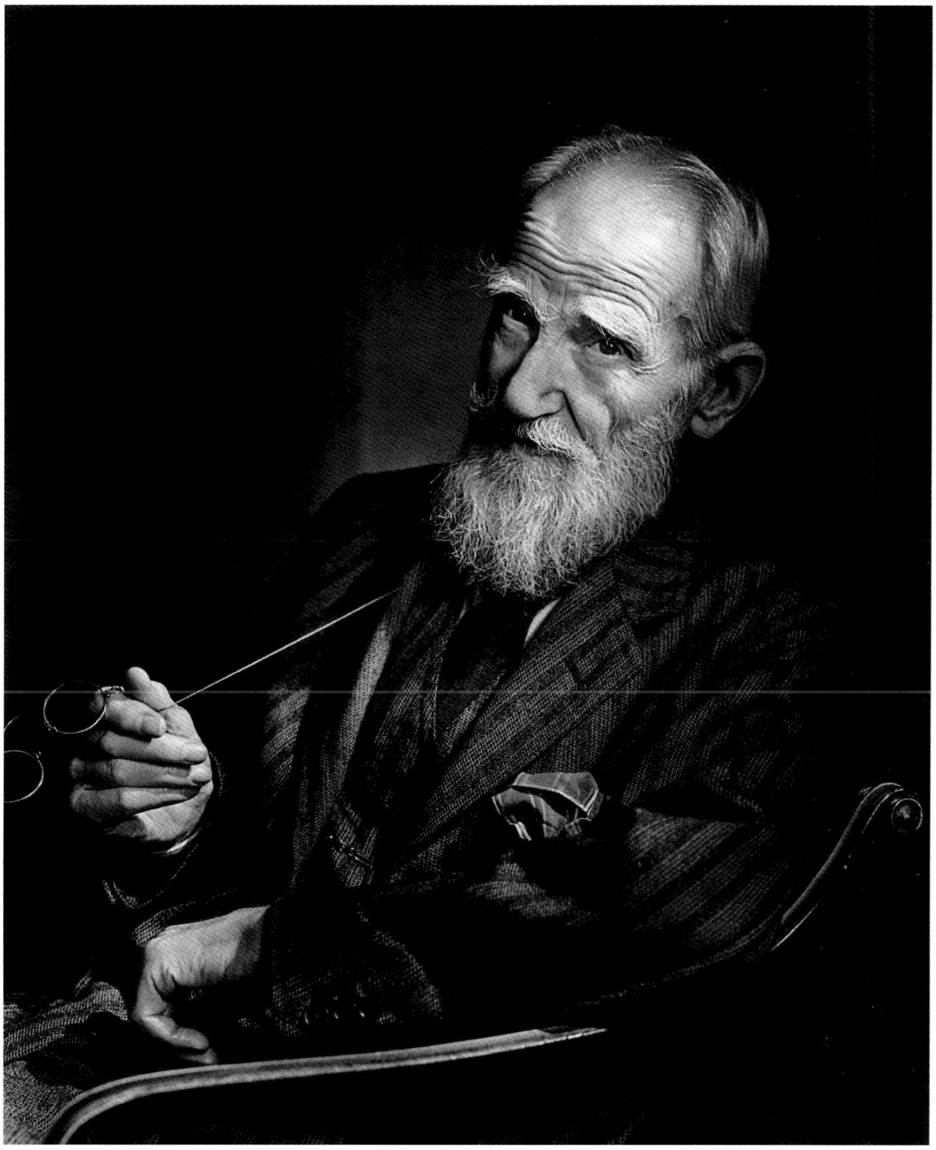

With assistance from staff at Canada House, Karsh scheduled important sittings during his two-month stay, including with notable figures such as Lord Beaverbrook, William Maxwell Aitken (the Canadian British newspaper magnate and wartime supply chain commander of aircraft production); literary figures such as George Bernard Shaw and H.G. Wells; and members of the British royal family. Also included in the portfolio were portraits from Karsh's 1945 commission by *LIFE* magazine to photograph political delegates attending the United Nations Conference on International Organization in San Francisco.

Karsh would receive even further recognition for his work. In 1947, the Canadian Citizenship Act came into effect, establishing a distinct identity for Canadian citizens, no longer considered a subclass of British subjects. In a special ceremony officiated by the Supreme Court marking the new act, Karsh was chosen to represent Ontario, and in recognition of his contributions to Canada's historical record, he received his official certificate designating him as Citizen No. 10.

Yousuf Karsh, *George Bernard Shaw*, September 12, 1943, gelatin silver print, 60 x 50.5 cm, Montreal Museum of Fine Arts.

On Assignment

By the end of the 1940s, with his international reputation firmly established, Karsh began to pursue photographic projects beyond commissioned studio portraits. Throughout his long career, he had accepted various commercial assignments, from photographing models for Burkholder Furs in the 1930s to creating advertising images for consumer products such as cigarettes, cars, liquor, watches, and cameras, as well as for government bodies.[24]

In 1950, Karsh accepted an invitation from Atlas Steel, the largest producer of stainless steel in the British Commonwealth, to create a series of images depicting steelworkers in the foundry based in Welland, Ontario.[25] He later remarked that an Atlas Steel representative had encouraged him to undertake the assignment by suggesting that after years of glorifying the prominent, he should turn his camera to "glorify the humble ones of the earth."[26] Karsh approached the project cinematically, touring the operation to find ideal settings while "casting" among the workers he observed.[27] He photographed activities such as pouring steel, roll grinding, hot strip, and coiling processes, staging one or two workers within the monumental industrial space. Where he could not bring his photographic equipment due to safety concerns, he later created composite negatives to achieve the best possible composition of the foreground figures and background machinery.

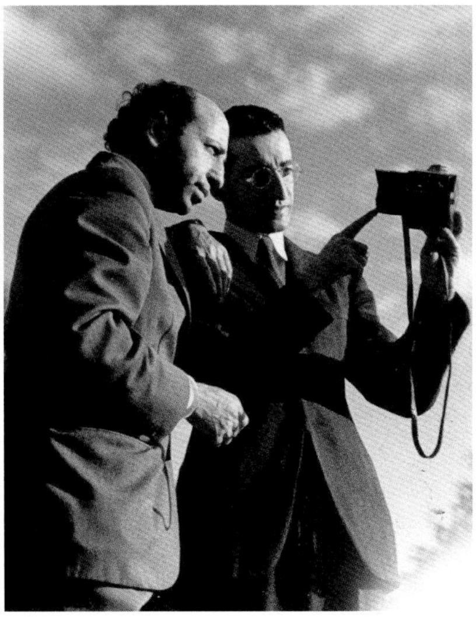

As with his portraits of illustrious sitters, Karsh aimed to ennoble the working men and dignify their labour. He received independent recognition for his editorial and commercial work in 1950 from the Art Directors Club of Chicago and in 1955 from the Art Directors Club of Montreal.[28] For Karsh, the success of the Atlas Steel assignment opened doors to further commercial and promotional projects.

In 1952, following the success of his first book, *Faces of Destiny*, and his commission for Atlas Steel, Karsh was approached by *Maclean's* to create iconic "portraits" of Canada's key cities, highlighting important industries and urban modernization. In 1953, the agreement was extended to include an additional six essays. Karsh collaborated closely with the editors at *Maclean's* to develop shooting scripts in advance and arrange access to specific locales and events.[29]

Yousuf Karsh (*left*) with his brother Malak Karsh (*right*), Ottawa, 1940s, photographer unknown. Opposite, clockwise from above left: Yousuf Karsh, *Saint John, New Brunswick*, 1952, printed 1989, gelatin silver print, 40.9 x 39.8 cm, National Gallery of Canada, Ottawa; Yousuf Karsh, *Sikh Workers at Logging Camp, British Columbia*, 1953, gelatin silver print, 23.8 x 19 cm (image), 25.3 x 20.5 cm (sheet), Estate of Yousuf Karsh; Yousuf Karsh, *Man Eating Lunch [Lawrence Heppler], Great Lakes Paper Company, Thunder Bay*, c.1953, gelatin silver print, 12.2 x 9.6 cm (image), 12.6 x 9.8 cm (support), Yousuf Karsh Fonds, Library and Archives Canada, Ottawa.

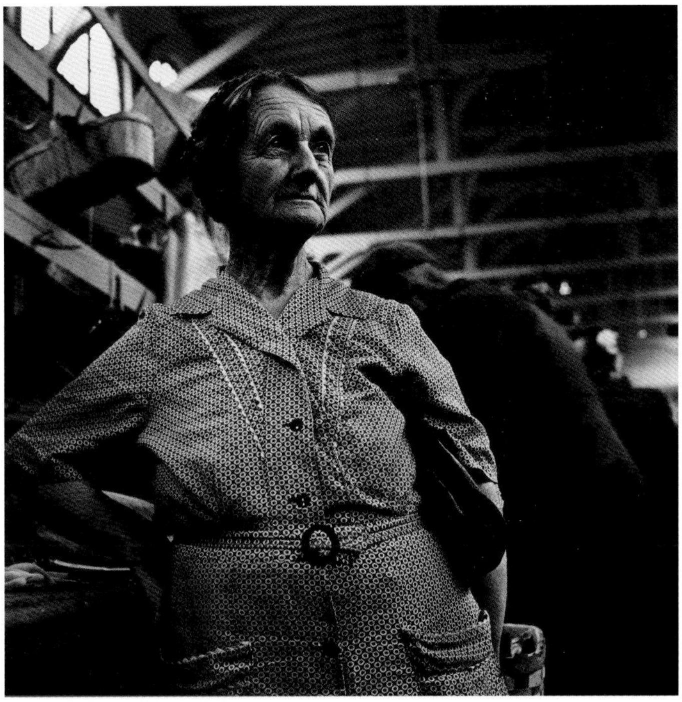

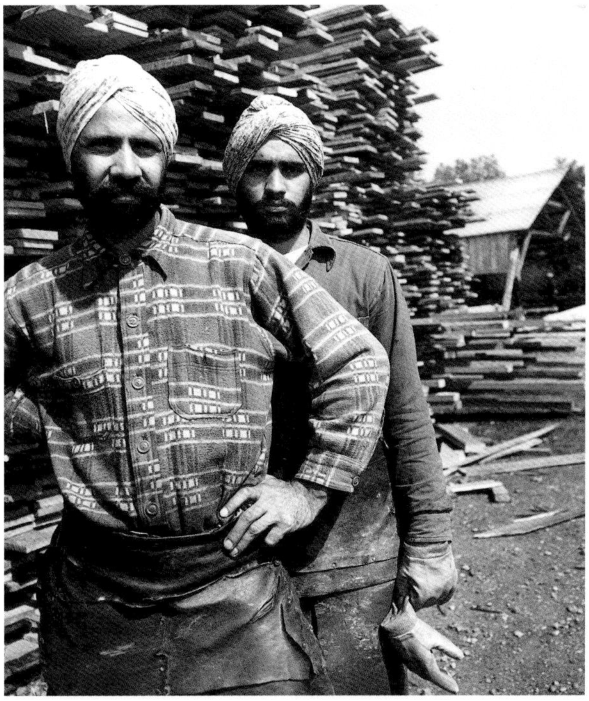

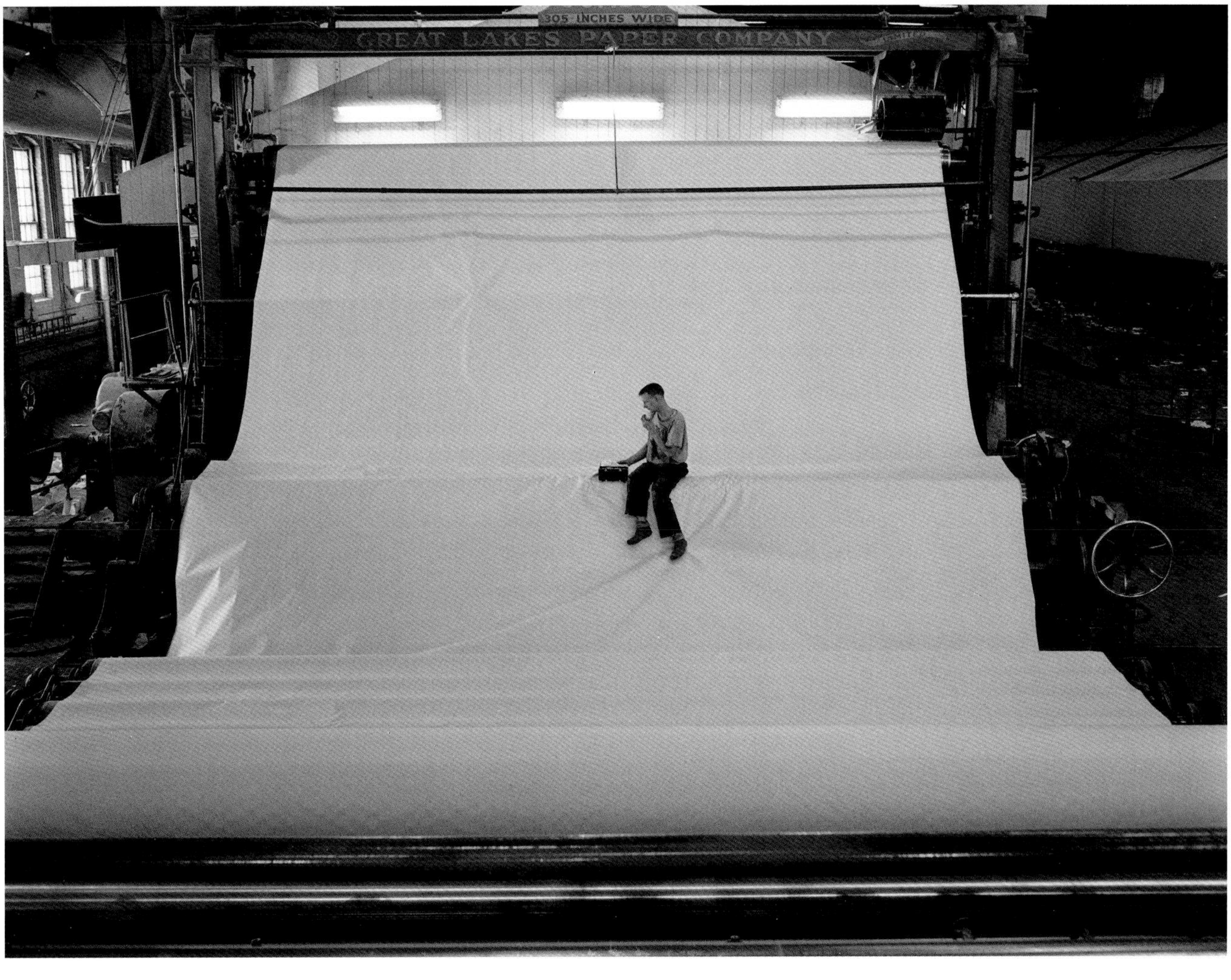
305 INCHES WIDE
GREAT LAKES PAPER COMPANY

The project appealed to Karsh, giving him an opportunity to photograph life in Canada as he saw it and to work with a smaller, more portable camera like his Rolleiflex. He was also aware of the growing success of his younger brother Malak Karsh (1915–2001) in the evolving genre of documentary photography.[30] Notable examples of this new field included photographic essays documenting America's Great Depression by Dorothea Lange (1895–1965), Walker Evans (1903–1975), Margaret Bourke-White (1904–1971), and others, as well as photo stories produced by the respected National Film Board of Canada photography unit.

Freed from the studio, Karsh used the *Maclean's* Canadian City project to explore new compositions and disjunctions of scale to convey a sense of monumentality in the depiction of the everyday.[31] Of the estimated eight thousand photographs taken by Karsh for this project, *Maclean's* published about three hundred in pictorial essays between November 15, 1952, and February 15, 1954.[32]

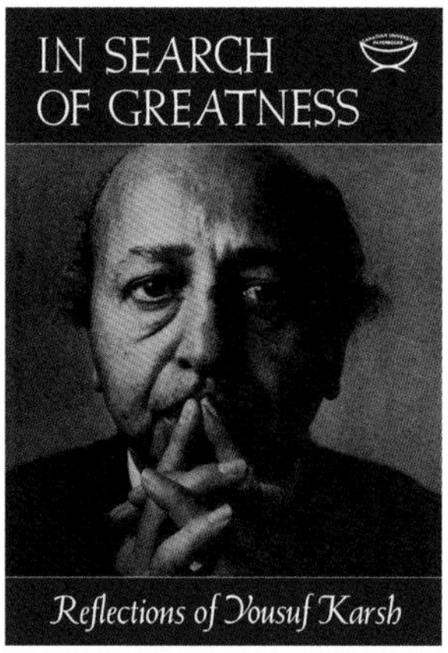

The Canadian City series achieved Karsh's goal of mastering the photo essay format through his visual storytelling talent, as applied to various documentary subjects, such as street scenes, folk traditions, farming, resource extraction, and manufacturing.[33] In particular, he was attracted to architecture: the modern vocabulary of industrial structures and the chance to use built forms to manipulate scale. Karsh depicted Canada's increasingly multicultural population, capturing Sikh millworkers and Chinese shopkeepers in British Columbia and Indigenous patients in an Edmonton hospital. He also portrayed the evidence of regional socio-economic disparity, featuring Saint John, New Brunswick, as a depressed relic of its nineteenth-century shipbuilding heyday and highlighting the hardships of Newfoundland's mining community.[34]

In his portrayal of modern Canada through its contemporary citizens, urban environments, natural resource industries, and surrounding scenic spots, Karsh applied his established methods of prior research and iconic composition to fulfill a triumphant economic narrative.[35] The Canadian City series also provided Karsh with a sabbatical of sorts, affording him the time to observe life outside the studio and create a visual record of his own experiences. Ultimately, he was celebrating the heroic in the everyday.[36]

In Search of Greatness

By the end of the 1950s, Yousuf Karsh was a household name, known for his iconic portraits seen by millions in widely circulated illustrated magazines. In 1959, these were compiled into a volume titled *Portraits of Greatness*, a new type of photography book,

Cover of Yousuf Karsh's memoir, *In Search of Greatness: Reflections of Yousuf Karsh* (Toronto: University of Toronto Press: 1962). Karsh's clasped hands at his lips create an air of deep reflection, as indicated in the title, but perhaps they also suggest that he is the keeper of secrets that he intends to spill in the memoir.

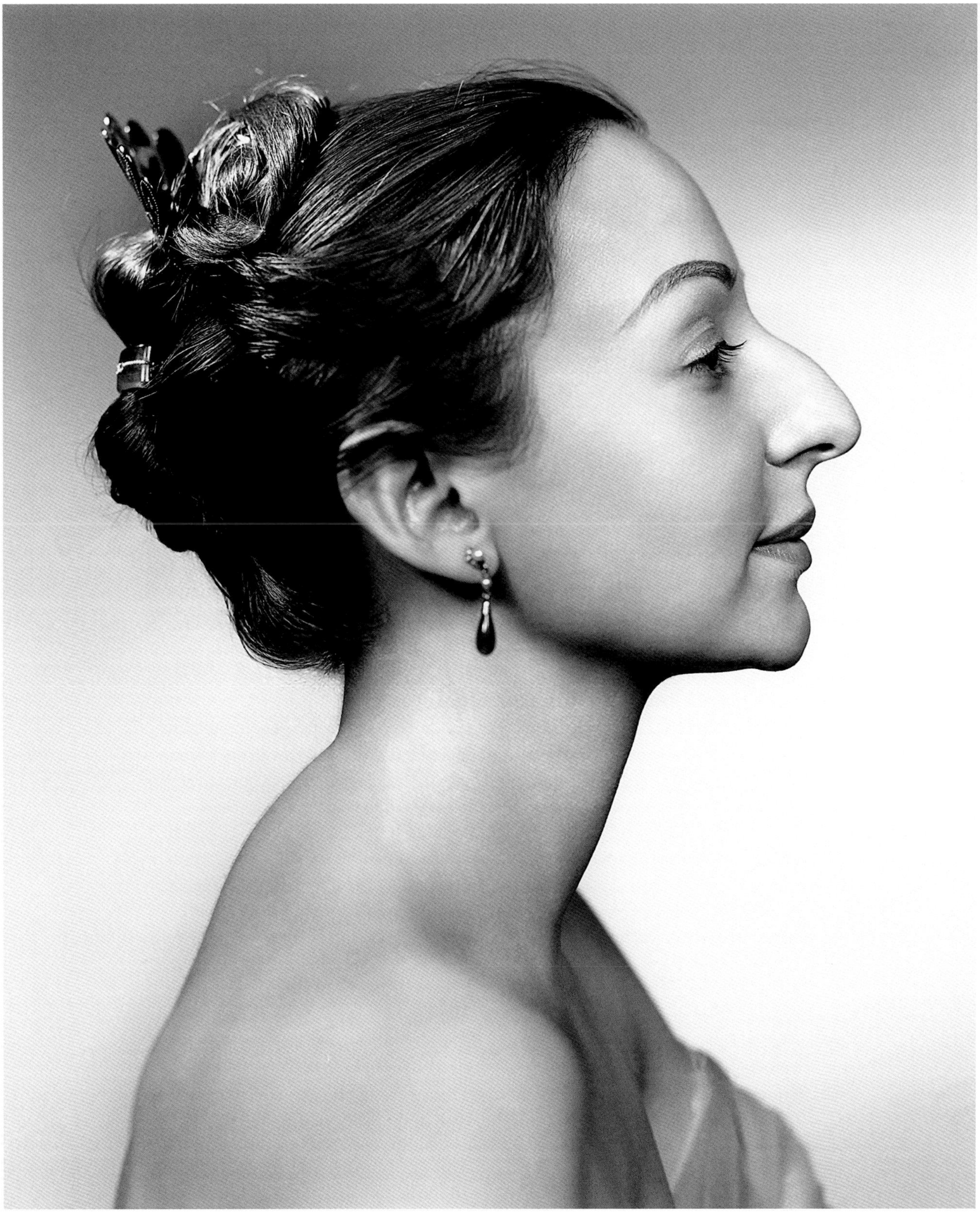

Yousuf Karsh, *Estrellita Karsh*, January 1, 1963, gelatin silver print, 60.3 x 49 cm, Montreal Museum of Fine Arts.

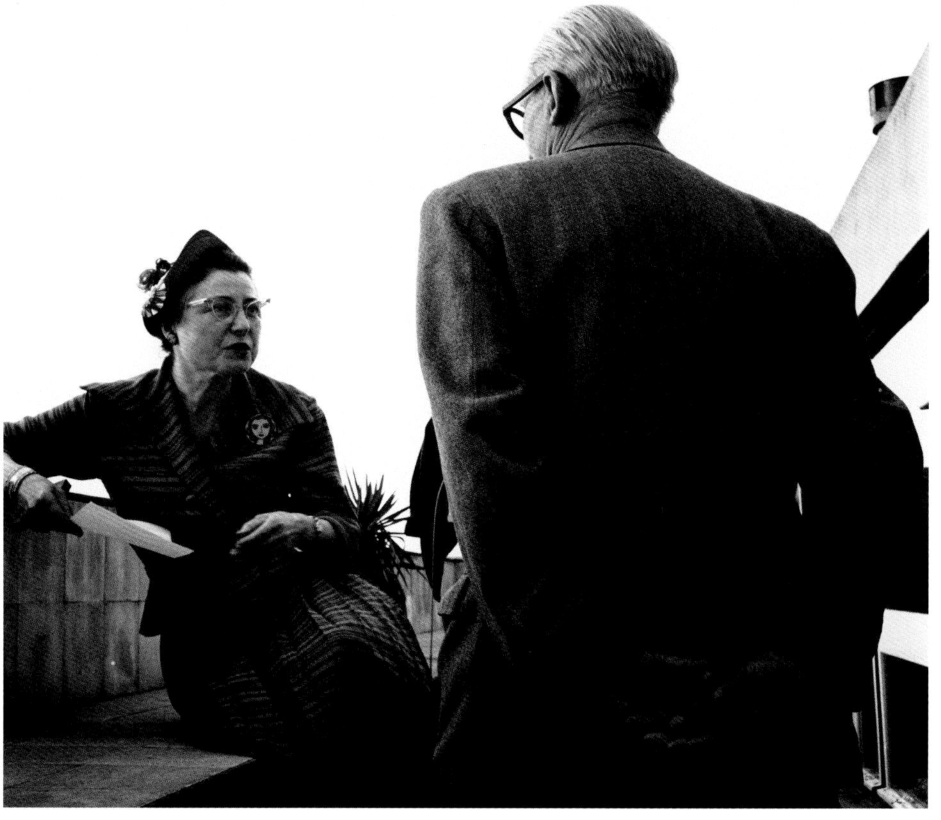

folio-sized and featuring high-quality printed images alongside polished biographical information and anecdotal texts on the facing pages.[37]

The title, *Portraits of Greatness*, highlighted the elevated stature of the book's subjects. For Karsh, greatness was linked to qualities of goodness and talent, and was distinct from the celebrity portraiture prevalent in movie idol magazines and tabloids. As a portrait artist, he sought to capture the essence of the preeminent figures of his time. Over the years, Karsh had received numerous queries from aspiring photographers seeking tips on how to replicate his style. Remarkably, he provided his exact equipment and darkroom specifications at the end of the volume. In this seemingly generous act, Karsh affirmed his belief in the portrait as a record of an event, a social moment in which he elicited an elusive truth.

In the introduction to the book, Karsh writes, "Here, in these pages, are some portraits of the gifted, the harvest of a long search. I hope they may bring my subjects a little closer to those who view them."[38] *Portraits of Greatness*, along with the popular travelling exhibition that followed, aimed to uplift humanity through images of its best exemplars. The large volume felt hefty in the reader's lap, connecting the space of their own body to the space of each portrait. The sense of proximity between the reader's life and that of the depicted subject was heightened by the monumental scale of the celebrated figure within the frame.

The wide variety in Karsh's work was the result of the strategic scheduling of portrait sittings in locations around the world where his illustrious subjects lived and worked. The price he paid for this bounty, accumulated over three decades, was chronic exhaustion. The demands of the constant travel, the physical and psychological strain of conducting portrait sittings, and the maintenance of a high volume of production in the darkroom for various commissions were enormous. Furthermore, Karsh was the public

Solange Karsh interviewing French architect Le Corbusier during a Yousuf Karsh portrait shoot in Europe, 1954, photograph by Peter Miller.

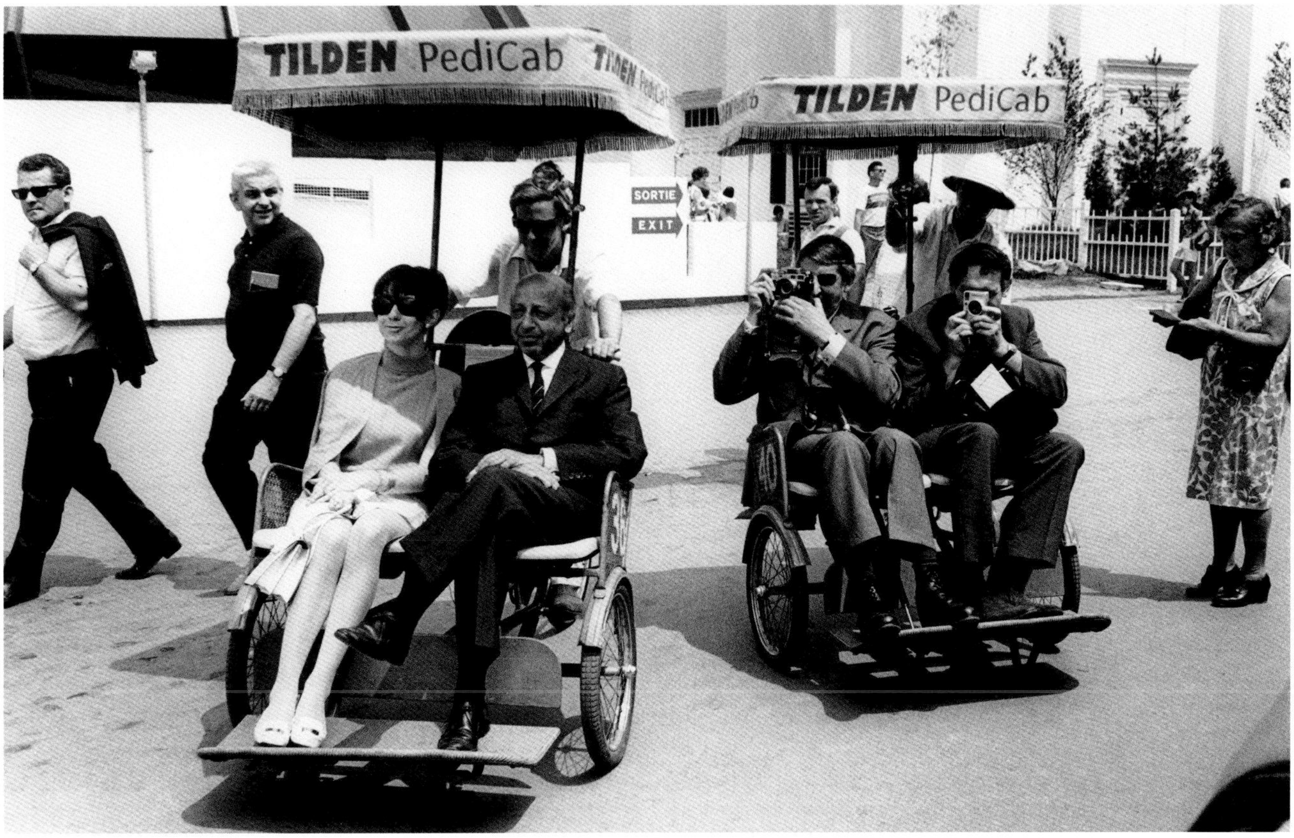

face of a large studio operation and a celebrity in his own right, dedicating his time to promoting his projects through magazine and television interviews.

Behind the scenes, Solange Karsh managed the business side of the studio, as well as arranging sittings and travel logistics and serving as the key liaison with museums and galleries. She travelled constantly with Karsh, fostering the pre-sitting social dynamic and taking the notes that would later become the basis for printed anecdotes. The Ottawa studio staff included a secretary/archivist, an expert printer, and assistants to pack, transport, and set up bulky photographic equipment. Beyond the studio, press agents in Europe and North America managed the flow of requests for new sittings and fine prints of Karsh portraits.

As production of *Portraits of Greatness* concluded, both spouses faced health crises. Karsh collapsed from a serious heart attack while working in Washington, D.C., requiring weeks of recovery in the hospital before returning to Ottawa. During his recovery, Solange was diagnosed with terminal breast cancer. They focused their efforts on one final collaboration, Karsh's memoir, *In Search of Greatness: Reflections of Yousuf Karsh*, with Solange preparing the text in the last months of her life. The 1962 book, which features a portrait of Karsh by celebrated fashion photographer Irving Penn (1917–2009), closely chronicles Solange's death the previous year,[39] and the text, a lively recounting of his rags-to-riches journey, interactions with notable people, and philosophical and practical reflections on portrait making, remained the definitive narrative of Karsh's life and career through to his death in 2002.

After Solange's death, work was Karsh's solace. But while photographing Chicago-based physician and medical columnist Dr. Walter Alvarez in 1962, he met Alvarez's

Yousuf Karsh at Expo 67, Montreal, 1967, photograph by Sam Tata.

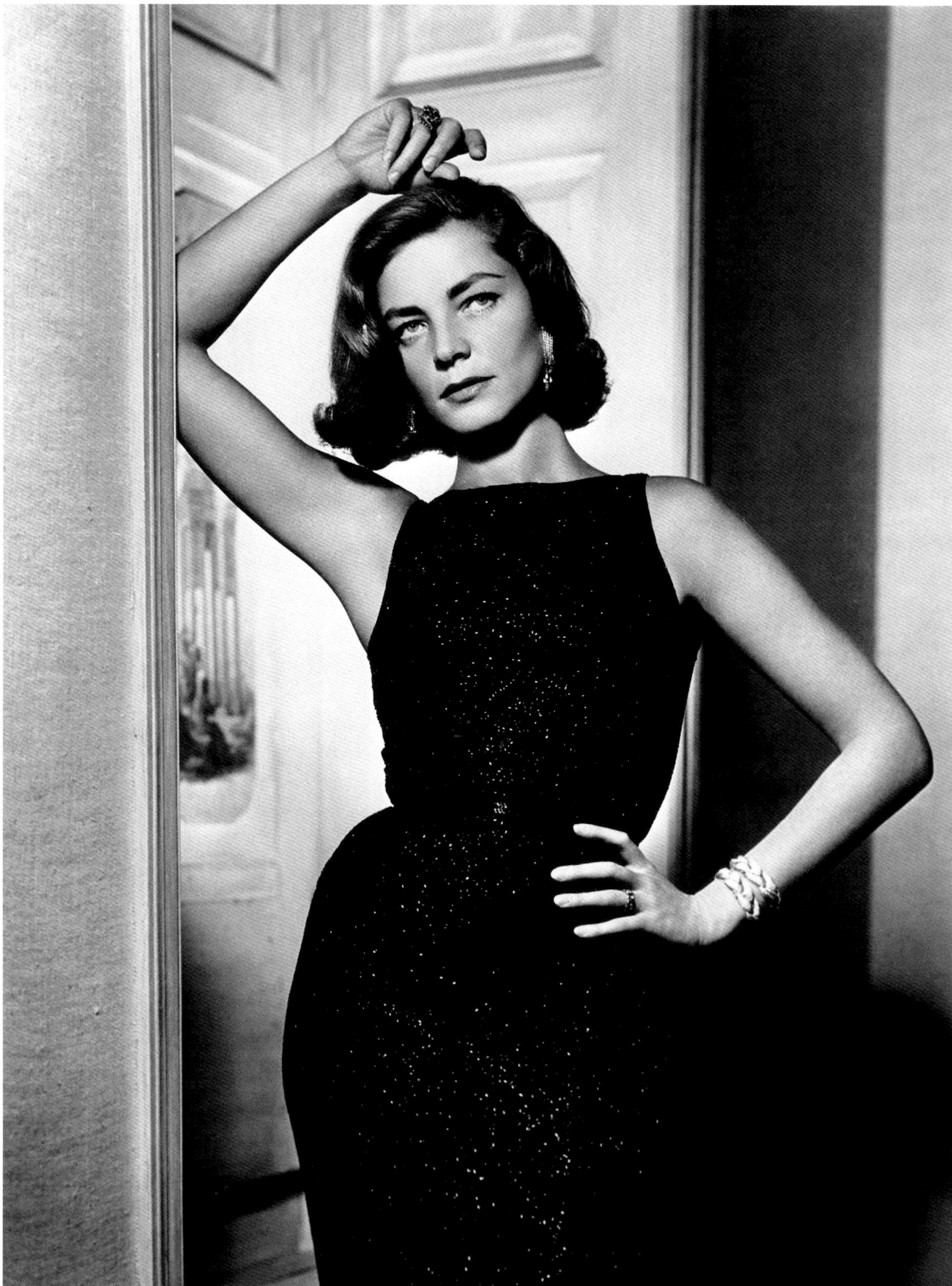

Yousuf Karsh, *Lauren Bacall*, March 27, 1957, Estate of Yousuf Karsh.

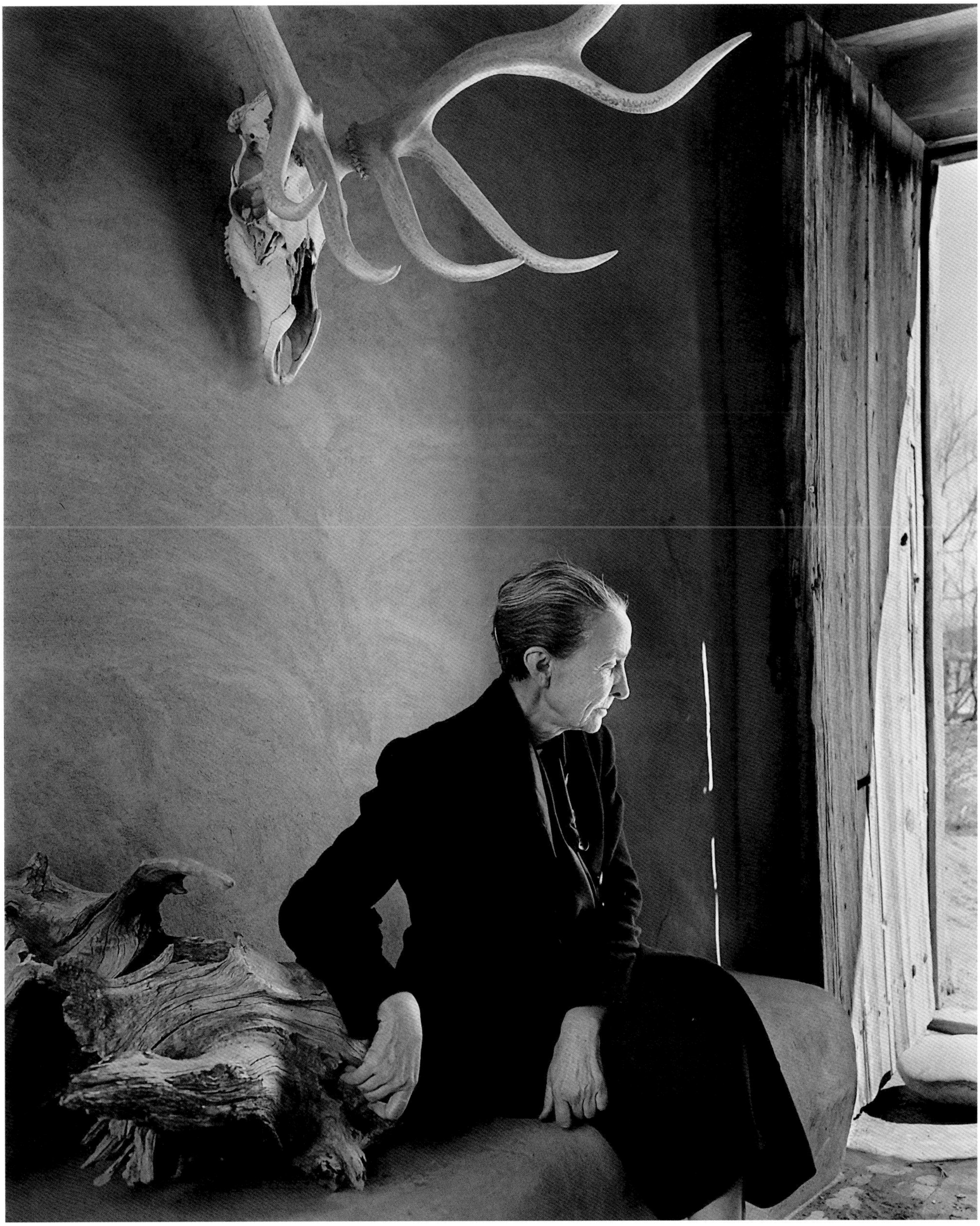

Yousuf Karsh, *Georgia O'Keeffe*, March 18, 1956, gelatin silver print, 59.7 x 47.9 cm, Montreal Museum of Fine Arts.

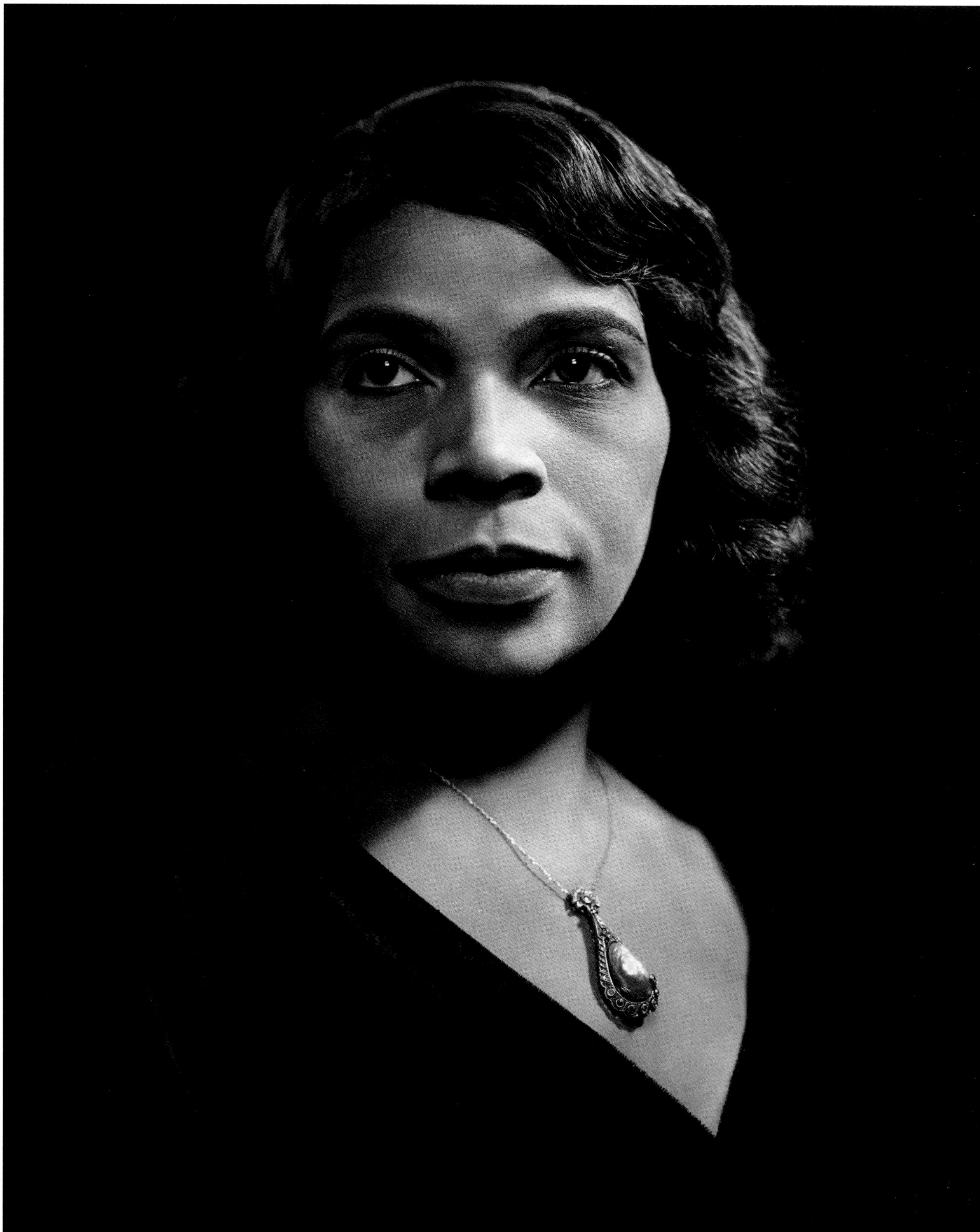

Yousuf Karsh, *Marian Anderson*, December 9, 1945, gelatin silver print, 42 x 34.4 cm, Estate of Yousuf Karsh.

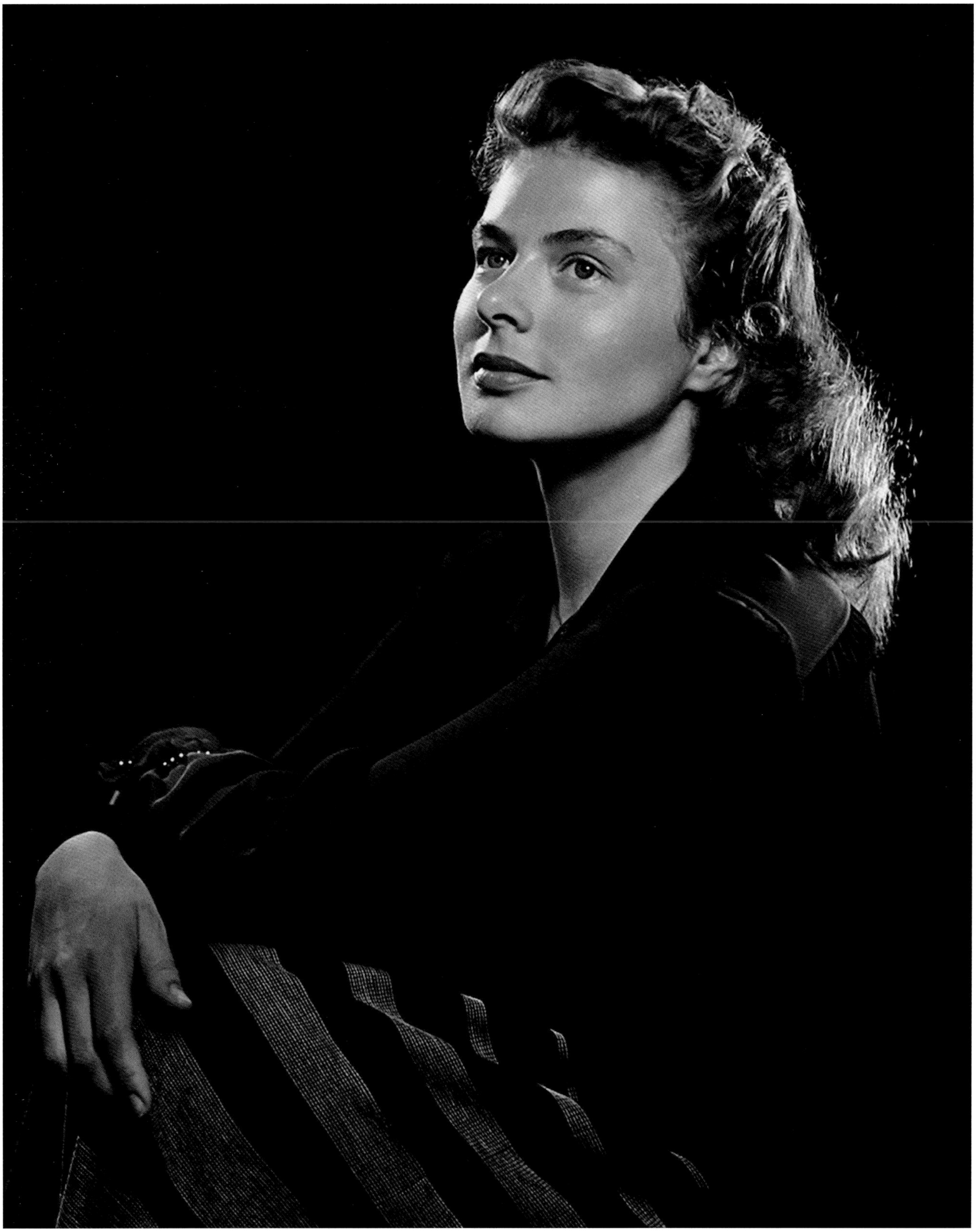

Yousuf Karsh, *Ingrid Bergman*, February 24, 1946, gelatin silver print, 26 x 20 cm, Montreal Museum of Fine Arts.

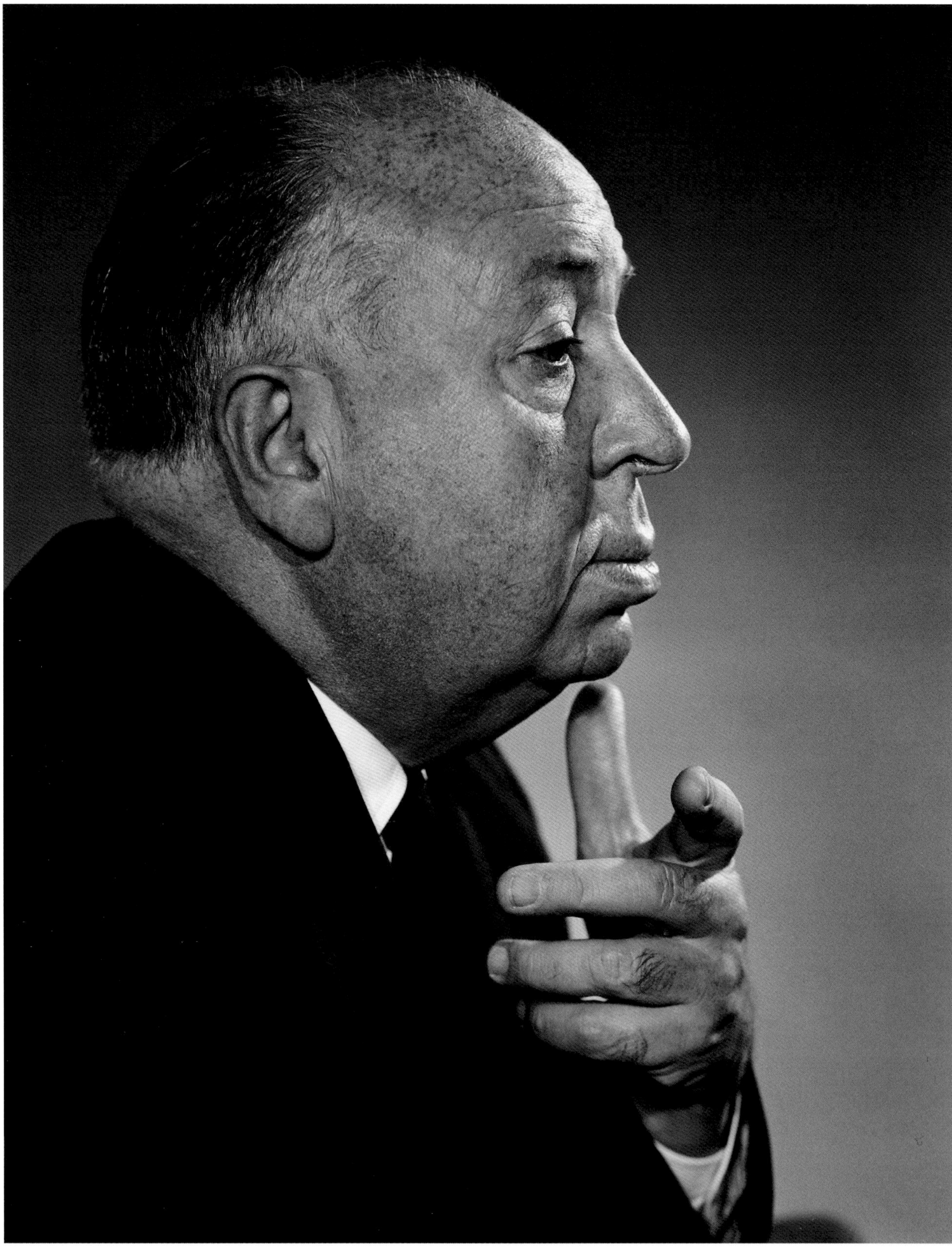

Yousuf Karsh, *Alfred Hitchcock*, December 14, 1950, Estate of Yousuf Karsh.

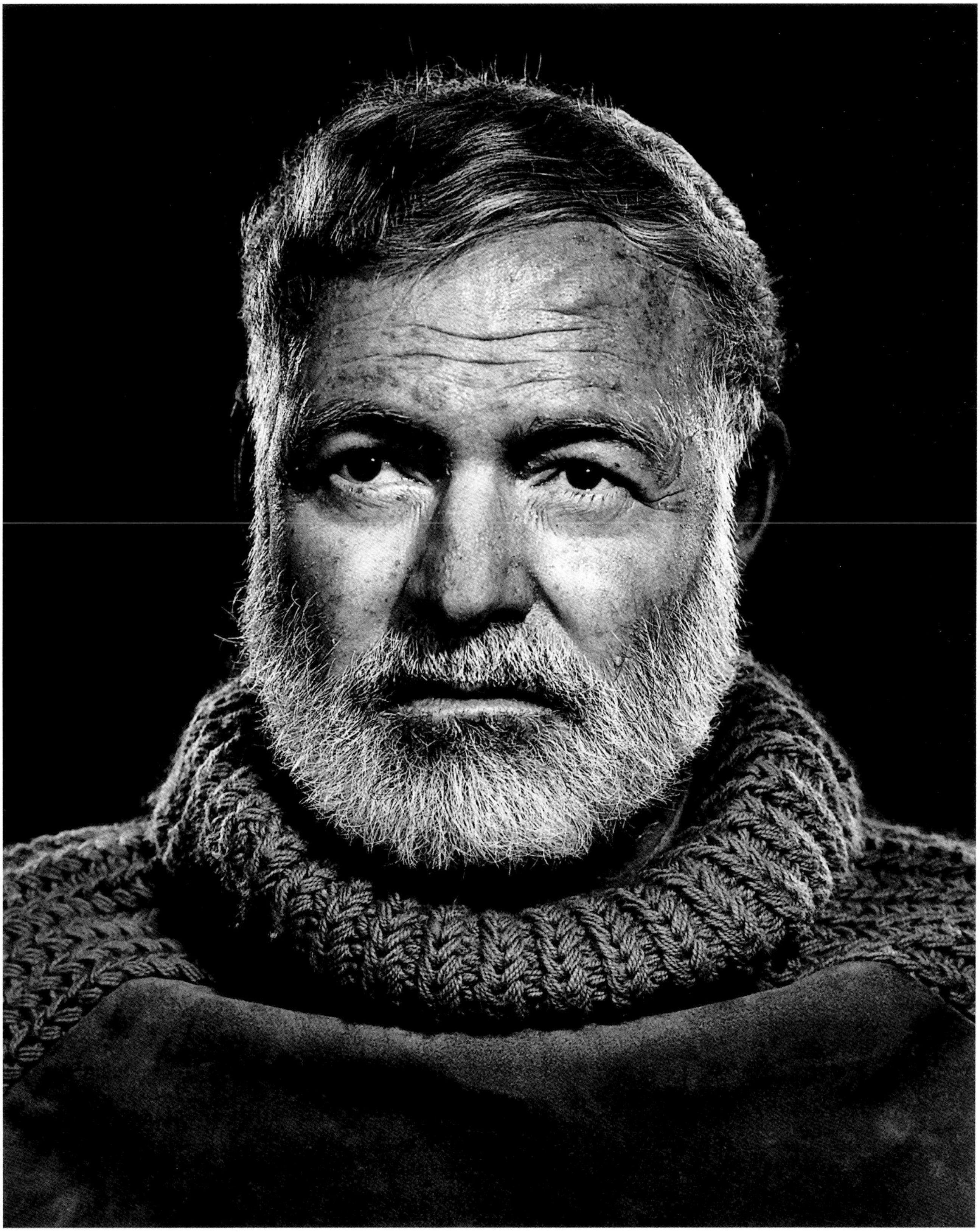

Yousuf Karsh, *Ernest Hemingway*, March 15, 1957, gelatin silver print, 60.3 x 50.5 cm, Montreal Museum of Fine Arts.

talented medical researcher and writer, Estrellita Nachbar. As *Newsweek* later quipped, "Something more than the camera clicked."[40] After their wedding later that year, Estrellita became a devoted partner in the studio's operation, managing major projects and working closely with Karsh during portrait sittings to help put sitters at ease.

Their partnership coincided with growing interest from museums in featuring photographic exhibitions. Influential curators such as Beaumont Newhall, Edward Steichen, and Nathan Lyons in the United States, and later James Borcoman at the National Gallery of Canada, acquired and exhibited photographs through newly established museum departments dedicated to the art form. Recognizing this expanding phenomenon, Karsh saw a significant opportunity for his audience to view his exquisitely produced prints in person rather than only in books and magazines.

New Perspectives

Following the success of the travelling version of *Portraits of Greatness*, Karsh was invited to serve as photographic advisor for Canada's Expo 67 world's fair in Montreal, where millions saw his prints featured in *Men Who Make Our World*.[41] The exhibition was immediately reprised in early 1968 at the Montreal Museum of Fine Arts before touring museums in the United States and Europe.

In his role as photographic advisor to Osaka's Expo 70, Karsh travelled across Japan to create portraits of prominent business leaders, artists, performers, and Nobel laureates considered "treasured by the entire nation."[42] The Japanese concept of living legends as honoured citizens resonated deeply with Karsh and inspired his next project, a published portfolio of notable Canadians.

A lavish coffee table book, *Karsh Canadians*, 1978, published by the University of Toronto Press, featured seventy-nine portraits arranged alphabetically, each accompanied by his customary commentary. The portfolio served as Karsh's love letter to the nation that had welcomed him and was dedicated "to the people of Canada and to my uncle, George Nakash, who brought me here."[43] The book's introduction includes Karsh's recounting of his arrival in Canada in 1924 as a refugee and his journey to "becoming" as a portrait master.

In addition to portraits from the 1940s and 1950s, Karsh included photographs of figures significant to contemporary Canadians. His portrait of Prime Minister Pierre Elliott Trudeau, for example, shows the newly elected leader in a leather jacket instead of a formal suit, signalling a maverick tenure to come. Karsh recalled, "The new head of government was very relaxed, very natural and, above all, candid.... [T]he voters already had found him compelling and charismatic but not yet controversial."[44]

By the end of the 1970s, as Karsh entered his sixties, his status as one of the great masters of twentieth-century photography was firmly established. Karsh had photographed and enjoyed the camaraderie many of the photographic giants of his era, such as Edward Steichen, Jacques Lartigue (1894–1986), Man Ray (1890–1976), Berenice Abbott (1898–1991), and Ansel Adams (1902–1984), as well as photo-based artists such as Andy Warhol (1928–1987). However, the practice of photographic portraiture had shifted away from his trademark style. Classical, staged portraiture embodying social or individual

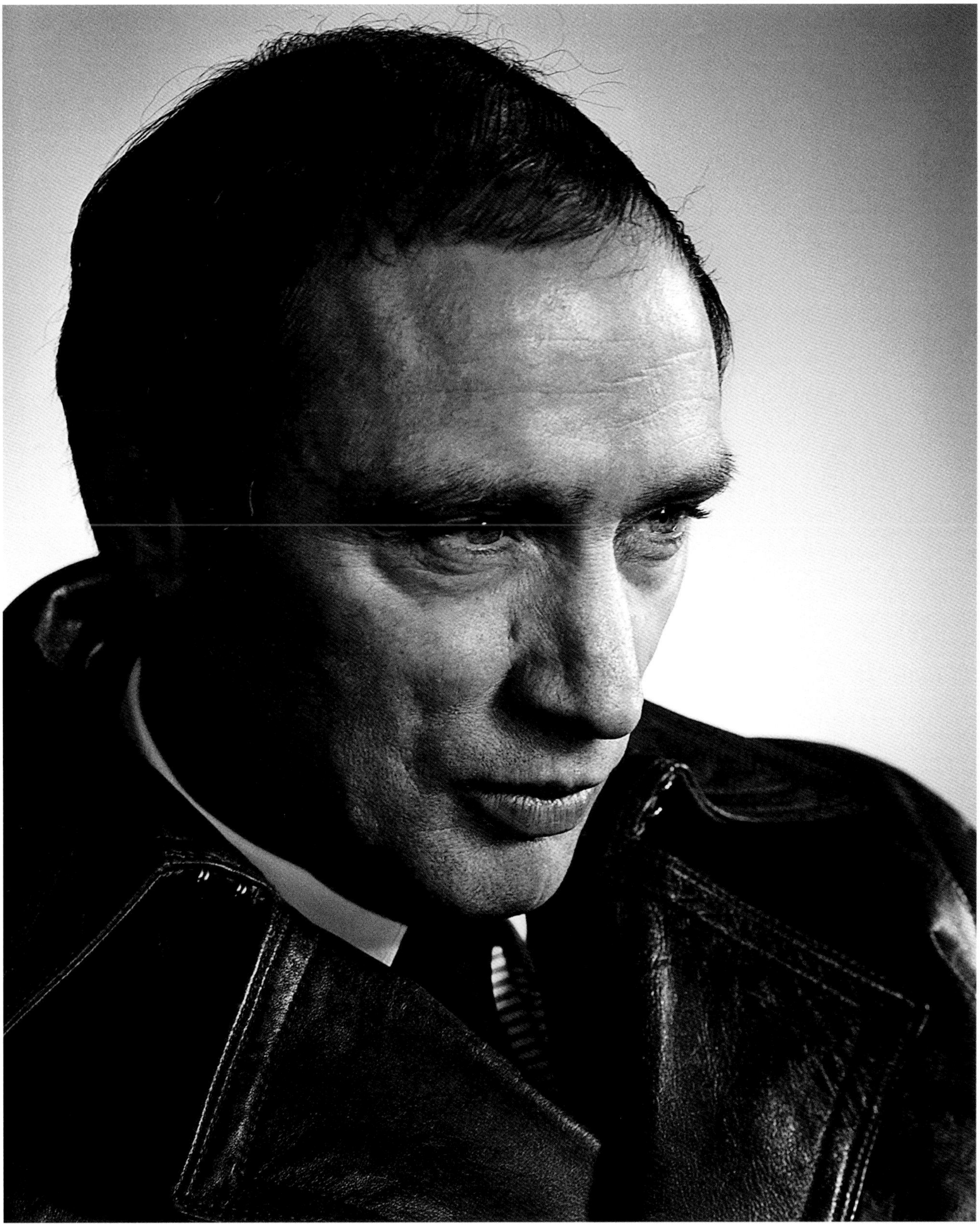

Yousuf Karsh, *Pierre Elliott Trudeau*, November 4, 1968, gelatin silver print, 43 x 35.5 cm, Montreal Museum of Fine Arts.

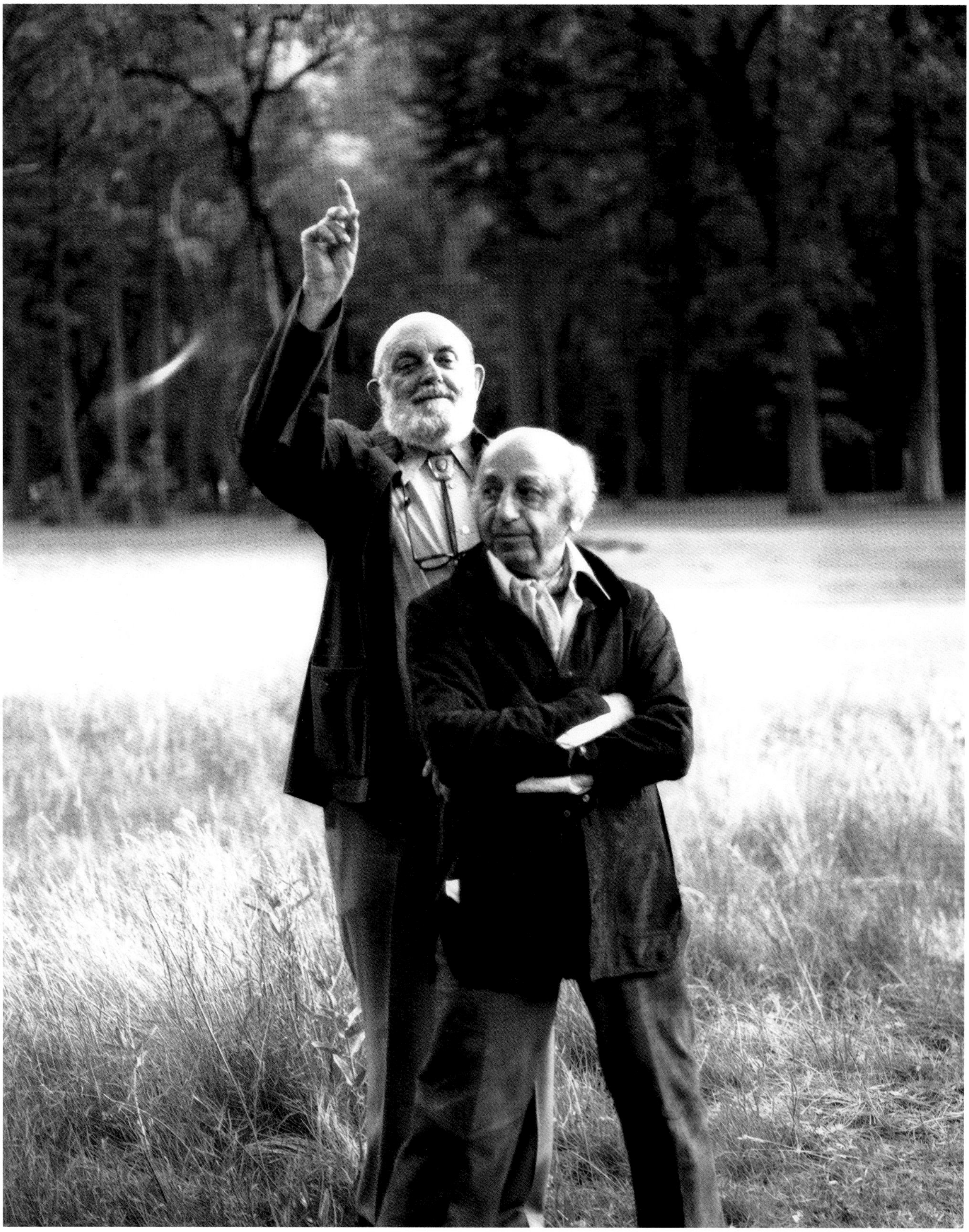

Yousuf Karsh (*front*) relaxing with Ansel Adams (*back*) during the Yosemite Photo Workshop, Yosemite National Park, California, June 1977, photograph attributed to Craig McFarland.

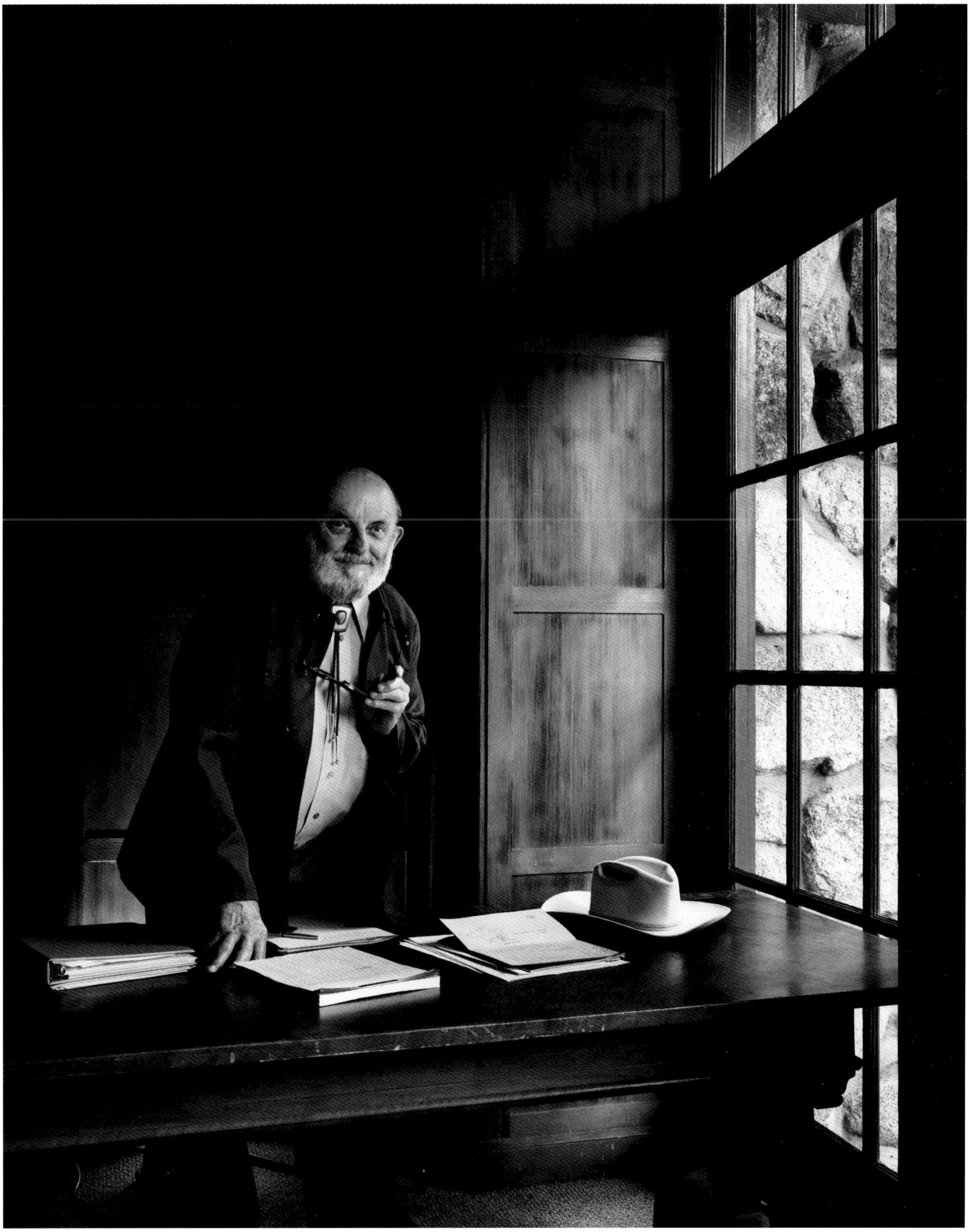

Yousuf Karsh, *Ansel Adams*, July 20, 1977, Estate of Yousuf Karsh.

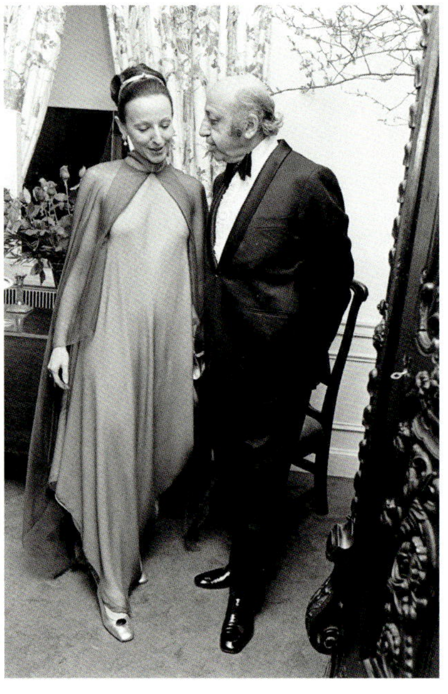

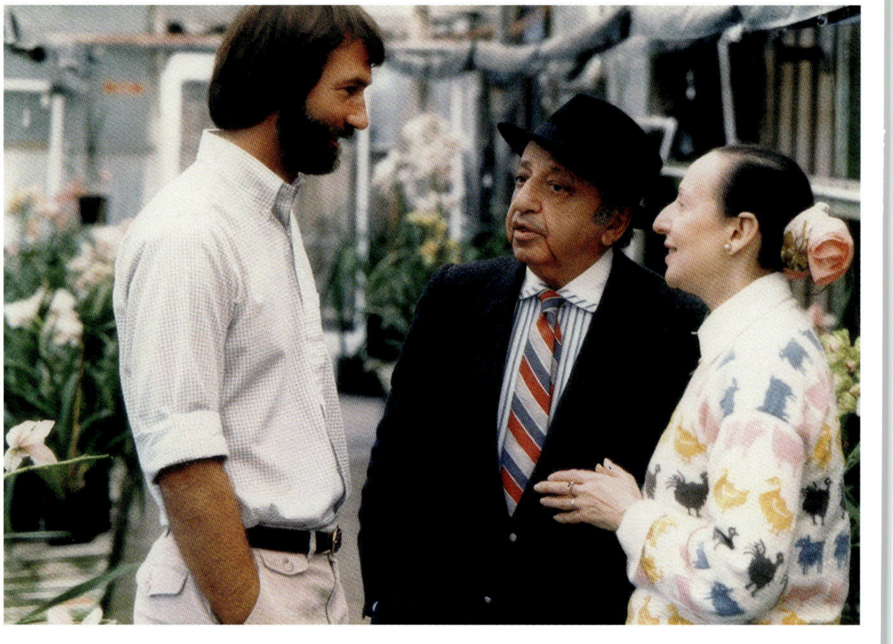

truths was replaced by a greater interest in subjective interpretations, which Museum of Modern Art curator Nathan Lyons would call "social landscape" photography.[45]

As Karsh continued his practice in later years, younger artists exploring portraiture studied his distinctive style while interrogating the practice itself. Photographers positioned themselves along a continuum between revelation and concealment, between direct observers and constructors of fiction.

Later Years

As Karsh grew older, his scheduled portrait sittings and extensive travels diminished. In 1973, he moved his studio from the Hardy Arcade at 130 Sparks Street to a suite of rooms on the sixth floor of the Château Laurier, Ottawa's grand hotel opposite Parliament Hill. As author Kevin Holland observes, "The arrangement provided the Karsh Studio with a prestigious and highly accessible address, and gave Canadian National's flagship hotel a prestigious tenant."[46] Karsh had become a celebrity in his own right, appearing on television shows and in documentaries. A born *flâneur* and popular local figure, he was a familiar presence in Ottawa's Parliament District and the lobby of the Château Laurier during his daily walks.

In his eighties, Karsh continued to satisfy the public's appetite for formal portraits of notable individuals and to collaborate on retrospective exhibitions of his work organized by major cultural institutions. In 1983, the International Center of Photography in New York hosted a retrospective of Karsh's career featuring lesser-known portraits from his assignment work in addition to well-known portraits. The National Gallery of Canada prepared a major exhibition, *Karsh: The Art of the Portrait*, in 1989, marking the institution's move to a new building designed by Canadian architect Moishe Safdie. Karsh's portfolio *American Legends* was published in 1992 and included many new works, such as a colour portrait of American soprano Jessye Norman, and he worked on retrospective publishing projects like *Karsh: A Sixty-Year Retrospective* (1996), which was later re-released as a revised edition, *Karsh: A Biography in Images* (2003).

Over his lifetime, Karsh received numerous honorary doctorates and the Canada

Left: Estrellita and Yousuf Karsh at the pre–Carnation Ball event held at the Waldorf-Astoria Hotel, New York, April 26, 1972, photographer unknown. Right: Yousuf and Estrellita Karsh with Jerry Fielder (*left*), Santa Barbara, 1985, photographer unknown.

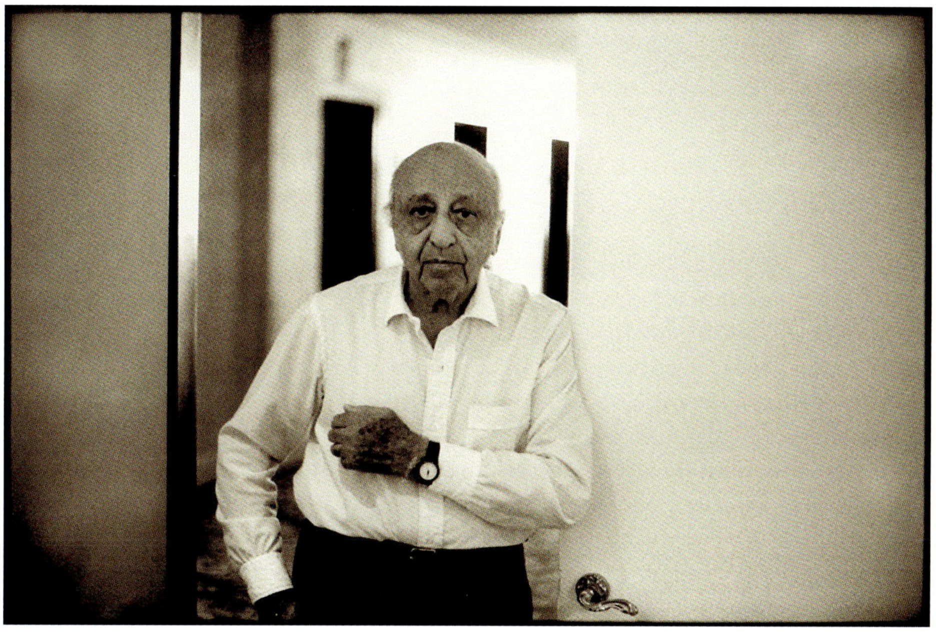

Council Medal in 1969; he was inducted into the Royal Canadian Academy of Arts in 1975 and was named a Companion of the Order of Canada in 1990. Perhaps the most fitting honour was being listed in *The International Who's Who 1998–99* (1998) as one of the one hundred most influential figures of the twentieth century. The only photographer and only Canadian among the distinguished selection, Karsh had made portraits of more than half of the honourees.[47]

In anticipation of the closure of his studio, his lifetime legacy was transferred to the then National Archives of Canada (now Library and Archives Canada) beginning in 1987. The acquisition included Karsh's creative output from the founding of his studio, comprising negatives, prints, and colour transparencies, as well as his business papers, publishing projects, artwork, personal correspondence, scrapbooks, awards, and honours. Karsh's photographic equipment was acquired by the Canada Science and Technology Museum.

In 1992, the Karsh Studio closed permanently, and Yousuf and Estrellita Karsh retired to Boston, Massachusetts, returning to the city that had been so instrumental in the formation of his life and work. At age ninety-three, Karsh died on July 13, 2002; he is buried in Ottawa's Notre Dame Cemetery.

In the years following her husband's death until her own in 2025, Estrellita sponsored multiple hospital and museum initiatives in his name.[48] In 2003, the city of Ottawa established the Yousuf and Malak Karsh Photography Award to recognize a mid-career local artist for their outstanding body of work and significant contribution to the artistic discipline in a photo/lens-based medium. Karsh's work continues to be studied and exhibited internationally and supported by the website Karsh.org—led by Karsh's longtime assistant, Curator and Director Jerry Fielder—which serves as an authoritative and comprehensive source about Karsh.

Karsh continues to be honoured, extending his earthly renown. In 2013, the Royal Astronomical Society of Canada named a small planet in honour of Yousuf and Malak Karsh jointly, and in 2015, the International Astronomical Union named a fifty-eight-kilometre-wide crater on Mercury after Yousuf Karsh. Fittingly, the "portrait" of the Karsh crater features his signature theatrical balance of light and shadow.

Yousuf Karsh in the doorway of his studio at the Château Laurier, Ottawa, 1998, photograph by George Pimentel.

Key Works

Through his iconic portraits, Yousuf Karsh sought to reveal the essence of an individual, stating in his book *In Search of Greatness*, "There is a brief moment when all there is in a man's mind and soul and spirit is reflected through his eyes, his hands, his attitude. This is the moment to record." Early in his career, Karsh developed a distinctive modernist style, and his portraits—found in books, magazines, and art exhibitions, as well as on stamps and currency—form a visual encyclopedia of the twentieth century. His practice embraced significant shifts in the history of photography: the rise of celebrity portraiture in magazines, the recognition of photography as collectible art, and the decline of large-format analogue photography.

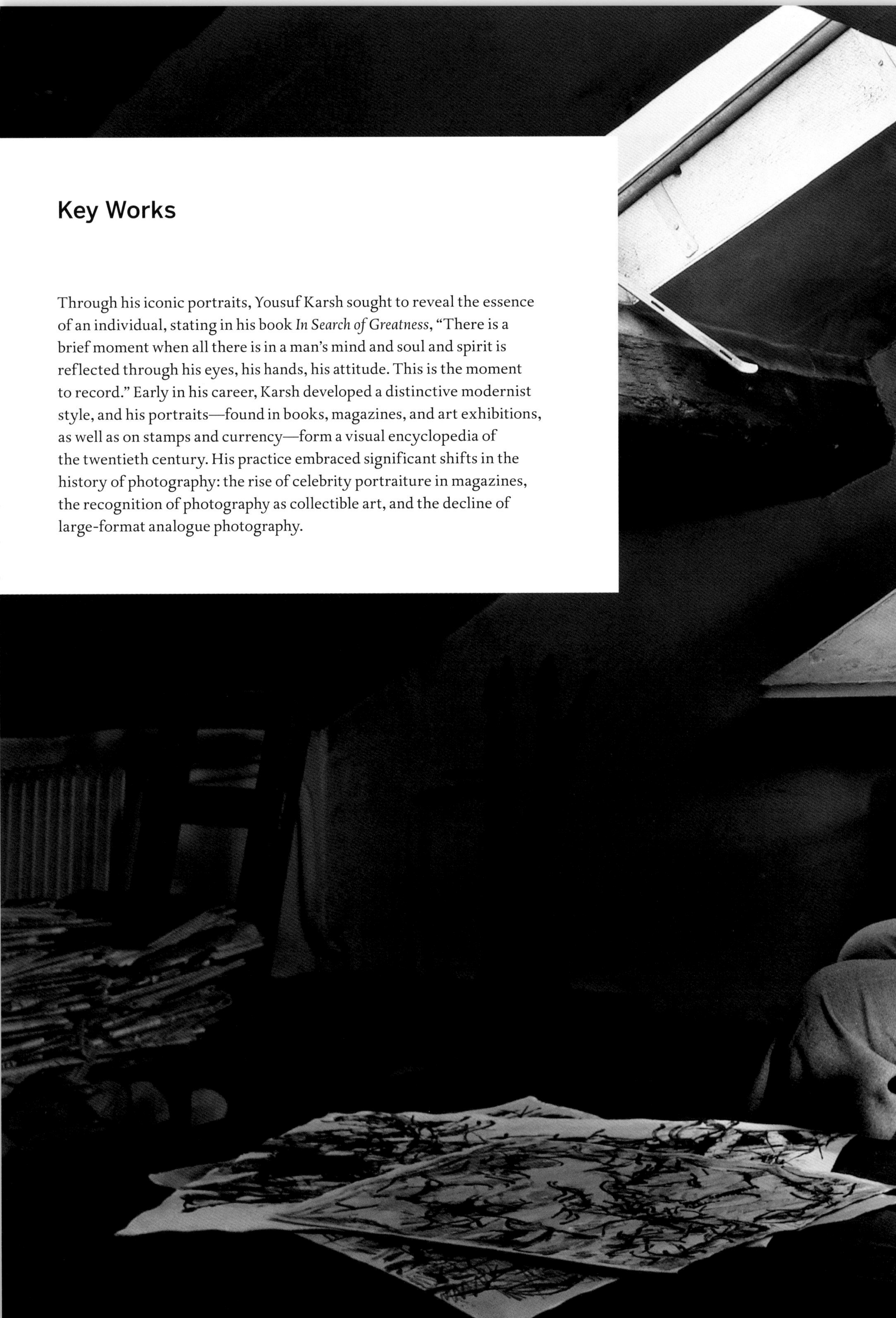

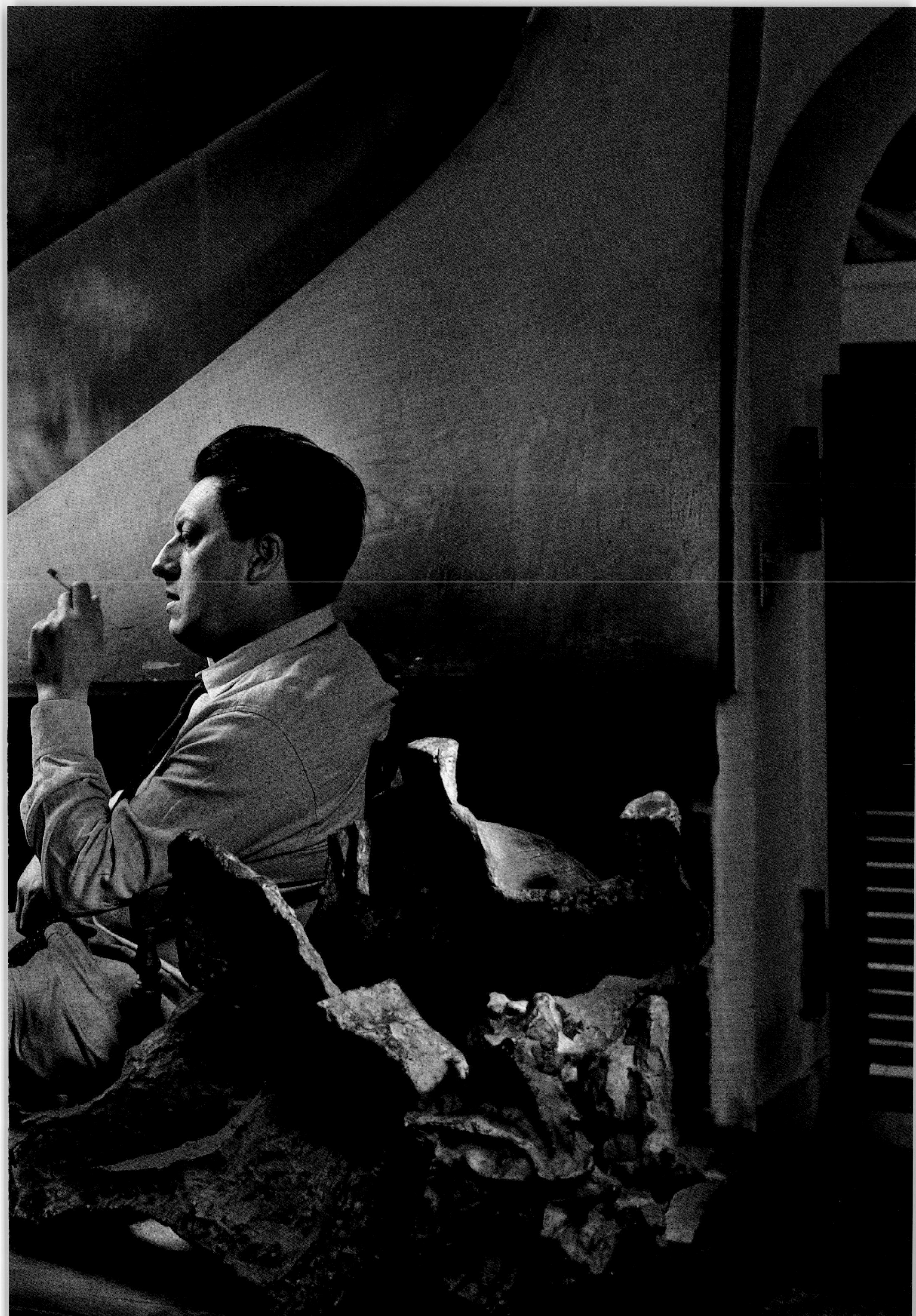

Woman in a Turban (Betty Low)
1936

Gelatin silver print, 34 x 27 cm (image), 50.8 x 40.6 cm (mount)
Estate of Yousuf Karsh

In 1936, Karsh made artistic studies of Betty Low—the daughter of Ottawa's mayor and a friend of Karsh's future wife, Solange Gauthier. Low would later become a celebrated Broadway actor and a dancer in the renowned Ballet Russe de Monte Carlo. This portrait exemplifies Karsh's signature style, formed early in his career, well before he achieved international acclaim. The extreme close-up composition emphasizes the monumentality of Low's head, with no background details visible. Her face seems to emerge from the shadows into sudden illumination, accentuating every contour.

In the early years of Karsh's portrait practice in Ottawa, the demands of establishing his business occupied most of his energy, leaving limited opportunities for self-directed creative work. Like his Boston mentor, John H. Garo (1870–1939), Karsh felt the pressure to balance client commissions with active membership in elite art photography circles. He regularly submitted work to national and international photography salons and was elected as an associate of the Royal Photographic Society in 1938. *Woman in a Turban (Betty Low)* is considered the finest among his salon submissions and was significant in establishing Karsh's credentials as a portraitist working in the fine art tradition.

When unconstrained by a client's schedule and expectations, Karsh felt free to try experimental approaches, balancing previsualization with sudden inspiration. During the portrait session with Low, he impulsively tore down his window curtains, draping the fabric around Low's head and shoulders to improvise a turban. This contrived headwear shifts the portrait from a specific personality in modern time to a character evoking antiquity.

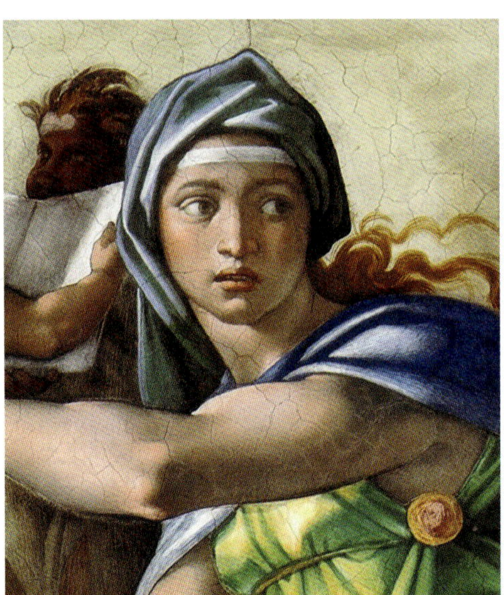

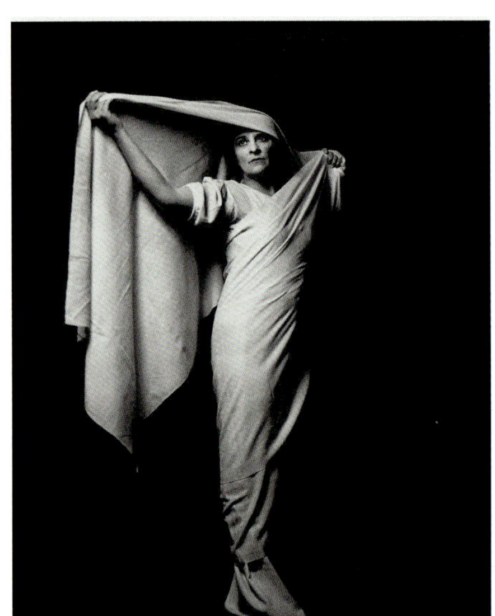

Previous spread: Yousuf Karsh, *Jean-Paul Riopelle, Photographed in His Paris Atelier* (detail), April 7, 1965, printed 1987, gelatin silver print, 33.2 x 40.9 cm (image), 60.6 x 50.9 cm (sheet), National Gallery of Canada, Ottawa. Left: Michelangelo, *Delphic Sibyl* (detail from the Sistine Chapel ceiling), 1508–12, fresco, Vatican Museums, Vatican City. Right: Yousuf Karsh, *Ruth Draper*, November 25, 1936, printed 1989, gelatin silver print, 48.6 x 37 cm, National Gallery of Canada, Ottawa.

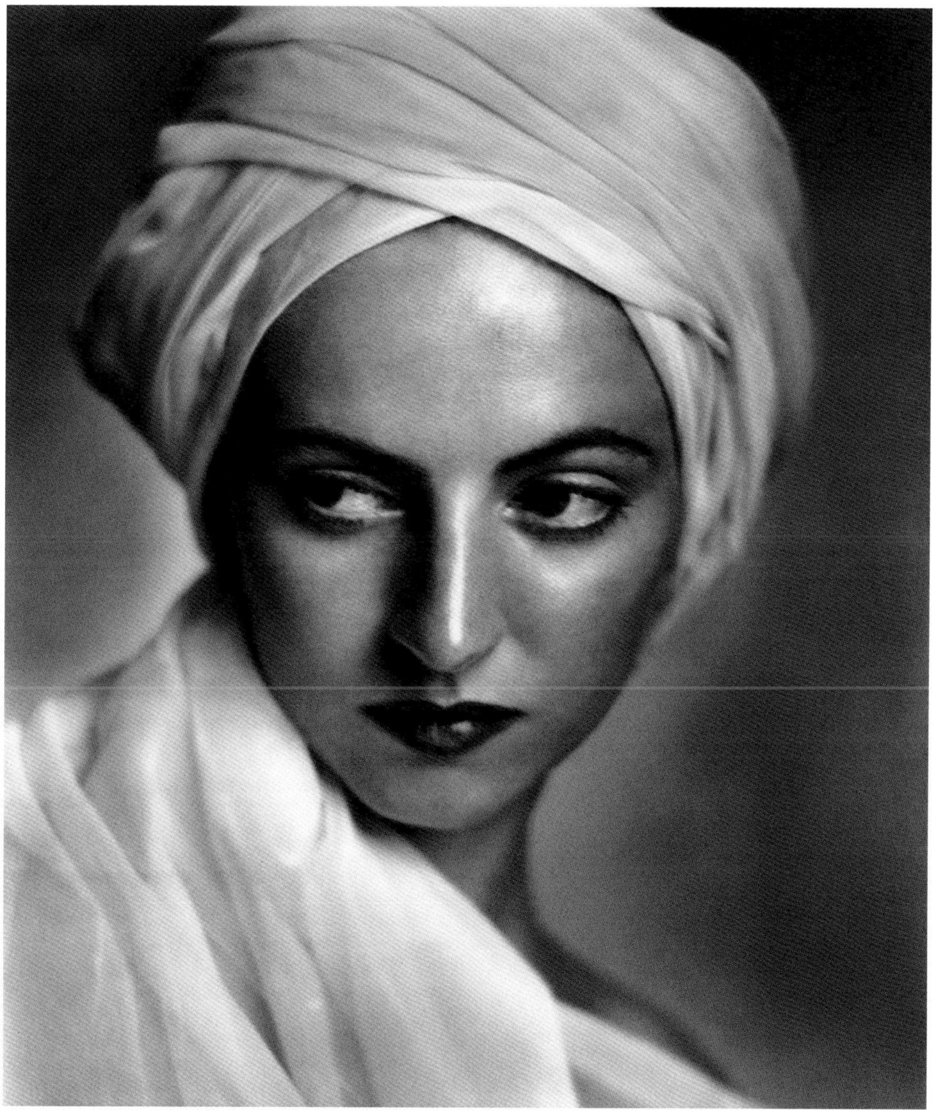

This portrait clearly reflects Karsh's study of classical painting. Under Garo's tutelage from 1928 to 1931, Karsh supplemented his technical skills by taking art classes at the Museum of Fine Arts in Boston and by studying masterworks of portraiture past and present. Through his visits to Boston's fine art museums and great libraries, Karsh became familiar with, for example, the monumental Sistine Chapel frescoes by Michelangelo (1475–1564) featuring figures of prophets, which were reproduced in books about Renaissance art. He had further direct exposure to works from his own era, including the suite of murals entitled *Triumph of Religion*, 1895–1919, by Garo's friend, the celebrated American painter John Singer Sargent (1856–1925), installed along the vaulted ceiling of the central Boston Public Library.

Karsh was also influenced by an established photographer he admired and later grew close to, Edward Steichen (1879–1973). A leading proponent of the Photo-Secession circle, established by Alfred Stieglitz (1864–1946), Steichen explored the dramatic potential of classical themes. His portrait of American actor Ruth Draper, published in *Vanity Fair* in 1928, features the performer portraying one of her stage characters, her mournful expression illuminated against a dark shroud. Karsh's attentive study of these precedents is evident in his own striking portrait of Draper, photographed in Ottawa in 1936.[1]

Winston Churchill
December 30, 1941, printed before 1972

Gelatin silver print, 50 x 39.7 cm
Art Gallery of Alberta, Edmonton

In December 1941, Yousuf Karsh made the most famous photographic portrait of his career: a powerful image of British Prime Minister Winston Churchill, who was seen as playing an integral role in defending liberal democracy against the spread of fascism during the Second World War. The publication of this portrait immediately catapulted Karsh into the international arena.

In the wake of Japan's attack on an American naval base at Pearl Harbor, Churchill made the perilous journey across the Atlantic to meet with President Franklin D. Roosevelt in Washington, D.C., to secure support for the Allied forces. Churchill arranged for a short side trip by train to Ottawa, arriving to cheers from throngs of war-weary Canadians supporting the battle commander. The following afternoon, Churchill delivered a rousing speech—which was transmitted live over CBC Radio—during a joint session of the Senate and House of Commons in Parliament, located just steps from Karsh's Sparks Street studio.

The prior evening, Karsh had been admitted to the Speaker's chamber, where he had set up his Agfa Ansco 8 x 10 large-format camera, six floodlights, two spotlights, and a background light.[1] He greeted the unsuspecting British prime minister moments after his electrifying speech and offered to memorialize the occasion. As Karsh later remarked:

> Churchill lit a fresh cigar, puffed at it with a mischievous air, and then magnanimously relented. "You may take one." Churchill's cigar was ever present. I held out an ashtray, but he would not dispose of it. I went back to my camera and made sure that everything was all right technically. I waited; he continued to chomp vigorously at his cigar.
>
> I waited. Then I stepped toward him and, without premeditation, but ever so respectfully, I said, "Forgive me, sir," and plucked the cigar out of his mouth. By the time I got back to my camera, he looked so belligerent he could have devoured me. It was at that instant that I took the photograph.[2]

Karsh had previsualized the portrait before Churchill's arrival. What he could not have anticipated was Churchill's indignant facial expression as his cigar was snatched away, an action demonstrating Karsh's interpretation of the decisive moment, a concept championed by French photographer Henri Cartier-Bresson (1908–2004).

The story of Karsh snatching the cigar from Churchill's mouth to provoke the "roaring lion" became legendary, eventually attaining mythic status. Karsh's wife, Solange, wrote to B.K. Sandwell, editor of *Saturday Night* magazine, to share the events behind the promised portrait.[3] She emphasized that the anecdote was Karsh's account and not hers: "Here are Yousuf's notes as given to me last night and I refuse to doctor them up."[4] The Churchill portrait was featured on the cover of the January 10, 1942, issue of *Saturday Night*, followed by a full-page reproduction the next month in *LIFE* magazine and *The Illustrated London News*.[5]

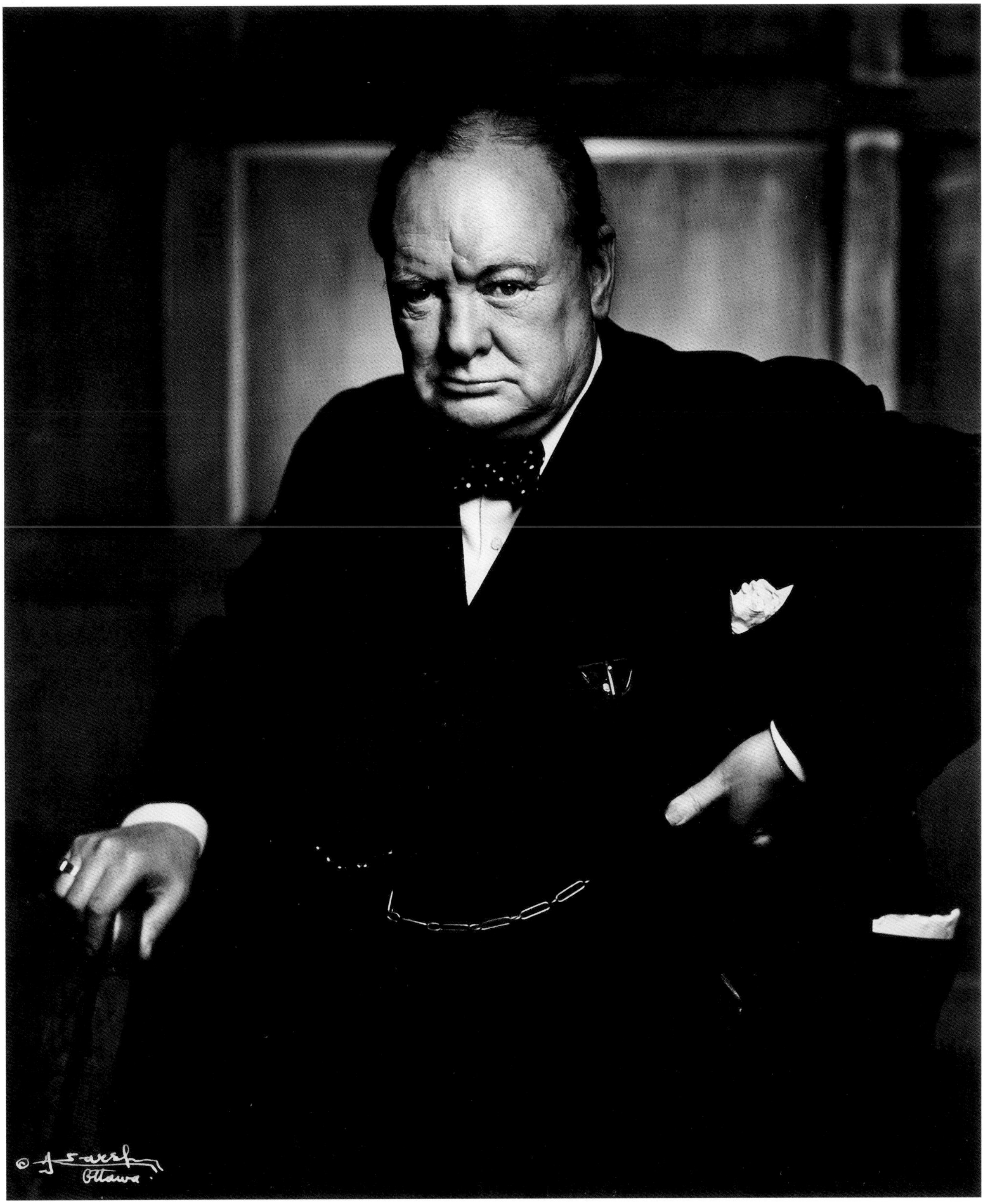
Ottawa

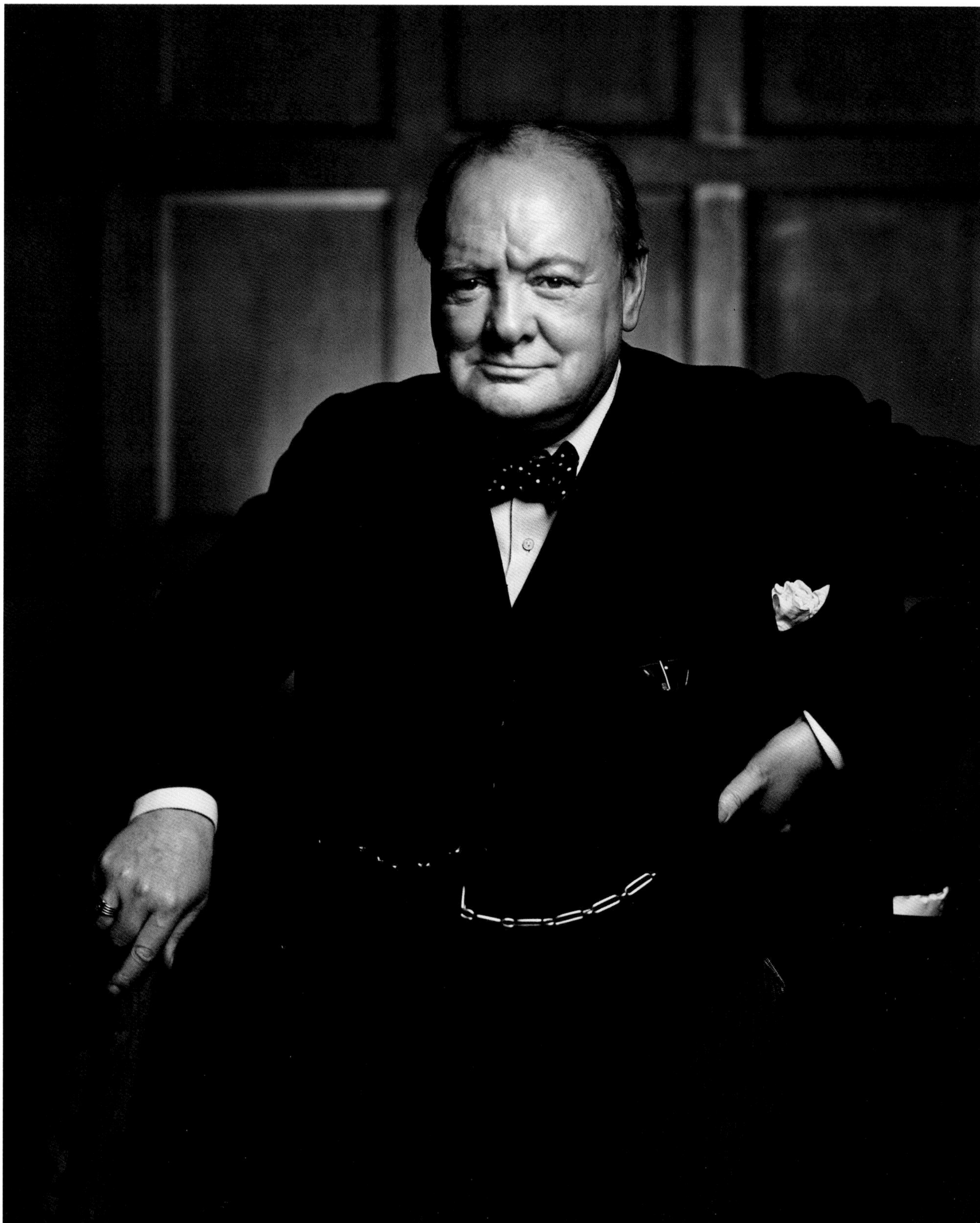

Yousuf Karsh, *Winston Churchill*, December 30, 1941, Estate of Yousuf Karsh. Moments after taking his first portrait of Churchill glowering in astonishment of his cigar being snatched away, the wartime leader relaxed and invited Karsh to take a second exposure, this time with a genial facial expression, remarking, "Well, you can certainly make a roaring lion stand still to photograph him."

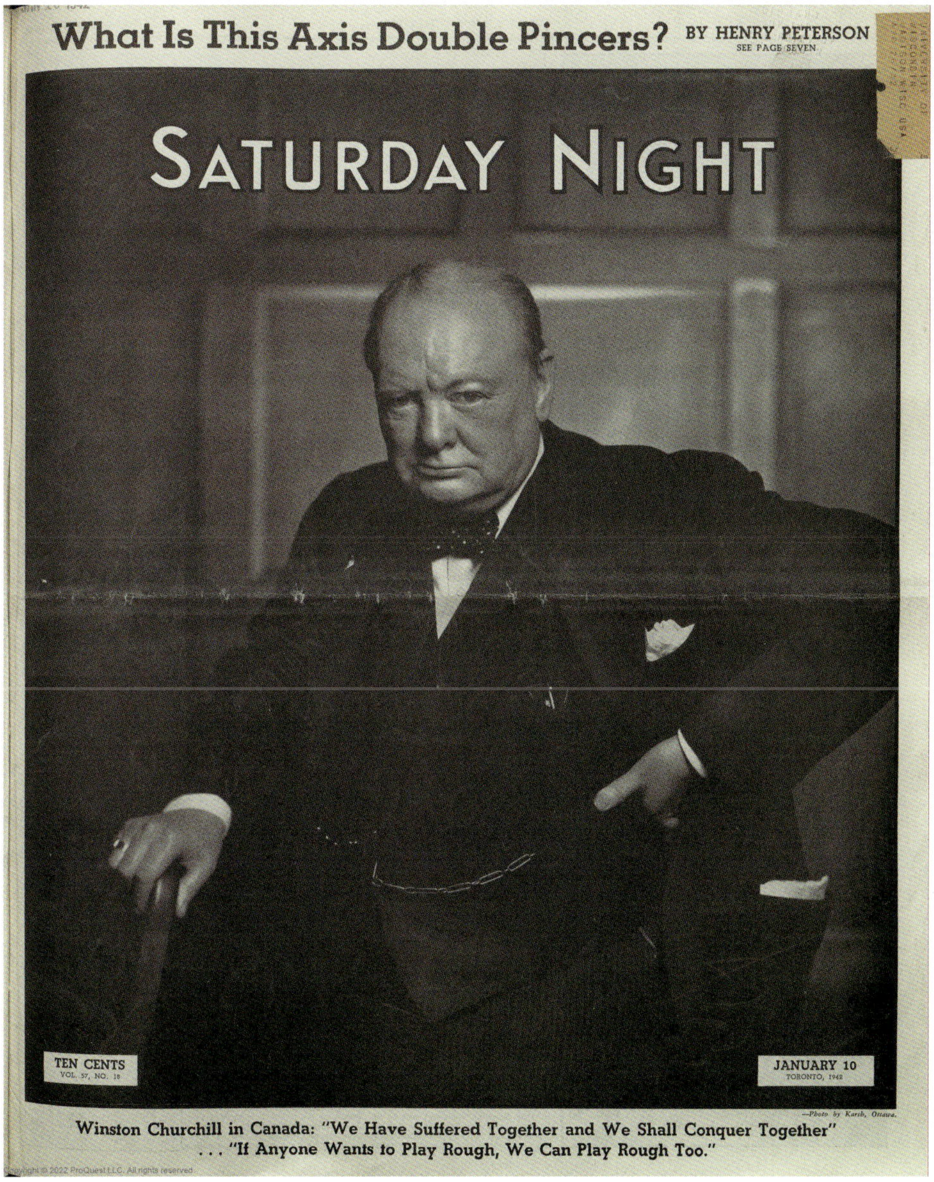

The photograph documenting a split-second interaction between impertinent photographer and scowling subject was transfigured into a powerful political address to allies and enemies alike and signified a stalwart and intimidating wartime leader.[6] Karsh's definitive portrait of Churchill was widely circulated through its reproduction on currency and stamps and as large-scale exhibition prints, and it has remained Karsh's most requested portrait.

In 2022, it was discovered that the Churchill portrait had been brazenly stolen from the lobby of Ottawa's Château Laurier hotel. The thief installed a facsimile in its place, delaying the discovery of the theft for months. It was later acquired by an Italian collector who was unaware of its provenance and returned the print to the hotel in 2024.

Cover of *Saturday Night*, January 10, 1942.

Princess Elizabeth July 30, 1951

Estate of Yousuf Karsh

In 1951, Karsh photographed the future Queen Elizabeth II, then a twenty-five-year-old princess, in an iconic series of portraits just six months before she ascended the throne. Several black-and-white and colour versions were circulated, playing a crucial role in creating a widely recognized image of the soon-to-be queen. Karsh photographed Elizabeth both alone and with her husband, Philip, and their young children, Anne and Charles, at her home, Clarence House, in London. One notable variant is a bust-length portrait of the princess wearing a tiara and draped in an off-the-shoulder gown that reveals her graceful neck. She appears to be in motion as she turns her head to gaze at the camera and, by implication, her future subjects.

Karsh's portraits later became the basis for some of the first official reproductions of Queen Elizabeth on currency and stamps. Design work began in 1952 to feature one of Karsh's 1951 portraits on Canadian banknotes (issued in 1954 as the Canadian Landscape series). The Bank of Canada had the tiara removed when preparing the transfer to an engraving plate, to differentiate it from a stamp series featuring the same portrait.[1]

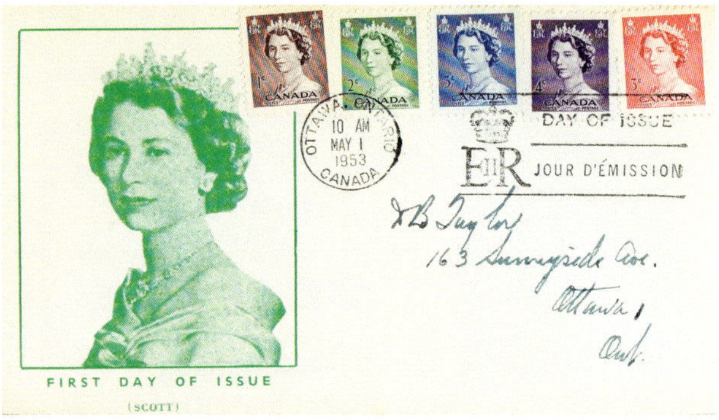

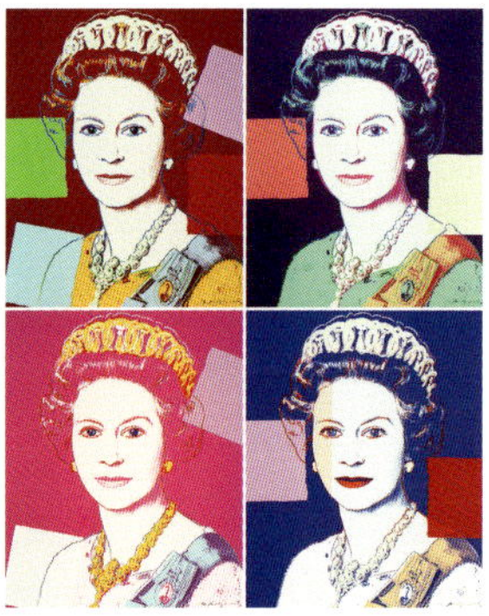

The widespread circulation of the Queen's portrait on currency and stamps resulted in a "Karsh in every pocket" for millions of Canadians from the 1950s onward. Official portraits of the Queen and her family were also circulated for display in government buildings and embassies worldwide. Karsh's regal portrayal of the Queen—enhanced by vibrant colouration—fostered the creation of a public persona of the young monarch prepared for her responsibilities with character and capability.

In 1985, American artist Andy Warhol (1928–1987), a leading figure in the Pop art movement, selected portraits of four royal heads of state as the basis for his series Reigning Queens: Queen Elizabeth II of the United Kingdom, Queen Beatrix of the Netherlands, Queen Ntfombi Tfwala of Swaziland (now Eswatini), and Queen Margrethe II of Denmark. In creating silkscreen versions of the portraits, Warhol applied his signature technique of outline tracing and the incorporation of abstract blocks of bright colours associated with modern advertising, and he reproduced the prints at a larger-than-life scale.

Although not a direct reference to Karsh's work, Warhol's treatment extends its cultural implications in terms of the mass diffusion of iconic images. In this work, reminiscent of postage stamps, Warhol both challenges the premise of royal portrait

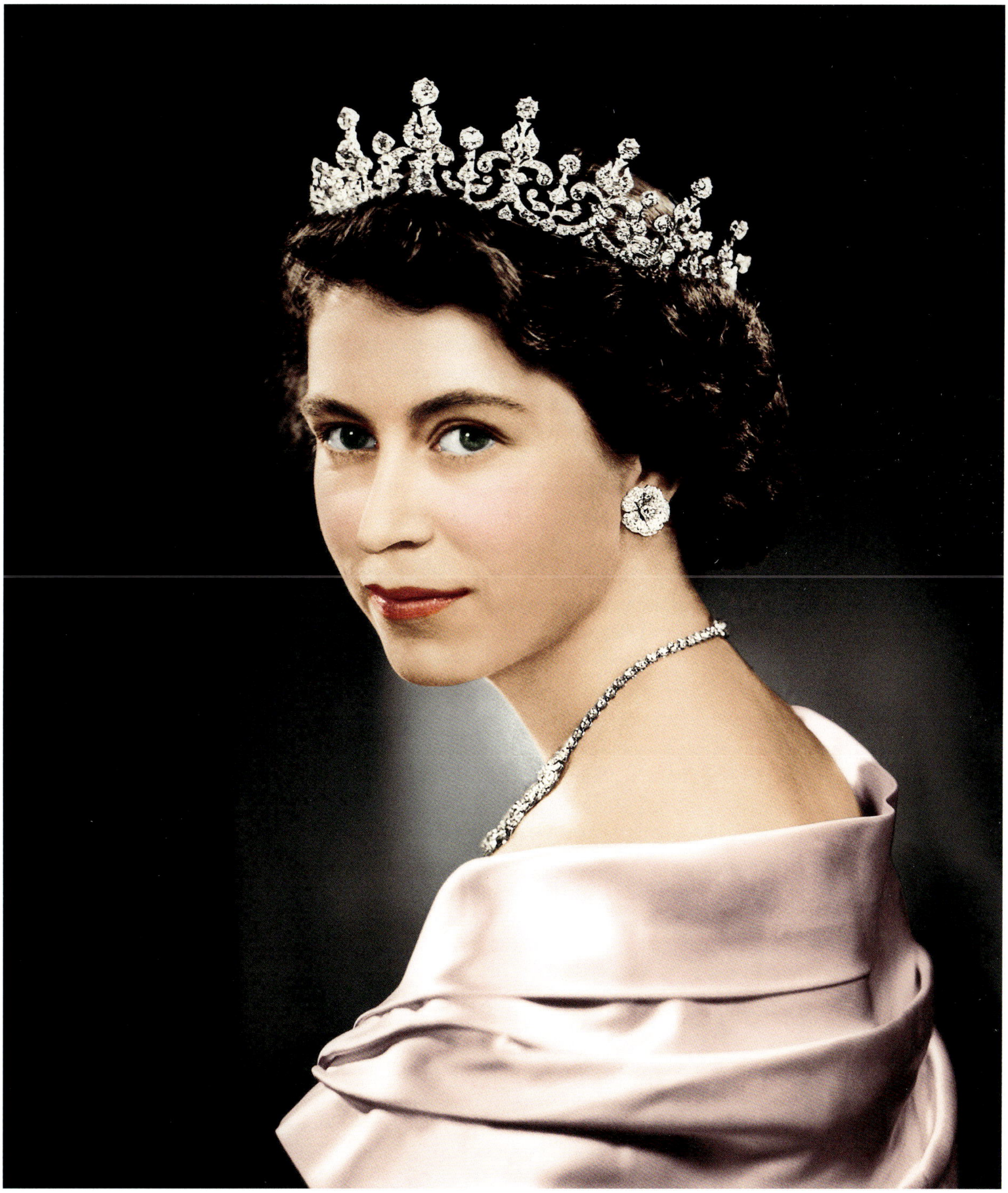

photography and reinvigorates it. In his portrait of the queen-in-waiting, Karsh signifies the dignified gravitas of Elizabeth's royal stature, her anticipated assent to the Crown bestowed by noble birth; by contrast, Warhol's Pop "translation" democratizes the mature monarch as simply another glamorous icon in the celebrity ecosystem.[2]

Opposite, left: First-day cover of the Canadian postage stamps featuring Yousuf Karsh's *Princess Elizabeth*, July 30, 1951; May 1, 1953, Elizabeth Hutchinson Collection, Library and Archives Canada, Ottawa. Opposite, right: Andy Warhol, printed by Rupert Jasen Smith, New York, published by George C.P. Mulder, Amsterdam, *Queen Elizabeth II of the United Kingdom*, from the series Reigning Queens, 1985, four colour silkscreen prints on Lenox Museum Board, each 100.1 x 80 cm, private collection.

Daniel Makokis, Edmonton 1952

Gelatin silver print, 31.3 x 26.7 cm (image), 50.7 x 40.6 cm (sheet)
CMCP Collection, National Gallery of Canada, Ottawa

By the early 1950s, Karsh's reputation as a portrait photographer was firmly established, largely through the reproducibility of his work. He soon began receiving projects beyond those he could execute in his Ottawa studio. Karsh took this portrait of trapper and hunter Daniel Makokis, an Indigenous patient receiving medical treatment at the segregated Charles Camsell Indian Hospital in Edmonton, Alberta, as part of a photo essay commission by *Maclean's* magazine.[1] It is a notable example of how Karsh's portraits were so effectively distributed across multiple media channels, each with its own encoded way to encounter images. Each time a photograph was reproduced or exhibited, its meaning shifted to suit the new context.

The Makokis portrait, positioned on a page with two others taken by Karsh at the Camsell Hospital, first appeared in *Maclean's* in the December 15, 1952, issue, under the subtitle "The Children of the Frontier." There, Karsh's text described his visit to Camsell, warmly congratulated the staff, and empathized with the patients in their care. As an elderly man, Makokis was clearly not a "child" of the frontier, especially when contrasted with the two images of younger patients: this terminology was a way of indicating the subordinate status of Indigenous people in the care of the federal government.

Later, the Makokis portrait was chosen for display inside the Karsh Studio in Ottawa. The portrait is visible in a shot by Chris Lund (1923-1983), an acclaimed photographer for the National Film Board of Canada (NFB). This photograph of the interior of Karsh's studio was featured in the May 27, 1958, NFB photo story "Portrait of Karsh: Close-Up of a Celebrated Canadian." Neither Karsh's studio display nor its citation in the NFB photo story identifies Makokis or indicates the original context of the photo, as the real subject of the story is Karsh himself.

Karsh's printed portfolio *Karsh Canadians* (1978) featured the Makokis portrait along with the following text:

> Daniel Makokis had been flown from the Saddle Lake Reserve to the Charles Camsell Hospital in Edmonton for a cataract operation. Meeting him there, I was impressed by the stoic determination of an Indian who had come on a long journey, with all his worldly belongings in a sack, his near blindness indicated by a white cane. I photographed him because he seemed to embody the ancient spirit of his people. This is a portrait of humble endurance and quiet courage in a hard northern land.[2]

In this account, written two decades after the portrait was taken, Karsh shares with the reader how he met Makokis and was moved by his resilience. By naming him and by transcribing their brief encounter, Karsh accords Makokis a place of recognition and respect on par with the other sitters selected for the volume, regarding him as a representative in his Canadian pantheon.

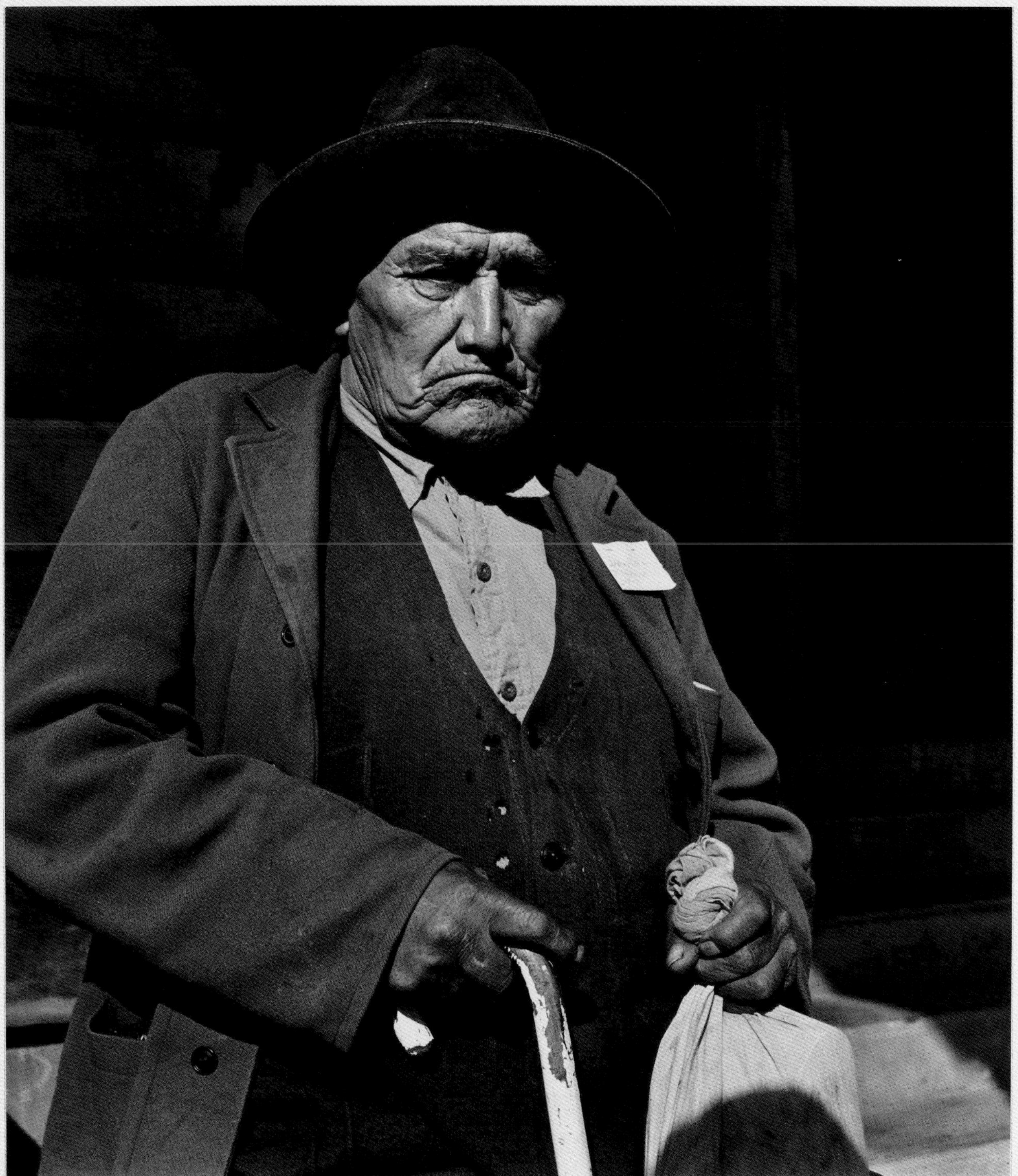

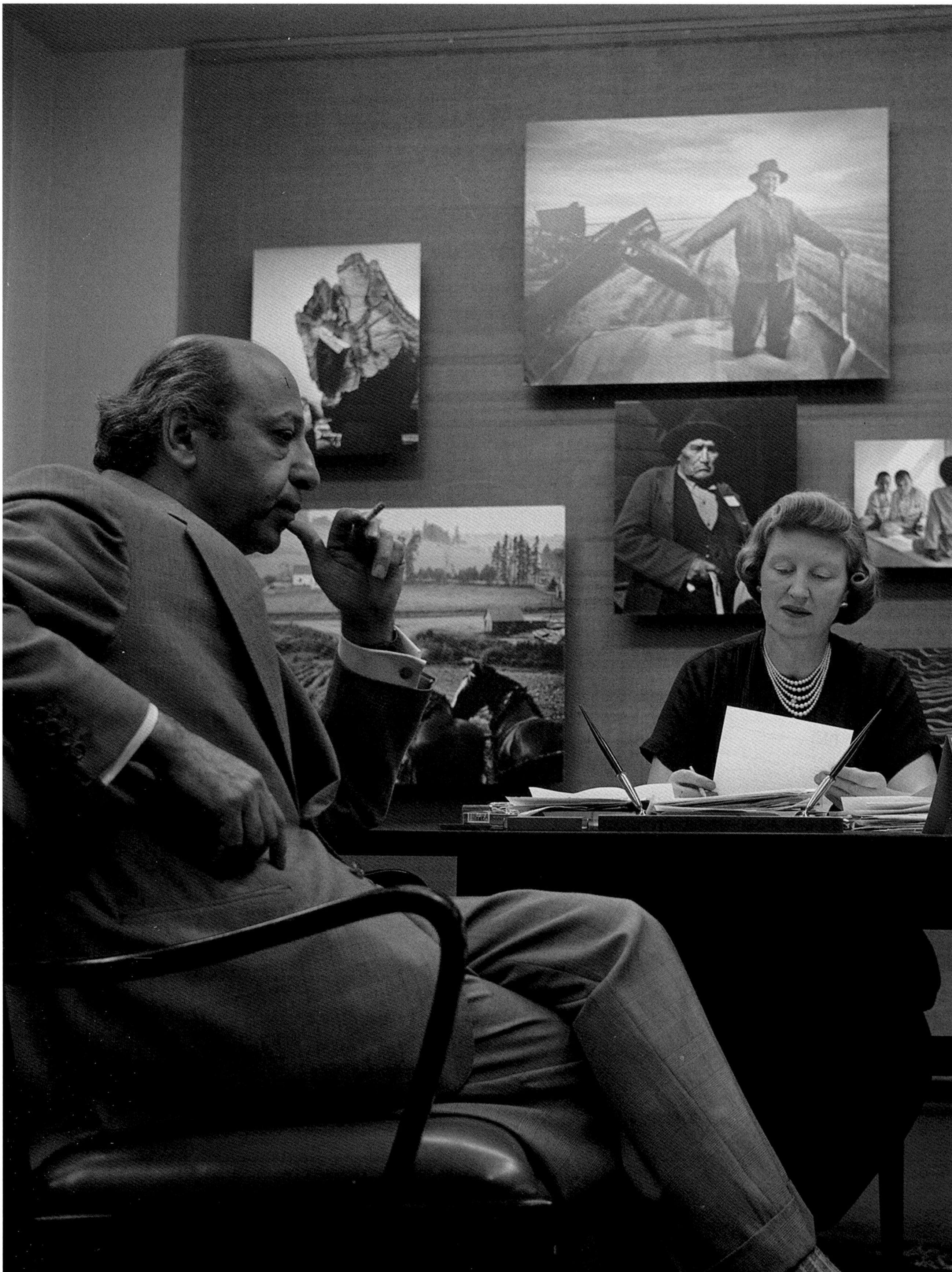

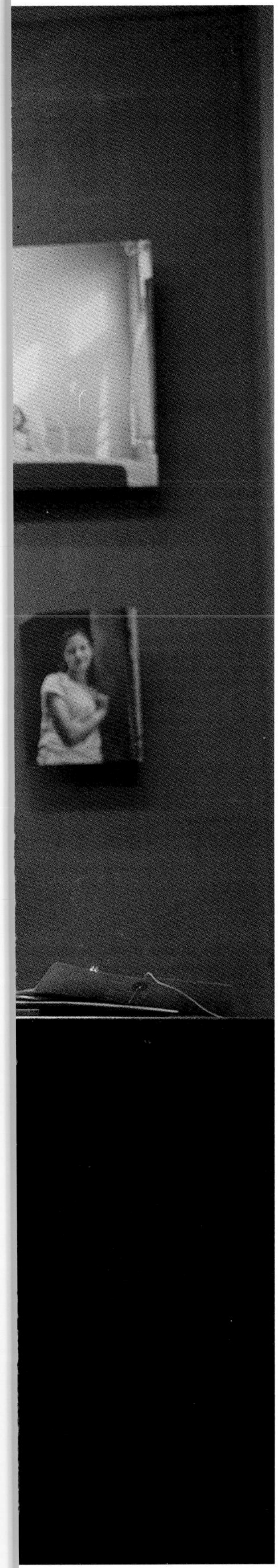

The emphasis on the individuality of the portrait's subject was lost, however, in its subsequent appearance in the major exhibition and catalogue *Karsh: A Fifty-Year Retrospective*, organized by the International Center of Photography in 1983. As part of an artist retrospective, the Makokis portrait represented Karsh's foray into assignment photography, yielding remarkable images that could also be appreciated as fine art. The caption for the image as it appeared in the exhibition reads, "Indian Man, 1953: To an Edmonton hospital he brought all of his worldly belongs wrapped in a knapsack, his name on a label, and a worn white cane."[3] This change in accompanying text resulted in the erasure of the subject's personal name and his treatment and recovery at a hospital far from his home community, as well as evidence of Karsh's interaction with him prior to the exposure of the camera's shutter. The portrait that had begun as a magazine assignment before shifting to a subsequent context as art portraiture was now reduced to a vague ethnography.[4]

Karsh demonstrates a rare moment of affinity with photographers working outside the portrait studio through comparison with New York street photographs by Paul Strand (1890–1976) and images of displaced families by Depression-era documentarian Dorothea Lange (1895–1965). As psychology is exchanged for physiognomy, individual name for descriptive label, the subject's face becomes aesthetic terrain.

Yousuf Karsh and Joyce Large at the Karsh Studio, 1957, photograph by Chris Lund. Karsh's Daniel Makokis portrait is visible on the wall.

Jawaharlal Nehru
December 22, 1956

Gelatin silver print
Estate of Yousuf Karsh

In the aftermath of the upheaval and violence of the Second World War and the establishment of the United Nations to foster diplomatic dialogue, Karsh's portraits of world leaders collectively envision an aspirational future of peaceful coexistence among nations and among peoples. A significant example is Karsh's portrayal of Jawaharlal Nehru, India's first and longest-serving prime minister, nearly ten years after the country gained independence from Britain.

Nehru is posed in near profile, with hands clasped, gazing contemplatively away from the camera. A soft diffusion of light surrounds his figure. Karsh pays tribute to Nehru's leadership during the 1947 Partition, which established India as a secular republic emancipated from British rule and Pakistan as an Islamic state. The portrait sitting took place in Washington, D.C., in 1956, after Nehru's meeting with President Dwight D. Eisenhower to secure American support for peaceful diplomacy in addressing the Suez Crisis, an Arab–Israeli conflict implicating global superpowers.

Karsh was unparalleled in his time as a portraitist with access to diplomats and political figures. He photographed Eisenhower as battle commander, as president of the United States, and finally, as a retired statesman with his hand placed on an enormous globe. Eisenhower does not rest his extended arm on the globe for support so much as he exerts influence upon it, his hand conspicuously poised above North America. Like Nehru's, Eisenhower's gaze is contemplative, his eyes downcast, a performance of *gravitas* in facing the geopolitical precarity of a world armed with nuclear weapons.

A key figure in the Suez Crisis was Canada's foreign minister, later prime minister, Lester B. Pearson, who was awarded the Nobel Peace Prize in 1957 for his role in mediating the crisis and proposing the deployment of the United Nations Emergency Force. Karsh attended Pearson's address in the House of Commons where he received congratulations from his parliamentary peers. Later, he restaged the scene with Pearson posed in profile, notes in hand, and Speaker of the House Roland Michener and a parliamentary page lit dramatically to the left.

Karsh's portraits of Nehru, Eisenhower, and Pearson demonstrate his remarkable ability to envision unique, iconic portrayals of political leadership. While each of the figures—who share a historical moment—is presented as a thoughtful leader seeking a peaceful future, Karsh's visual cues define their different perspectives: for Nehru, non-violent activism; for Eisenhower, strategic military dominance; for Pearson, persistent dialogue.

The portrait of Nehru is also significant because Karsh was singular among his peers in seeking to represent the cultural and racial diversity of the world he lived in. His portrayal of Nehru expresses his own world view, one formed from his childhood experience as a survivor of Armenian persecution and his later experience as an ethnic outsider admitted to Canada in 1924 as an exception to the prohibition against so-called Asiatic immigrants.[1] With his heavy Arabic accent and olive complexion, Karsh was regarded as "other" in 1930s Ottawa society. He understood well the challenge of difference, as did Nehru, who had spent many of his formative years living in the United Kingdom.

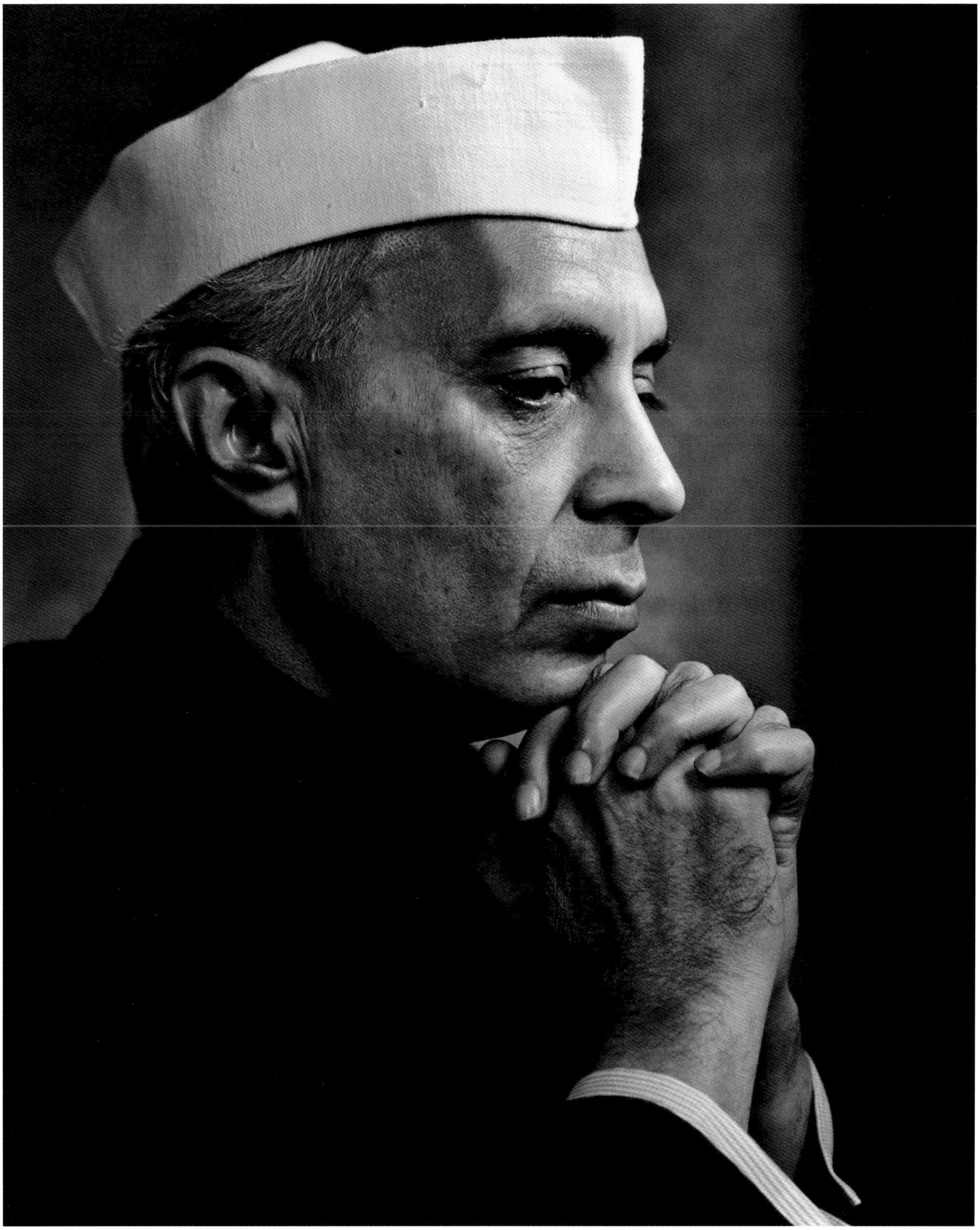

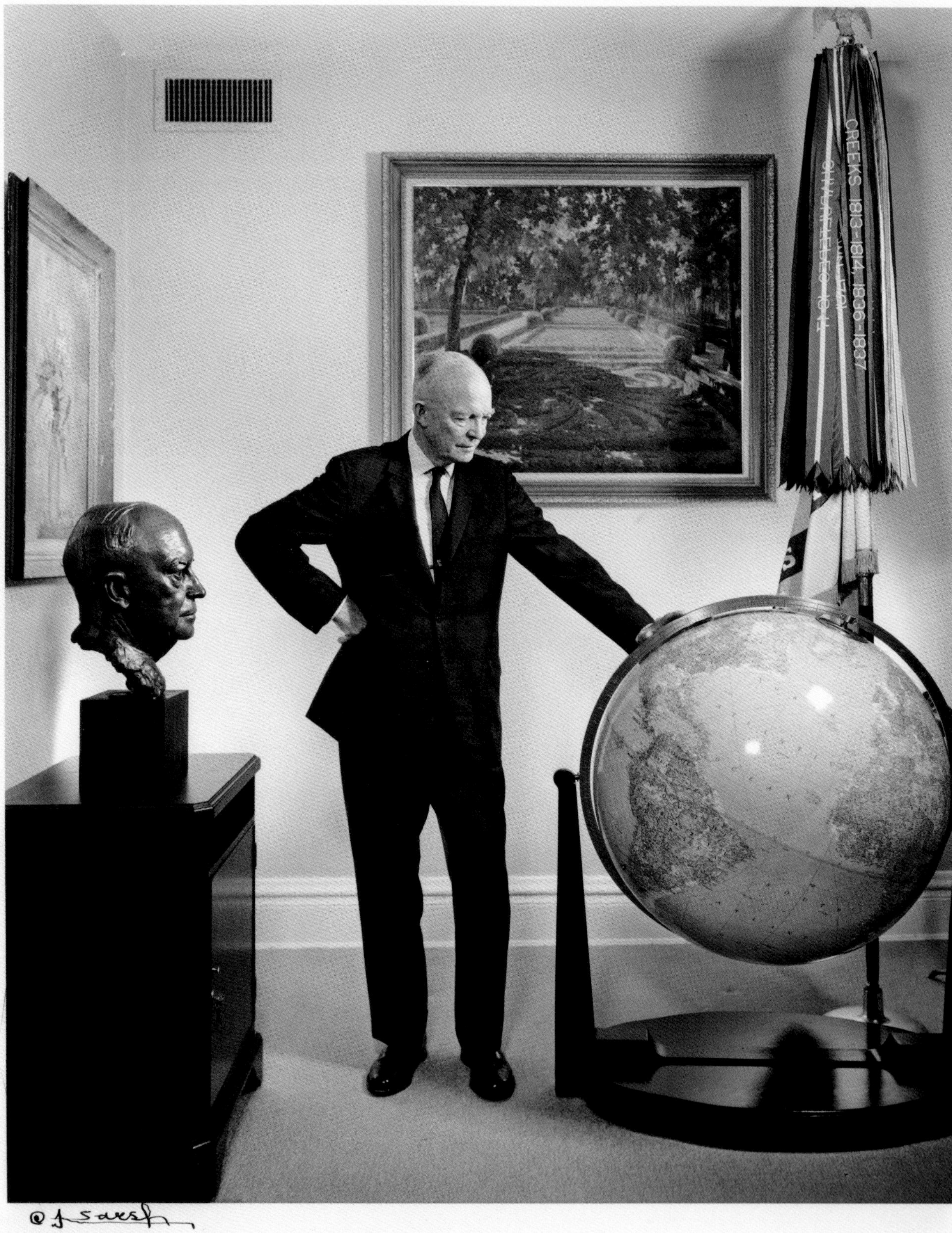

Yousuf Karsh, *President Dwight Eisenhower*, July 20, 1966, gelatin silver print, 24.1 x 19.1 cm, Yousuf Karsh Fonds, Library and Archives Canada, Ottawa.

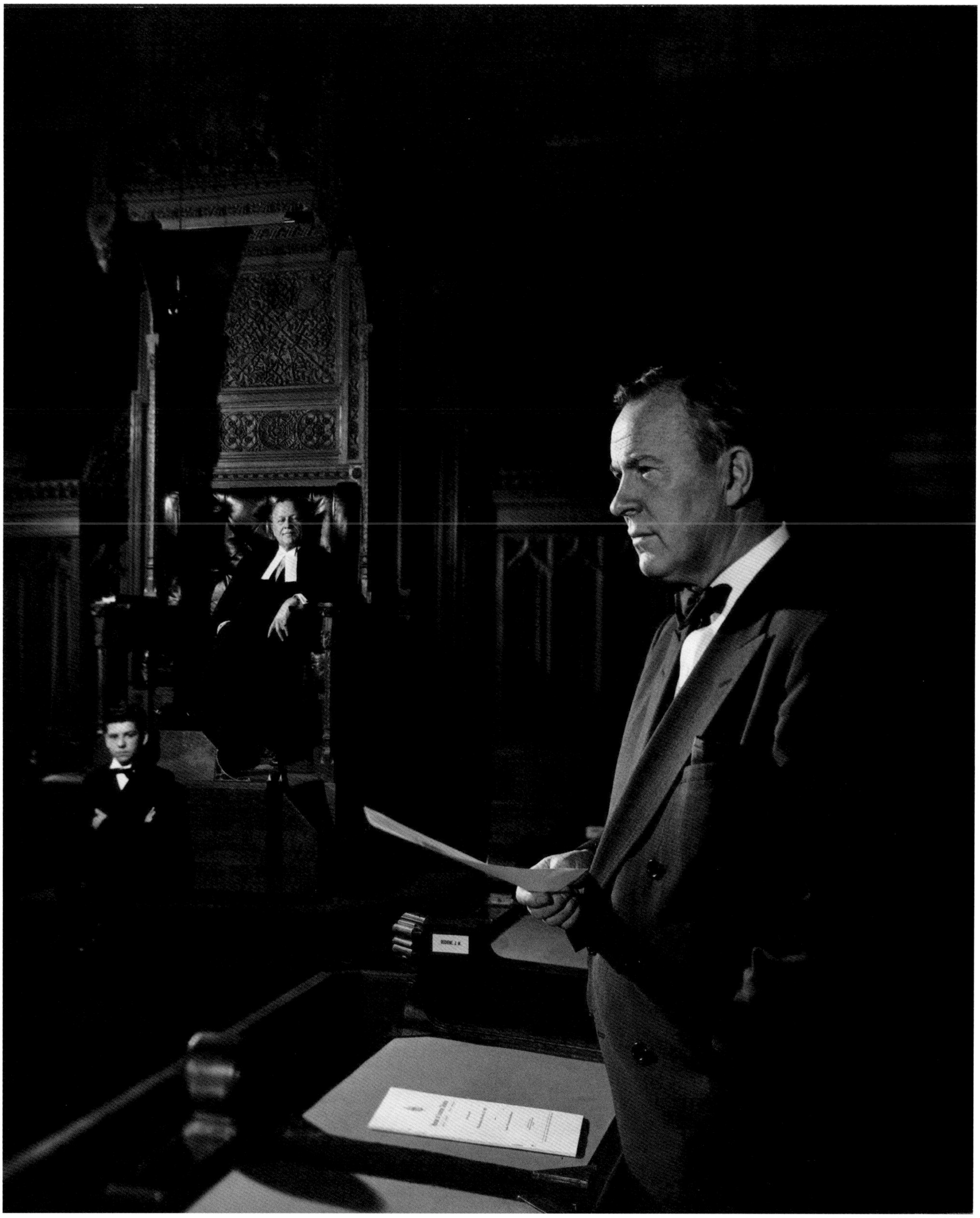

Yousuf Karsh, *Lester B. Pearson*, November 23, 1957, gelatin silver print, 50.4 x 40.5 cm (image), 50.4 x 40.5 cm (support), Yousuf Karsh Fonds, Library and Archives Canada, Ottawa.

Anna Magnani
May 1, 1958

Gelatin silver print, 59.6 x 48.1 cm
Montreal Museum of Fine Arts

At many points during his long career, Karsh took care to photograph mature women with respect and dignity—as talented individuals with autonomy and agency in directing their lives. In his portrait of Italian actor Anna Magnani, Karsh creates psychic and compositional space for the assertion of her command as a performer who is resisting prevailing definitions of gender. Posed before Karsh in 1958, Magnani addresses the camera with a direct stare and bold frontal stance, cigarette in hand. Although a movie star, she does not wear feminine clothes, reveal her body, smile, or otherwise invite an admiring gaze.

Magnani, a celebrity of Italian neorealist cinema, was known for playing feisty working-class characters navigating the hardships of poverty, sexual politics, and political upheaval. Unlike the glamorous and polished American movie stars working on studio sets, Magnani dispensed with vanity, portraying extraordinary ordinary women in their everyday settings. Playwright Tennessee Williams (also photographed by Karsh) created the character of Serafina in *The Rose Tattoo* (1955) specifically for her. She received an Academy Award for Best Actress for the role, making her the first Italian—and first woman whose native language was not English—ever to win an Oscar.

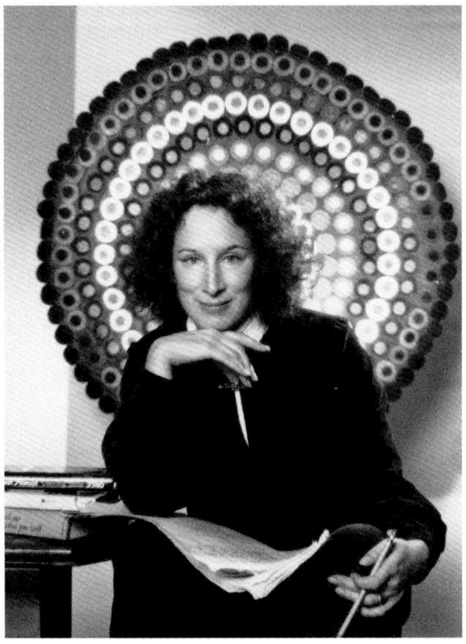

For Karsh, the portrait sitting was a social and aesthetic act entwining the artist, the subject, and the eventual viewer. His portrait of Magnani visually frames his own experience of meeting the Italian actor *and* his respectful witness of Magnani's assured conception of self.

This accordance of social—and ultimately, political—space can be located throughout Karsh's oeuvre; for instance, in his 1977 portrait of poet, author, and activist Margaret Atwood, he shows her at her home, posed with a circular patchwork quilt radiating around her head like a mandala. Karsh later confessed that he "wondered if she would be as caustic and provocative as some of her books: on the contrary, as I soon found, she was as natural, friendly, and unassuming as her home."[1] Atwood smiles as she regards the camera with pencil in her hand and pages of a manuscript in her lap, her own books nearby. The placement of Atwood's hand near her brooch creates the illusion that she is sweetly wielding a stiletto knife, a complement to her pencil, both weapons at the ready. As with the Magnani portrait, Karsh captures this instant as aesthetically optimal as a composition, but more significantly, it frames the individual's performance of her social and political agency.

Yousuf Karsh, *Margaret Atwood*, November 5, 1977, gelatin silver print, 23.8 x 17.4 cm (image), 27.4 x 17.4 cm (sheet), Yousuf Karsh Fonds, Library and Archives Canada, Ottawa.

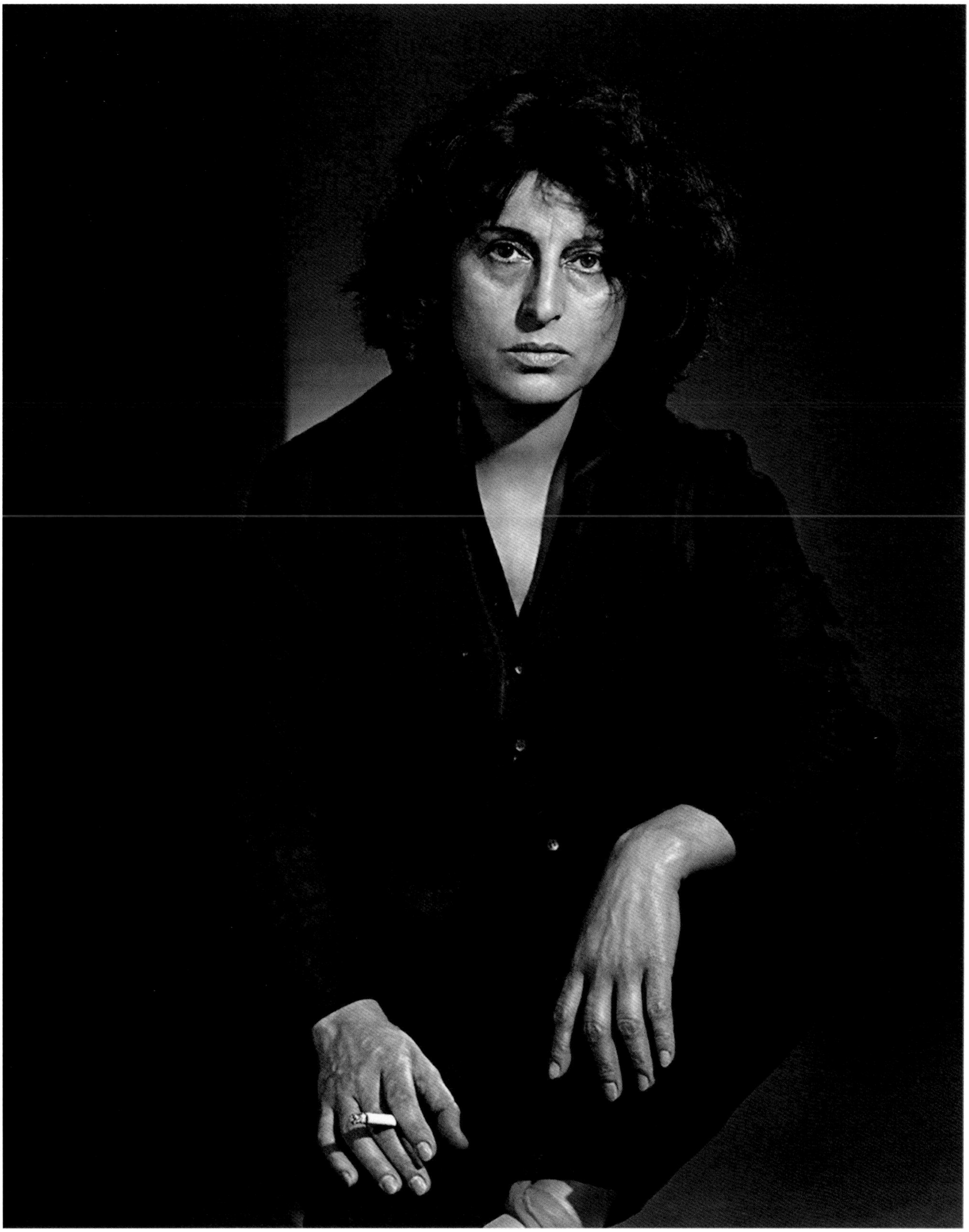

Jean-Paul Riopelle, Photographed in His Paris Atelier April 7, 1965, printed 1987

Gelatin silver print, 33.2 x 40.9 cm (image), 60.6 x 50.9 cm (sheet)
National Gallery of Canada, Ottawa

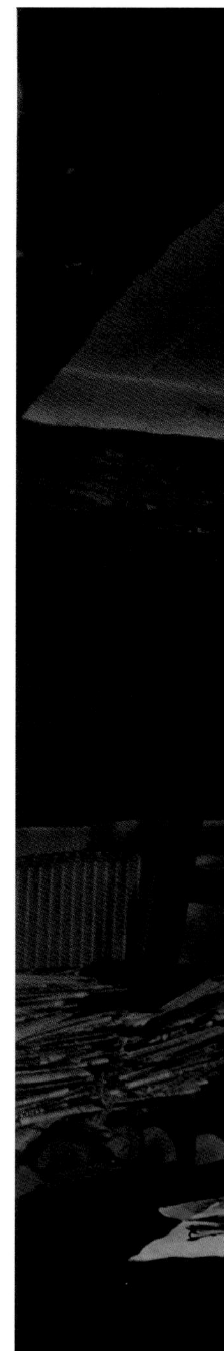

Jean Paul Riopelle (1923–2002) was a founding member of the Automatistes, the revolutionary Montreal-based Abstract Expressionist group. Karsh's portrait session in Riopelle's Paris studio yielded a dozen distinct poses. Karsh selected this image, capturing Riopelle bathed in the natural light of the atelier window as if momentarily pausing from his creative work, as the iconic version. His accompanying text amplifies the trope of the artist as a tormented genius: "He will go for weeks, or even months, without lifting a brush. Then, all of a sudden, will come a period of intense, almost frantic activity when art simply explodes in him. He will paint for weeks; he will not eat; he will not sleep; he will cover canvas after canvas with his highly individual, textured interlacings of bright impasto. Only when the compulsive surge has been fulfilled will his creative labours also subside."[1]

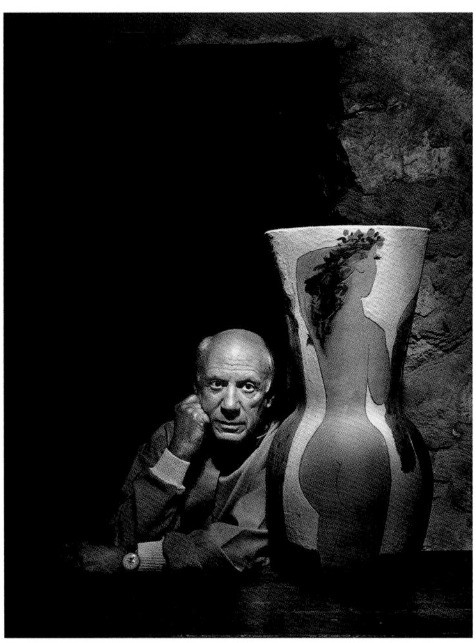

Karsh's narrative highlights Riopelle's apparent disregard for being commemorated in a portrait. Just three years earlier, Riopelle was selected as the sole artist representing Canada at the 1962 Venice Biennale, the international showcase for contemporary art. Karsh's portrait of Riopelle in his studio was selected as an early acquisition for the National Gallery of Canada photographic archive.[2]

Karsh typically photographed artists gazing at the camera, posed next to one of their works, whether painting, sculpture, or textile art. In turn, the artist collaborated by posing for Karsh fully aware of the subsequent mass circulation of a defining image. Karsh's 1954 portrait of Pablo Picasso (1881–1973), for example, does not depict the artist in the act of creation but as a summative representation of Picasso's unique talent, immortalizing him with the tangible result of his creative act.

Karsh's portrait of Riopelle emphasizes a sense of immediacy, as the artist is immersed in his creative work, unconcerned about external praise. Riopelle also arguably resists the expectation of compliance as a portrait sitter as he refuses to meet the camera's gaze.

Yousuf Karsh, *Pablo Picasso*, July 2, 1954, gelatin silver print, 60.1 x 50 cm, Montreal Museum of Fine Arts.

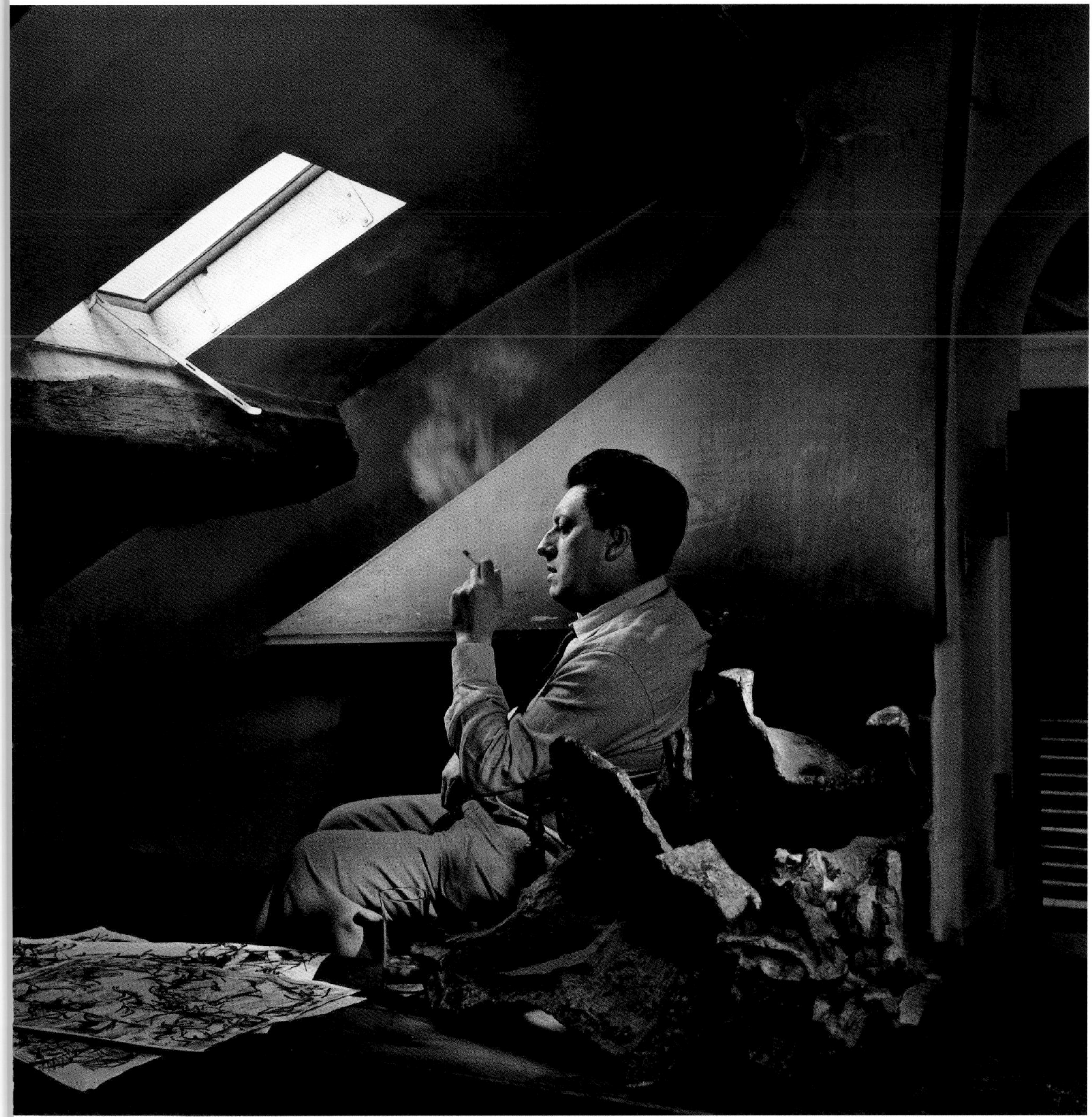

Roppeita Kita, with Grandson Nagayo Kita
November 1, 1969

Gelatin silver print, 50 x 39.7 cm
Estate of Yousuf Karsh

Rooted in the classical traditions of portrait painting, Karsh's works present subjects as timeless figures, effectively immortalizing them. This sense of permanence underscored Karsh's belief in portraiture as a visual tribute that endures far beyond the subject's moment in history, a significant aspect of his work over the span of his six-decade career.

By the 1960s, Karsh's status as photographer emeritus earned him an appointment as special photographic advisor to Expo 70, held in Osaka, Japan. In 1969, Karsh travelled in advance to Japan to photograph leading Japanese business leaders, artists, performers, and Nobel laureates, considered Living National Treasures (*Ningen Kohuko*).[1]

Among his portrait subjects was the eminent master of Noh theatre, Roppeita Kita. As Karsh later recounted, "Roppeita Kita is more than a legend in Japan, he is a living shrine—so revered that all who entered the theatre when he is on stage fell to their knees in respect. At 90-plus, he is one of the greatest actors of the Noh drama, a form of theatre which has been so meticulously refined over seven centuries, so filled with subtle symbolism, that even few contemporary Japanese can fully appreciate all the nuances of the performance."[2] In this work, soft light falls on the wrinkled face and hands of the venerable actor, alluding to the passage of time. The presence of Kita's grandson, Nagayo, who was also a Noh performer, introduces a sense of familial tenderness, reverence for one's elders, and the continuance of the mentorship tradition.

For Karsh, living legend status was not restricted to celebrated figures who achieved a long life—it extended to those of talent at any age. His 1969 Japan portfolio also featured internationally acclaimed younger figures, notably the filmmaker Akira Kurosawa, lauded for his experimental techniques in films such as *Rashomon* (1950) and *The Seven Samurai* (1954). Karsh also photographed physicist Hideki Yukawa, Japan's first Nobel laureate and an outspoken advocate for nuclear disarmament. Both Kurosawa and Yukawa were close to Karsh's own age at the time, in their early sixties, and in the prime of their careers. Rather than representing Japan's enduring traditions, they exemplified the country's emerging influence in the modern era.

During his trip, Karsh became profoundly interested in the Japanese government's heritage designation system—in particular, its distinction of Preservers of Important Intangible Cultural Properties, which resonated with his lifelong work seeking to chronicle the best of humanity and produce a visual language to express goodness, talent, and achievement. The concept of immortalizing a nation's living legends as a collective portrait representing both tradition and innovation informed Karsh's later projects chronicling the dramatis personae of his own time in his published portfolios *Karsh Canadians* (1978) and *Karsh: American Legends* (1992).

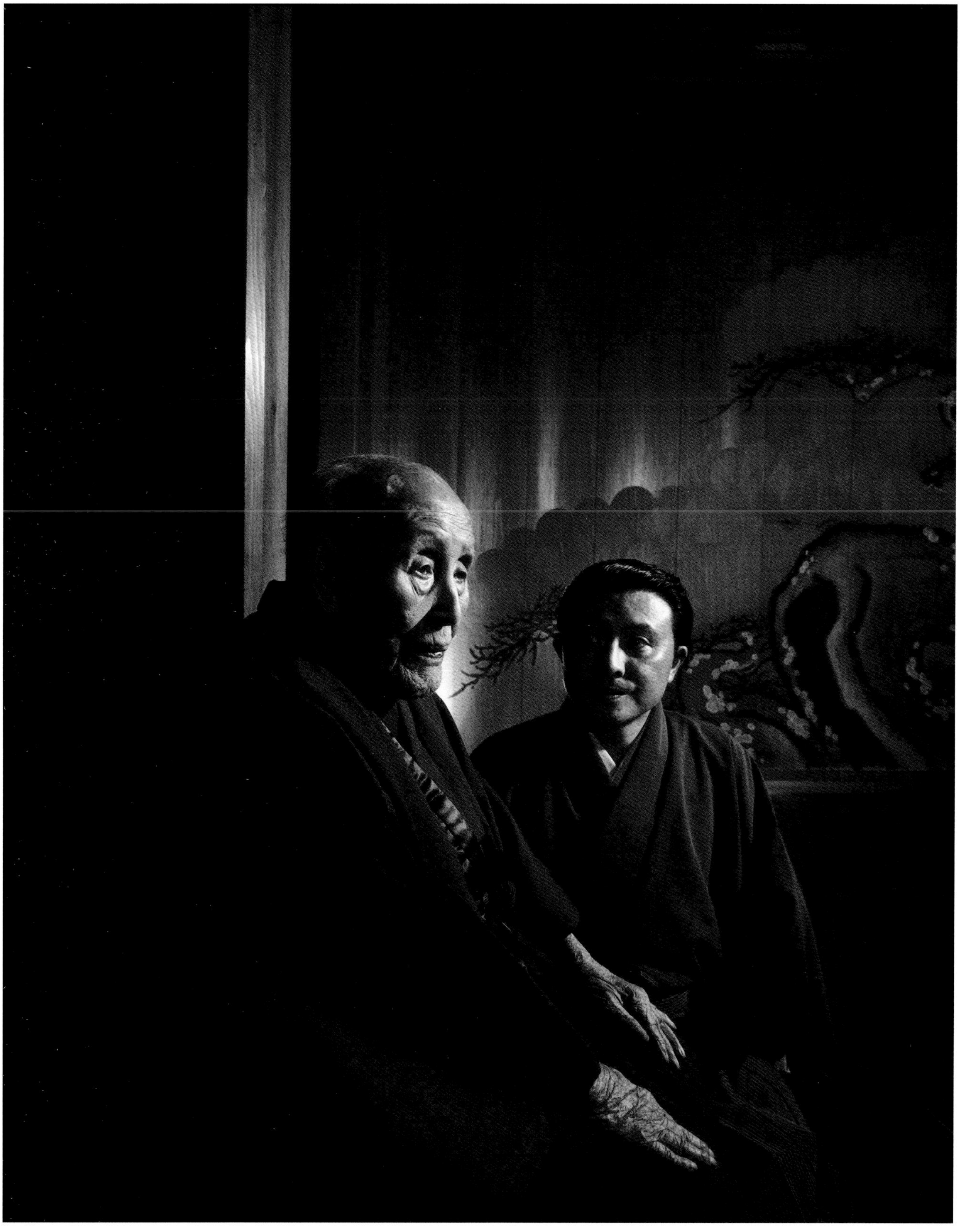

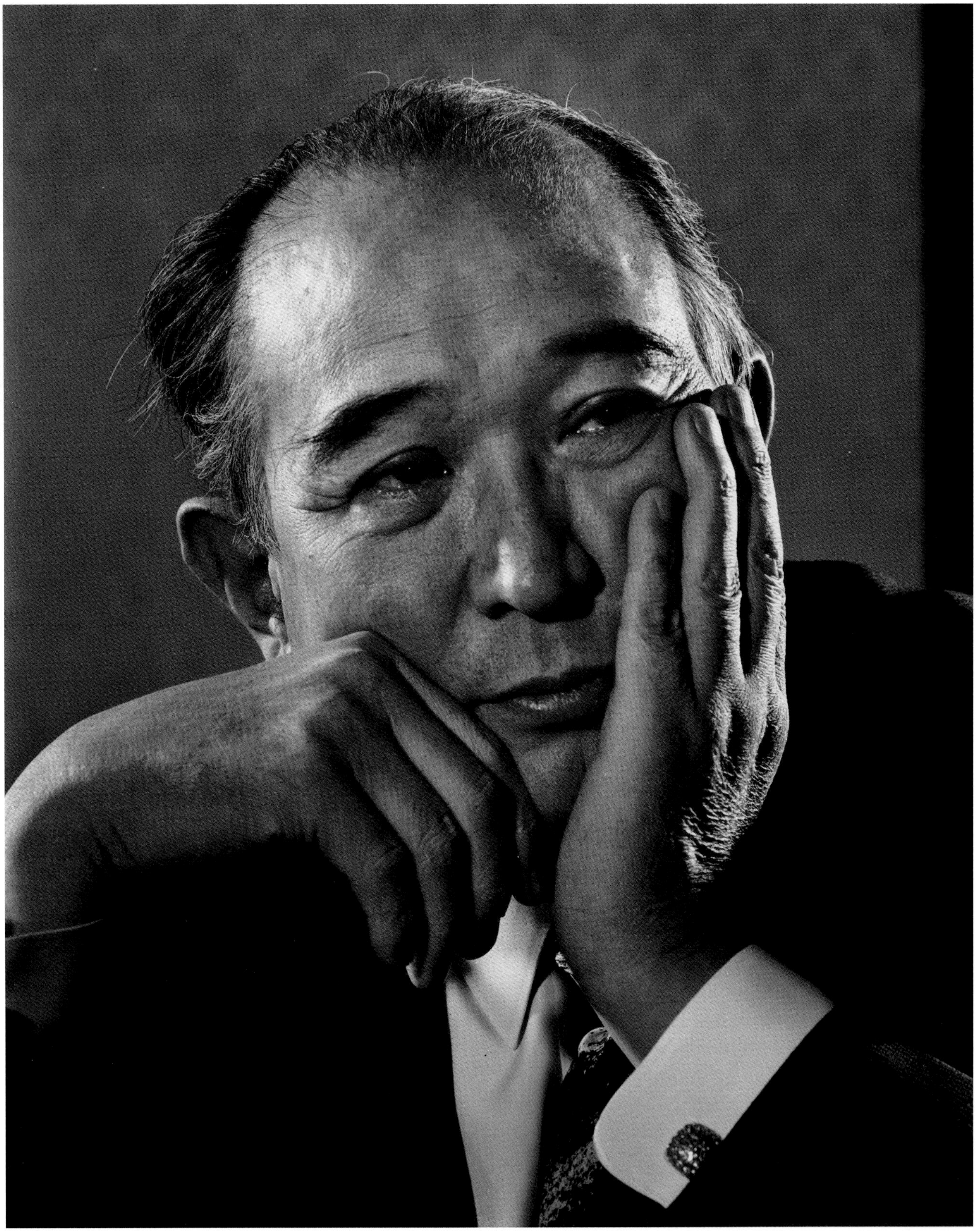

Yousuf Karsh, *Akira Kurosawa*, November 1, 1969, gelatin silver print, 34.1 x 27.2 cm, Yousuf Karsh Fonds, Library and Archives Canada, Ottawa.

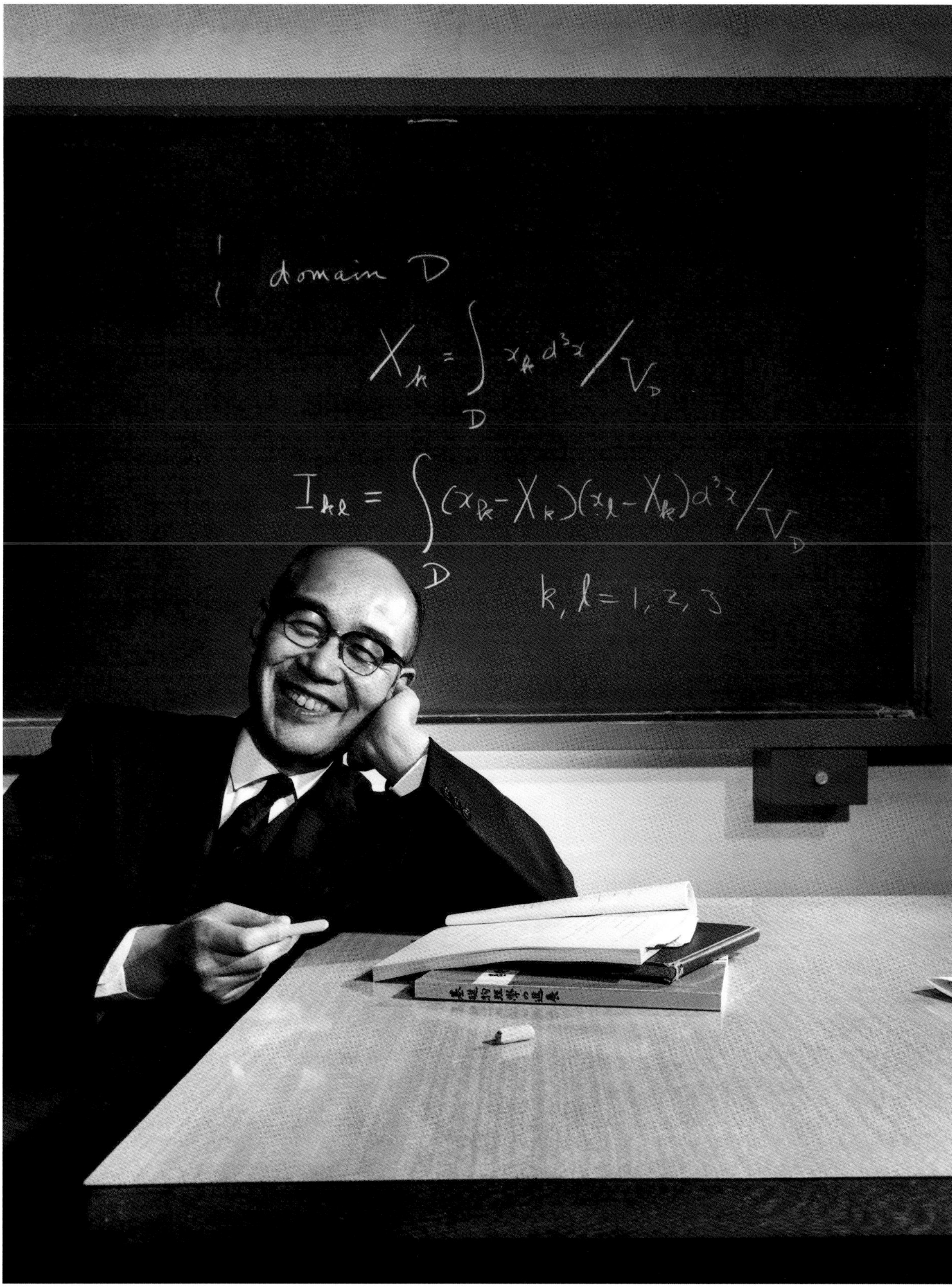

Yousuf Karsh, *Hideki Yukawa*, November 1, 1969, Estate of Yousuf Karsh.

Andy Warhol
November 21, 1979

Gelatin silver print, 59.4 x 49.3 cm
Montreal Museum of Fine Arts

In 1979, Yousuf Karsh, the most famous portraitist of his time, photographed Andy Warhol (1928–1987), the most famously controversial artist of his time. Arguably, they had more in common than it might seem: both were household names due to the widespread proliferation of their images, and both were prolific creators supported by a cadre of assistants and agents. The portrait session was commissioned by Warhol's print magazine, *Interview*, which was founded in 1969 as "the crystal ball of Pop" and featured interviews with and by celebrities

As Karsh often did in portrait sessions, he took multiple exposures, selecting a few images for public release. In one black-and-white shot, with its characteristic sharp focus and deep shadows, Warhol embodies the purported banality of his Pop art aesthetic by holding a housepainter's brush to his face.[1] Warhol playfully draws attention to criticism of his "factory-like" artistic method, which involved many hands working in a large New York studio called the Factory.

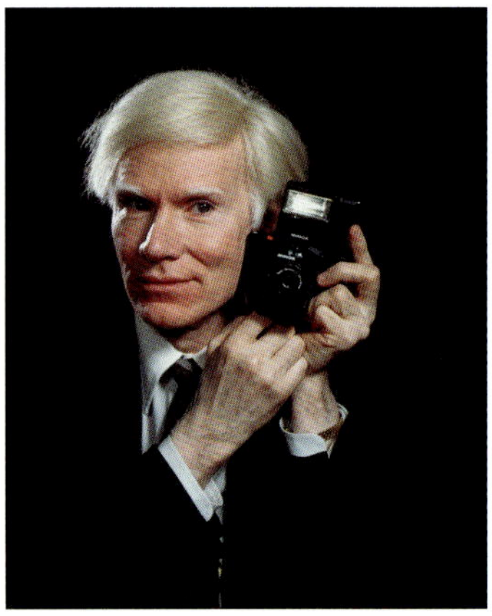

A colour portrait from the same session features Warhol posing as if for an advertisement, holding a camera up to his face with playful reverence. Famous in his own right for photograph-based portraits of celebrities, Warhol—unlike Karsh—explored "low art" automatic camera technologies like the Polaroid camera and photo booth pictures as the basis for reproduction as screenprints.

In his portraits, Karsh aimed to distill a cumulative portrayal of his subject, capturing Warhol as a disruptor of art conventions. Karsh's classic style of formal portraiture contrasts with that of his almost exact contemporary, the fashion and art photographer Richard Avedon (1923–2004), challenging the viewer to reconsider what a portrait truly depicts. Avedon's close-up of Warhol's torso, covered in deep scars—evidence of an assassination attempt by Valerie Solanas[2]—is posed against a stark white background: the absence of proof of life in the form of Warhol's living face results in an unsettling, clinical "portrait" reminiscent of post-mortem photography. Avedon also monumentalized Warhol by printing this piece in massive, larger-than-life dimensions.

While both Karsh and Avedon highlight photography's evidentiary role—namely, to bear witness—they pursue completely different approaches to representing the individual. Karsh records moments in the collaborative interplay between photographer and subject, capturing Warhol's coyly self-acknowledged role as a provocateur. In this way, Karsh codifies Warhol's already (in)famous persona. Avedon disrupts portrait convention by supplanting Warhol's famous face with a topography of his trauma and survival.

Yousuf Karsh, *Andy Warhol*, November 21, 1979, Estate of Yousuf Karsh.

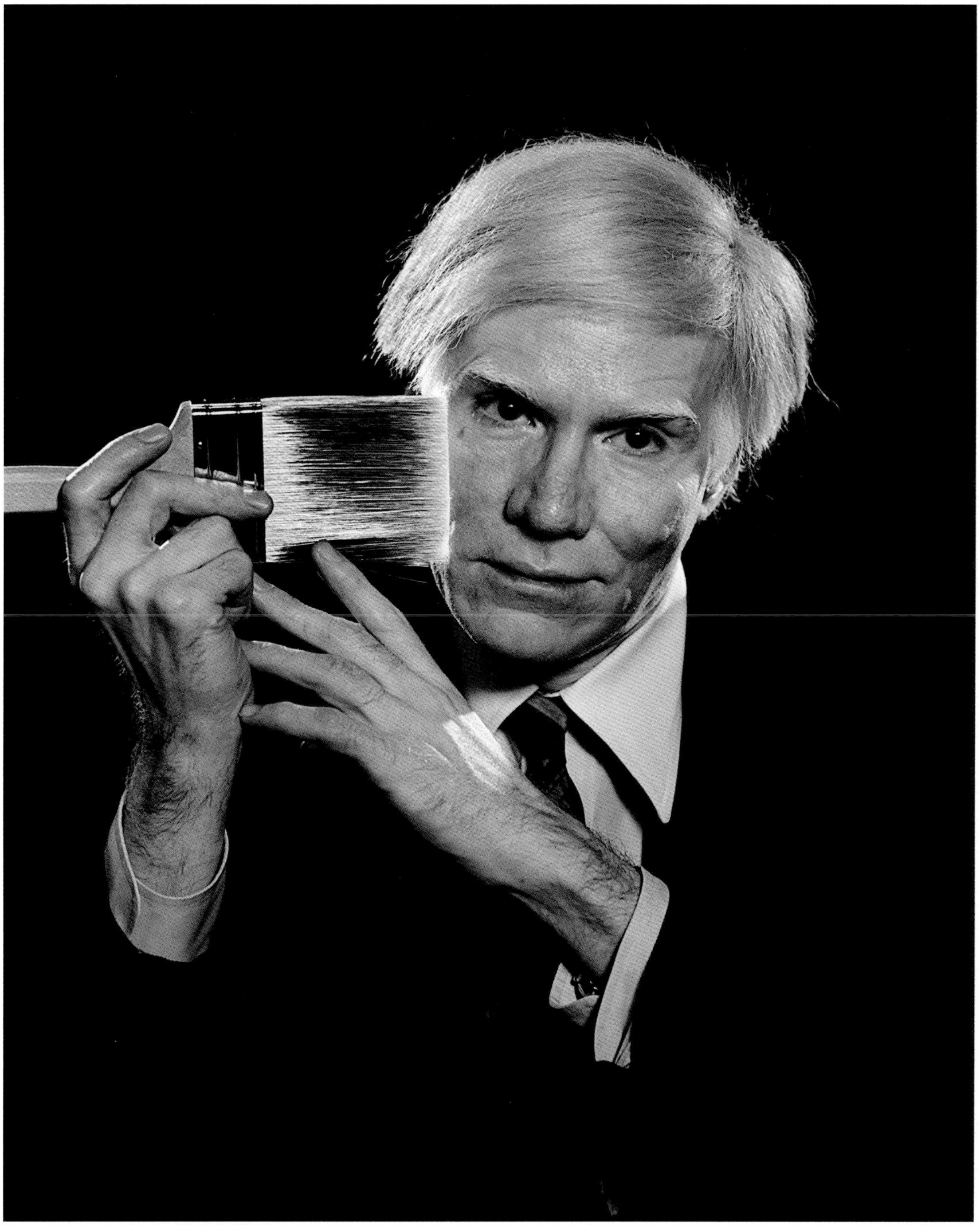

The timing of Karsh's portrait session with Warhol, which took place in the late 1970s, is particularly significant, as it occurred at a liminal moment when photographic practice began to change radically, with artists exploring postmodern concepts of the constructed self rather than seeking to capture the true essence of an individual in a single image. It also heralded Karsh's arrival at the last phase of his career and the twilight of film photography, as digital photography emerged as the new paradigm.

Lilly Koltun
August 10, 1987

Gelatin silver print, 25.4 x 19.1 cm
Yousuf Karsh Fonds, Library and Archives Canada, Ottawa

In 1987, as Karsh prepared to close his studio, the extensive Karsh archive was acquired on behalf of all Canadians by the National Archives of Canada (now Library and Archives Canada). The lead negotiator was Lilly Koltun, an acclaimed art historian and director of the archives' prestigious photographic collection. Karsh offered to photograph Koltun, who eagerly accepted the first-hand experience of a typical sitting in the name of research. The resulting image shows Karsh, still at his full powers at age eighty-nine, creating an arresting portrait recalling the stylish elegance of 1930s celebrity photography.

Koltun later recounted her experience:

> I'll always remember my delight one day, when I heard the courteous tones of Yousuf Karsh's voice on the telephone asking me if he might photograph me! He said that it had long been his wish, and if I agreed, could I please wear a dress which he had always admired. To my astonishment, he described it exactly!
>
> After I arrived in his studio at the appointed hour, wearing the dress of course, he then spent all morning completing my sitting.... [A]t the very moment when I was about to give up, it seems I put my hands on my hips, and there it was! He took it instantly, and I admit to this day that remains my favourite pose. I insist it makes me look a little like Ava Gardner![1]

Although Karsh achieved fame as the creator of a remarkable portrait gallery of notable figures from his time, his roots remained in his Ottawa studio. Beginning in the 1930s, Karsh's studio business was open to ordinary people seeking iconic portraits: business executives, diplomats, and socialites who could afford his fees could book a sitting even during the height of his international projects. Between Karsh's agents booking magazine assignments and his own self-selected sittings for book projects, everyday clients who were neither celebrities nor famous politicians formed the core work that kept the studio at full capacity. Sitters knew in advance that the resulting images would reflect Karsh's signature aesthetic and portray them with dignity.

Susan Sontag famously observed that photography confers importance upon the person being depicted.[2] Posing for Karsh also indirectly connected the subject to the famous figures he had already photographed, elevating their own stature and providing them with an anecdote to proudly recount when showing the portrait, signed by Karsh, to others.

As Jerry Fielder, who worked alongside him for decades, remarked, "Karsh was impressed by talent, intelligence, humour and accomplishment. But most of all, he was impressed by kindness and integrity. He treated everyone the same, whether they were a headwaiter or a head of state. When you were with Karsh, you felt as if you were the most important person in the world because his focus was entirely upon you."[3]

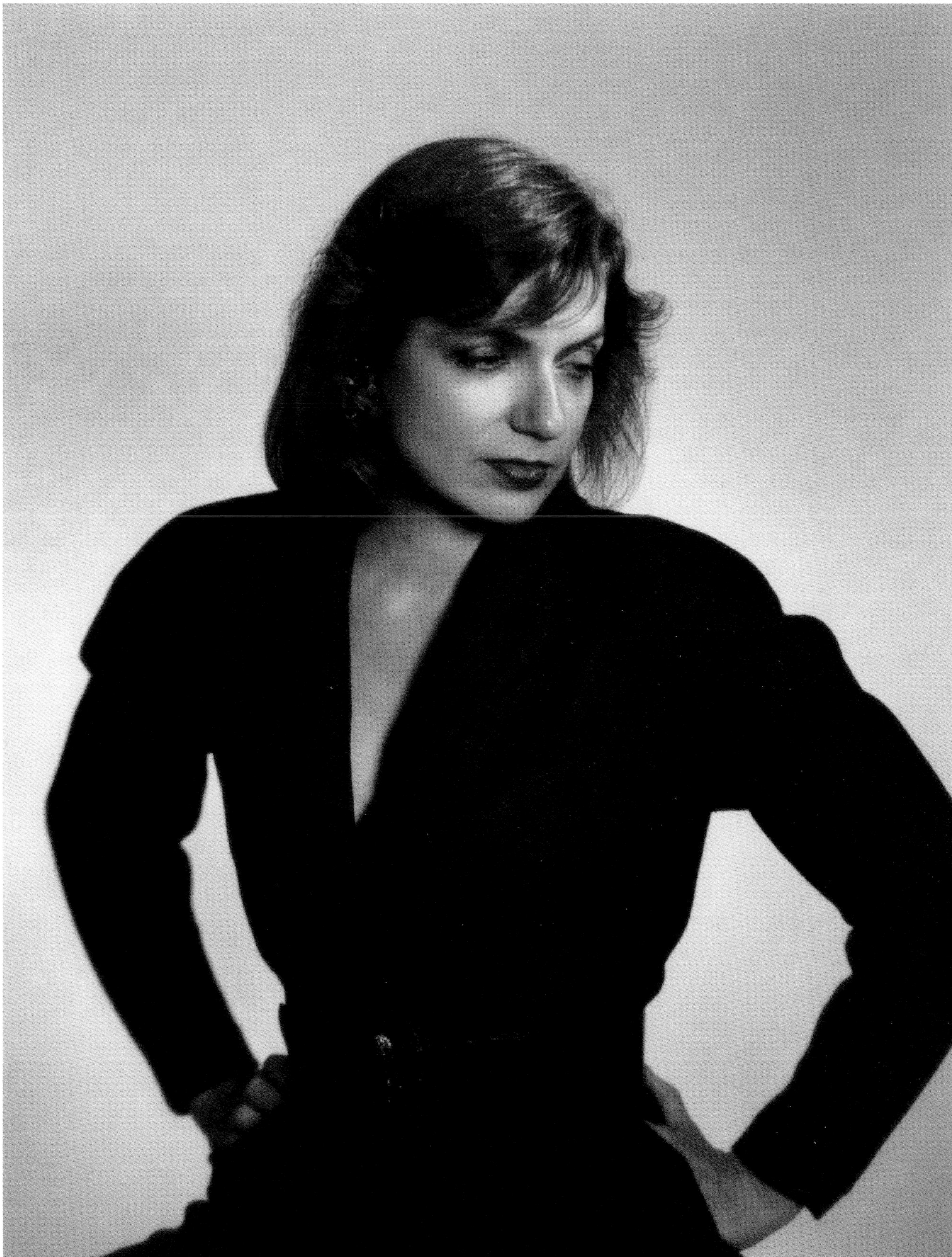

Jessye Norman
April 4, 1990

Chromogenic print, 101.6 x 76.2 cm (image), 121.9 x 90.5 cm (sheet)
Estate of Yousuf Karsh

In 1990, Karsh photographed American soprano Jessye Norman. She faces the camera in regal splendour, a serene and confident woman, her powerful frontal pose filling the frame. Arguably Karsh's greatest portrait in colour, it is also significant as a collaboration between photographer and performer, a powerful visual statement of individual and racial emancipation. Karsh photographs Norman at nearly full length, emerging from shadows as she directs her attention to the camera and, beyond that, the eventual viewer. She commands the entirety of the visual space as a declarative act—"I am"— laying claim to her right to occupy it.

Indelibly associated with the dramatic tonal range of black-and-white portrait photography, Karsh also worked with colour film throughout his career. He was regularly commissioned to provide colour portraits for illustrated magazines, one of the key channels for distributing his images. Although he accepted colour portrait commissions, he did so sparingly: it was his preference, by training and temperament, to seek a more psychologically powerful portrait defined by an infinite monochrome palette rather than the bravura of colour to replicate the range of human vision.

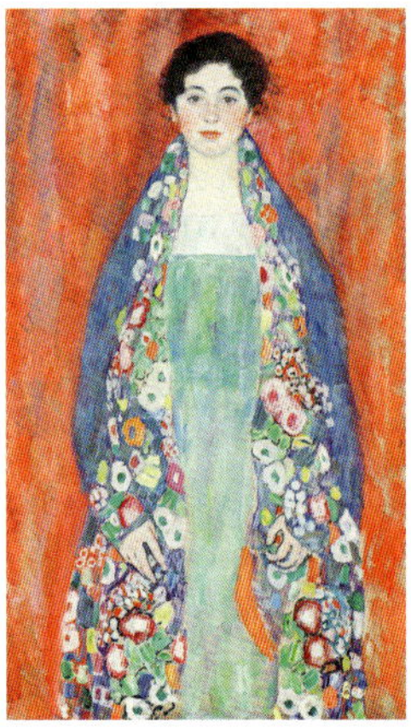

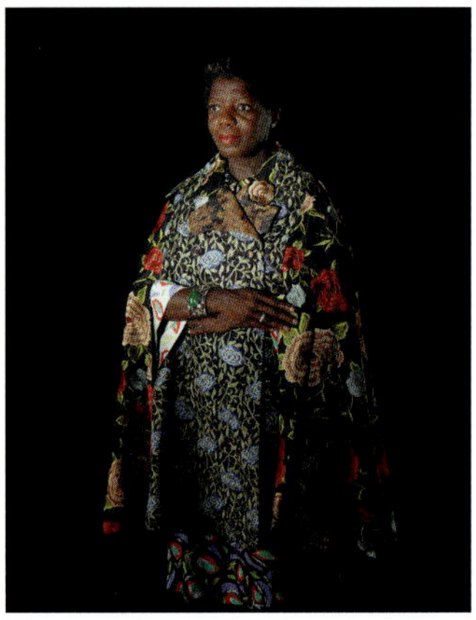

Posing for Karsh, Norman addresses our gaze as her individual persona rather than as an operatic character. The singer is backlit, radiating soft light around her. Her nearly full-length figure creates a triangular brocaded composition evocative of the richly patterned textiles in the work of Vienna Secessionist painter Gustav Klimt (1862–1918). For her portrait sitting with Karsh, Norman donned this magnificently brocaded garment that she had worn a few weeks earlier during her performance on March 18, 1990, singing gospel spirituals with fellow soprano Kathleen Battle at New York's Carnegie Hall.

Norman's powerful presence is amplified by the glowing aura that surrounds her, announcing her mastery as an unparalleled performer. Karsh's conception of this portrait celebrates Norman not only as a gifted diva but also as a forceful figure of political change. Norman, who grew up in the segregated state of Georgia in the 1940s and 1950s, assumes majestic proportions to challenge the slow change in the classical music community. "Racial barriers in our world are not gone," Norman once said, "so why can we imagine that racial barriers in classical music and the opera world are gone?"[1]

Left: Gustav Klimt, *Portrait of Fräulein Lieser*, c.1917, oil on canvas, 140 x 80 cm, private collection.
Right: Catherine Opie, *Thelma*, 2017.

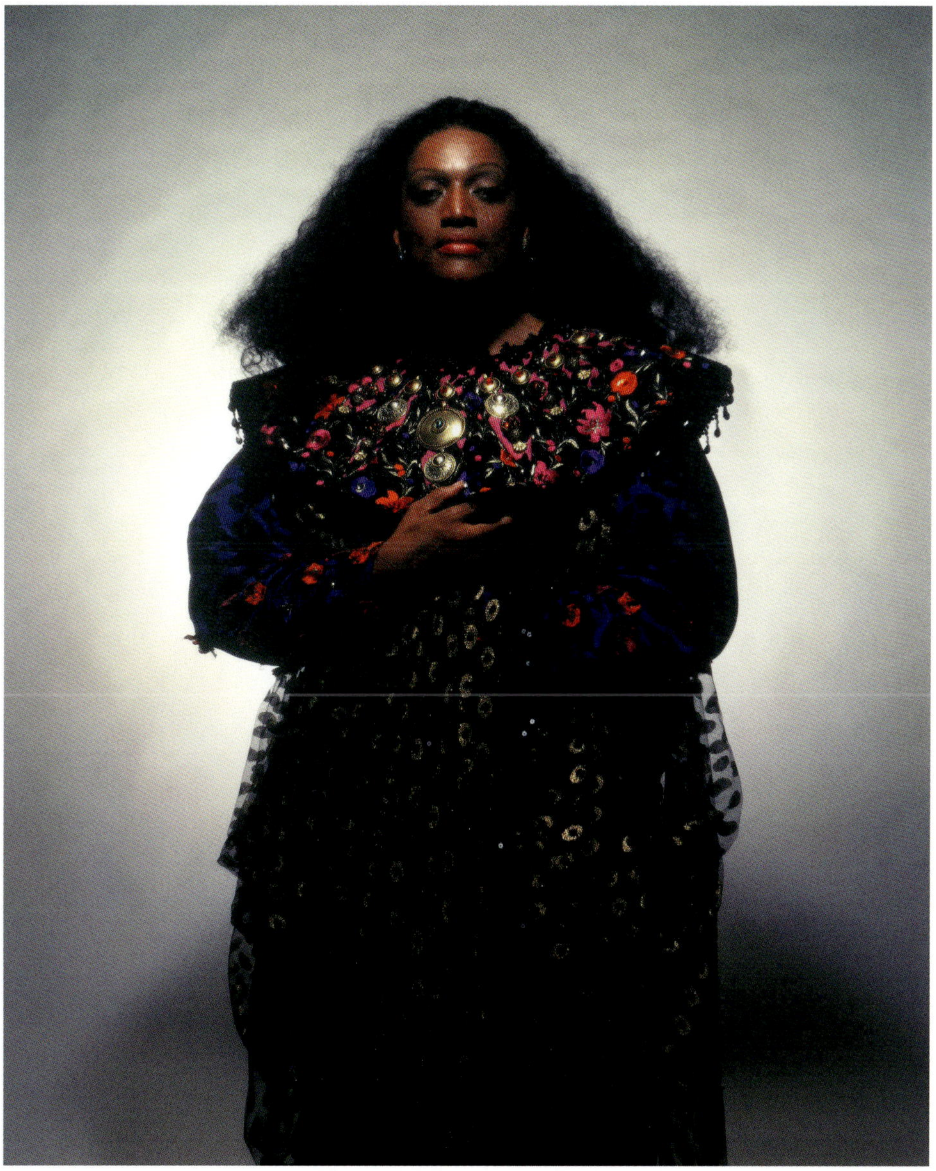

Nearly three decades later, Los Angeles–based photographer Catherine Opie (b.1961) extends this impact of declaration in the social space, creating dramatic colour portraits that draw upon classical portraiture traditions to convey power and respect.[2] In her series of portraits made around 2017, Opie worked with large-format 8x10 film, posing her subjects in front of a black backdrop. *Thelma*, 2017, recalls Karsh's tour-de-force portrayal of Norman: the subject, Thelma Golden, renowned director and chief curator of the Studio Museum in Harlem, New York, is photographed as a nearly full-length figure emerging from a dark background, draped in tapestry-like garments with ornate floral patterns.[3] Golden's assured demeanour declares her command of both personal and political space as the producer of groundbreaking exhibitions by contemporary artists of African descent.

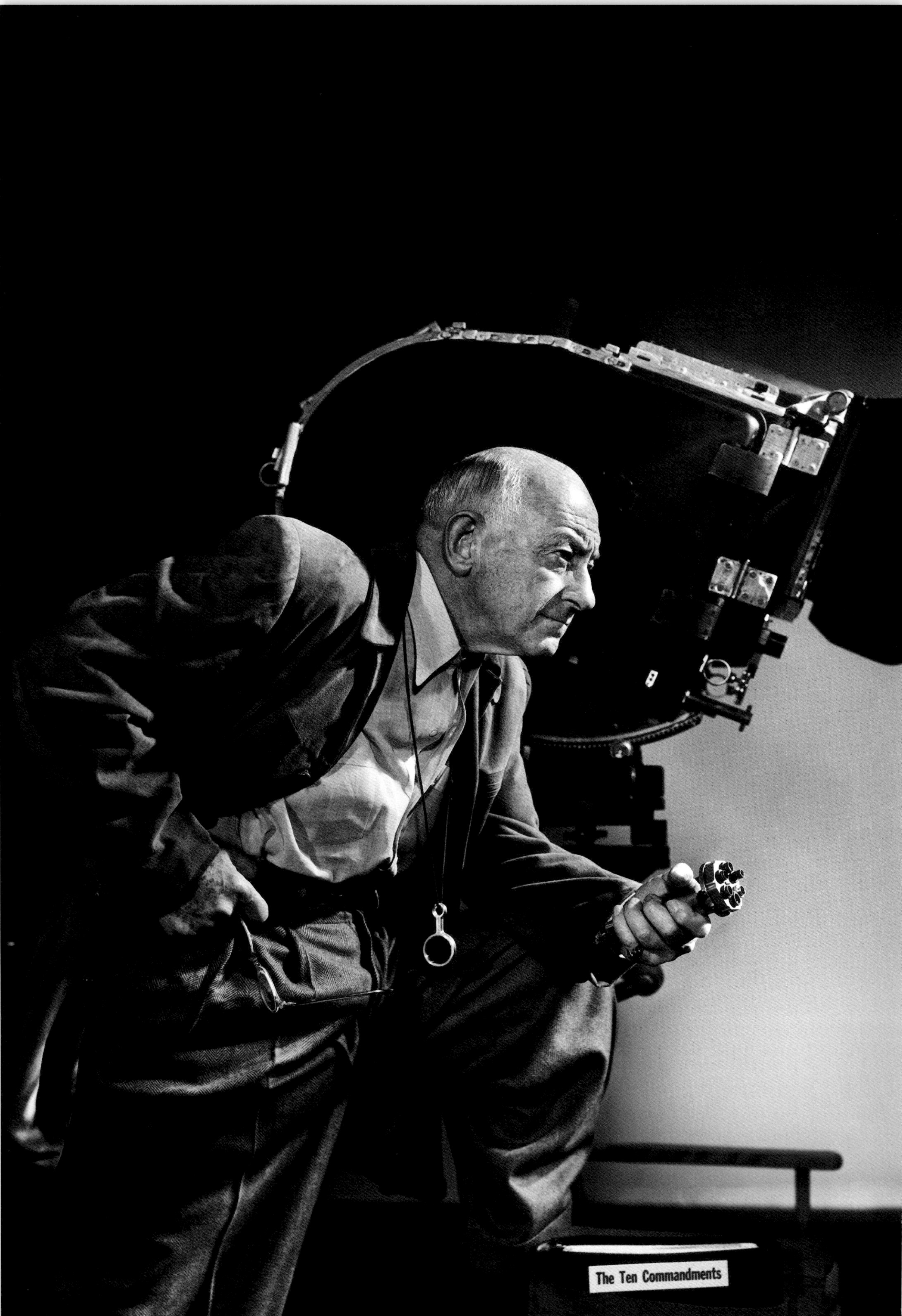
The Ten Commandments

Significance & Critical Issues

Yousuf Karsh's portraits are a visual encyclopedia of the twentieth-century Western world, a theatre of personality showcasing timeless individual qualities such as greatness and beauty amid collective alienation, fragmentation, and relentless change. Karsh believed the camera could reveal a person's true self if distilled by a skilled photographic interpreter. Analyzing selected aspects of his work raises new questions about classical portraiture as a modern expression, the complex dynamic between photographer and sitter, and the role of portraits in constructing identity. Karsh's works define and challenge concepts of truth and objectivity, perspective and performance, and question what we can truly know from a portrait.

Karsh the Storyteller

Karsh's dramatic 1941 portrait of British Prime Minister Winston Churchill launched his international reputation, but equally as famous was his first-hand account of the sitting, in which he related his own nervous impertinence as a young photographer snatching a lit cigar from the wartime leader's lips. In this sense, Karsh created a narrative that operates on two levels: the first is a charming origin story marking his own experience of making the portrait, and the second is the portrait's symbolic meaning, which accrued with each reproduction. The key to Karsh's success as a master portraitist was his remarkable skill as a storyteller.

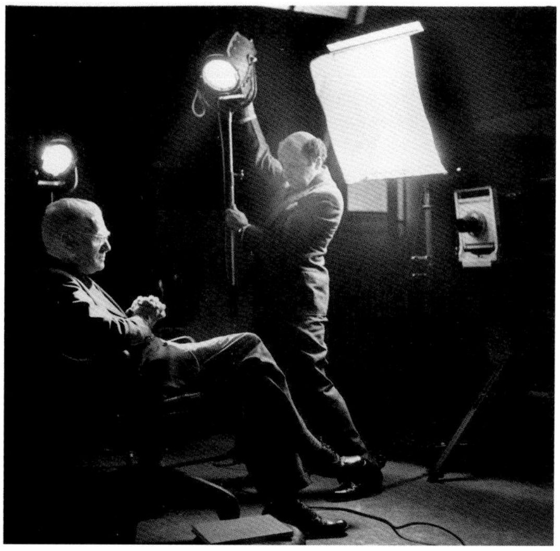

Karsh's strategy was to link three perspectives—the subject, the artist, and the viewer—each one an active agent in fabricating the meaning of the image. Specifically, Karsh envisioned the image as the carrier of the visual narrative through pose, setting, props, and expression. To deepen the audience's engagement in viewing the portrait, Karsh then inserted himself into that narrative. For him, "the photographer of personages is necessarily a storyteller.... And his encounters with great personalities can hardly fail to move him to recount his experiences with them later."[1] His interest in connecting the visual image to a printed or oral anecdote was distinctive and set a template for his later work, especially in the production of his many portfolios of portraits, with each image accompanied by text.[2]

Opposite: Yousuf Karsh, *Cecil B. DeMille* (detail), March 21, 1956, Estate of Yousuf Karsh.
Above: Yousuf Karsh in-studio with sitter Leonard Brockington, January 12, 1945, photograph by Eric Schaal.

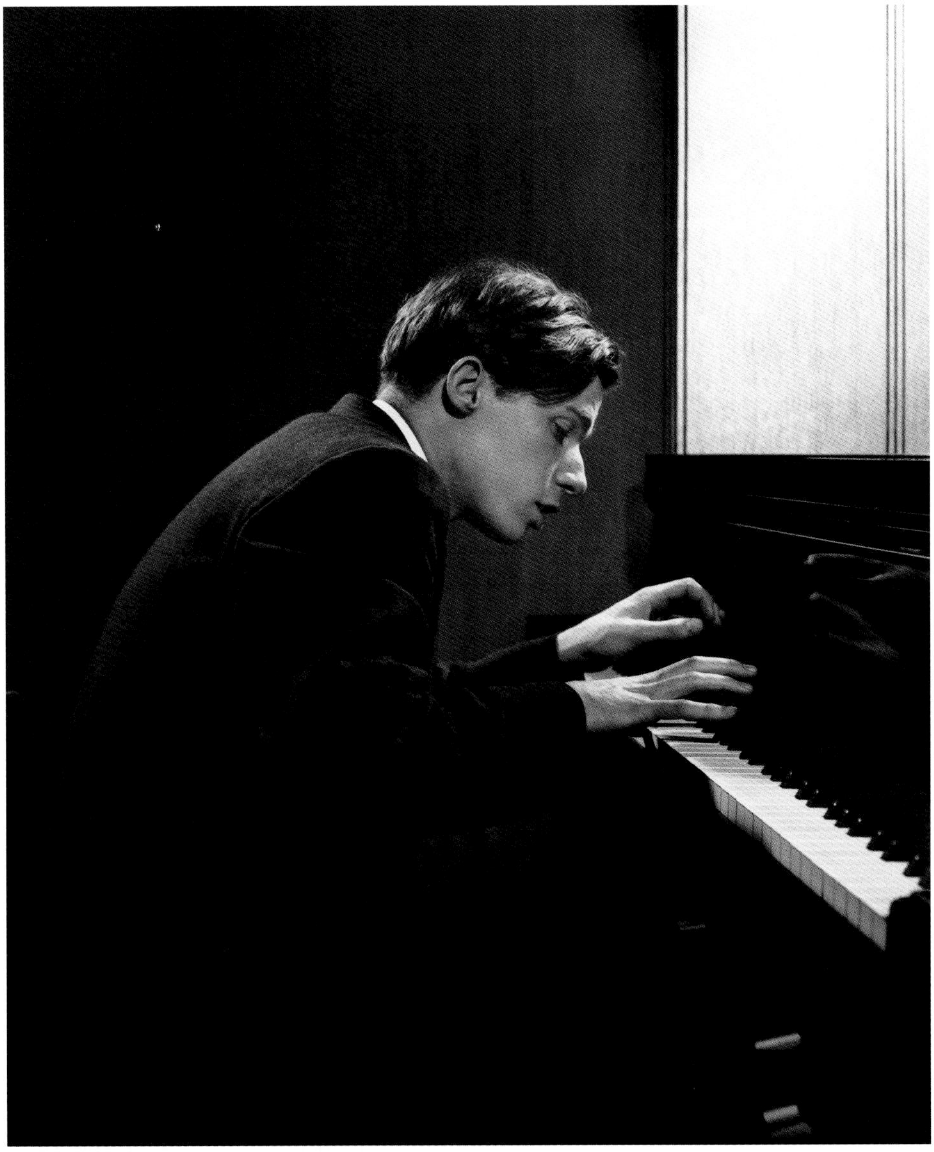

His portrayal of Canadian pianist Glenn Gould—renowned for his interpretations of Johann Sebastian Bach and for his eccentric movements and humming during performances—shows him entirely engaged in the music, seemingly oblivious to the photographer and his camera. In sharing this portrait, Karsh inserted himself into the narrative by relaying the story of his encounter with the famous sitter and emphasizing his own special access as artist and director. In his collection *Karsh Canadians* (1978), the accompanying text on the page facing the portrait begins with Karsh's experience photographing Gould and then relates Gould's impressions of his recent tour of the Soviet Union:

> While I photographed Glenn Gould at his Toronto home, in 1957, he never stopped playing the piano for a moment. The music, Bach and Alban Berg, was so arresting that I found myself captivated, forgetful of camera shutter and lights. Critics have often muttered about Gould's unconventionality,

Yousuf Karsh, *Glenn Gould*, February 21, 1957, gelatin silver print, 60.6 x 49.9 cm, Estate of Yousuf Karsh.

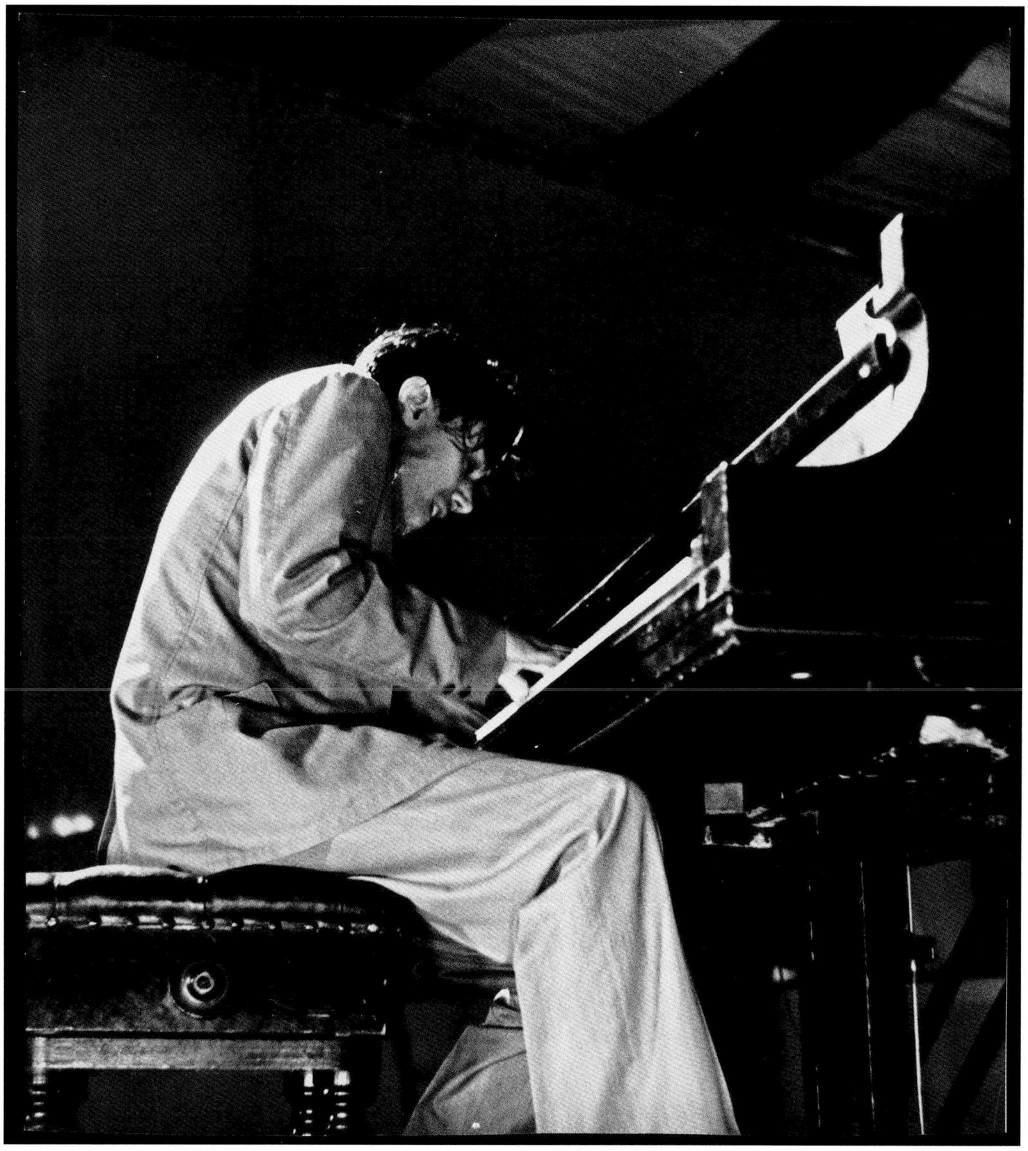

> but it seemed to me that his mittens, the frequent hand-soakings before a concert, his facial contortions and audible humming were all in keeping with his personality. There was, I thought, no deliberate eccentricity, only a total absorption in art.[3]

Karsh shared this story for a future audience, to convey what it was like to spend time with Gould during the sitting and to emphasize their kinship as artists. The overall narrative—Gould as musical genius—is conveyed by the image of Gould absorbed in his music paired with Karsh's revealing account of being likewise captivated.[4]

German philosopher Walter Benjamin considered the role of the storyteller to be that of a carrier of cultural truths, a performer who unmasks social and political myths.[5] Karsh's role as storyteller serves not to *unmask* a hidden truth behind a public persona but to weave a new narrative, a personification distilled in image and text, prepared specifically for an imagined audience.[6]

Lisette Model, *Horace Silver, Newport Jazz Festival, Rhode Island*, c.1954–57, gelatin silver print, 30.7 x 27 cm, National Gallery of Canada, Ottawa.

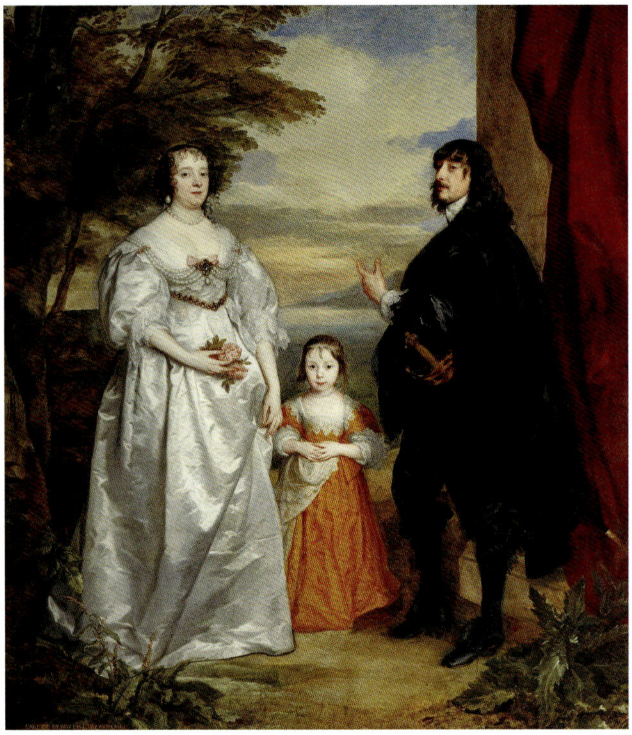

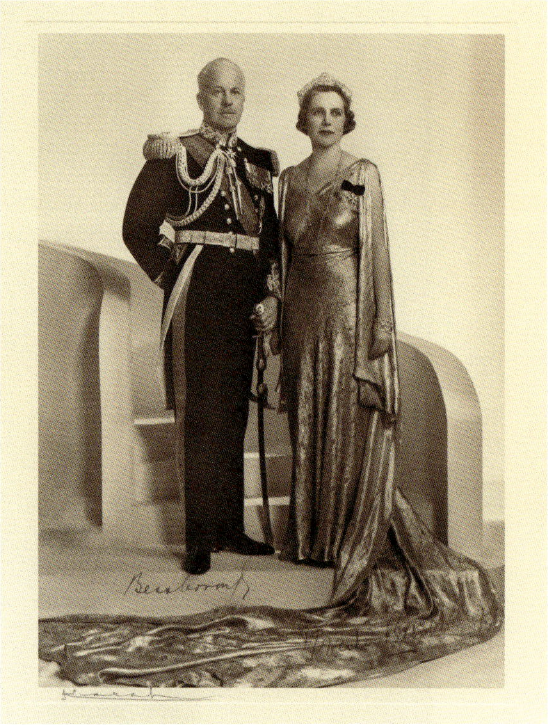

Karsh's limited command of English (it was, after all, his fourth language) meant that he had to develop strategies for creating polished writing from raw notes and verbal reportage. For much of his career, the work of composing and editing this text was undertaken by his spouse—first Solange and later Estrellita. Both women were skilled communicators and were essential to Karsh's realization of engaging personal stories. In large-scale projects, such as his portfolio *Portraits of Greatness* (1959), the accompanying biographies and details about meeting the sitters were complex undertakings involving advance questionnaires, interviews during the session, and post-sitting development with professional editors to create a consistent narrative voice. In this way, Karsh worked against the tide of contemporary art photography—notably the work of Henri Cartier-Bresson (1908–2004), Robert Frank (1924–2019), and Lisette Model (1901-1983), who provided minimalist titles or scant caption information to allow for an open-ended formation of a narrative on the part of the viewer.

Although Karsh worked largely in a classical portraiture tradition—delivered in a dramatic modernist style—he was an important innovator when presenting his portraits to a mass audience. As an artist, Karsh entwined his own experience with the narratives of the subject and the eventual viewer. He carefully considered how to portray an individual through a single, summative portrait combined with a personal anecdote. For the viewer, Karsh's pairing of image and text fostered a greater sense of familiarity with a celebrated stranger. The final construction of the narrative lay with the viewers, who formed their own intellectual and emotional responses to beholding the portrait with Karsh's accompanying first-person account.

Left: Anthony van Dyck, *James Stanley, Lord Strange, Later Seventh Earl of Derby, with His Wife, Charlotte, and Their Daughter*, c.1636, oil on canvas, 246.4 x 213.7 cm, The Frick Collection, New York. Right: Yousuf Karsh, *Official Portrait of Sir Vere Brabazon Ponsonby, Ninth Earl of Bessborough, Governor General of Canada from 1931 to 1935 and His Wife Roberte Ponsonby (Born Neuflize), Countess Bessborough*, March 19, 1935, gelatin silver print, 24.1 x 17 cm (image), 29.2 x 22.9 cm (mount), Yousuf Karsh Fonds, Library and Archives Canada, Ottawa.

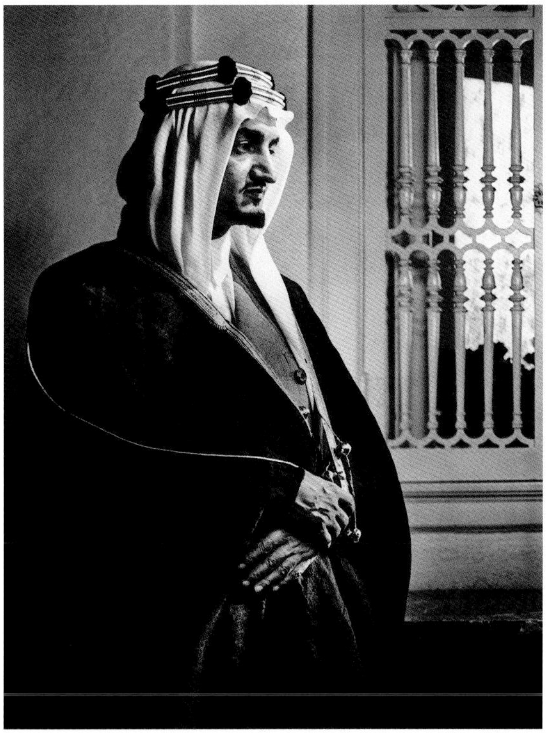 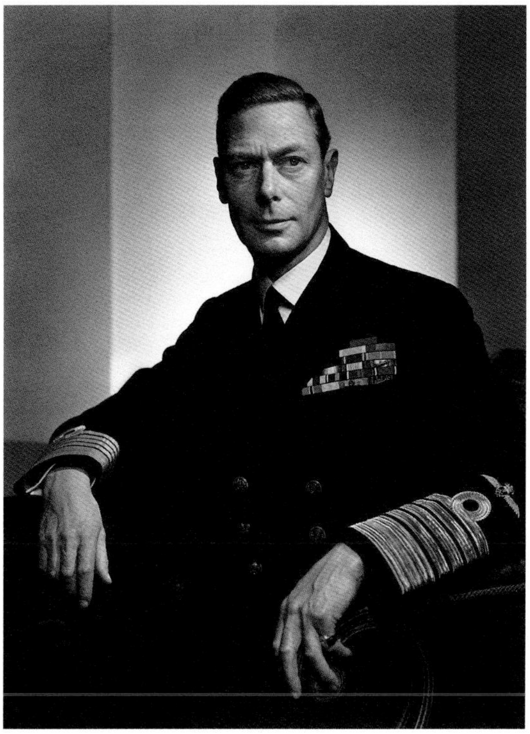

A Courtly Tradition

Spanning six decades across the intersection of modern and postmodern photography, Karsh's practice was rooted in the classical tradition of courtly portraiture. Karsh had been encouraged to study examples by portraitists such as Flemish painter Anthony van Dyck (1599–1641) during his apprenticeship in Boston, and he understood how to portray his patrons in a way that would invite an admiring gaze from the viewer. The careful selection of setting, pose, and prop conveyed coded signs of social stature, personal comportment, or notable achievement. In both his commissioned studio portraits and his sittings with famous figures, Karsh aspired to depict his subjects at their best, treating each sitting as an opportunity to create an immortal image.

In 1935, Karsh made what he considered his first important commission, a regal depiction of Governor General Lord Bessborough and his wife. Upon photographing the Bessboroughs, Karsh was granted the honour "By Appointment to Their Excellencies, The Governor-General and Lady Bessborough"—later printed on the Karsh Studio portrait cover—and continued to be endorsed by his successor, Governor General Lord Tweedsmuir, John Buchan. Karsh leveraged this significant commission to elevate his status as an artist, hone his interpersonal and professional skills, and expand his clientele.[7]

After the publication of his iconic portrait of Churchill, Karsh conceived an ambitious series that received financial backing from his editor at *Saturday Night*, B.K. Sandwell. In 1943, Karsh crossed the Atlantic on an explosives-laden Norwegian freighter, travelling to London to photograph leading British wartime figures and cultural luminaries, including King George VI, H.G. Wells, and Noel Coward. Among his portrait subjects during this 1943 trip was Princess Elizabeth, then eighteen years old and serving as an ambulance mechanic and driver. The portrait session took place at

Left: Yousuf Karsh, *HRH Ibn Abdul Aziz (later King Faisal of Saudi Arabia)*, May 7, 1945, gelatin silver print, 49.1 x 39.7 cm, Estate of Yousuf Karsh. Right: Yousuf Karsh, *King George VI*, September 12, 1943, Estate of Yousuf Karsh.

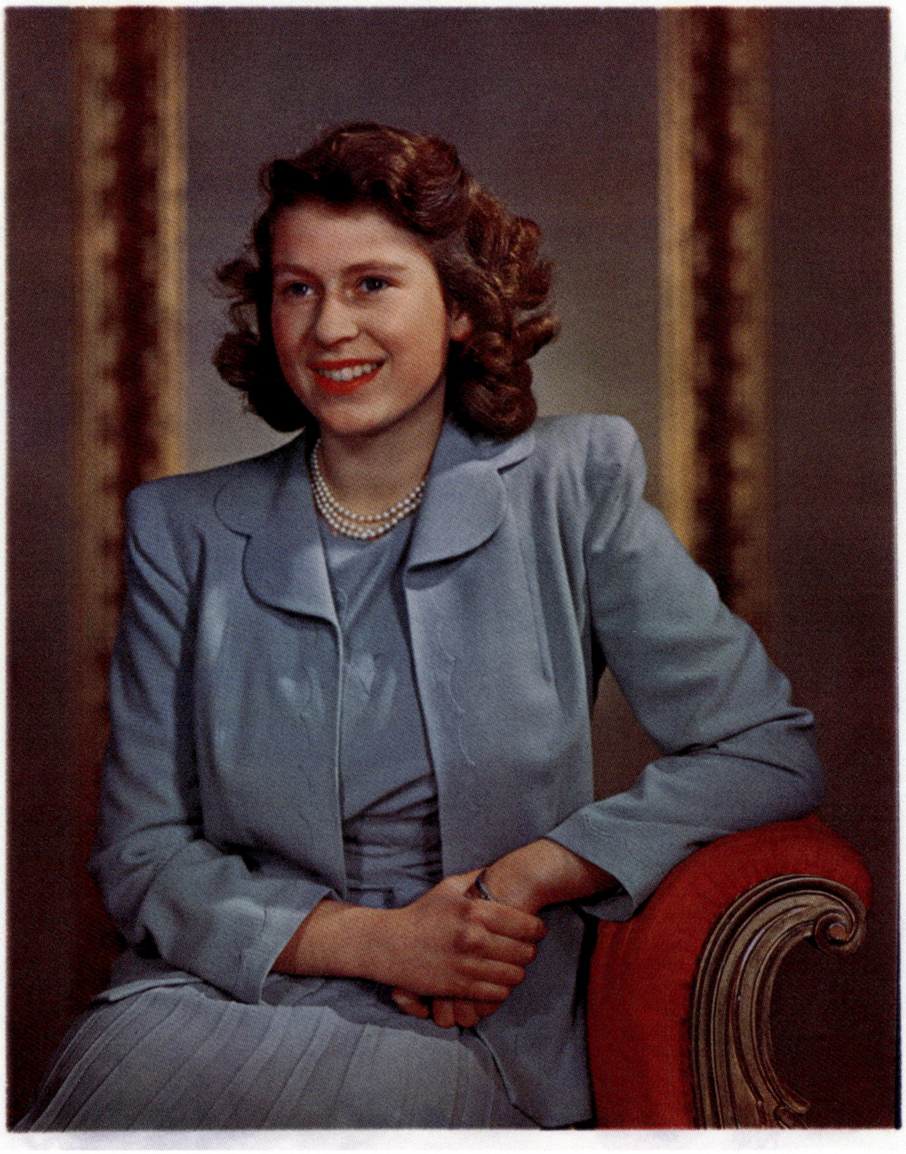

Buckingham Palace, and Karsh later recalled being impressed by her "wholesome charm, good humor, and entire lack of affectation."[8] He would go on to take official portraits of her and her family on multiple occasions over the next forty-four years, including one of Elizabeth that was disseminated widely upon her ascension to the throne in 1952.

Later, in advance of Canada's Centennial in 1967, Karsh was selected to create new official portraits of Queen Elizabeth II alone and with her husband, Prince Philip, dressed in their regal splendour in the Music Room at Buckingham Palace. As official portraits representing the Crown in Canada, they were reproduced for formal display in federal buildings and in Canada's consular and embassy spaces worldwide.

The impact of such portrayals on viewers has been described by artist and theorist Allan Sekula (1951–2013) as "the look up," in which we confer admiration or respect on the subject of the portrait.[9] In these acts of looking, we engage in creating social distinctions, positioning our own identities by judging the identities we construct about

Yousuf Karsh, *Princess Elizabeth*, November 1, 1943, Kodachrome print, 34.1 x 27.1 cm (image), 35.4 x 28.2 cm (support), Yousuf Karsh Fonds, Library and Archives Canada, Ottawa.

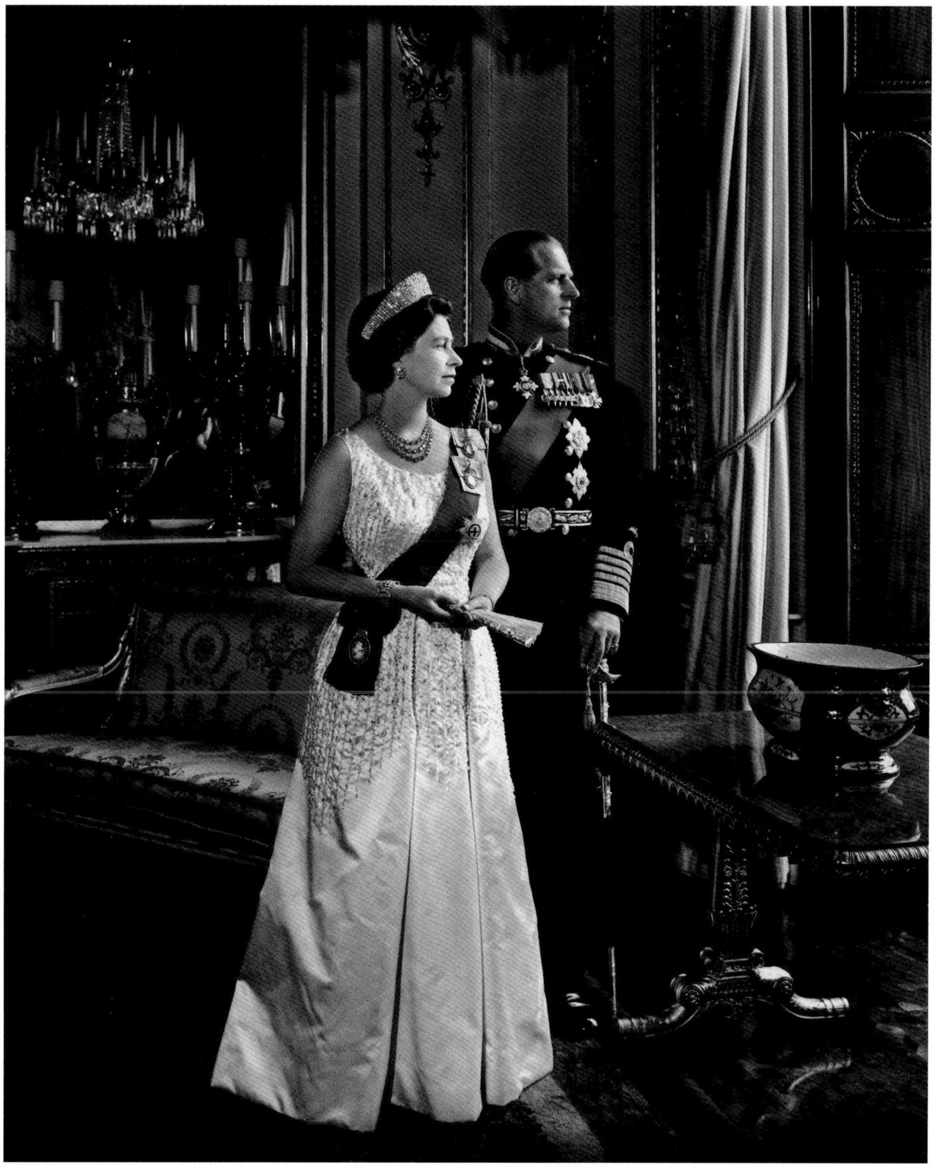

the subject of the photograph. The portrait became foundational to Karsh's enduring interest in the concept of greatness. Later, remarking on his role as a portrait photographer tasked with revealing the ennobling qualities of his sitters, he said: "The question… is whether I should record the legend, or something else about the personality.… I am satisfied that no purpose would be served if I were consciously to seek to convert what could be a portrait of greatness into a moment of weakness."[10]

Framing the Hero

Karsh believed that a person's essence, or true self, could be revealed before the camera and distilled by a skilled photographic interpreter. His interest lay in perceiving and recording a psychological moment of truth. As he wrote of his own work in *Karsh Portfolio* in 1967, "Within every man and woman a secret is hidden, and as a photographer it is my task to reveal it if I can. The revelation, if it comes at all, will come in a small

Yousuf Karsh, *Queen Elizabeth and Prince Philip*, August 2, 1966, gelatin silver print, 60 x 49 cm, Estate of Yousuf Karsh.

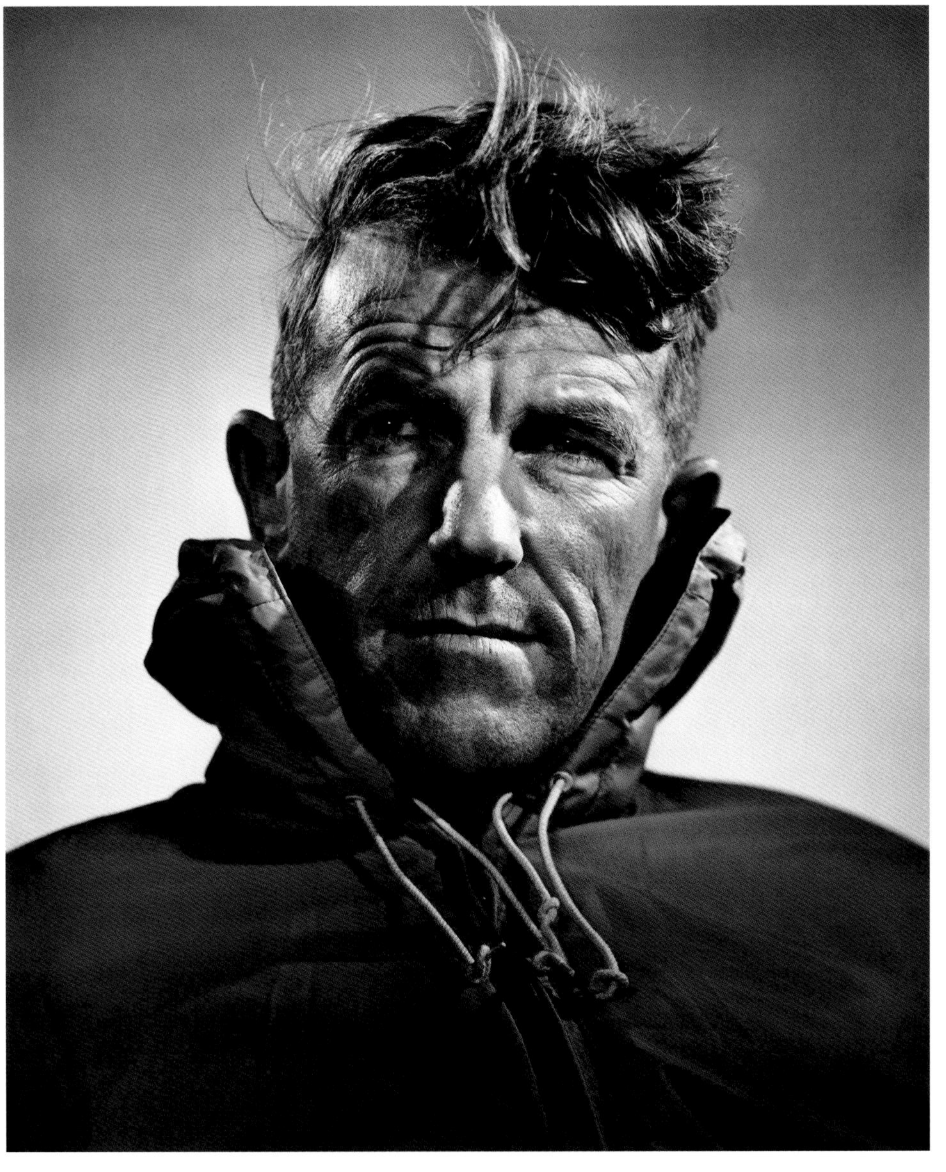

fraction of a second with an unconscious gesture, a gleam of the eye, a brief lifting of the mask that all humans wear to conceal their innermost selves from the world."[11]

Karsh's project, built one portrait at a time, sought to assemble a pantheon representing the best of humanity, a theatre of personalities emphasizing individual character, talent, and beauty. Conscious of a public audience avidly viewing his portraits of celebrated individuals, Karsh grappled with the dilemma of creating portrayals that combined *fact* (this person is posed in front of the camera at a specific moment) and *fiction* (the photographer tells you a story through specific technical and artistic choices).

Karsh's portrayal of greatness as aspirational depended on factors unique to his time. His approach reflected contemporary ideas found in the work of Austrian psychiatrist Sigmund Freud and Swiss psychologist Carl Jung, theories of the modern self composed of ego and subconscious, as well as a collective consciousness populated by universal archetypes. Additionally, Karsh, a devout Catholic, subscribed to a profound spiritual "hope for humanity and faith in the Infinite," and sought to elicit a portrait of the soul.[12]

Yousuf Karsh, *Sir Edmund Hillary*, January 30, 1960, gelatin silver print, 49.8 x 40 cm (image), 71.3 x 56 cm (mount), Estate of Yousuf Karsh.

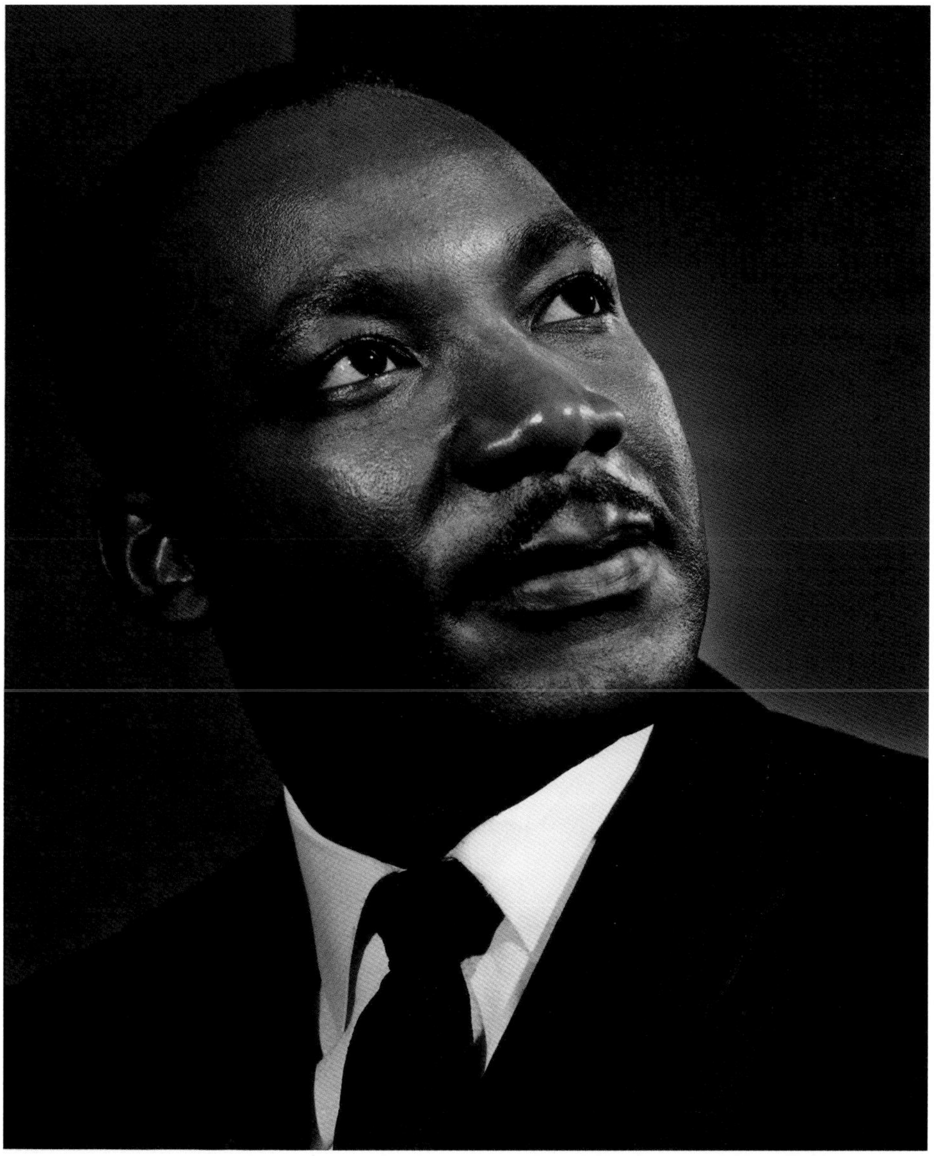

Karsh's narrative choices originated from the "allegorical impulse"[13] of late Pictorialism practised by his mentor, John H. Garo (1870–1939), and supplemented by the influence of historical painting and modern photos of Hollywood idols. His aesthetic emphasized sharp focus, dramatic tonal contrast, and minimalist setting and served to enhance attention on the facial expression.[14] For example, Karsh photographed New Zealand explorer and mountaineer Sir Edmund Hillary seven years after he and Sherpa Tenzing Norgay became the first climbers to reach the summit of Mount Everest.[15] By framing his subject in a tight close-up, Karsh monumentalizes Hillary through the dominance of pictorial space. The triangular composition frames Hillary as a colossal summit, signifying his achievement.[16]

In 1962, Karsh photographed Dr. Martin Luther King, leader of the American civil rights movement, one year before he delivered his historic "I Have a Dream" speech. King's faith-based commitment to social justice is signalled through his upward gaze. His face radiates fortitude and certainty in his mission to secure racial equality. The

Yousuf Karsh, *Martin Luther King, Jr.*, August 18, 1962, gelatin silver print, 49.7 x 39.7 cm (image), 49.5 x 39.7 cm (support), Yousuf Karsh Fonds, Library and Archives Canada, Ottawa.

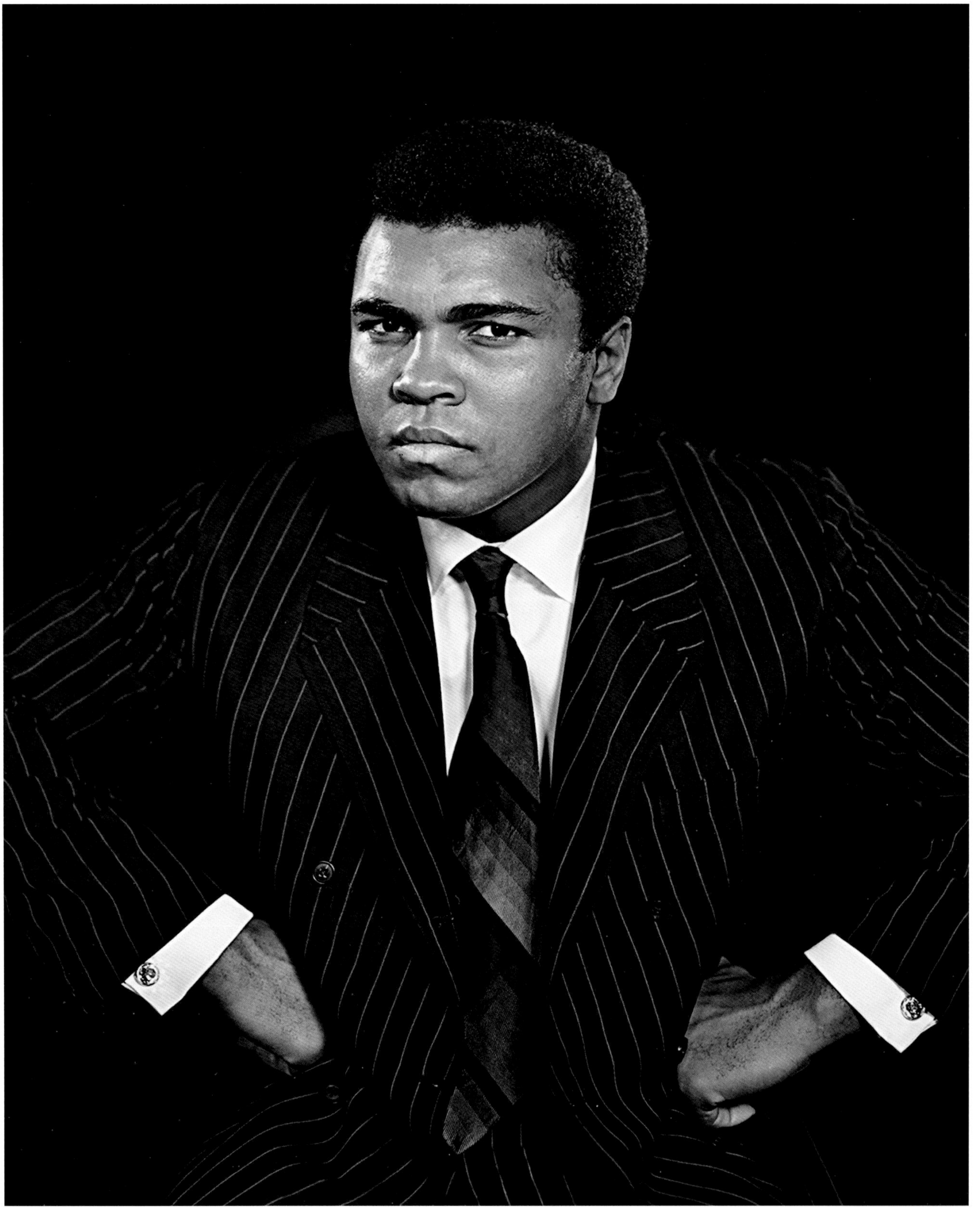

Yousuf Karsh, *Muhammad Ali*, March 27, 1970, gelatin silver print, 50.6 x 60.1 cm, Montreal Museum of Fine Arts.

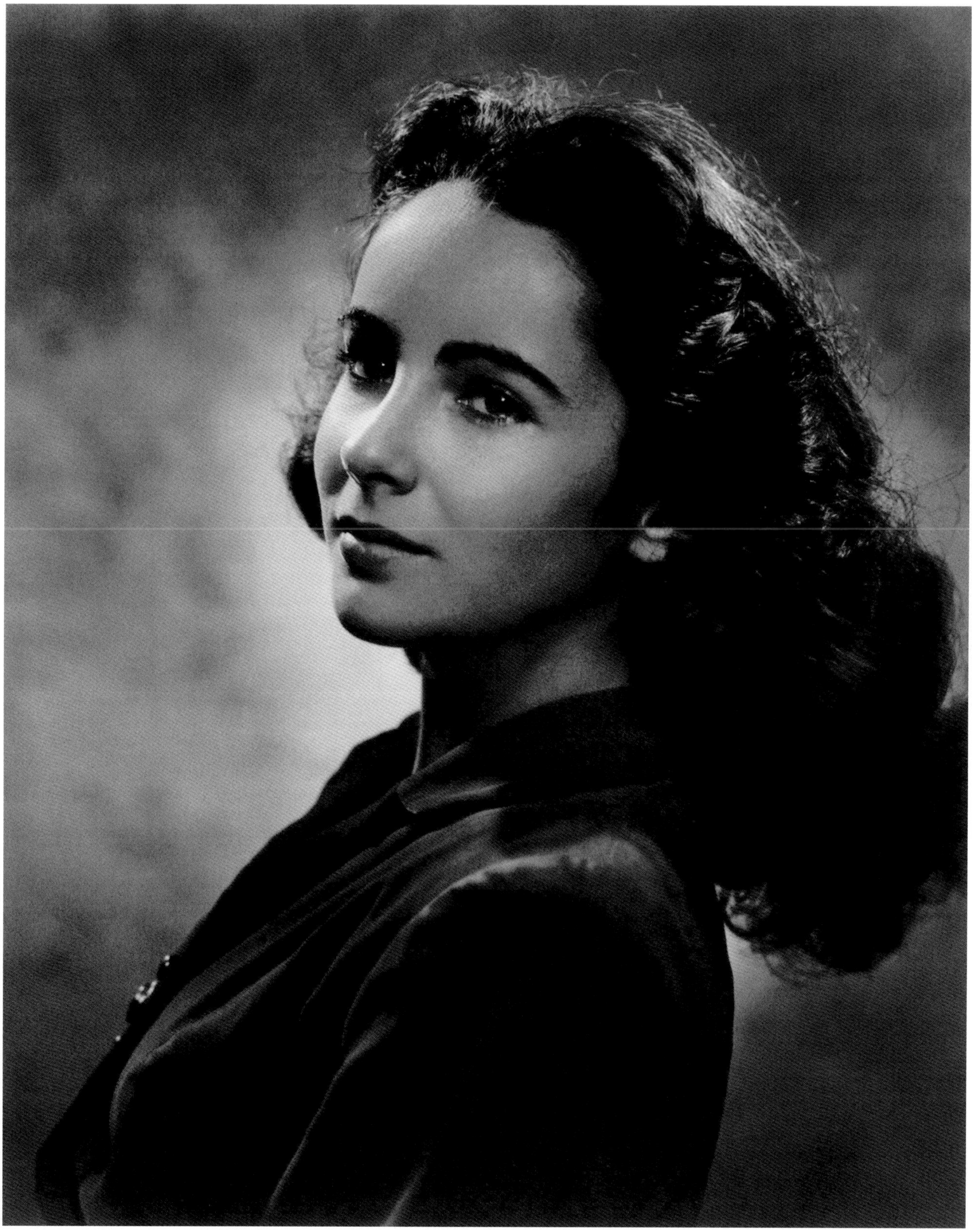

Yousuf Karsh, *Elizabeth Taylor*, February 14, 1946, Estate of Yousuf Karsh.

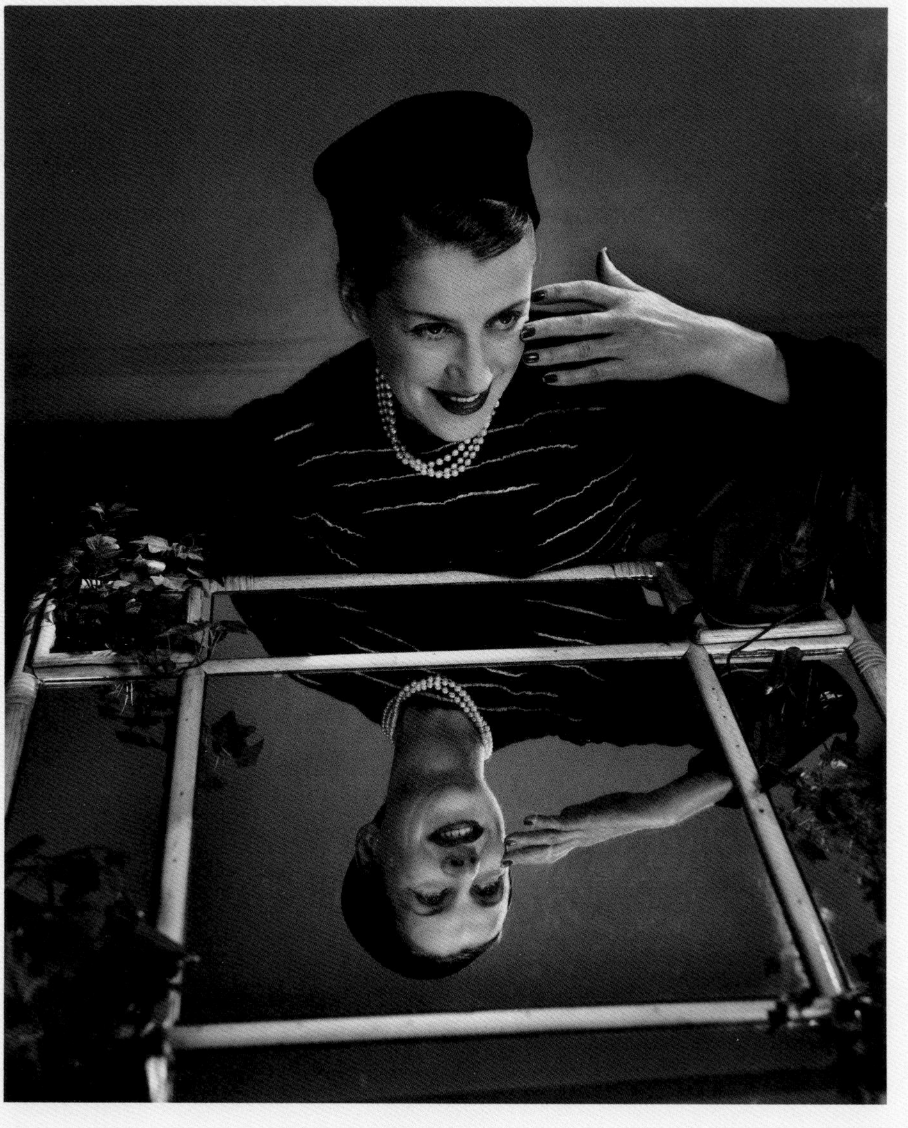

portrait—of a hero leading the battle for justice—took on a reverent significance following King's assassination in 1968.

The monumentality of Karsh's portrayal in both visual and psychological terms demanded a willingness from the viewer to see those depicted as heroes and not, as later proved to be true for so many, complex and flawed individuals. Karsh admitted as much, conceding, "While I am a hero worshipper, I do not expect my heroes not to show signs of the humanity that they share with us all."[17] Across time, certain portrait subjects were unmasked as villains; for example, Karsh's 1988 portrait of American financier Bernard "Bernie" Madoff features the confident businessman who had been entrusted with investors' life savings posed with his hands prominently placed across the arm of an ornately carved chair. In 2009, Madoff was found guilty on eleven counts of robbing tens of thousands of victims of their funds, amounting to an estimated $65 billion.

It is significant that Karsh's portraits may be interpreted as either *revealing* an essential character or *distilling* a staged performance of it. During most of Karsh's career,

Yousuf Karsh, *Beatrice Lillie*, March 18, 1948, gelatin silver print, 23.9 x 29.2 cm (image), 25.2 x 20.3 cm (sheet), Yousuf Karsh Fonds, Library and Archives Canada, Ottawa.

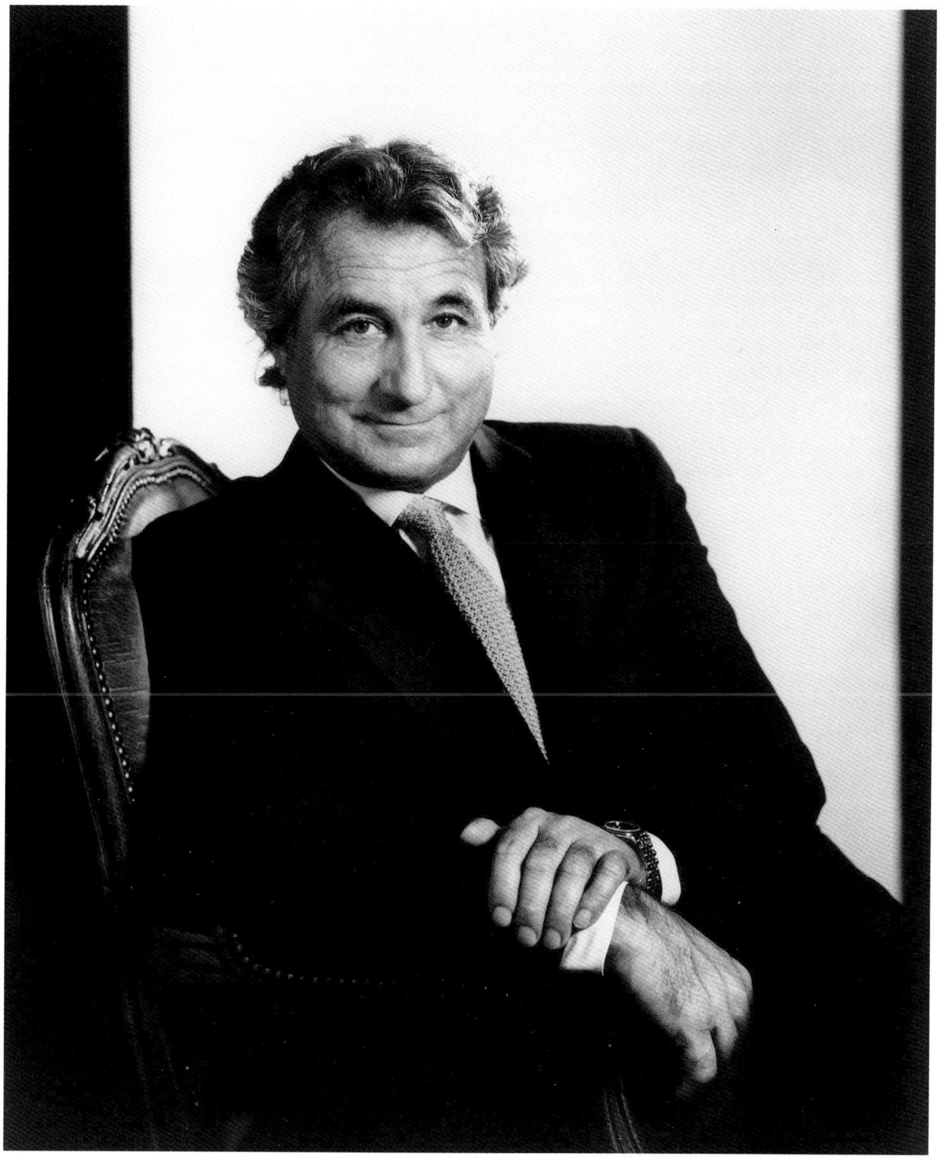

a firm boundary existed between the people's public and private lives. Famous personalities and ordinary people alike were expected to behave with decorum in their public lives, and Karsh was relied upon by his portrait subjects not to reveal any embarrassing or unflattering images. This tacit understanding has largely disappeared with the advent of cameras in every cellphone, ready to record and upload any human experience, and the proliferation of non-consensual photography, such as paparazzi snapshots, closed-circuit observation, and security scans.

Picturing Indigeneity

Consideration of Karsh's portrayals of Indigeneity begins with two portraits of non-Indigenous men. Karsh photographed celebrated British writer and conservationist Archibald Stansfeld Belaney, better known to Canadians by his self-styled Anishinaabe identity, Grey Owl, in 1936, before the public revelation of his non-Indigenous identity. This portrait, a close-cropping of the sitter's sharply defined face gazing beyond

Yousuf Karsh, *Bernard Madoff*, October 3, 1988, Estate of Yousuf Karsh.

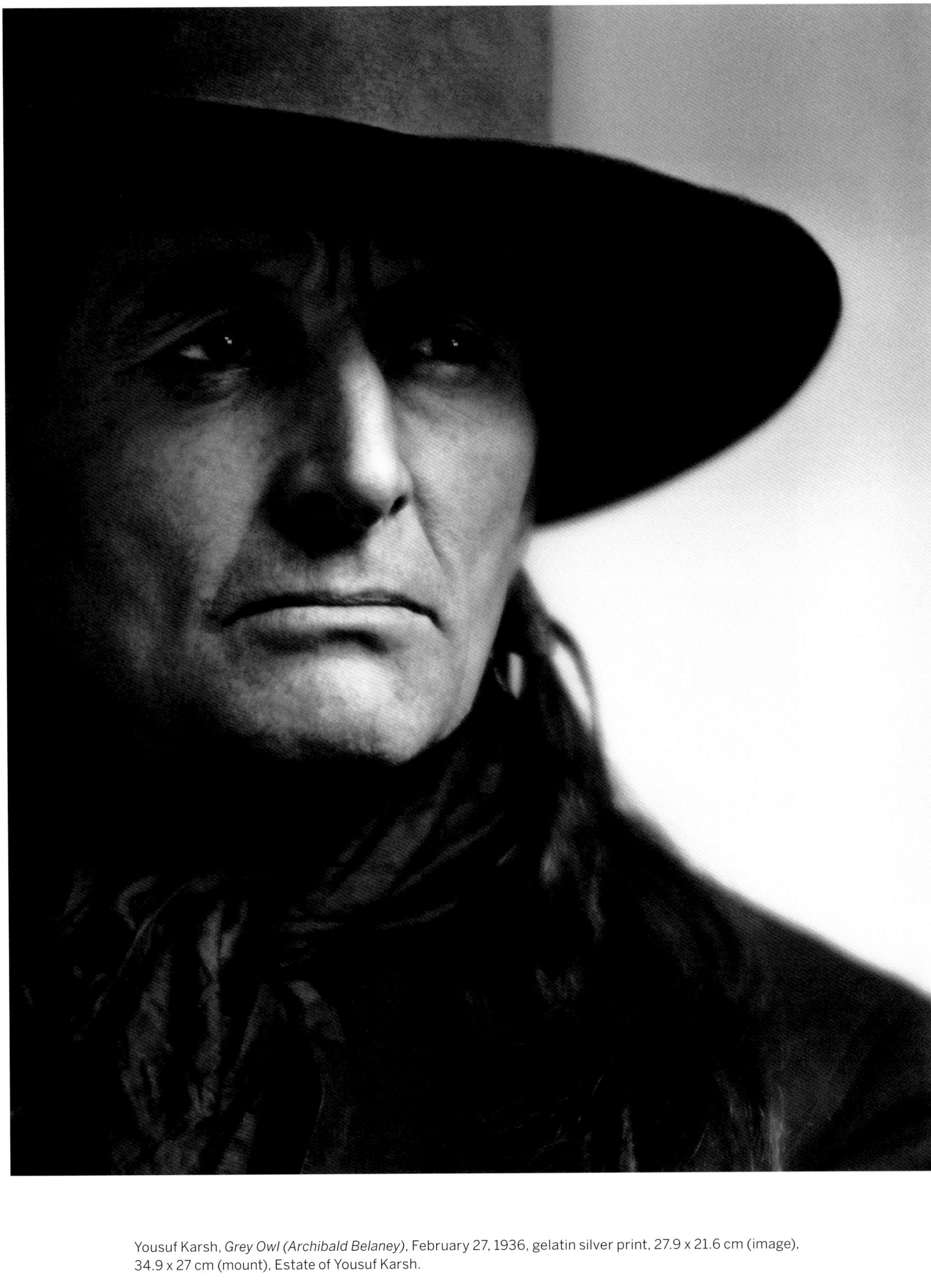

Yousuf Karsh, *Grey Owl (Archibald Belaney)*, February 27, 1936, gelatin silver print, 27.9 x 21.6 cm (image), 34.9 x 27 cm (mount), Estate of Yousuf Karsh.

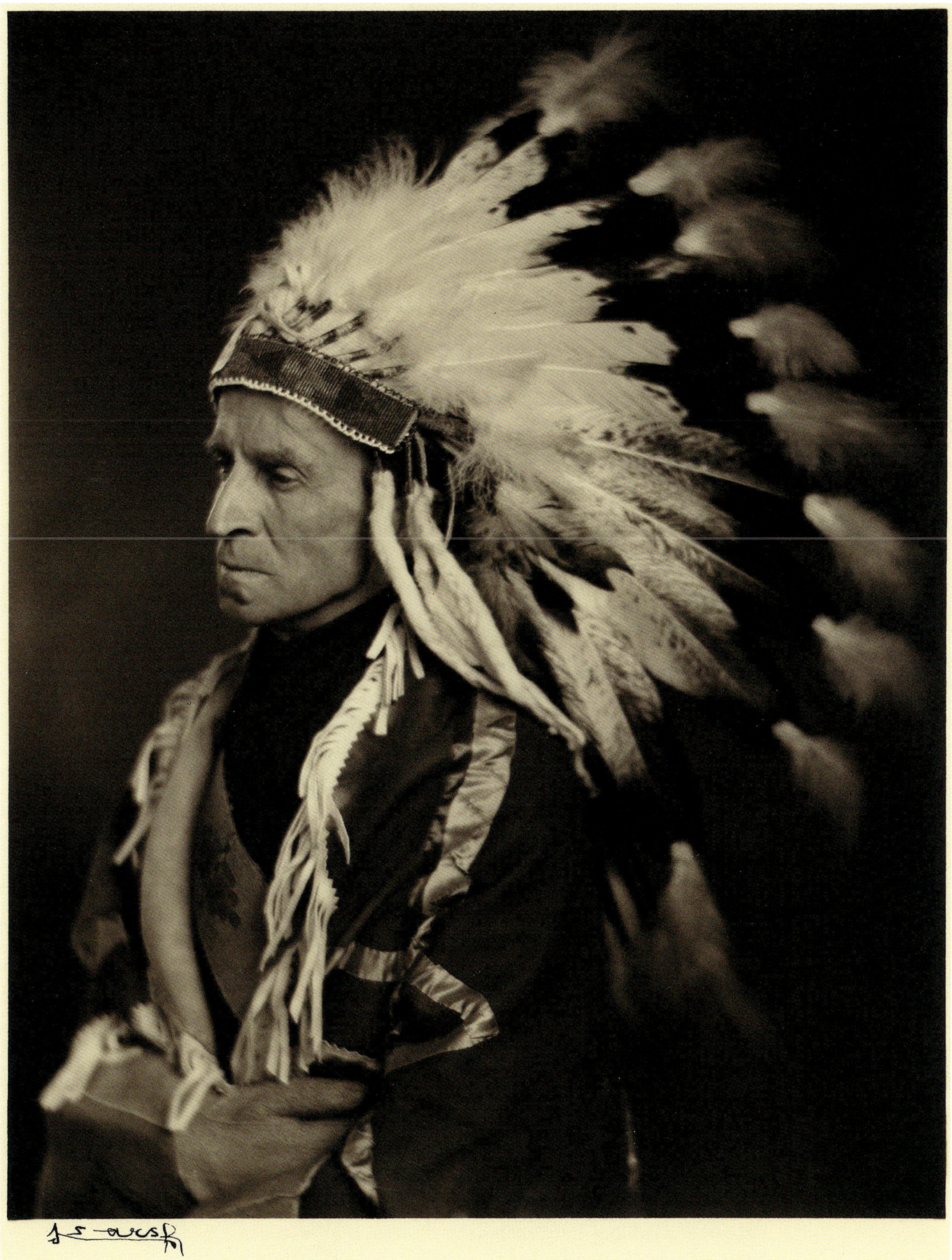

Yousuf Karsh, *Governor General Lord Tweedsmuir, John Buchan, Posed in His Honorary Chief Eagle Head Regalia*, May 5, 1937, gelatin silver print, 21.8 x 16.9 cm (image), 24.2 x 18.4 cm (sheet), Yousuf Karsh Fonds, Library and Archives Canada, Ottawa.

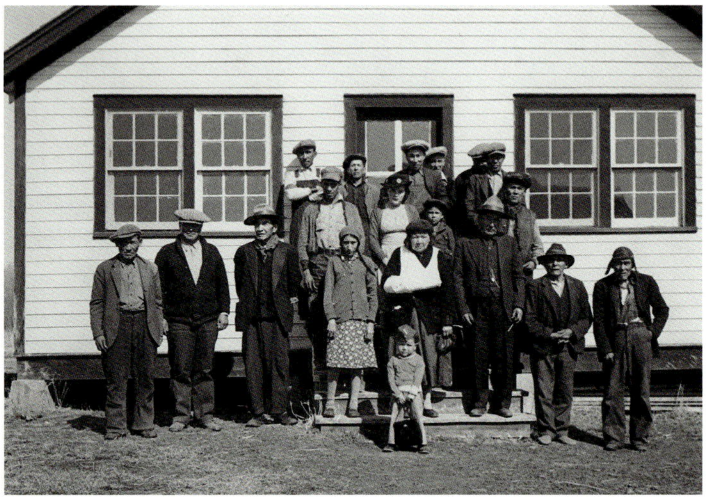

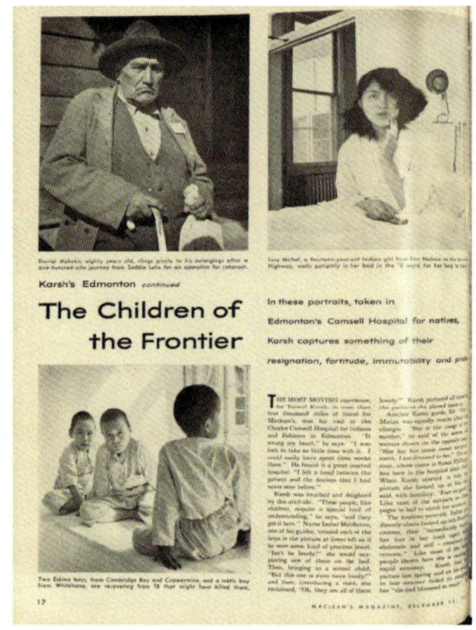

Karsh's Edmonton *continued*

The Children of the Frontier

In these portraits, taken in Edmonton's Camsell Hospital for natives, Karsh captures something of their resignation, fortitude, immutability and

the picture frame, garnered acclaim in art photography circles and was selected by Canadian artist Bertram Brooker (1888–1955) for the 1936 edition of *Yearbook of the Arts in Canada*.

In 1937, Karsh photographed Scottish novelist John Buchan, Lord Tweedsmuir, who had been appointed two years earlier as Canada's fifteenth governor general. According to records in the Karsh archive, he photographed the governor general and his family in at least thirty sittings. In one variation of the traditional portrait sitting, Karsh depicts Tweedsmuir wearing regalia presented to him as honorary Chief Eagle Head by the Kainai Chieftainship in 1936. As a formal portrait, it serves as a ceremonial acknowledgement of the honorific gesture to forge diplomatic links with the incoming governor general, who was deeply interested in Canada's history and culture. But the portrait also invites the possibility of misreading the figure as an Indigenous person, which indeed occurred. Karsh later recalled that a copy of this portrait was requested by Queen Elizabeth (the future Queen Mother) "to show the little Princesses what a real North American Indian looks like."[18]

Nearly a century later, the portraits suggest many interpretations. Karsh was, undoubtedly, a product of his time as a non-Indigenous person sharing the romantic notion of the "noble savage," as depicted in art history. Both portraits were created at the apex of European and North American interest in, and nostalgia for, Indigenous identity, knowledge, and culture—reframed as "vanishing," a euphemism for deliberate extinction.[19] Throughout the first half of the twentieth century, documentary photographers working for Canada's Department of Indian Affairs depicted their subjects as conquered and inferior. The photographers focused their lenses on individuals who were enduring material poverty and adverse health conditions as part of governmental efforts to assimilate them into mainstream (settler) culture.

In his later portraits of Indigenous individuals, Karsh operated within this non-Indigenous double perspective: settler subjects commissioning portraits of themselves romantically posed as Indigenous people, and actual Indigenous people captured on camera as subjects of documentation and subjection.

In 1952, Karsh was commissioned by *Maclean's* magazine to photograph Canadian cities, ultimately publishing sixteen photo essays between 1952 and 1954. On March 20,

Left: Portrait of members of Alexander First Nation (including Chief Alexis Arcand and Councillor Mark Bruno) standing in front of Ration House, Calgary, c.1918, photographer unknown. Right: Page from Yousuf Karsh's photo essay "Karsh's Edmonton: The Threshold of the Frontier," featured in the December 15, 1952, issue of *Maclean's* magazine.

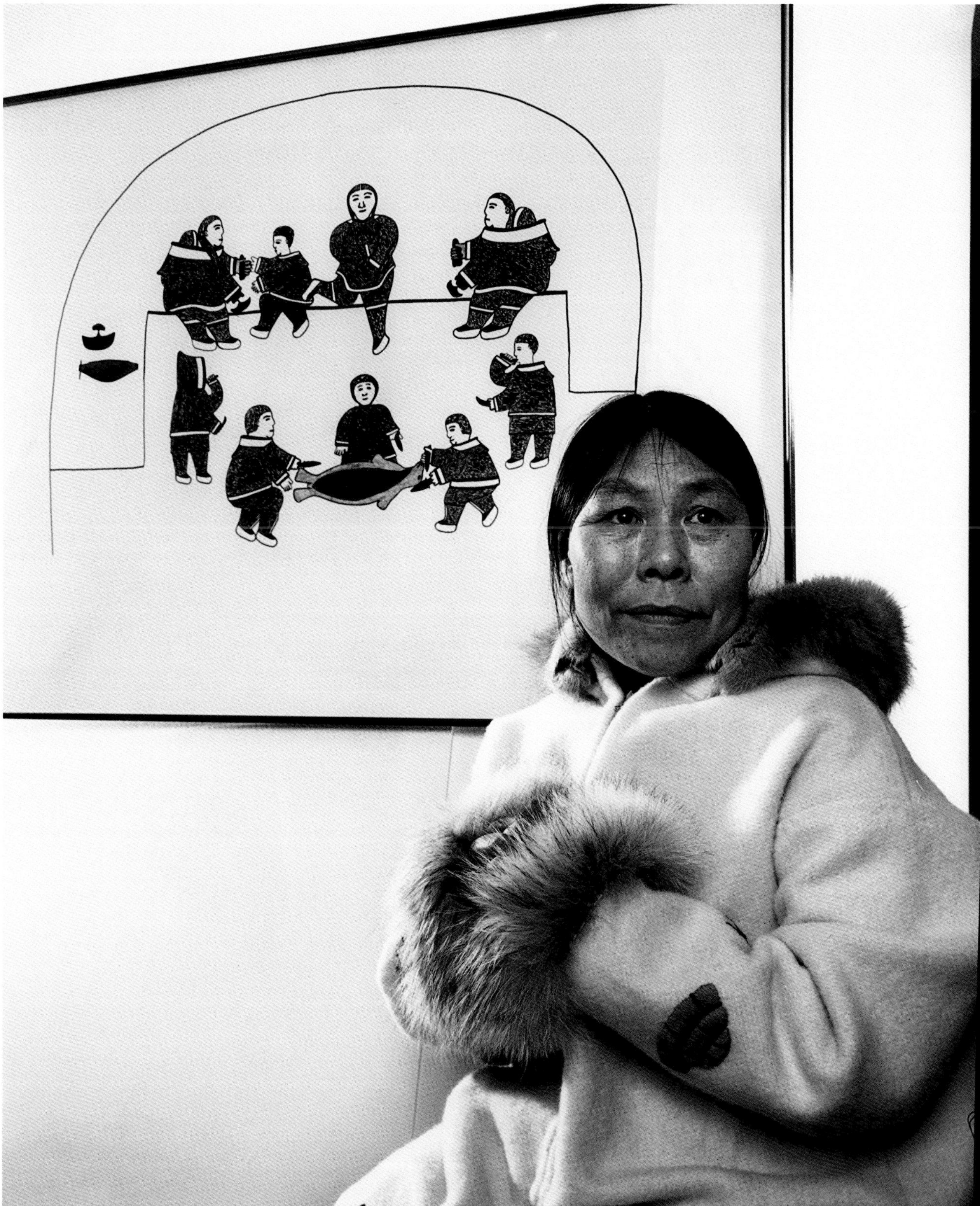

Yousuf Karsh, *Kenojuak Ashevak*, April 8, 1976, gelatin silver print, 25.3 x 20.3 cm, Montreal Museum of Fine Arts.

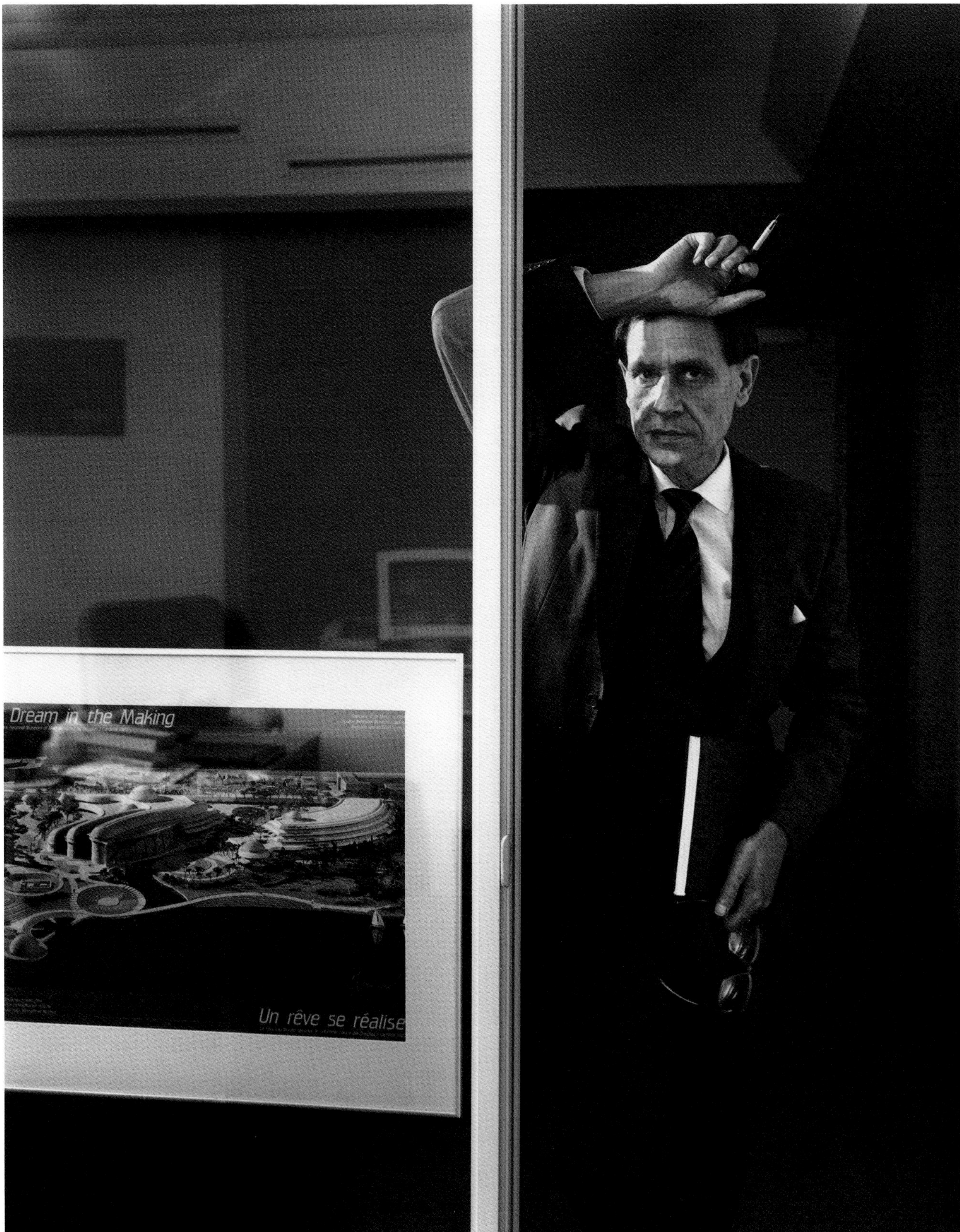

Yousuf Karsh, *Douglas Cardinal*, April 7, 1989, gelatin silver print, 28 x 21.5 cm (image), 35.5 x 27.7 cm (sheet), Yousuf Karsh Fonds, Library and Archives Canada, Ottawa.

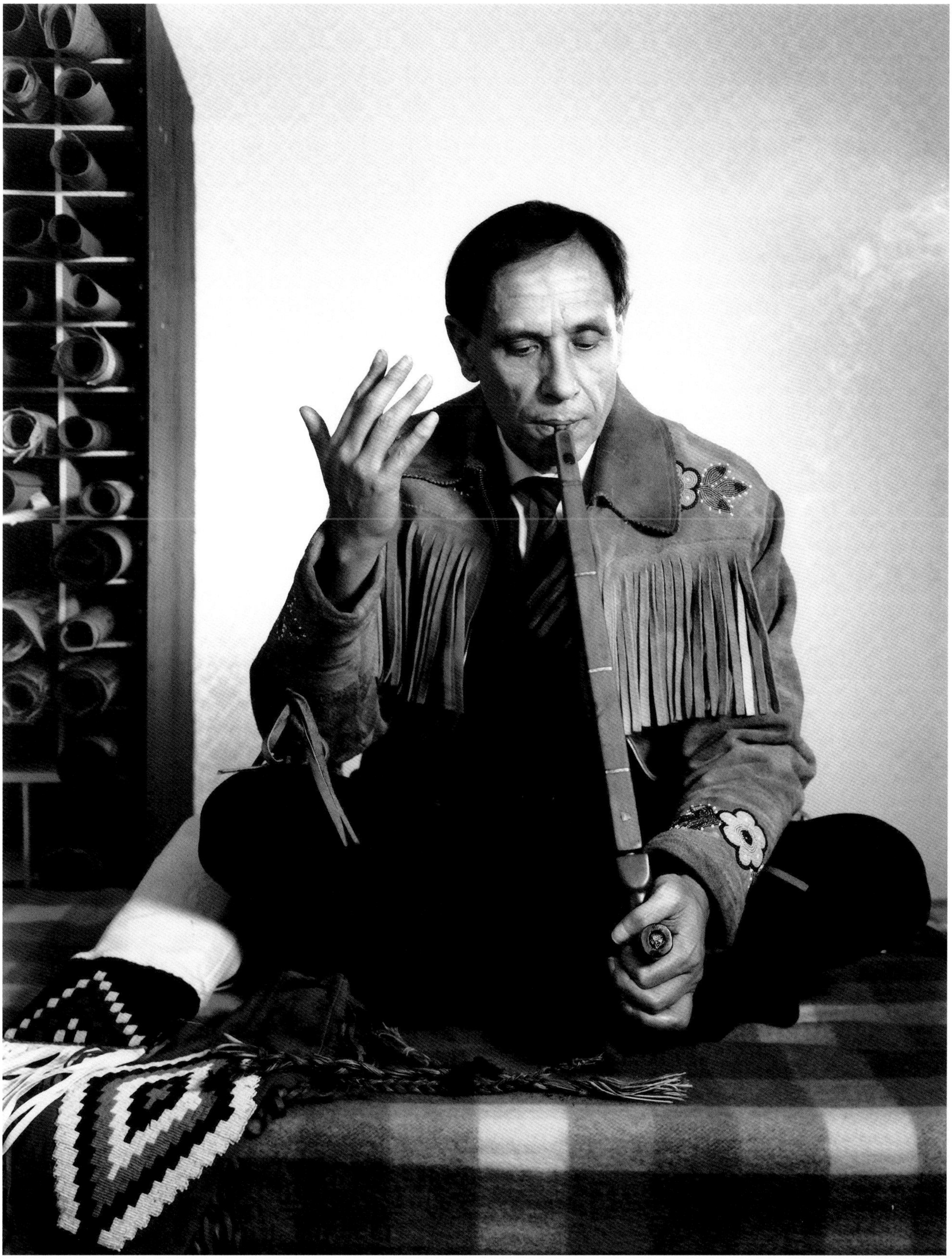

Yousuf Karsh, *Douglas Cardinal*, April 7, 1989, Estate of Yousuf Karsh.

1952, Karsh photographed Indigenous patients at the Charles Camsell Indian Hospital in Edmonton, Alberta.[20] Karsh's access was arranged by hospital authorities; he had little time to establish rapport with patients—most of whom were assigned temporary settler names during their treatment.

Portraits from this series were published as part of "Karsh's Edmonton: Threshold of the Frontier," a photo essay featured in the December 15, 1952, issue of *Maclean's*. The piece included a two-page display of four images, introduced with the words "Children of the Frontier: In these portraits, taken in Edmonton's Camsell Hospital for natives, Karsh captures something of their resignation, fortitude, immutability and pride."[21] This problematic text, added during production by *Maclean's* writers, obscures Karsh's perspective in photographing the Camsell patients. In the context of his era, Karsh's view was not particularly distinct from other documentary photographic practices, such as journalism, anthropology, or street photography, where the photographer's benevolent intentions, the power imbalance with the portrait subject, and the interests of a publisher may coexist.[22]

Though Karsh's portraits of Indigenous individuals reflected his experiences as an ethnic outsider as well as his respectful demeanour, he also photographed Indigenous subjects through the lens of the prejudices of his time. He later adapted, as Indigenous advocacy shifted Canadian attitudes toward addressing injustice.

In 1976, Karsh photographed celebrated Inuit artist Kenojuak Ashevak (1927–2013), a leading figure in the Kinngait (Cape Dorset) printmaking community, known for her captivating portrayals of Arctic birds and scenes of daily life.[23] Kenojuak is posed next to her felt pen drawing *Happy to Eat Together*, 1974, which was featured in a travelling exhibition organized in 1975 by members of the Canadian Conference of Catholic Bishops, who invited artists to illustrate a new Sunday Missal.[24] Karsh portrays Kenojuak as an independent artist and storyteller, in control of her narrative, rather than as an anonymous documentary subject. But the portrait, shot in a gallery environment, may not have used the artificial lighting so essential to Karsh's signature dramatic contrast of light and shadow. Instead, the overall tonality of the picture is very light, with minimal contrast between the artist, her artwork, and the setting, and suggestive—intentionally or otherwise—of a snowbound Arctic environment.[25]

Toward the end of his career, Karsh photographed acclaimed architect Douglas Cardinal during the construction of the Canadian Museum of Civilization (now the Canadian Museum of History), across the river from Ottawa's Parliament Hill. Born in Calgary of Métis, Blackfoot/Kainai, German, and Algonquin heritage, Cardinal created an organic curvilinear design that defined an Indigenous style of modern architecture. One variant from the 1989 photo session shows Cardinal in a suit and tie, standing in the doorway of his office next to a rendering of the museum design. A second version shows the architect sitting cross-legged on a blanket, with rolled architectural drawings on shelves to the left, wearing a fringed and beaded jacket and smoking a long-stemmed ceremonial pipe. Together, the portraits reveal an intensely personal integration of multiple traditions in Cardinal's distinctive practice.

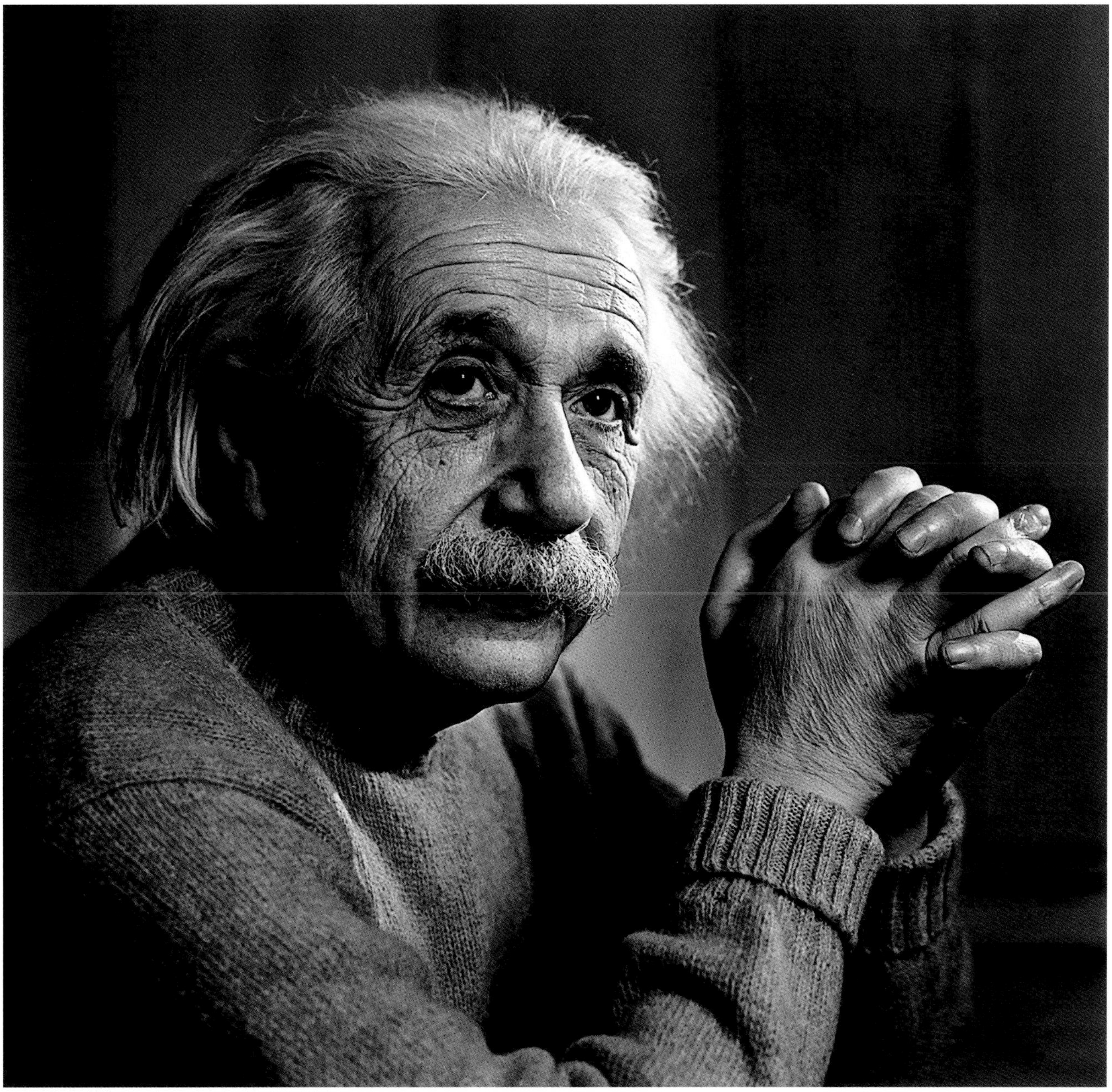

Hope and Catharsis

Karsh lived through the Armenian massacres he witnessed as a child, the barbarism of two world wars, and the threat of nuclear annihilation from the Cold War. He saw his portraits as beacons of hope and believed that progress in politics, business, and culture could be embodied in individuals of high achievement. In Karsh's optimistic world view, portraits could alleviate the anxieties of a troubled world.

One of his most reproduced works, the 1948 portrait of Albert Einstein seated at his desk at Princeton's Institute for Advanced Study, draws our gaze: the Nobel physicist known for his theory of relativity appears wise and genial, and was later described by Karsh as "a simple, kindly, almost childlike man."[26] For the viewer, Einstein's gentle

Yousuf Karsh, *Albert Einstein*, February 11, 1948, gelatin silver print, 48.9 x 53.1 cm, Montreal Museum of Fine Arts.

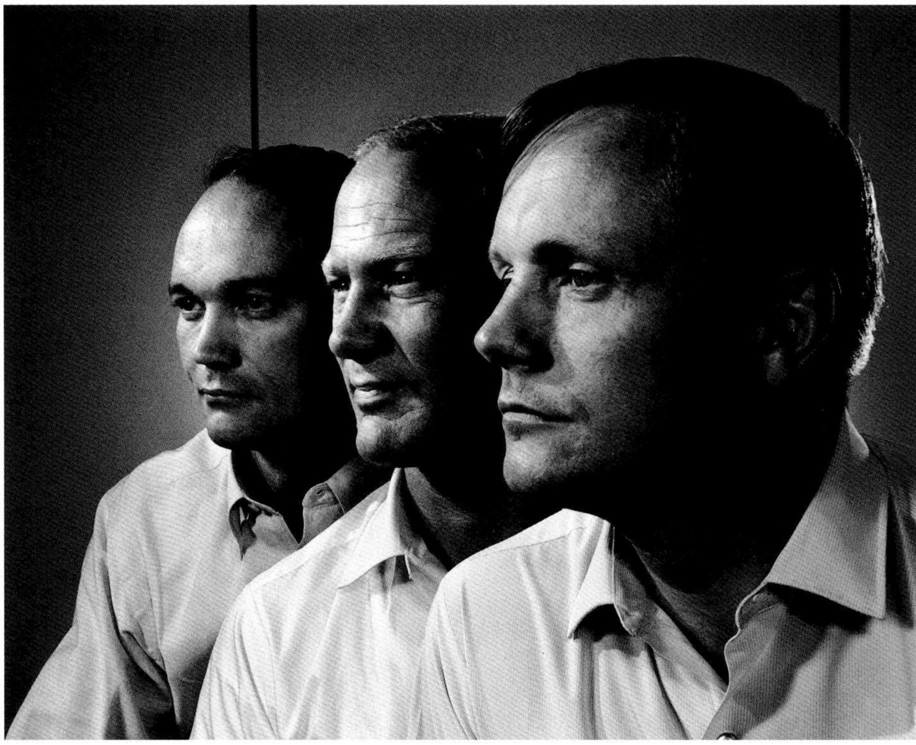

demeanour imparts a resigned acceptance of the human-generated threat to life on Earth following the convulsive twentieth-century discoveries of the universe and its laws. Karsh's text commentary for the portrait reinforces this perspective: "He spoke sadly, yet serenely, as one who had looked into the universe far past mankind's small affairs. When I asked him what the world would be like were another atomic bomb to be dropped, he replied wearily, 'Alas, we will no longer be able to hear the music of Mozart.'"[27]

Karsh believed it was the artist's job to accomplish at least two things: to stir the viewer's emotions and to lay bare the soul of his subject.[28] The emotional response to viewing images, or reception, is a significant aspect of photographic theory. Ultimately, it is the viewer, responding to the experience of beholding Karsh's portrait, who ascribes meaning to it.

Lilly Koltun considered Karsh's objective in his approach, arguing that from his early years as a portraitist, he pursued an intention clearly defined in terms of cathartic purgation, or emotional release, to relieve the viewer's anxiety about the self and the world's admired achievers and leaders.[29] Accompanying this objective, though perhaps not explicitly, was the portrait's function of alleviating any anxiety that Karsh's pantheon of exalted figures might be fallible, or worse, malevolent.[30]

Karsh photographed individuals associated with world events, never the events themselves. In front of his camera, politicians appear visionary, war leaders dignified, and business moguls benevolent. In this historical chronicle, Karsh suspends moral judgement over his collection of talented individuals to present a universe of exceptionalism. His project aimed to give visual language to concepts of imagination and innovation, achievement and altruism, benevolence and courage.[31] In this way, his work embodies a belief that humanity could be less cruel and more accepting of difference, a utopian realization of geopolitical harmony.

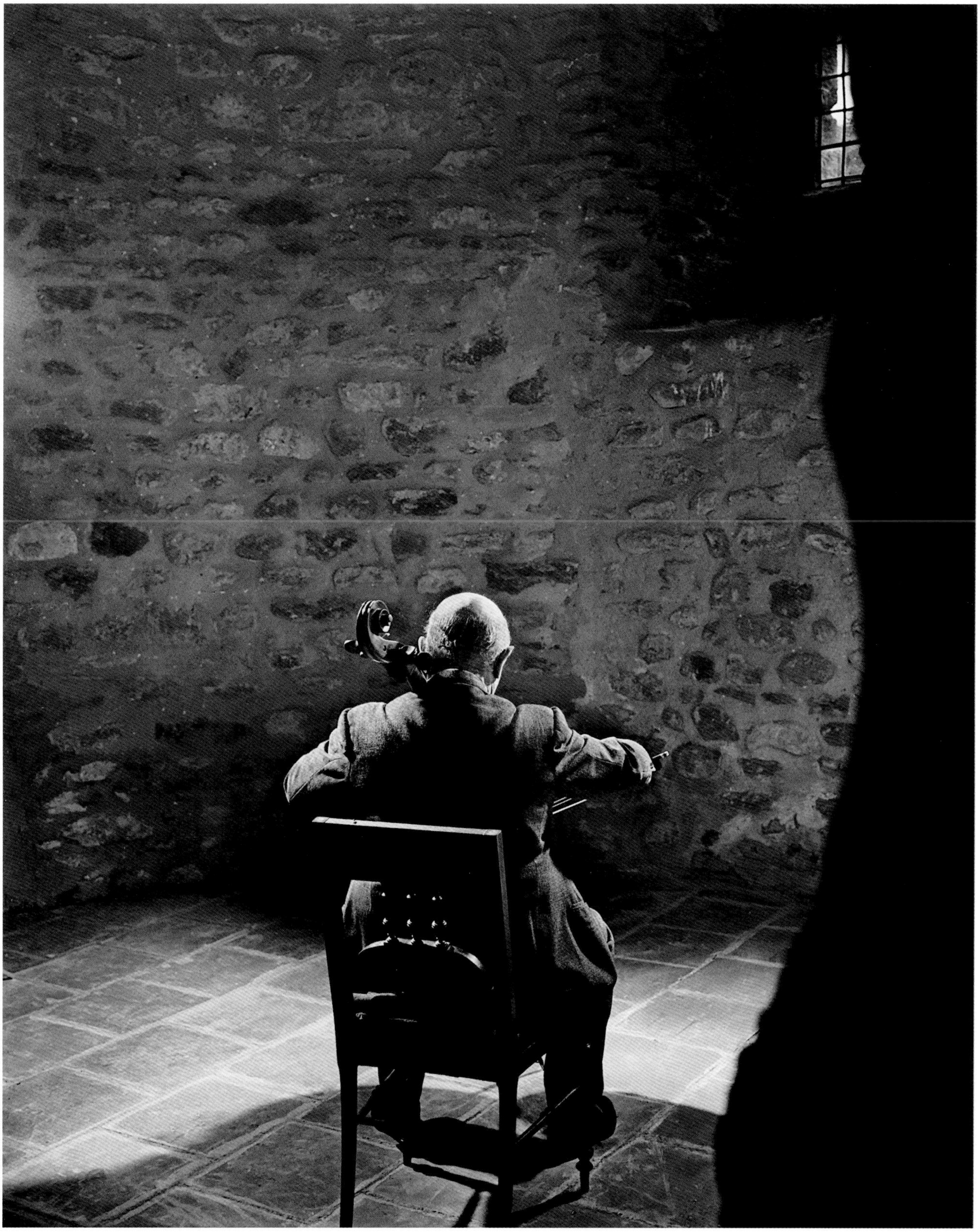

Opposite: Yousuf Karsh, *Apollo XI Crew*, 1969, gelatin silver print, 40 x 49.9 cm (image), 55.9 x 71.1 cm (mount), Estate of Yousuf Karsh. Above: Yousuf Karsh, *Pablo Casals*, June 30, 1954, gelatin silver print, 60.3 x 49.1 cm, Montreal Museum of Fine Arts.

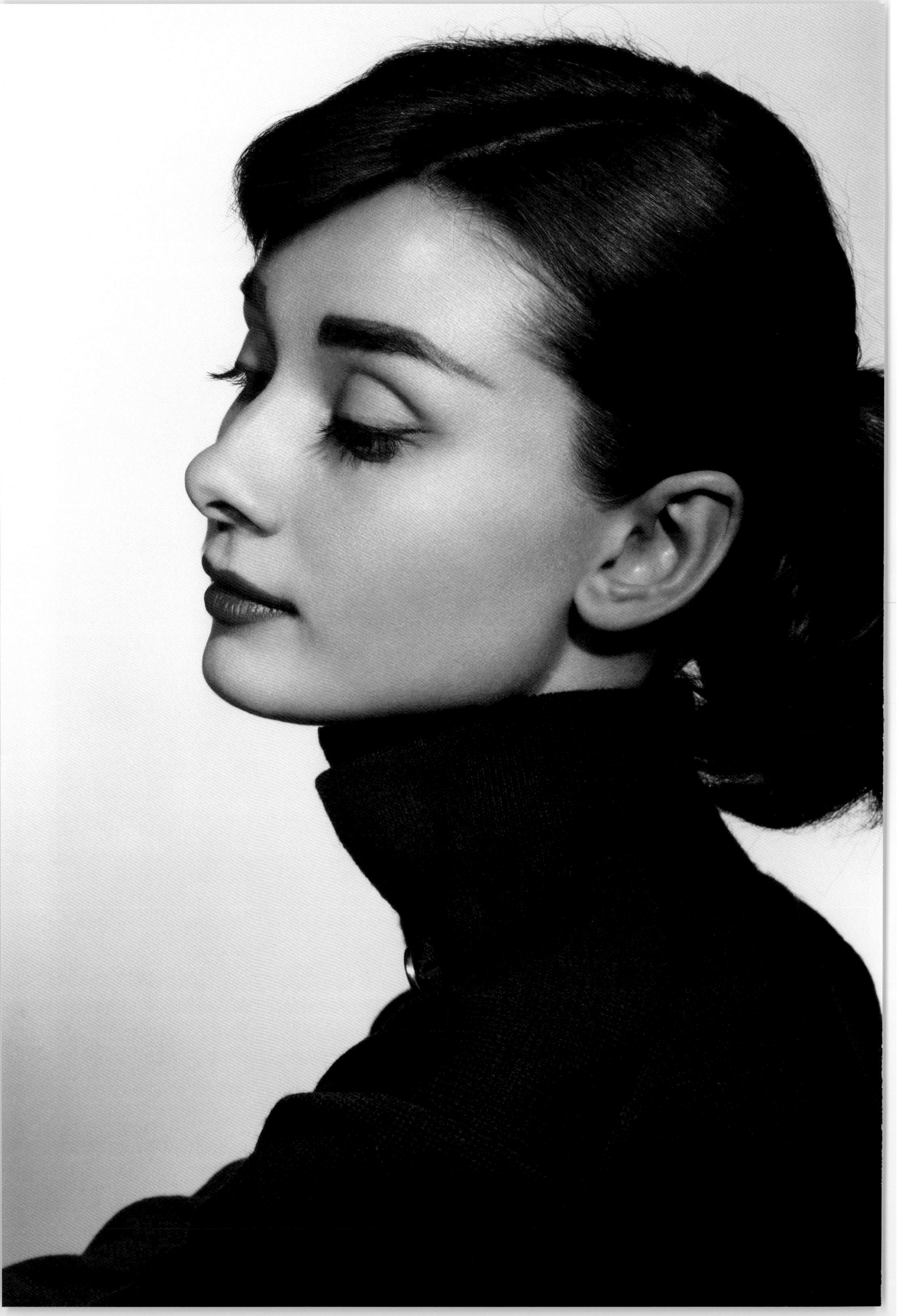

Style & Technique

Yousuf Karsh's signature style was the hallmark of modernist photography for much of the twentieth century: dramatic lighting, minimalist settings, sharp focus, and rich, velvety prints. For the public, a single frame from a portrait sitting would become an iconic image. But a Karsh portrait was carefully constructed, never simply "snapped"—the result of numerous artistic and technical decisions, from initial booking through to final printing. His mastery of photography spanned tremendous shifts in technology, from natural light to artificial illumination and from glass-plate negatives to film photography using large-format and small portable cameras. The end of Karsh's era of formal portraiture using film photography coincided with the rise of self-made digital images created with smartphone cameras.

The Portrait Sitting

Under the tutelage of John H. Garo (1868–1939), which ended in 1931, Karsh mastered the photographic styles and techniques of soft-focus Pictorialism. He photographed using natural light with a large bellows camera anchored on a tripod, taking exposures on cumbersome and fragile 14 x 17-inch or 16 x 20-inch glass negatives. By the time he opened his Ottawa studio in early 1933, Karsh had embraced a modernist portrait style that aligned with his generation. His work demonstrated an awareness of the sharp focus delineation that characterized work by American contemporaries such as Edward

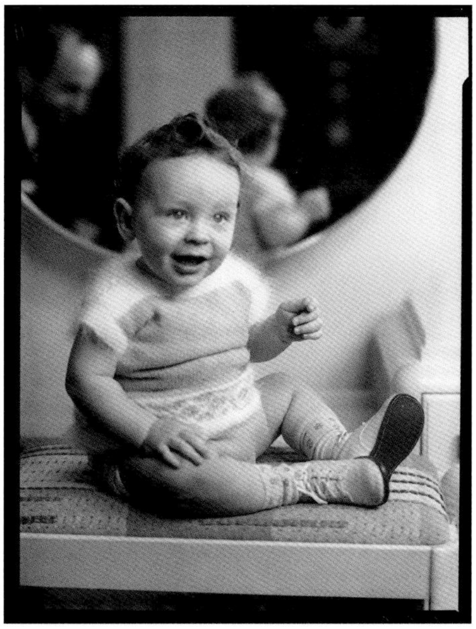

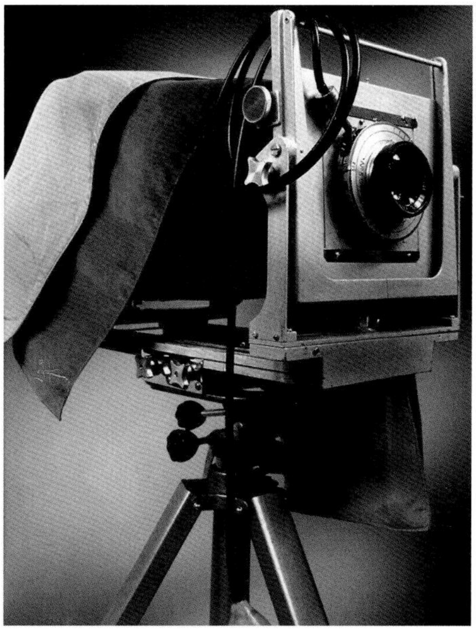

Opposite: Yousuf Karsh, *Audrey Hepburn*, March 23, 1956, Estate of Yousuf Karsh. Above left: Yousuf Karsh, *Master Michel Pharand*, March 19, 1937, interpositive made from original 25 x 19.9 cm nitrate negative, Yousuf Karsh Fonds, Library and Archives Canada, Ottawa. Karsh is seen in the background mirror reflection using his large-format camera while interacting with the baby. Above right: The 8 x 10 bellows Calumet, Yousuf Karsh's main camera, draped with a focusing cloth made for Karsh by his assistant and librarian, Hella Graber, date unknown, photograph by Ingenium.

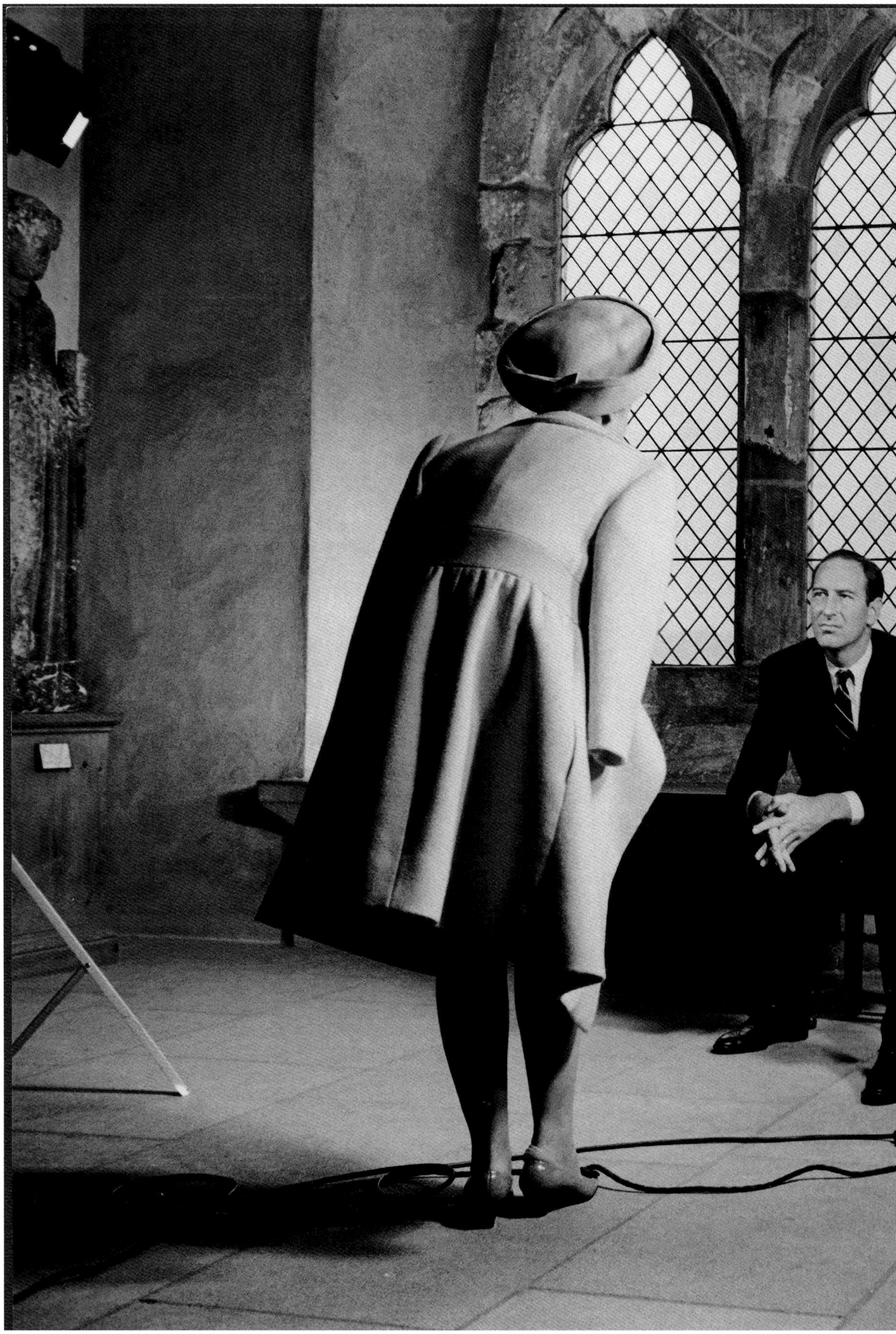

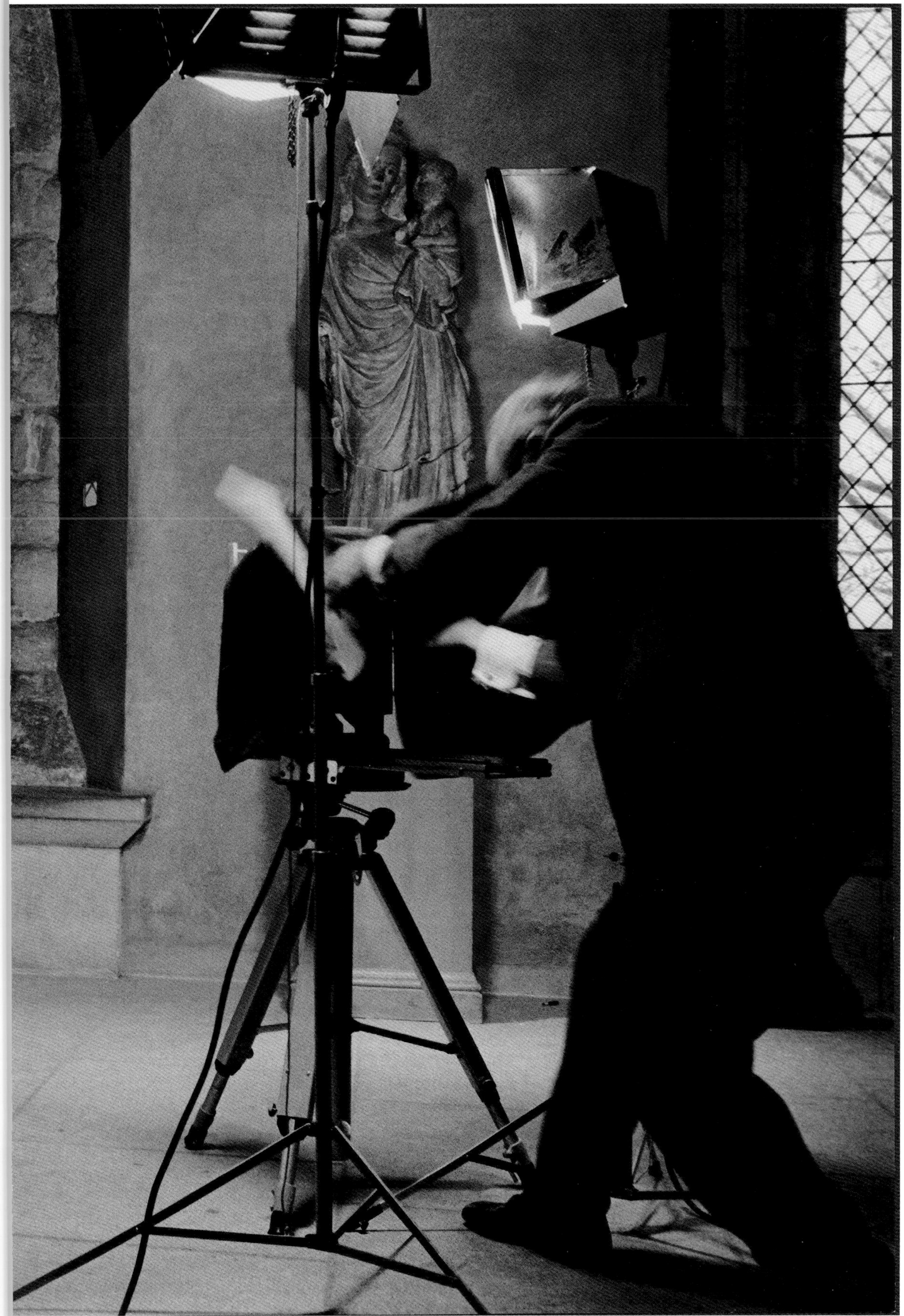

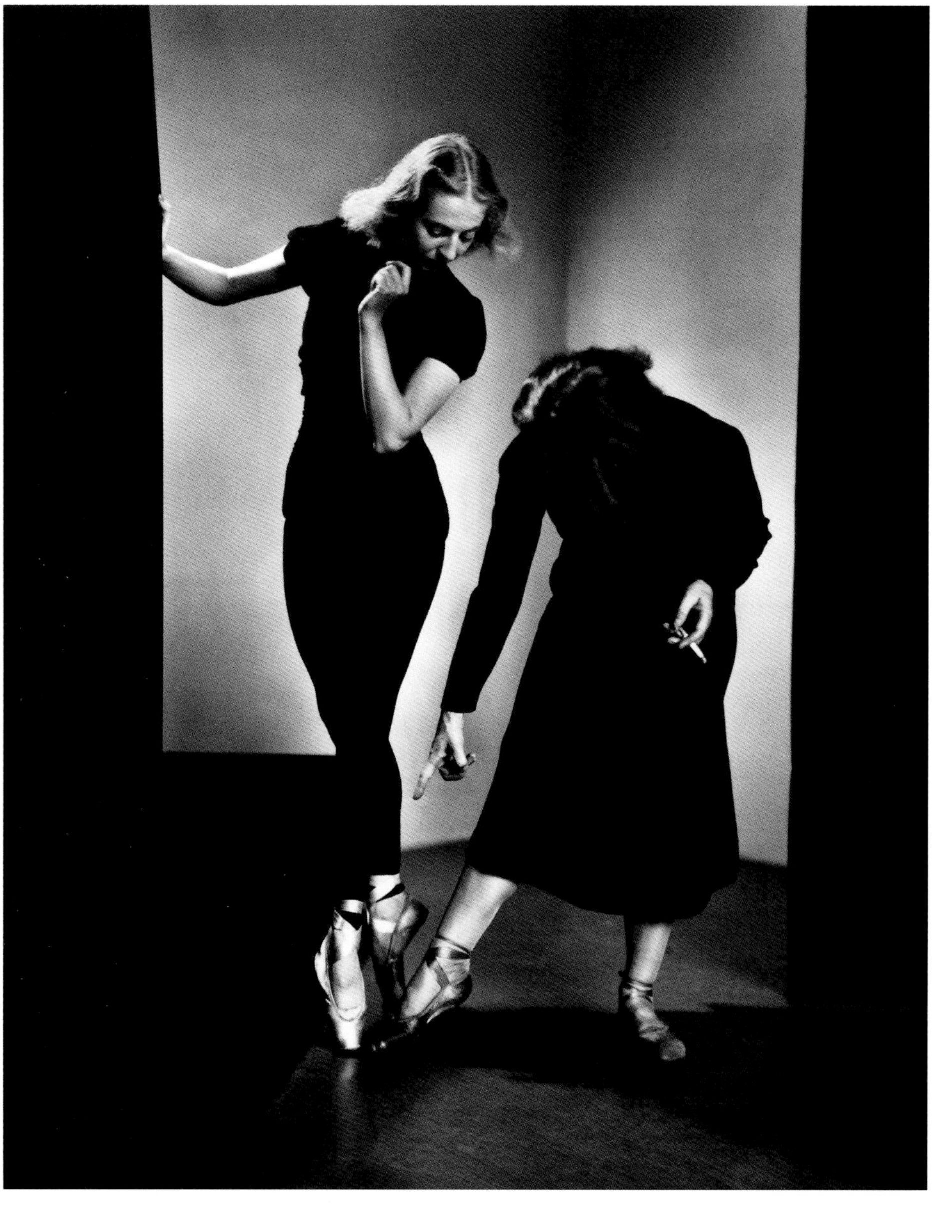

Steichen (1879–1973), Berenice Abbott (1898–1991), Edward Weston (1886–1958), and Ansel Adams (1902–1984).[1]

Karsh used a variety of photographic equipment and materials, but most of his portraits were made using a large-format camera. Working with this camera, he could produce high-resolution, large-format exposures on 8 x 10-inch film negatives from which multiple prints of various sizes could be made.[2] Though Karsh used lightweight Rolleiflex cameras for photojournalism assignments and personal photography, he rarely used them for formal portrait sessions.

An even more significant shift was Karsh's mastery of the dramatic potential of artificial lighting, which was already well established in theatre and cinema productions, as well as in the stylish portraits of movie stars featured in *Vogue* and *Vanity Fair.* As Lilly Koltun astutely observed, Karsh's experience working with theatre directors and their

Previous spread: Estrellita and Yousuf Karsh during a portrait session with Thomas Hoving (*centre*), April 17, 1967, photograph by Ivan Dmitri. Above: Yousuf Karsh, *The Lesson*, January 1, 1935, gelatin silver print, 34.1 x 26.7 cm (image), 35.4 x 28 cm (mount), Estate of Yousuf Karsh.

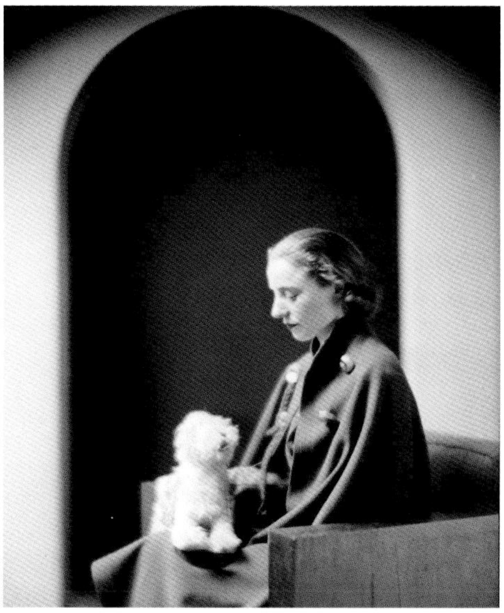 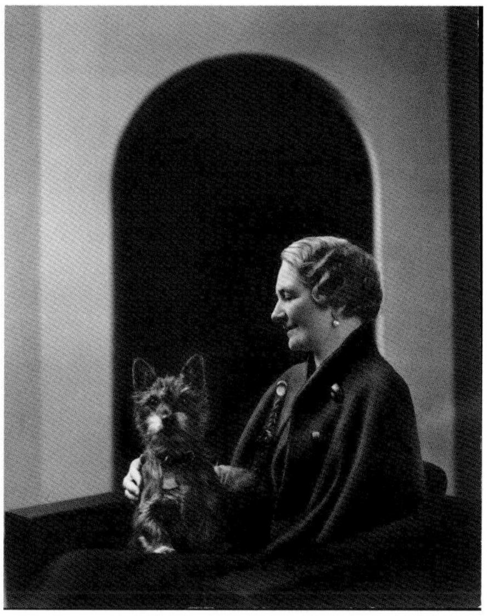

casts during the 1930s went far beyond expanding his technical skills. By detaching the expressive potential of illumination from the limitations of natural light, Karsh was able to assume directorial control and invoke an otherworldly dimension in his portraits, such as his portrayal of playwright and actor Madge Macbeth in 1936, creating psychologically impactful images that were pictorially distinct from the realm of the everyday.[3]

During a typical photo session, Karsh's key light was placed slightly behind and about one and a half metres to the right of the camera. This provided the main illumination, modelling the sitter's features and establishing the essential light and shade pattern of the image. He always positioned two light sources behind his subject on both sides—to act as either fill or rim lights—which resulted in light bouncing off the side of the subject's face and toward the camera.[4] By gently illuminating shadows, the fill light reduced the extreme contrasts produced by the main light. This made details in dark areas more visible in the final image. The ground-glass screen of the camera back showed Karsh the exact view captured by the lens (appearing upside down), allowing him to frame and focus with precision. To block ambient light, Karsh viewed the image under a heavy velvet cloth and ensured that all necessary lighting and camera adjustments were ready, and that the portrait subject was ideally posed.

Karsh was meticulous in his advance research of his portrait subjects, particularly those who were in the public eye and especially those with restricted schedules, such as heads of government. Each shot was based on planning and previsualization to ensure a portrait that was both compositionally effective and psychologically insightful. The sitter's pose and environmental factors such as lighting and the selection of props were carefully considered even before Karsh and his subject formally met.

Especially in the early years of operating his portrait studio, Karsh tested aesthetic and technical approaches to increase his confidence in directing the portrait session. For example, his future wife, Solange Gauthier, posed with a stuffed dog in preparation for a portrait sitting with Lady Anne Elizabeth Clark, wife of British High Commissioner Sir William Henry Clark, and her dog, Angus, in August 1934. This early portrait demonstrates the strong perfectionism that compelled Karsh to plan in advance, enhance

Left: Yousuf Karsh, *Solange Gauthier posing with a stuffed dog in preparation for a portrait sitting with Lady Anne Elizabeth Clark*, about August 9, 1934, interpositive made from original cellulose nitrate negative, Yousuf Karsh Fonds, Library and Archives Canada, Ottawa. Right: Yousuf Karsh, *Lady Clark, with dog Angus*, August 9, 1934, gelatin silver print, 23.5 x 18.8 cm, Yousuf Karsh Fonds, Library and Archives Canada, Ottawa.

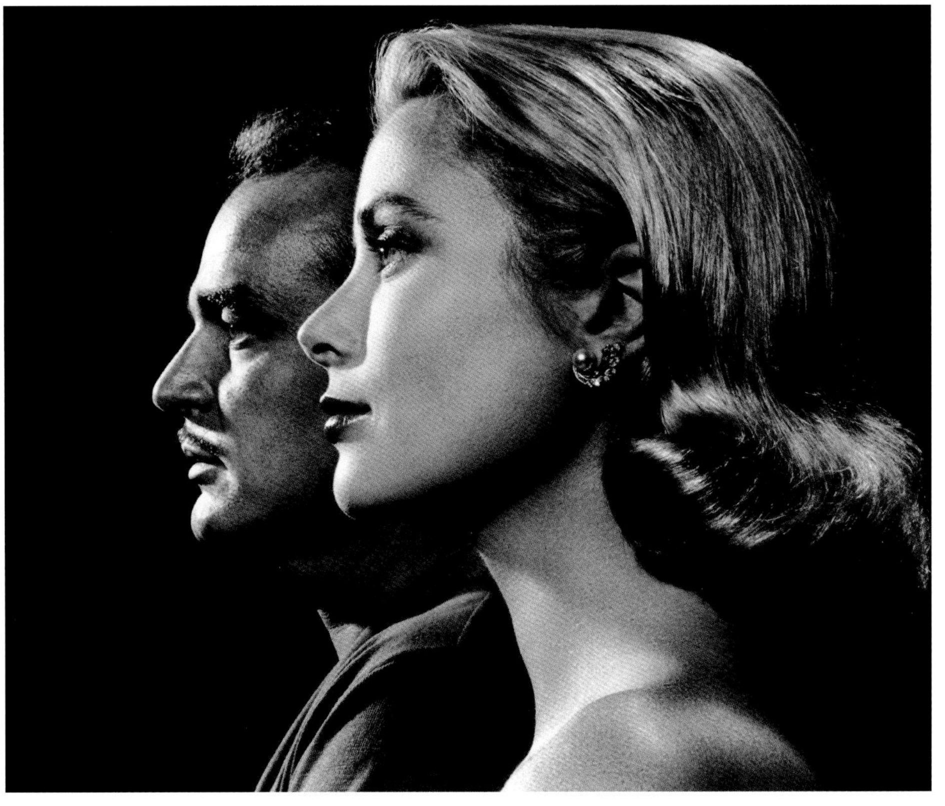

each portrait environment, whether in the studio or on location, and lead each session with confidence. By contrast, Karsh's 1936 *Woman in a Turban (Betty Low)* was created for circulation in prestigious photographic salons in a playful, unpremeditated moment. Karsh had spontaneously draped a window curtain around his sitter, friend and model Betty Low, resulting in a dramatic study evocative of classical art.

In the studio, Karsh ultimately made a reputation for himself as a thoughtful auteur. In addition to his careful attention to technical aspects, his focus on the person before him was absolute.[5] Sitters felt the strong pull of Karsh's attention, especially as he became a celebrity, a lesson he learned well from Garo. The portrait session involved negotiation—sometimes subtle, sometimes not—between performer and director to achieve a compelling final image. As one client, a young debutante who sat for him in the 1930s, remarked, "I recall that Karsh had a gentle manner but was very busy setting up various poses. He would come over and move my foot or my arm into position, and then return to his camera, and with a cloth over his head, he would have a look at me. He took about six pictures in total and my family was pleased with the results."[6]

As an experienced portraitist, Karsh drew upon a broad repertoire of compositions in the planning and execution of a portrait sitting. He typically shot many exposures and sometimes alternated the poses of the sitter in each session, then he selected the best images when viewing the first contact prints.

Setting and Symbolism

The force of the sitter's personality was established not only through pose and lighting but also through striking backdrops and props used to convey a sitter's talent, profession, or social position. Karsh often used visual cues as aids to an interesting composition and

Yousuf Karsh, *Prince Rainier III and Princess Grace of Monaco*, September 22, 1956, gelatin silver print, 14.9 x 13.5 cm, Yousuf Karsh Fonds, Library and Archives Canada, Ottawa.

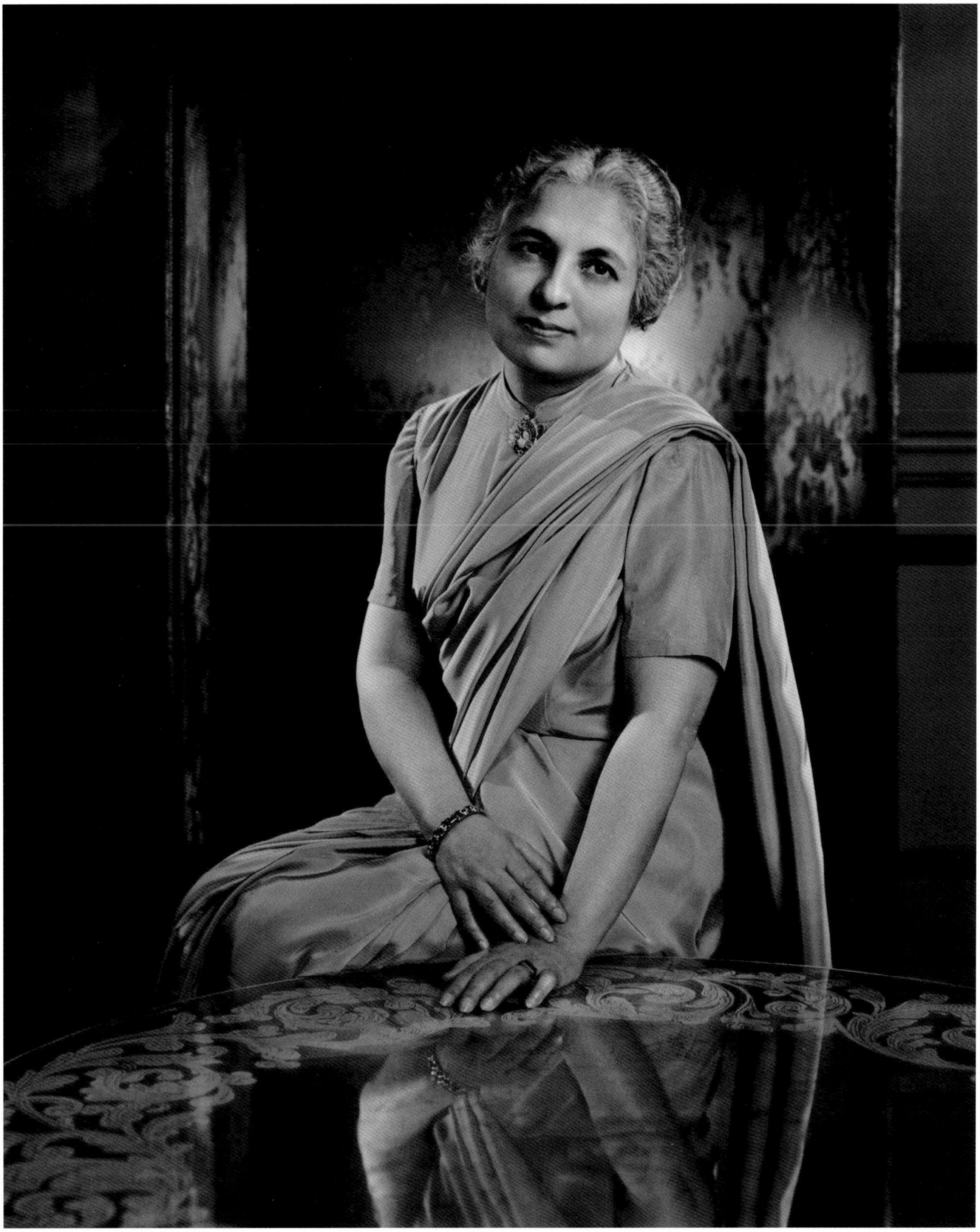

Yousuf Karsh, *Ambassador Vijaya Lakshmi Pandit*, October 2, 1949, gelatin silver print, 24 x 19.2 cm (image), 35.3 x 28 cm (sheet), Yousuf Karsh Fonds, Library and Archives Canada, Ottawa.

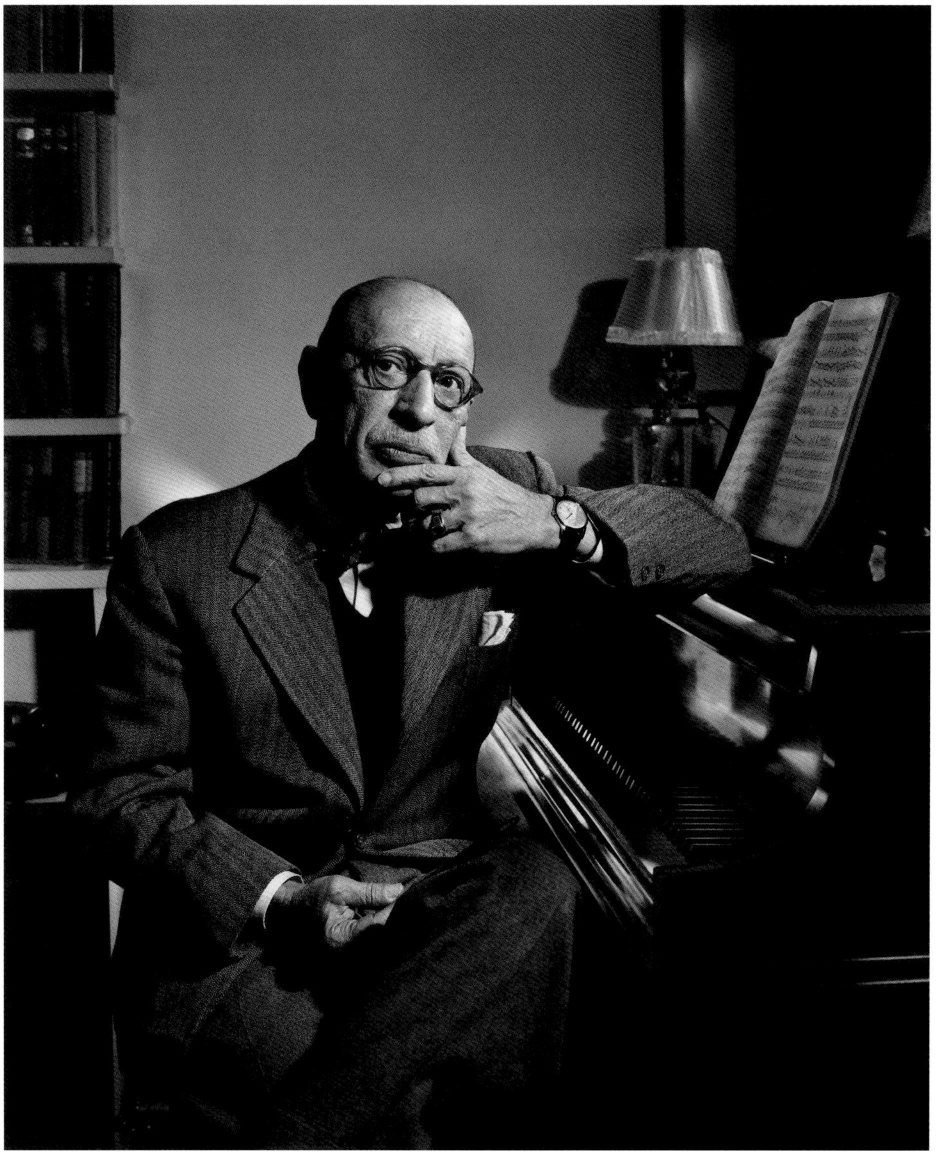

as symbolic objects to help his audiences recognize famous personalities. For instance, Ambassador Vijaya Lakshmi Pandit, the sister of India's first prime minister, Jawaharlal Nehru, gracefully poses at the edge of a polished round table. Pandit headed the Indian diplomatic delegations to the United Nations and served as India's ambassador to several countries, and Karsh's portrayal suggests that she casts her influence across the globe. Similarly, Karsh's portraits of composers and musicians frequently feature the artists posed with their instruments or actually playing them, such as a 1956 portrait of Igor Stravinsky, a proponent of modern atonal composition, seated at his piano as if taking a momentary pause during a composition session.

In another memorable portrait, Robert Oppenheimer, who was instrumental in the creation of the atomic bomb during the Second World War, is shown with pipe in hand, paused before two blackboards covered in scientific formulas. At the time of this sitting, the controversial physicist had had his security clearance revoked for his post-war

Yousuf Karsh, *Igor Stravinsky*, March 20, 1956, gelatin silver print, 31.8 x 25.7 cm (image), 40.6 x 33 cm (mount), Estate of Yousuf Karsh.

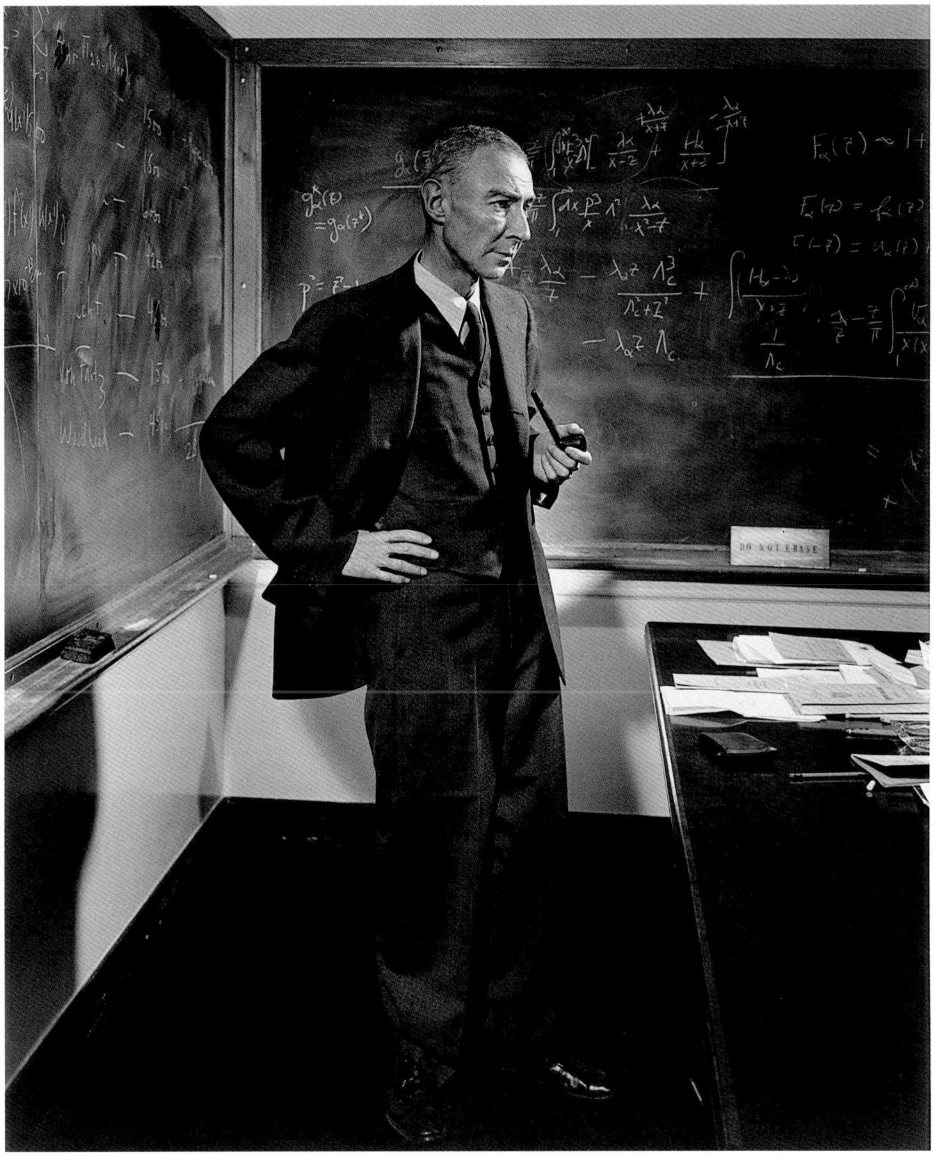

opposition to nuclear weapons. Karsh's vantage point in setting up the portrait also captures, ironically, a small sign placed to protect the work in progress: "Do Not Erase."

Though Karsh endeavoured to create each image as a unique tribute to the individual, he acknowledged there was a limit, particularly in view of a career that produced more than fifteen thousand sittings:

> But I cannot always avoid some duplication, and I think that it would be wrong if I were to endeavour to do so. Thus, I have at times repeated a composition or duplicated an arrangement where I have felt that this was natural. But I have done it with full awareness; as long as I can feel that I am conscious of such decisions, neither repetition nor freshness of composition will become ends in themselves, nor do I think they should.[7]

Yousuf Karsh, *Robert Oppenheimer*, February 9, 1956, gelatin silver print, 49.5 x 39.4 cm (image), 71.1 x 55.9 cm (mount), Museum of Fine Arts, Boston.

The iconic significance of a portrait was also grounded in Karsh's respect for the individual's gift and in his belief in a modern society founded on meritocracy, a conviction for which he himself was an exemplar. Karsh was acutely sensitive to posing his subjects so that the resulting portrait embodied their aspirations and achievements, as well as the public's perception of them.

Like many portrait photographers past and present, Karsh developed a signature approach that depended on consistently applied aesthetic choices across the breadth of his practice. Successful because of his established hallmark style, Karsh sought to optimize the possibilities of lighting, pose, and setting during each portrait occasion. He regarded the resulting image not only as intrinsically artistic but also as important evidence of a creative moment between himself and his sitter, an ineffable fragment of time distilling the photographer's unique sensitivity as a perceptive observer guiding the camera's mechanical eye.

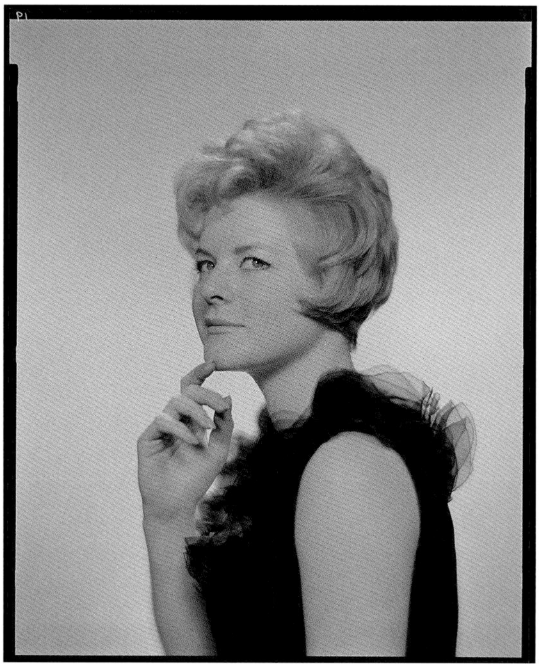

In the Darkroom

Although Karsh is celebrated for his entertaining anecdotes of portrait sittings with the luminaries of his time, and while he boldly shared his photographic method with the eager readers of his 1962 biography, *In Search of Greatness*, he closely guarded the mysteries of his back-of-house aesthetic and technical choices.

In the darkroom, exposed film was immersed in a chemical developer to produce a negative image from which multiple positive prints could be made on photo-sensitive paper. In Karsh's time, most photographers tracked the development of the negative by carefully monitoring the immersion time and the temperature of the solution, but Karsh had mastered the ability to judge it by visual inspection under a dim safelight.

For most of his career, Karsh produced reference prints known as "red proofs" that required exposure to daylight but no further processing. He used these to examine each exposure, select negatives for printing, and mark faults for correction on the original negative, as seen in the red proof and negative of his 1965 portrait of Christl Thalhammer

Yousuf Karsh, *Christl Thalhammer*, May 1965, interpositive made from the original negative, 25.2 x 20.1 cm, Yousuf Karsh Fonds, Library and Archives Canada, Ottawa.

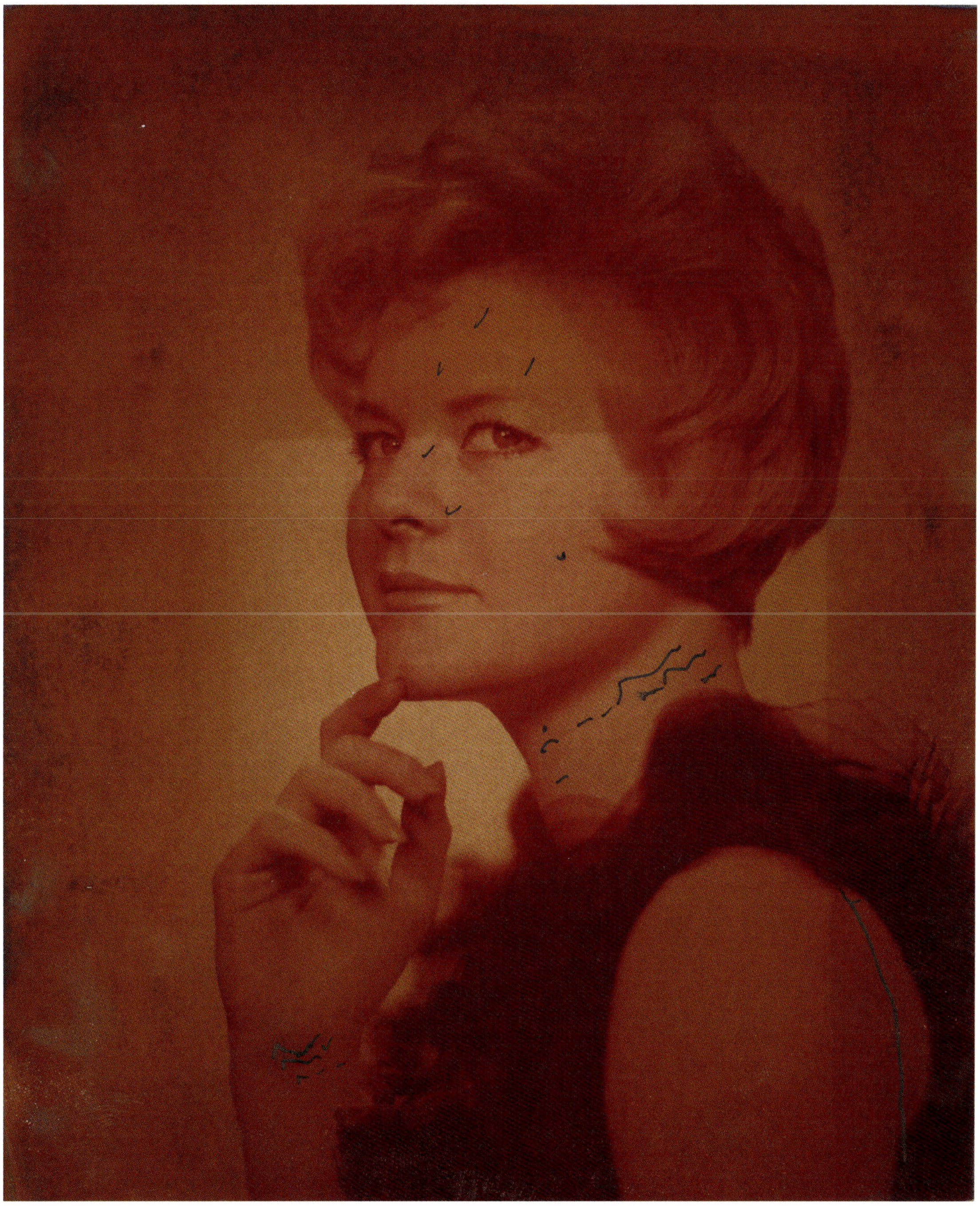

Yousuf Karsh, *Christl Thalhammer*, May 1965, red proof, 19.2 x 15.4 cm, Yousuf Karsh Fonds, Library and Archives Canada, Ottawa. Karsh manipulated this portrait to reduce an unwanted emphasis on the sitter's shoulder and upper arm. He first scraped away part of the negative's emulsion to create a dark area in the print and then retouched the negative to blend this area with the original background. To soften facial lines and wrinkles, Karsh shaded these areas on the negative with fine retouching pencils so they would appear lighter on the final print.

Next spread: Christine Fitzgerald, *Karsh's Finishing Pencils*, 2024, tri-chromate gum print on rag paper, 40.6 x 52.1 cm. Ottawa-based artist Christine Fitzgerald photographed Karsh's finishing pencils, preserved by Ingenium, upon being named the Karsh Award laureate by the city of Ottawa in 2023.

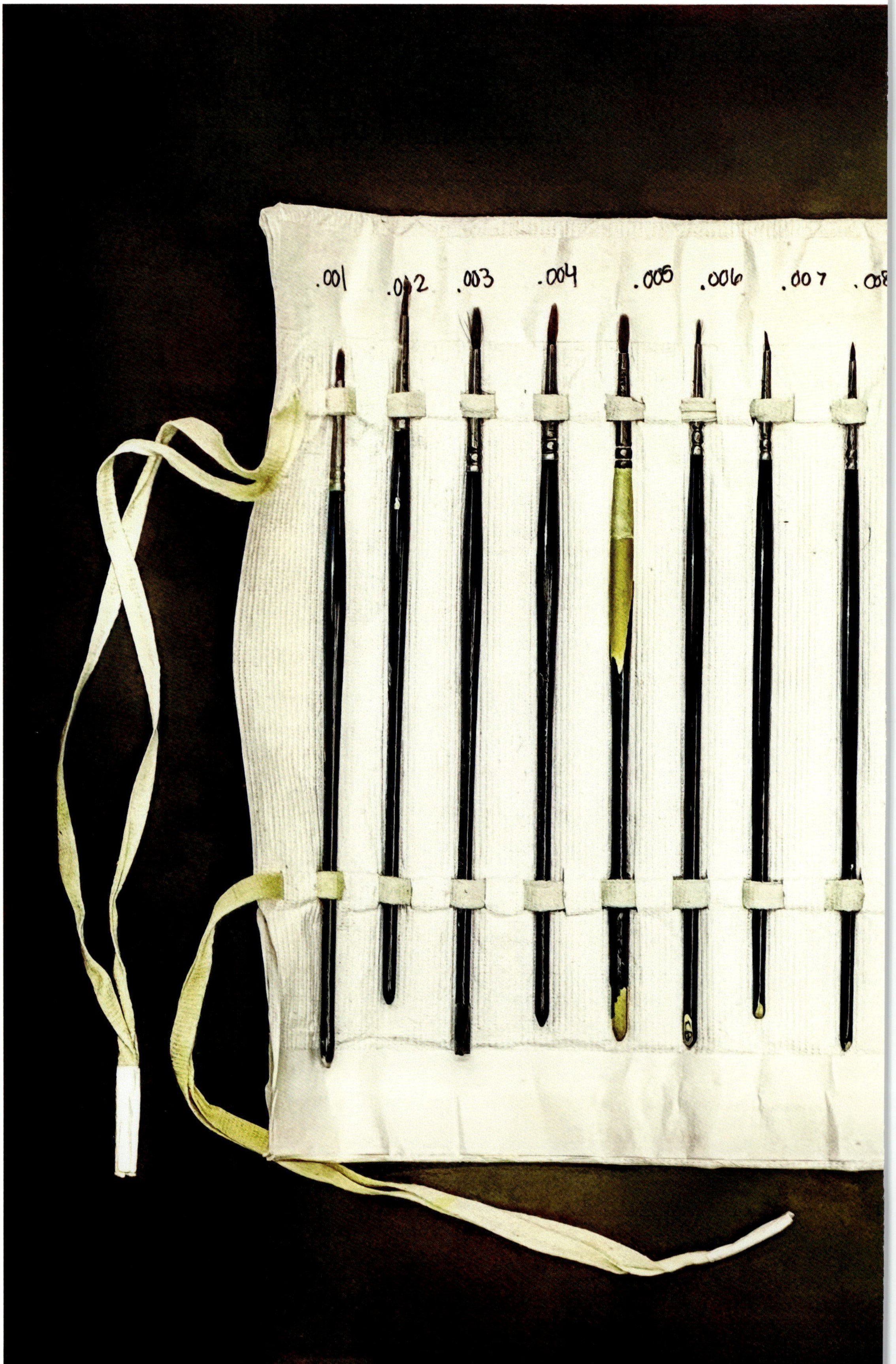
.001
.002
.003
.004
.005
.006
.007

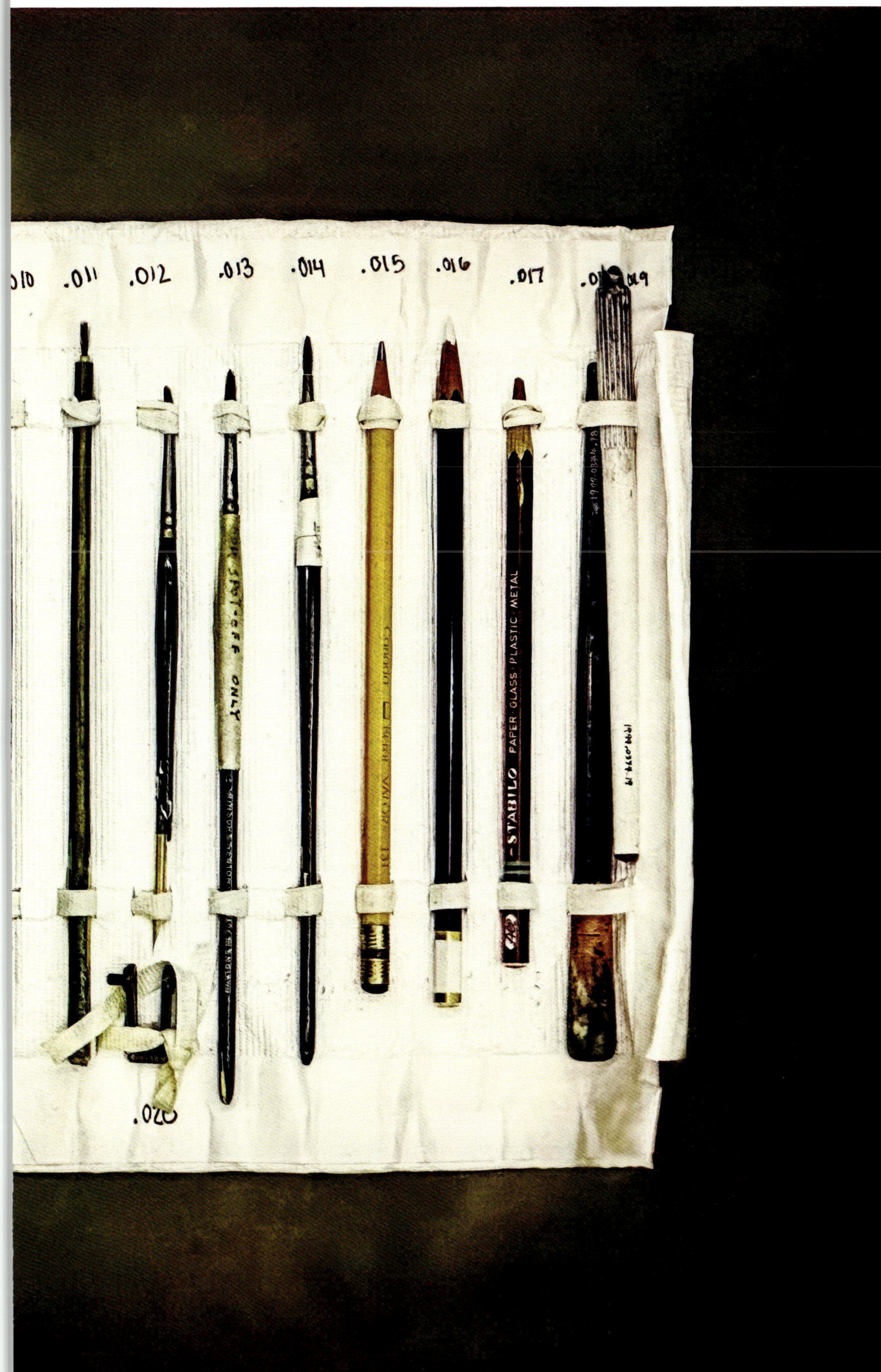
.011
.012
.013
.014
.015
.016
.017
.020
STABILO PAPER · GLASS · PLASTIC · METAL

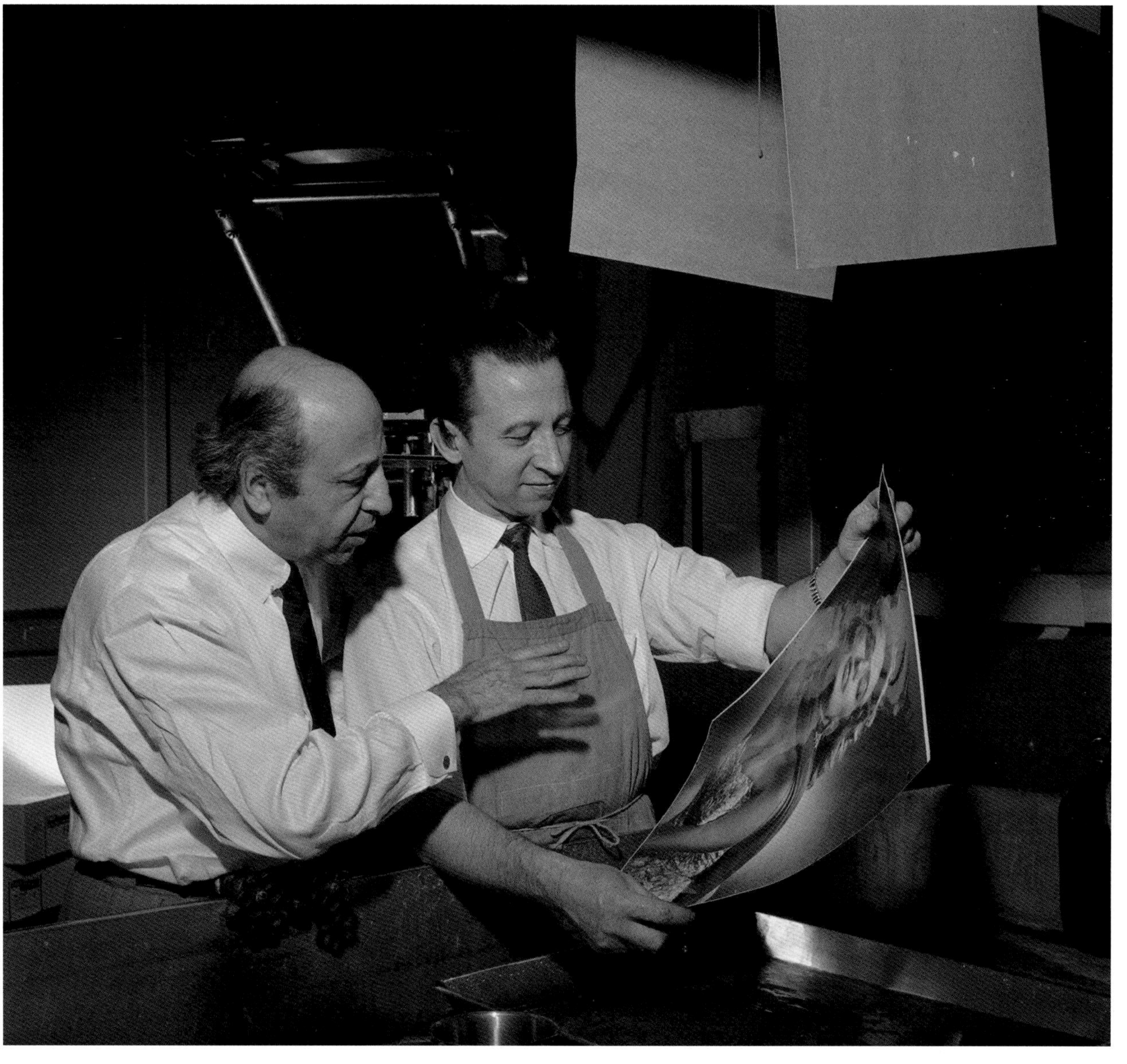

(shown with the film emulsion side up to reveal the retouching marks). Working on the developed negative, Karsh and his assistants then used various techniques and tools to correct flaws or create visual effects. For example, they would darken areas of a negative to produce more intense highlights in a sitter's hair when the tonalities were reversed in the finished positive print.

To create finished, museum-quality prints, the portraits were exposed on special printing paper under the light of an enlarger. Karsh developed photographs on Opal V paper, a textured Kodak product that produced a rich, velvety finish, sometimes compared to suede. He would select specific developers, papers, and toners to emphasize warm or cool tones in the final print. Other critical decisions came into play in this phase of production to determine size, tonal contrast, cropping, finish, and placement of the artist's signature. Final prints were delivered to the sitter, displayed in a gallery, or published.

Yousuf Karsh (*left*) and his long-time master printer, Ignas Gabalis, inspecting a print of Anita Ekberg, 1957, photograph by Chris Lund.

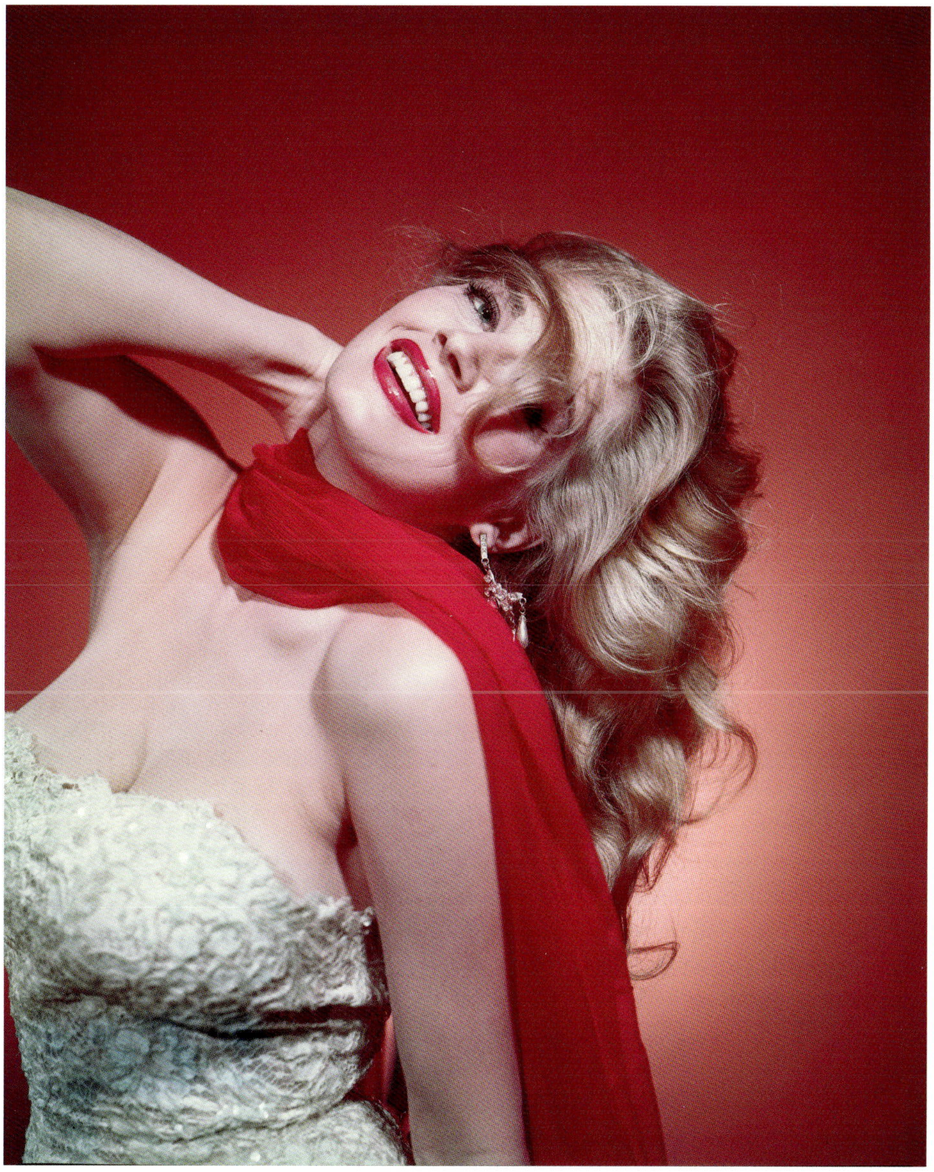

Over the course of his long career, Karsh created hundreds of thousands of negatives, transparencies, and prints from approximately fifteen thousand portrait sittings. Unlike many notable photographers of the twentieth century, such as Edward Weston, who directed that his negatives be destroyed after his death in the belief that only the prints were true expressions of his artistic vision, Karsh saw his archive as a wellspring for creating future fine art prints and reproductions of his celebrated portraits. When his comprehensive collection was acquired by the National Archives of Canada (now Library and Archives Canada) in 1987, Karsh included his negatives and red proofs along with his annotations on sitting envelopes and the negatives for montage printing. The decision to reveal his artistic choices was significant, as it supports ongoing research into his working methods and sheds light on the critical decisions involved in transforming a portrait from camera lens to final print.

Yousuf Karsh, *Anita Ekberg*, March 28, 1956, colour transparency, 25.4 x 20.3 cm, Yousuf Karsh Fonds, Library and Archives Canada, Ottawa.

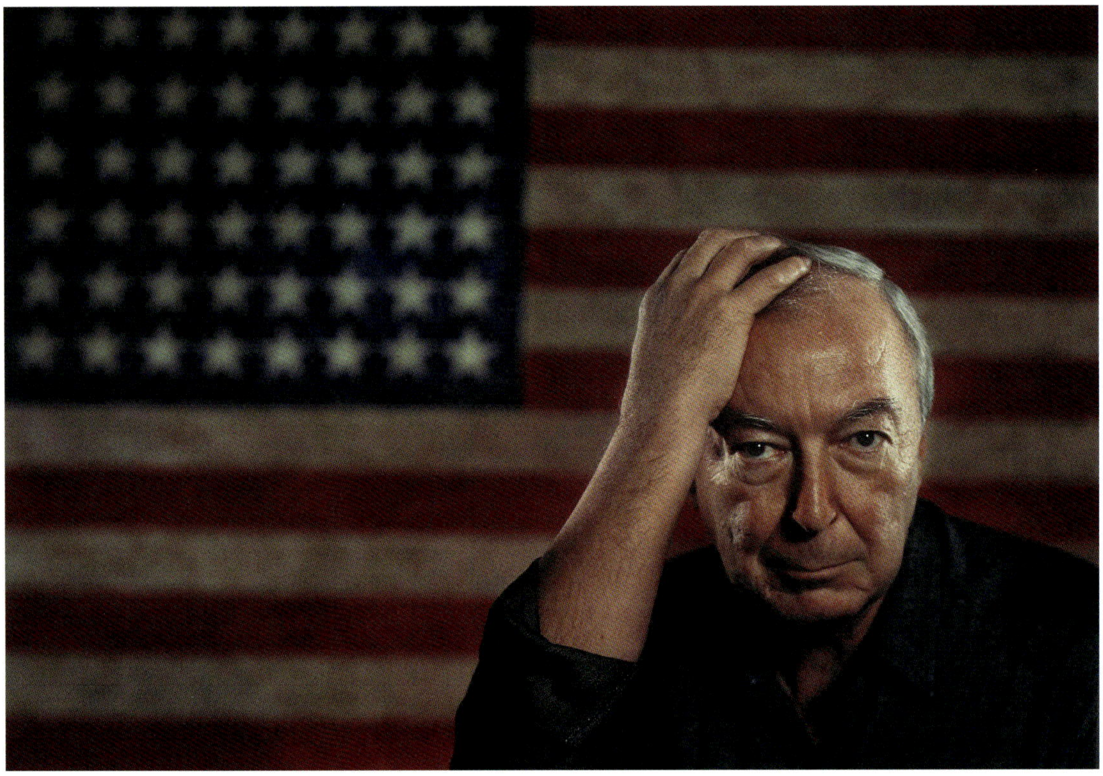

Karsh in Colour

From the 1940s onward, Karsh occasionally departed from his trademark dramatic and minimalist black-and-white portrayals in favour of lush colour-film photography and colour-separation commercial printing. Although black-and-white photography was considered essential in elite fine art photography circles, Karsh's commissions for illustrated magazines often required highly saturated portraits.

An early example of Karsh working with colour film is his 1947 portrait of Prime Minister William Lyon Mackenzie King. Karsh had photographed the Canadian prime minister on several formal and informal occasions. In 1947, he posed King with the Peace Tower of the Parliament Buildings visible through the window. A prolific diarist, King reflected on the sitting later that day, noting that Karsh initially worked with black-and-white film before switching to colour, taking about fifty exposures in all: "Once or twice, in photographing, Karsh made the significant remark that he wanted to get the picture of me that I would like to be remembered by. I can see that, from different sides, people have in their minds, that my public career and perhaps life itself may be drawing nearer to a close."[8] King's observation confirms Karsh's long-range view of portraits as immortalizing the subject. Images from this sitting were reproduced in *Maclean's* magazine and featured in King's impending political campaign. After King's death three years later, Karsh's portrait was used as the basis of a commemorative stamp in 1951.

Karsh was frequently commissioned to take colour portraits of Hollywood stars for reproduction in magazines. In 1956, he photographed Swedish actor Anita Ekberg in Los Angeles, California. Ekberg lived and worked mostly in Italy and is best remembered for her starring role as Sylvia in Federico Fellini's film *La Dolce Vita* (1960). When photographing cinematic femmes fatales, Karsh generally emphasized their sexual allure, and the choice of sumptuously chromatic film enhanced the viewer's sensory experience.

Yousuf Karsh, *Jasper Johns*, December 7, 1990, Estate of Yousuf Karsh.

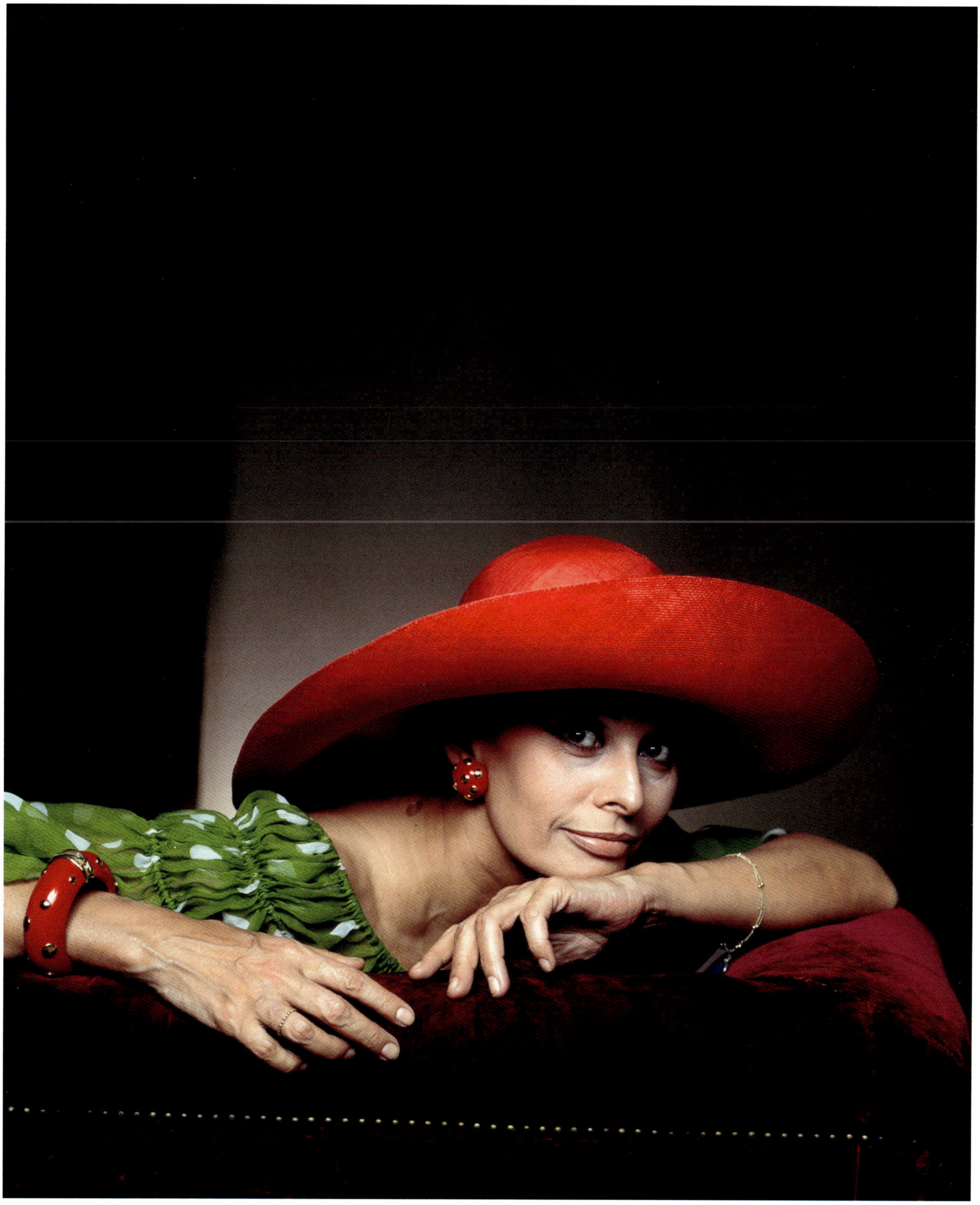

Yousuf Karsh, *Sophia Loren*, March 12, 1981, Estate of Yousuf Karsh.

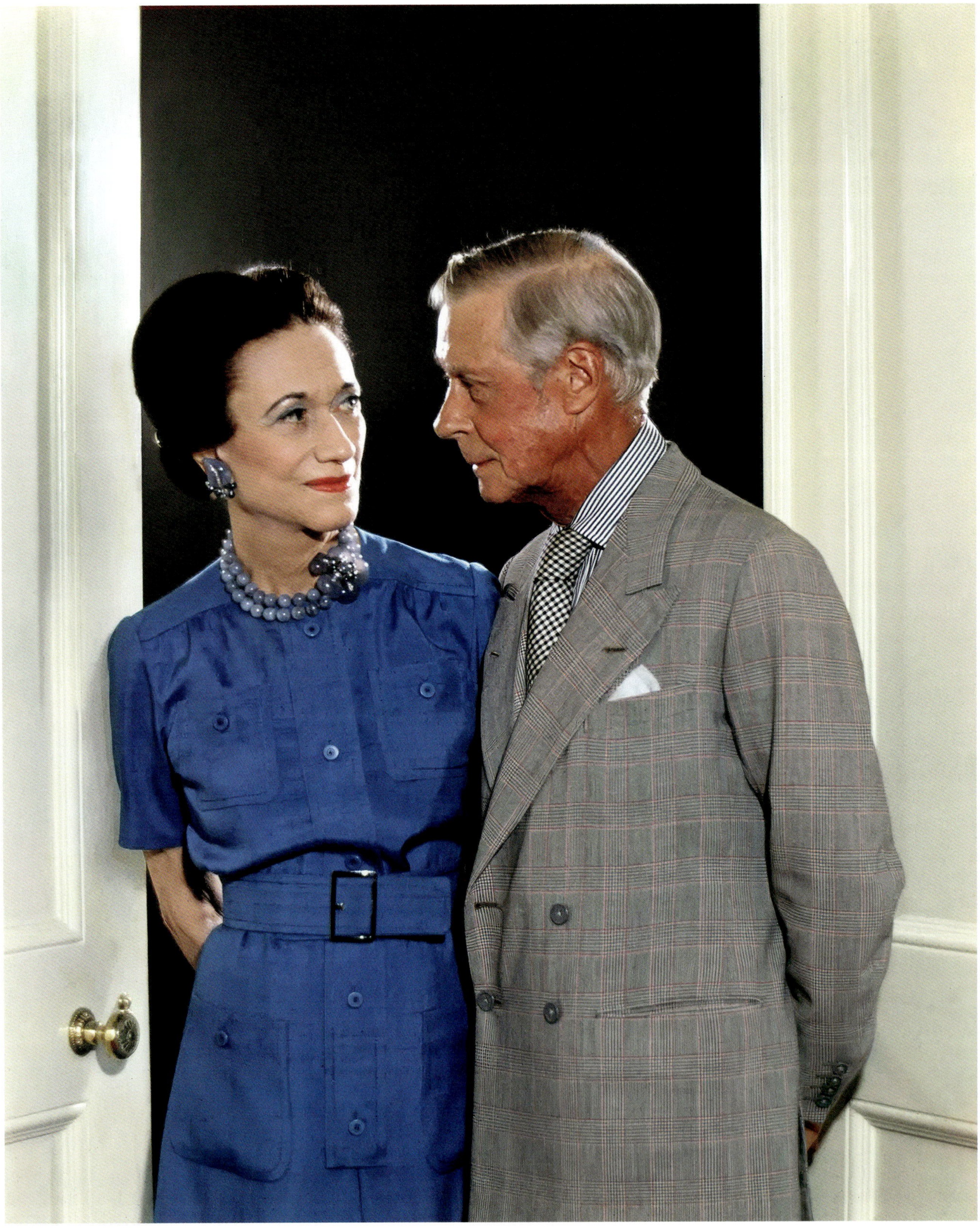

Yousuf Karsh, *Duke and Duchess of Windsor*, June 7, 1971, Estate of Yousuf Karsh.

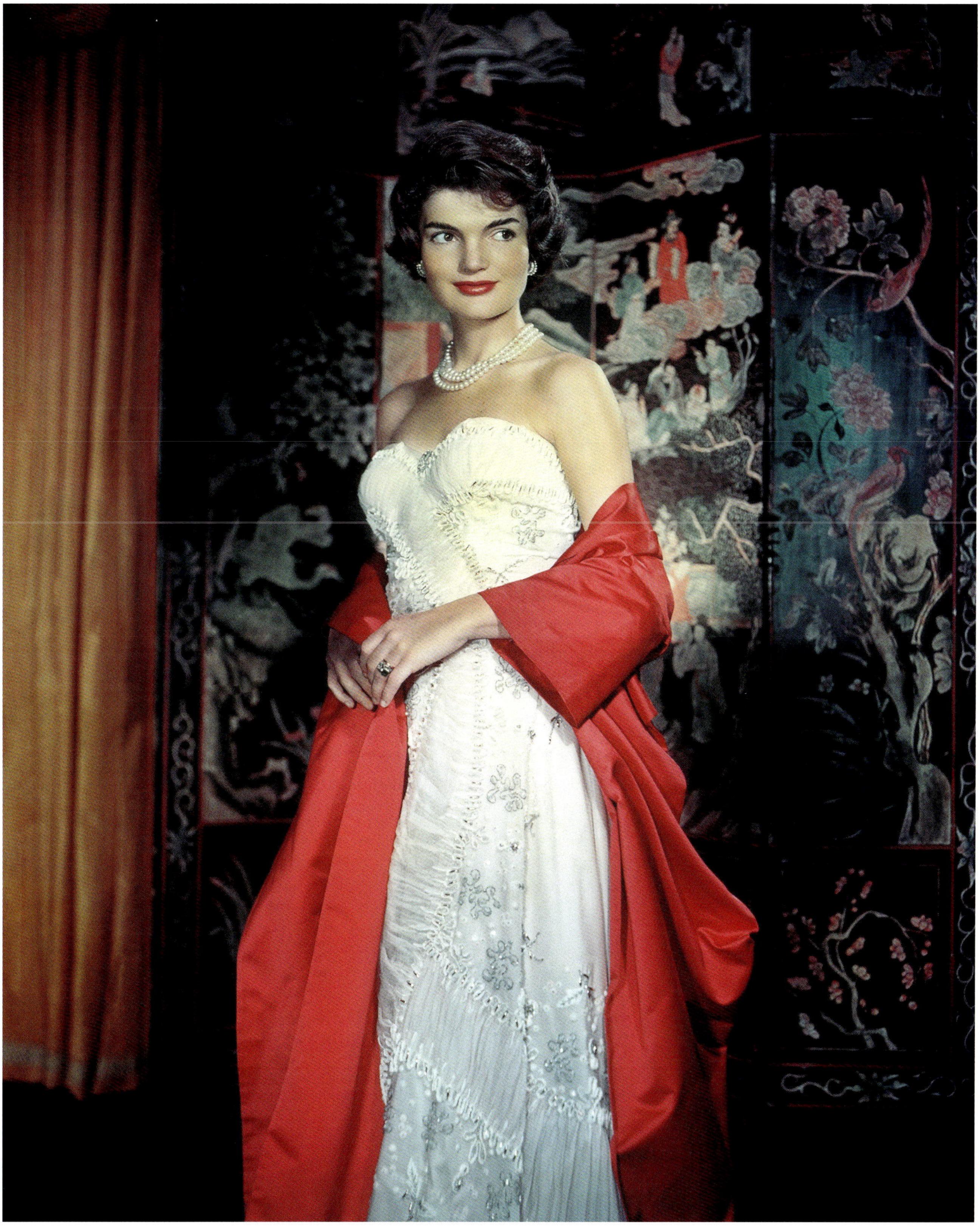

Yousuf Karsh, *Jacqueline Kennedy*, June 14, 1957, Estate of Yousuf Karsh. This translation from an original colour transparency made by Camera Press was created by Yousuf Karsh on October 22, 1990.

Karsh, a devout Catholic throughout his life, photographed church leaders and published collections that included lavish colour photographs depicting individuals and ceremonies in volumes such as *This Is the Mass* (1958), *This Is Rome* (1959), and *These Are the Sacraments* (1962). Although Karsh photographed ecclesiastical portraits using both black-and-white and colour film, the colour versions enhanced the rich reds associated with the ceremonial robes and the theatrical spectacle of spiritual rituals. Karsh's iconic 1949 portrait of Pope Pius XII, posed in reverential prayer, conflates the mortal with the divine and does not hint at the controversial legacy of Pius's action and inaction during the Second World War. The single colour transparency was reproduced as fifty thousand lithographs commissioned by the Vatican for distribution to parishes around the world.[9]

Karsh worked in colour mainly to meet the demands of the publishing market. Although he did create acclaimed portraits using colour film, it was not his preference. As he remarked in 1962, "Even though I had done a great deal of colour portraiture, I do not think there are many colour photographs that provide true artistic satisfaction. Too much of the mechanical element must always be involved; it is not possible—at least not yet—for the photographer to be in full control of the process, rather, he is likely to be its servant.... When the colour picture succeeds, nothing is left for the imagination of the viewer."[10]

Karsh understood the public demand—created and nourished by major publications—for proximity to cherished idols through gazing upon their lifelike, albeit pictorial, presences. He also understood the technical demands in the translation and transmission of his colour portraits for mass circulation. Although he accepted colour portrait commissions, Karsh did so sparingly, aware of the stigma of commercialization that they would accrue from fine art circles. His preference, by training and temperament, was to create less "real" but more psychologically "true" portrait afforded by an infinite monochrome palette.

Experimentation

Although Karsh had crafted his signature approach to commissioned studio portraits and portraits of famous figures, his interest in exploring the creative possibilities of camera-based art persisted. As the demands of his studio commitments, international travel, and publishing projects grew, it became a challenge to find time for self-directed expression. Karsh's exploration of straight photography, montage, and surrealism attests to his keen awareness of contemporary experimentation.

Karsh trained in the soft focus of late Pictorialism, whose adherents, including his mentor, John H. Garo, created photographs with a painterly look, often referencing allegorical or classical themes. As he established his own portrait practice in the 1930s, Karsh worked in the prevailing style of sharp-focus straight photography. This approach gained popular appeal from several directions: his modernist contemporaries of the New Objectivity movement in Germany; illustrated magazines featuring glamorous portraits of Hollywood movie stars; and American photographers exploring the

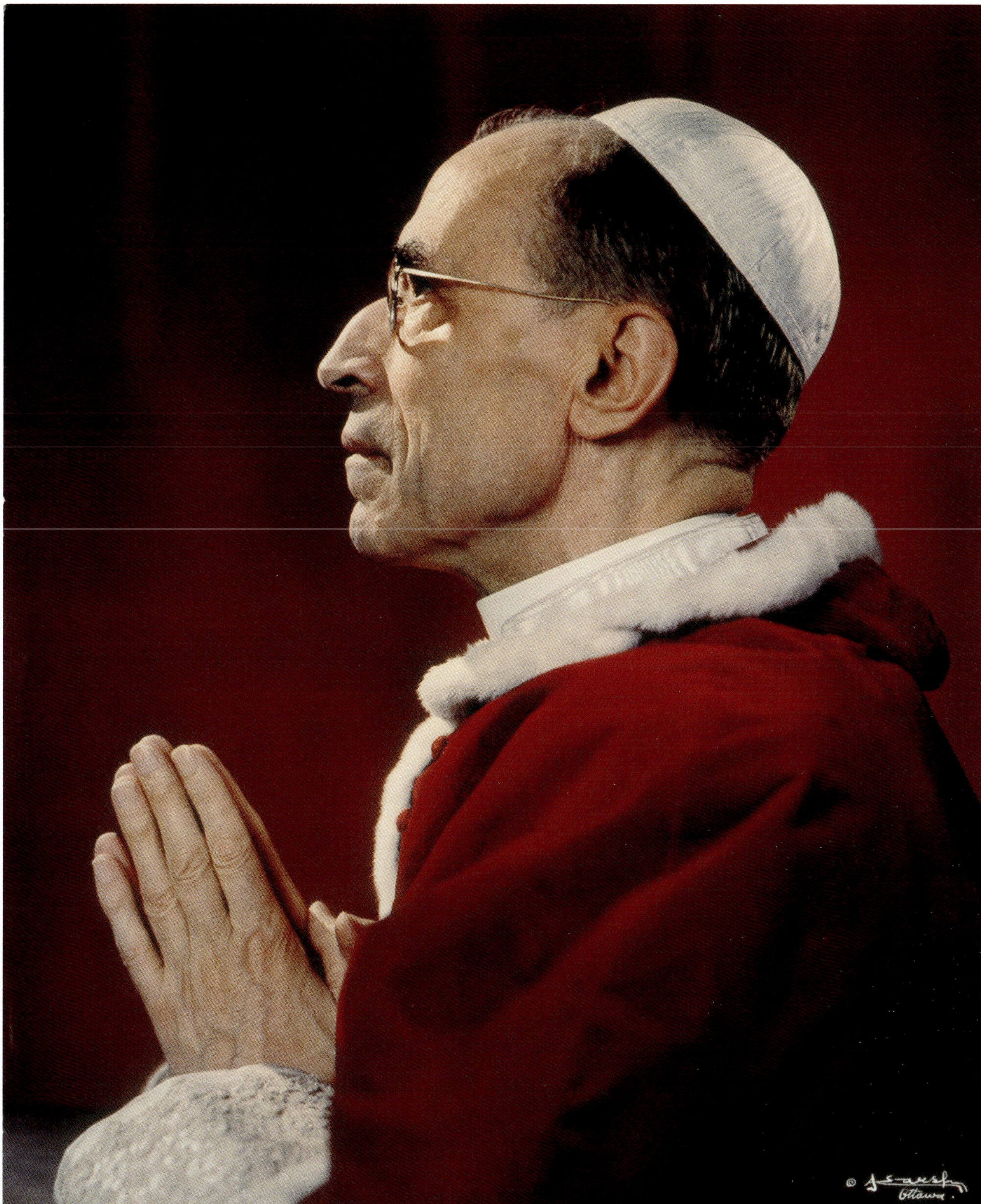

Yousuf Karsh, *Pope Pius XII*, June 16, 1949, positive paper colour dye transfer, 51.4 x 41 cm, Yousuf Karsh Fonds, Library and Archives Canada, Ottawa.

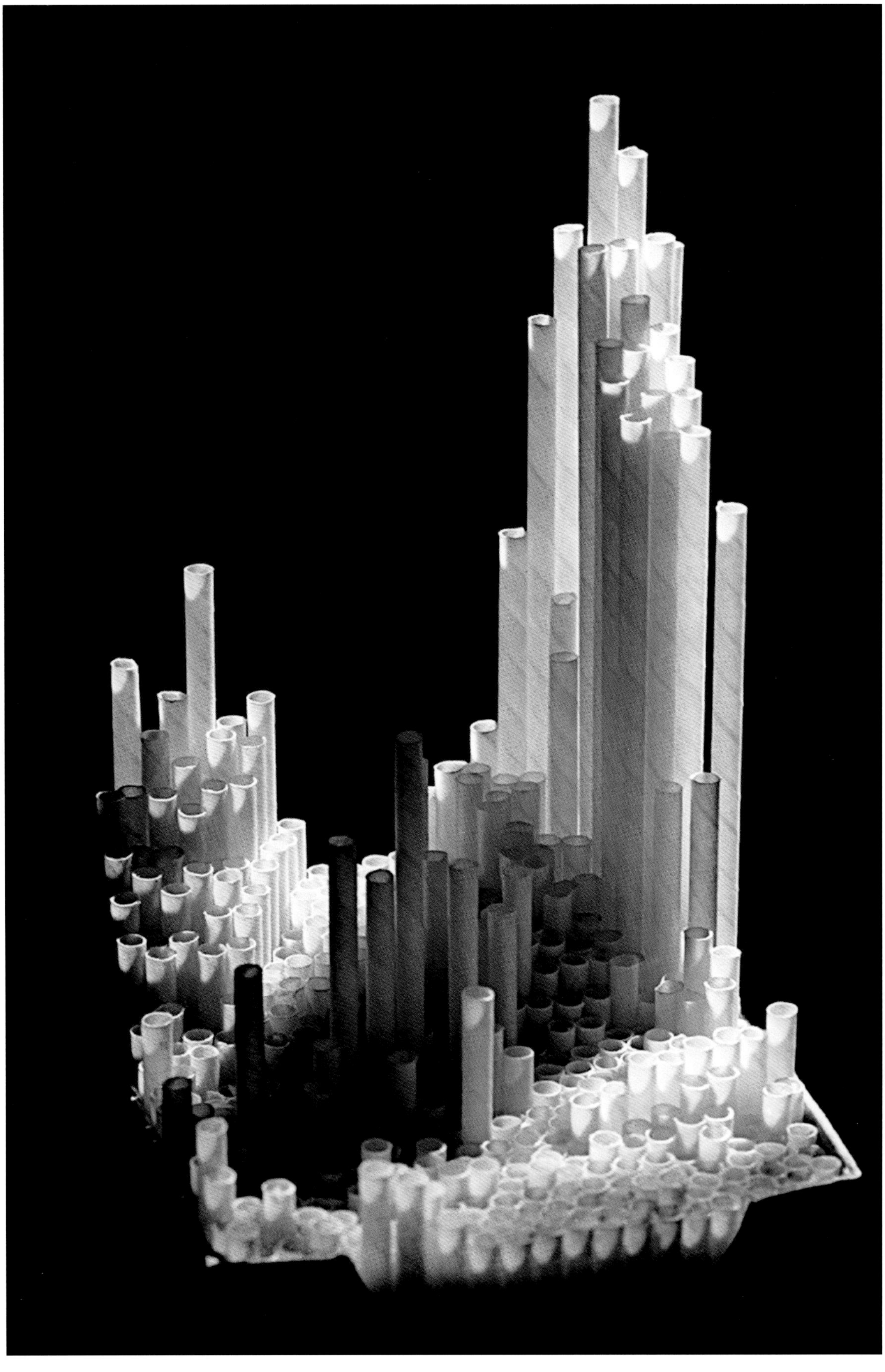

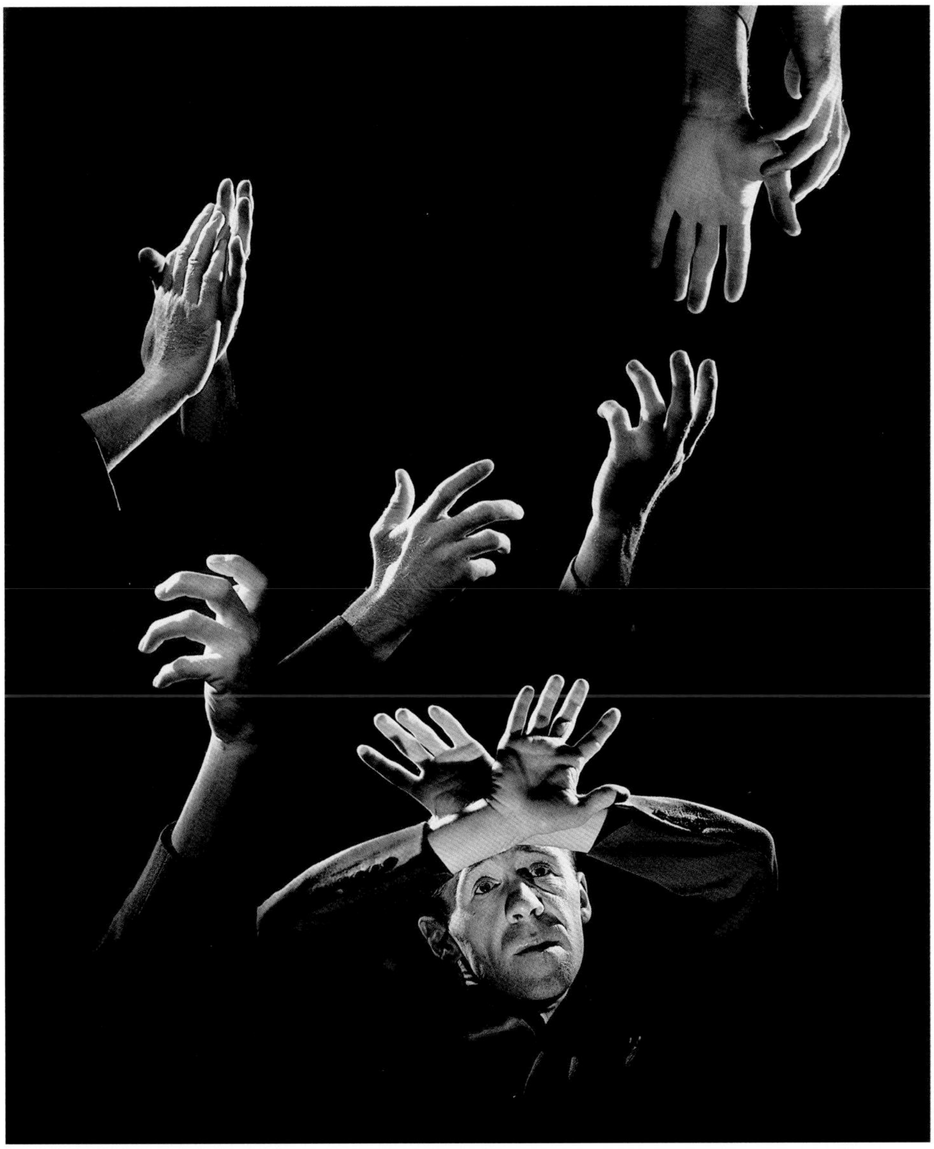

aesthetic possibilities of everyday objects, plants and vegetables, industrial machines, and innovative architecture of the period.

Karsh's first visit to New York City in 1936 left an indelible impression of both the accelerated pace of life and the scale of the built environment of a huge metropolis. In 1940, he created a tabletop tableau composed of drinking straws that uncannily resembled towering skyscrapers. The title of this experimental work, *City of Straws*, 1940, is typical of the ennobling and allegorical titles that art photographers often gave to still-life subjects of the period. The vertiginous perspective of the camera and the variation in the heights of the straws link Karsh to contemporary photographers working in the straight style to create dramatic portraits of real New York City streets, such as Alfred Stieglitz (1864–1946) and Berenice Abbott (1898–1991), who worked under the auspices of the Works Progress Administration.

Opposite: Yousuf Karsh, *City of Straws*, 1940, gelatin silver print, 59.9 x 49.2 cm, Montreal Museum of Fine Arts. Above: Yousuf Karsh, *Hands of Gratien Gélinas*, March 29, 1945, gelatin silver print, 61 x 50.5 cm, Montreal Museum of Fine Arts.

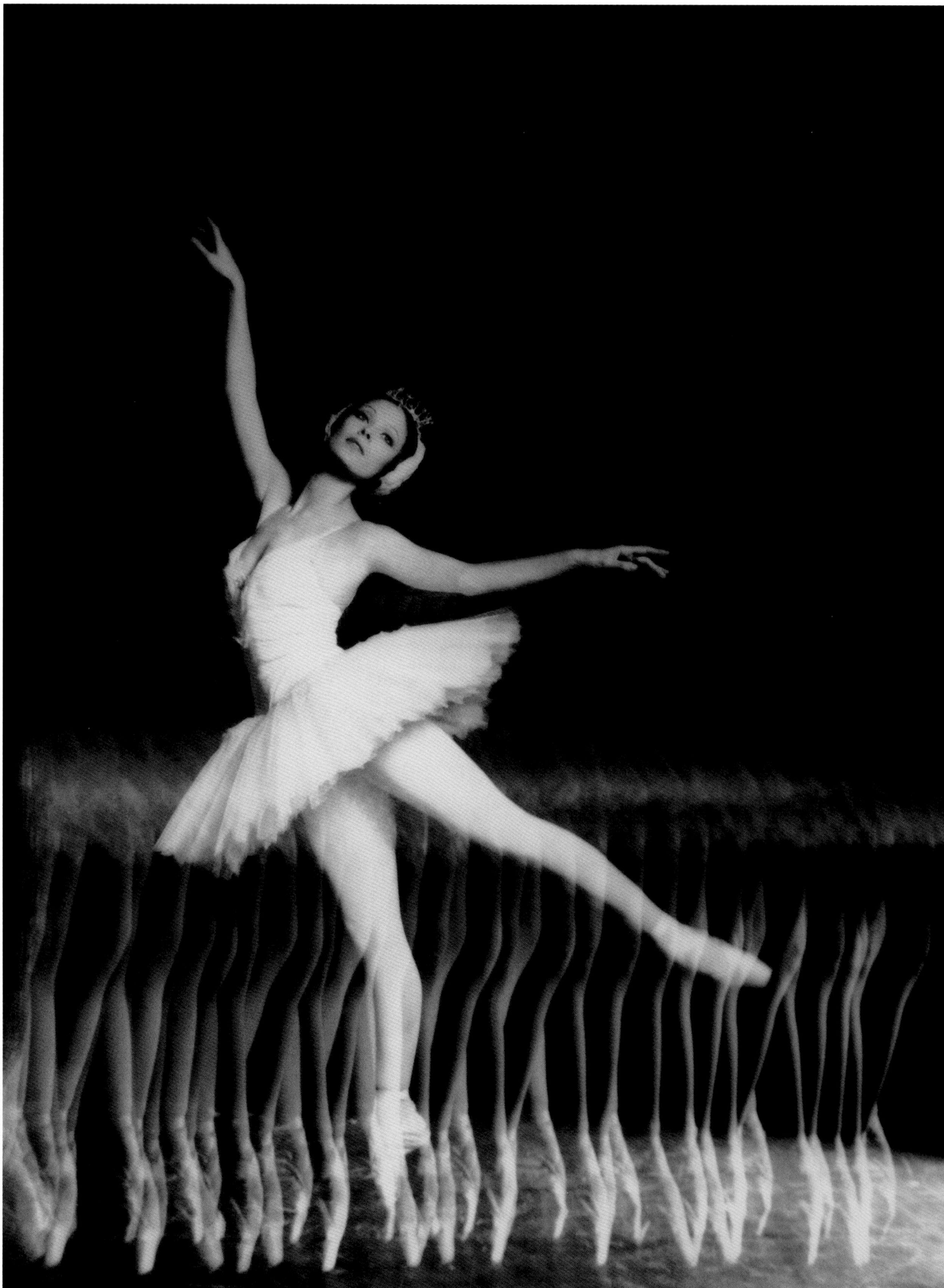

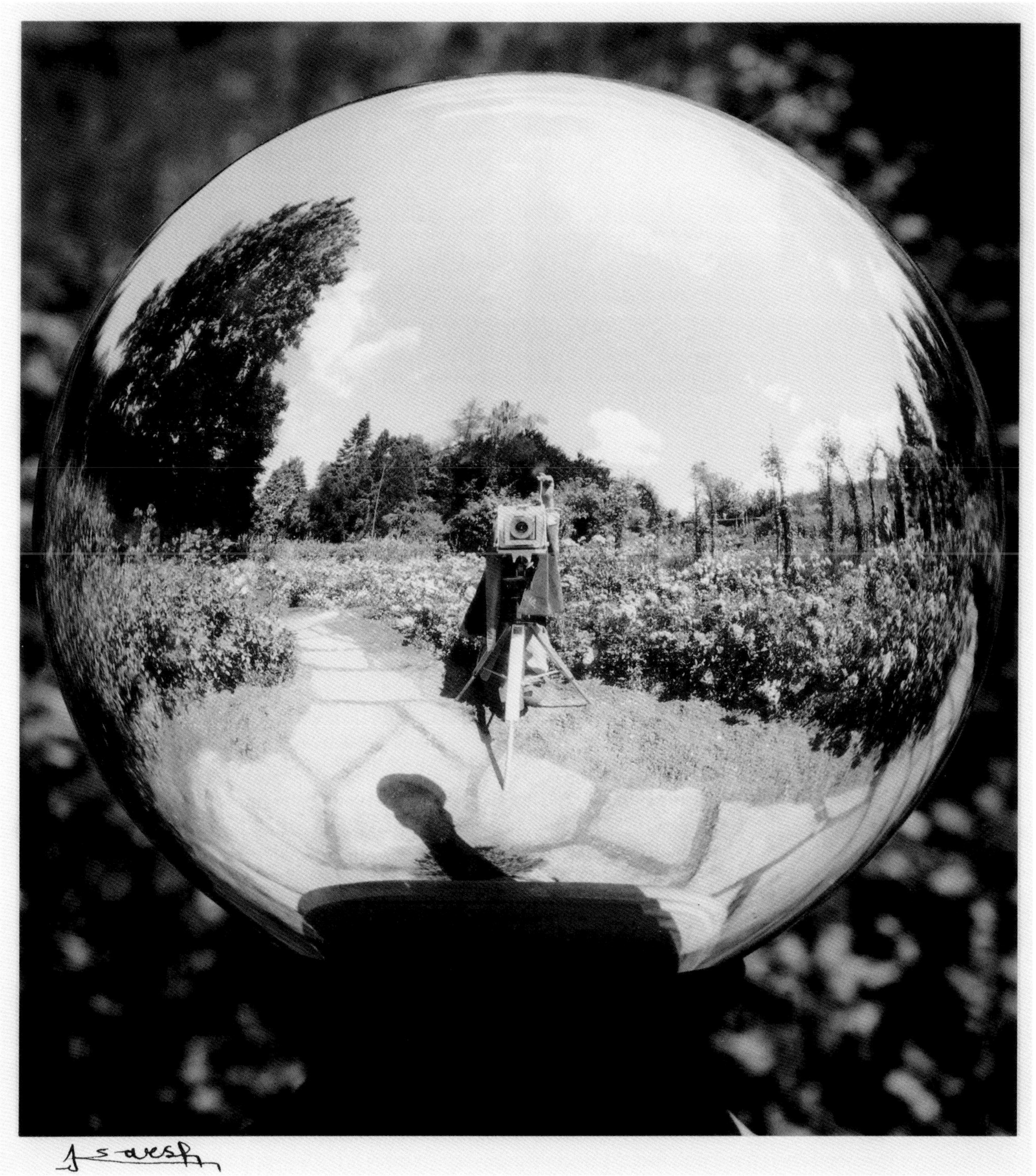

Opposite: Yousuf Karsh, *Karen Kain*, July 1, 1977, gelatin silver print, 50.1 x 40.3 cm, Montreal Museum of Fine Arts. Above: Yousuf Karsh, *Self-Portrait,* 1956, gelatin silver print, 22.2 x 19 cm, Yousuf Karsh Fonds, Library and Archives Canada, Ottawa.

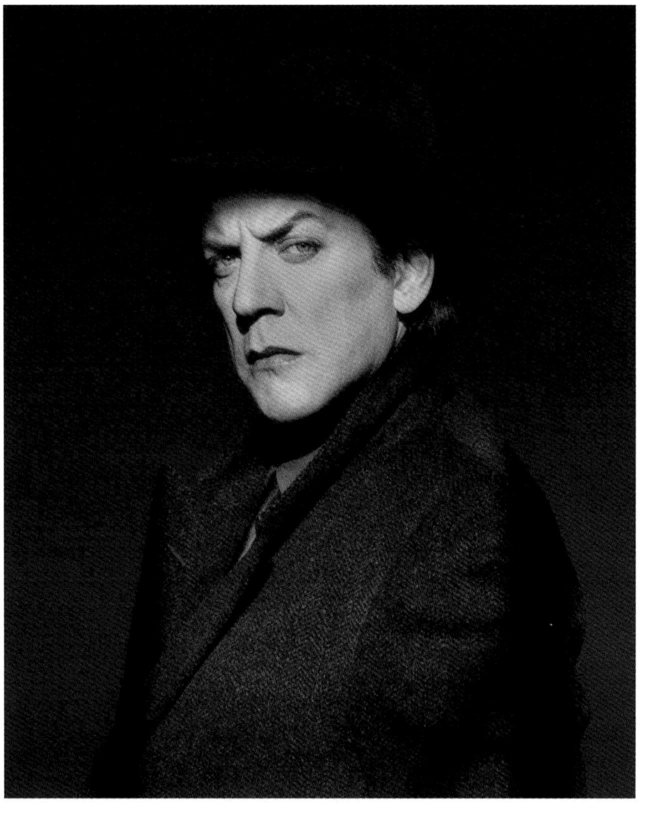

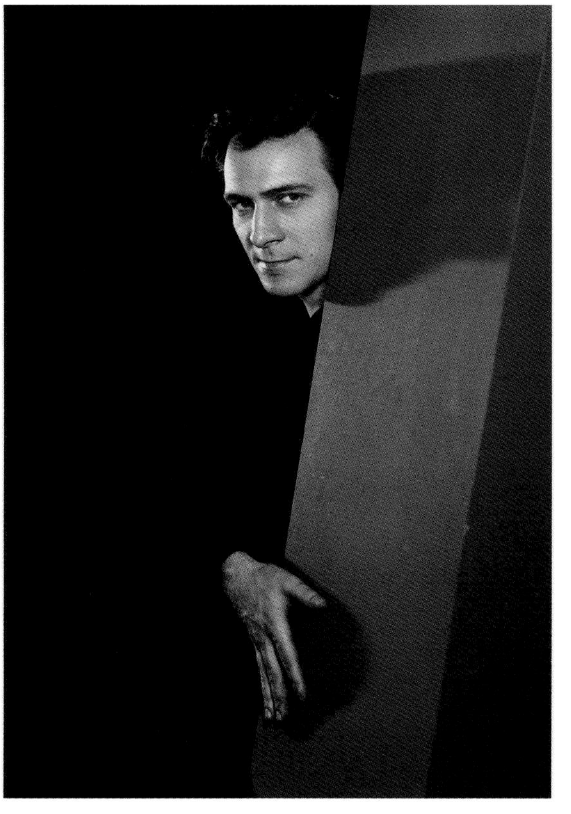

Although most modern photographers preferred the so-called straight print, or direct print, of a single negative, Karsh occasionally combined negatives to create a single composition. By using multiple images to form a final print, Karsh was able to create ideal lighting conditions for both figure and background before merging them. He used this technique extensively in his industrial and commercial photography but also occasionally in his portrait photography when existing backgrounds were inadequate.

He also experimented with combination printing to achieve special effects, as he had done in his print *Elixir*, 1938. In 1945, Karsh photographed celebrated Canadian actor, playwright, and director Gratien Gélinas. He depicts the founder and lead player of the popular Quebec revue *Les Fridolinades* as the everyman anti-hero surrounded by his own gesturing hands, a composition based on several negatives. The composite image suggests the character is being tormented by the winged creatures flying about him.

Karsh experimented with optics and surrealist distortions as well, but this was limited to his personal work rather than paid commissions. In a 1956 self-portrait, Karsh set up his newly acquired large-format Calumet camera along a garden path facing a mirrored orb. Several surrealist tropes are present in this self-portrait: the figure of the photographer is fused with that of his mechanical instrument; it is self-referential, in that both the portrait maker and his subject are present in the mirrored reflection; and the fish-eye distortion prevents the illusion of depth of a vanishing point perspective.

Although Karsh had little time for creative experimentation, his occasional departures demonstrate his awareness of and interest in other photographic genres, giving expression to a playful dimension in his work.

Left: Robert Mapplethorpe, *Donald Sutherland*, 1983, gelatin silver print, 48.7 x 38.6 cm, private collection. Right: Yousuf Karsh, *Christopher Plummer*, April 13, 1959, gelatin silver print, 34.2 x 23.2 cm, Yousuf Karsh Fonds, Library and Archives Canada, Ottawa.

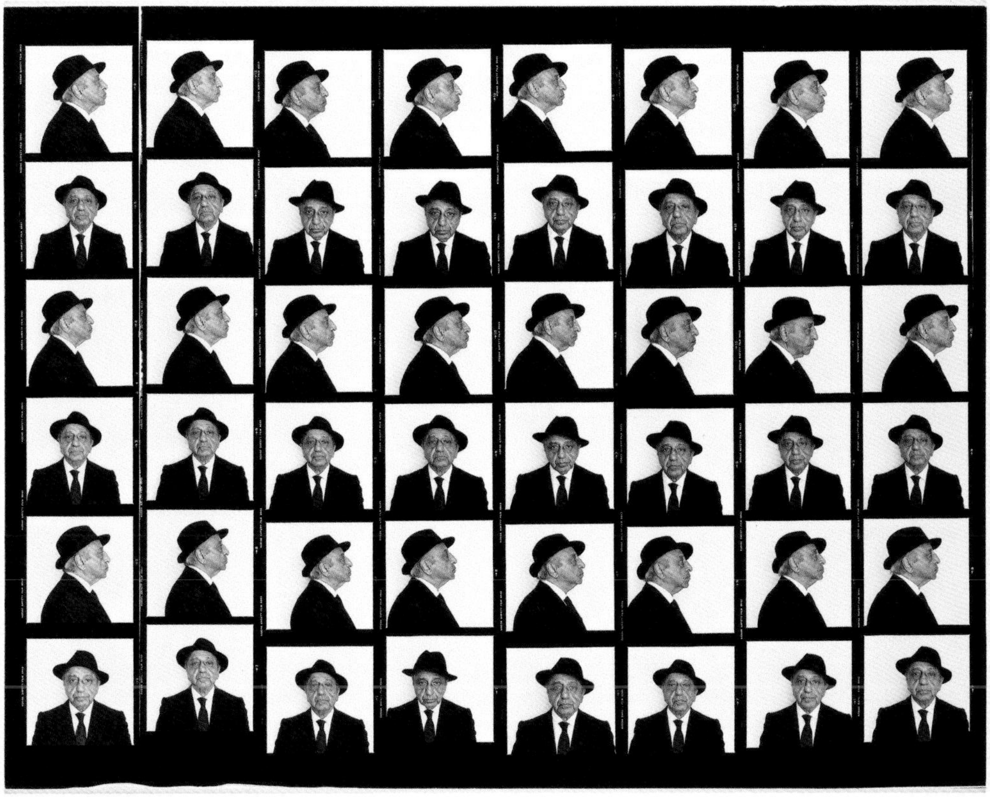

After Karsh

As Karsh approached the final years of his practice, younger artists exploring portraiture began to extend his distinctive style while also questioning the nature of the portrait itself as a fusion of revelation and concealment, direct observation, and constructed fiction.

Karsh's signature classicism can be traced in the work of New York–based Robert Mapplethorpe (1946–1989), whose still-life, nude, and portrait photographs are linked by an emphasis on an austere, dramatic, hard-edged minimalism. Mapplethorpe's portrait of Canadian actor Donald Sutherland features intense light illuminating the actor's face and his wary gaze addressing ours. This intensity echoes Karsh's approach to close-up portraiture, particularly the theatrical impact created by the dramatic lighting in his portrait of another Canadian actor, Christopher Plummer.

With the advent of postmodernist practices during the 1980s, many artists began to decode and reimagine the history of art. Critical to this perspective was an interrogation of the premises of classical portraiture itself: character revealed through facial expression, the authenticity of identity, and the purported portrayal of truth.

In contrast to Karsh's quest for the ultimate singular portrait to define personality, Canadian artist Arnaud Maggs (1926-2012) explored portraiture as a sequence of images. In the series *48 Views*, Maggs depicts his sitters—including Yousuf Karsh—in the manner of police mug shots, directing them to turn toward the camera, and then to the side 48 times. Each frame represents an exact moment in time and is placed within a grid of 48 images. In viewing the resulting "quilt" formed from dozens of nearly identical portraits, the viewer oscillates between perceiving the multitude of parts and desiring to create a continuous and coherent picture.

Arnaud Maggs, *48 Views of Yousuf Karsh*, 1981–83, gelatin silver contact print, 40.6 x 50.8 cm, Stephen Bulger Gallery, Toronto.

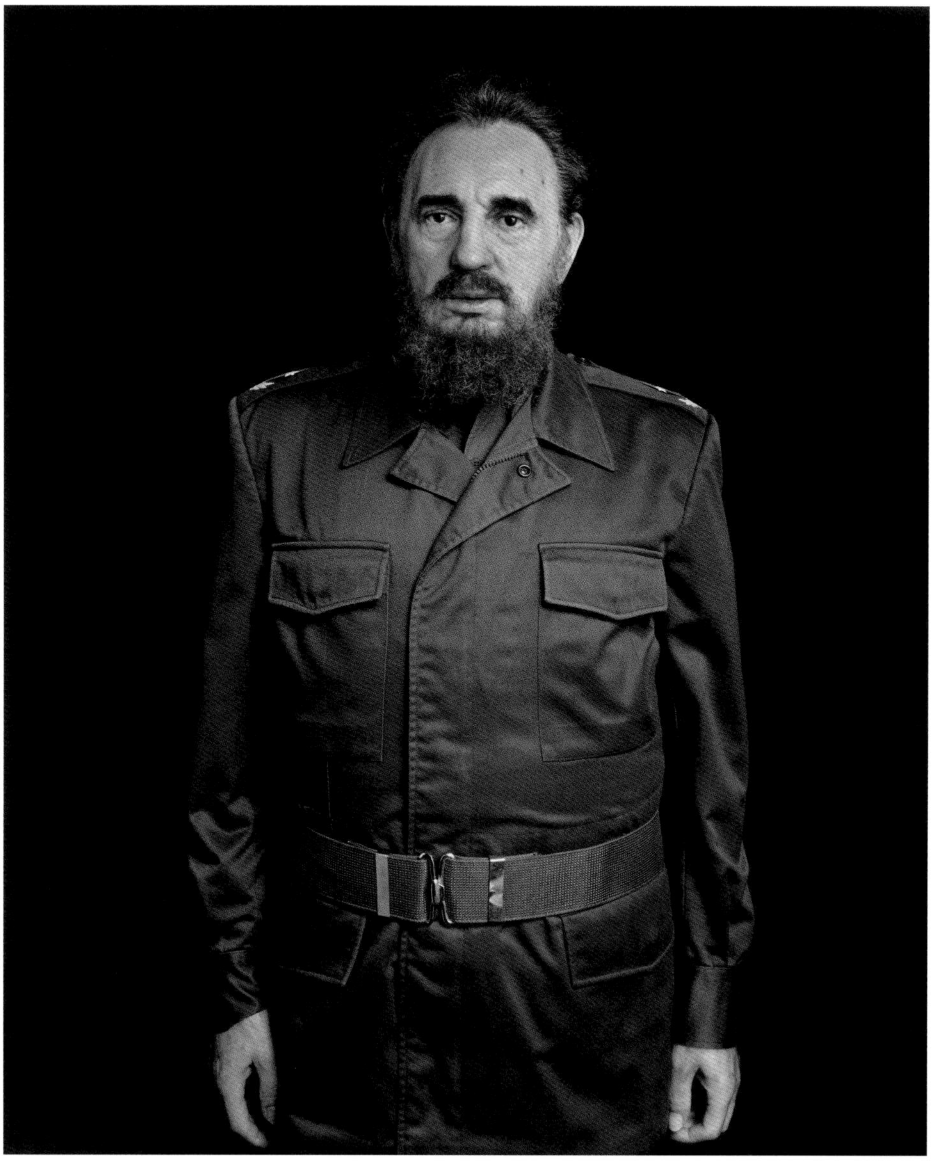

Japanese conceptual artist and architect Hiroshi Sugimoto (b.1948), for example, examines the practice of formal portraiture in his Portraits series, 1994–99. Sugimoto's photographs of historical figures are based on subjects from Madame Tussauds's wax museum. Sugimoto "poses" his sitters, such as Cuban president Fidel Castro, in studio conditions reminiscent of Karsh's style to achieve portraits of sitters who are undeniably famous, yet also inanimate representations of a living figure. Karsh's earlier portrait of Castro is a representation of a living sitter, accorded an authenticity based on Karsh's aesthetic choices, his prestige as a portraitist, and his first-person account of the sitting. Sugimoto disrupts these conventions in his photographic portrayal of a wax figure, provoking an unsettling tension between visual perception and intellectual understanding, and prompting viewers to question how they project and perceive authenticity in the constructed spectacle of personality.

Karsh's signature style was the hallmark of modernist photography for much of the twentieth century: dramatic lighting, minimalist settings, sharp focus, and rich, luscious

Hiroshi Sugimoto, *Fidel Castro*, 2001, gelatin silver print, 93.7 x 74.9 cm, Fraenkel Gallery, San Francisco.

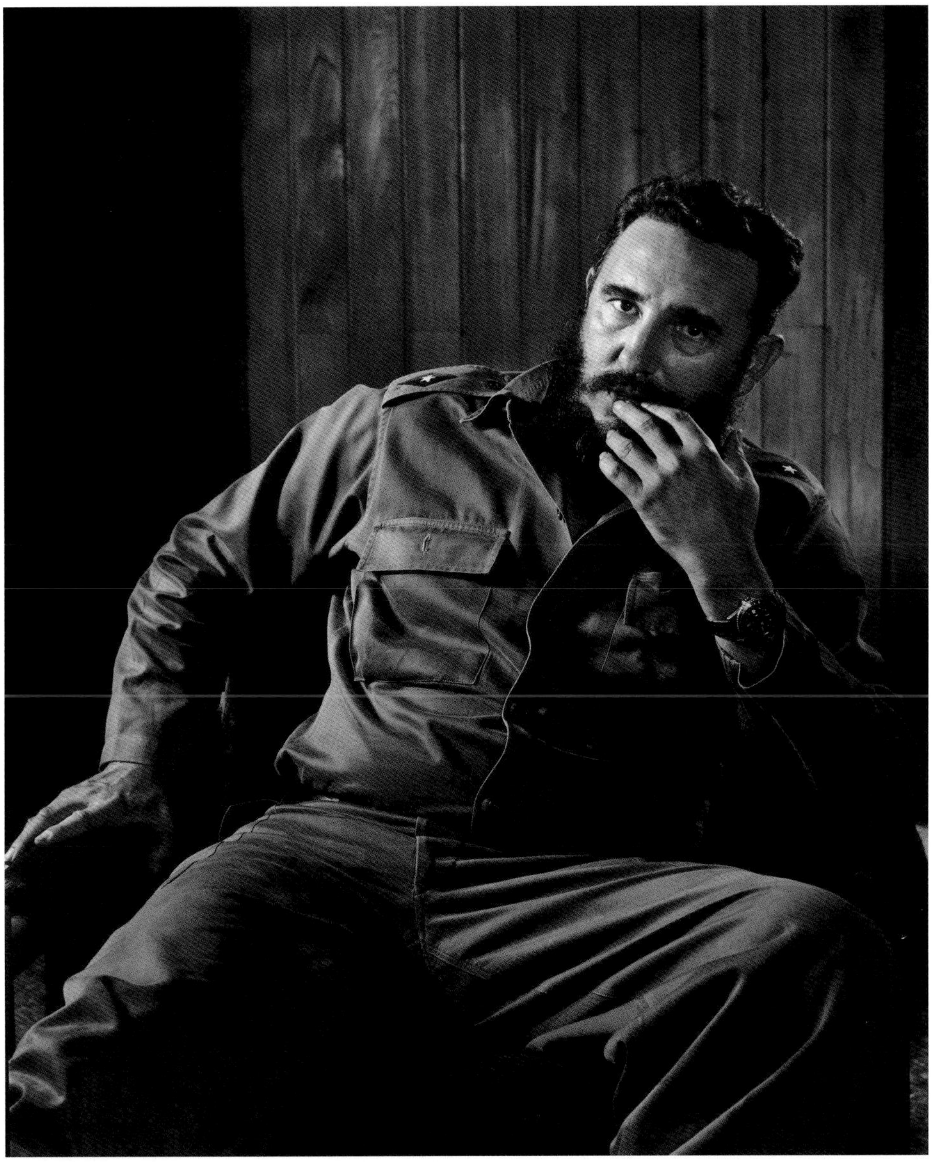

prints. The end of his era of formal portraiture created using film photography coincides with the rise of self-made digital images taken with smartphone cameras. But the so-called memeification of Yousuf Karsh during the first two decades of the twenty-first century has spawned websites dedicated to creating new portraits that pay homage to the master image maker. Browsing crowdsourced media platforms such Flickr and Vimeo reveals content creators exploring Karsh's approach and sharing their results, as well as the mechanisms they use to generate Karsh-style portraits through artificial intelligence.[11]

Through these acts of emulation and interpretation, play and experimentation, Karsh's method of portraiture continues to inspire dynamic engagement. His approach not only endeavours to capture the essence of the individual but also places that individual within the broader context of the social collective. Portraiture, as a blend of vulnerability and performance—expressing both self and of others—remains a potent catalyst for fostering conversation and connection.

Yousuf Karsh, *Fidel Castro*, August 1, 1971, Estate of Yousuf Karsh.

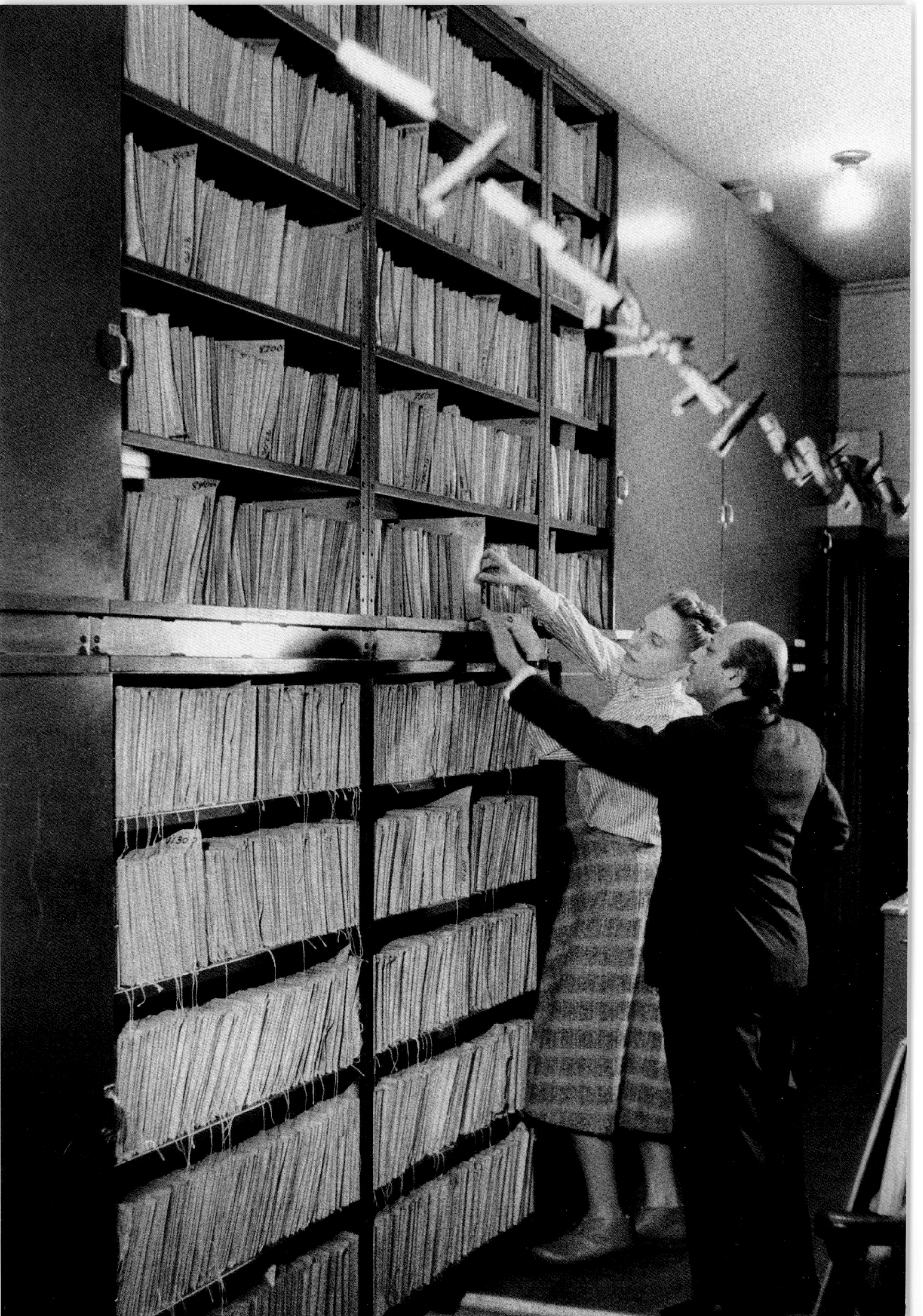

Sources & Resources

Yousuf Karsh's lifetime work is preserved as an extensive archive dispersed across three institutions. Collections of selected portraits are held by many major institutions, and since his death in 2002, Karsh's work continues to attract public interest through major travelling exhibitions. Throughout his career, he produced many luxury editions featuring biographical notes and personal recollections. His 1962 autobiography, *In Search of Greatness*, established the narrative of his formation as a photographer, rise to international acclaim, and interactions with his famous sitters.

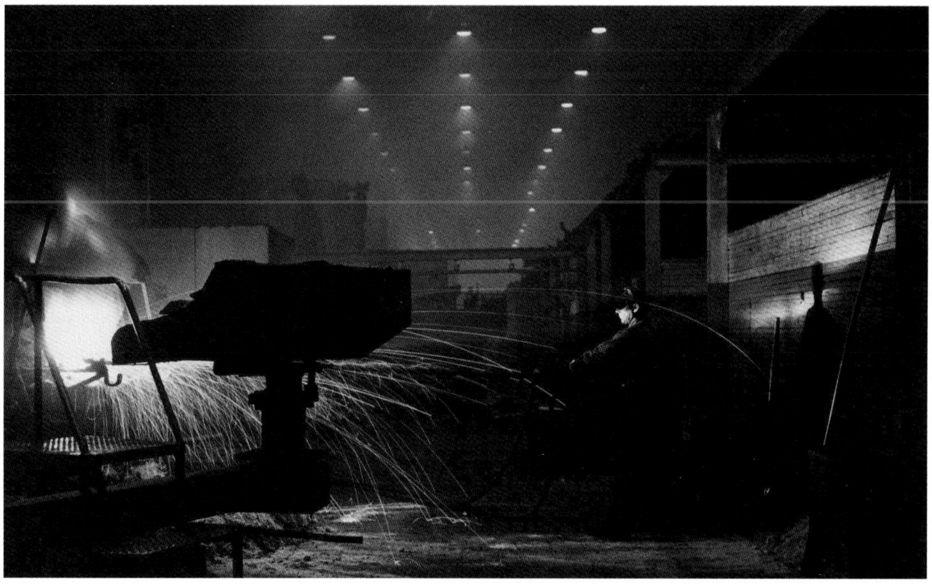

Yousuf Karsh, *Unidentified, Foundry* (detail), 1951, gelatin silver print, 50.5 x 40.1 cm, Art Windsor-Essex.

Key Exhibitions

1938–44
Karsh's work was featured in small displays at the flagship Simpson's store in Toronto, the Château Laurier in Ottawa, and photographic salons at the National Gallery of Canada.

1951
The Men of Ford Canada, Canadian National Exhibition, Toronto

1952
Karsh Portraits, Art Institute of Chicago
Men Who Make Atlas Steel, Charles Francis Press Gallery, New York
Karsh Photographs, N.W. Mutual Exhibition, Layton School of Art, Milwaukee

1953
Karsh, Ford of Canada, Oakville

Opposite: Yousuf Karsh and Librarian/Technician Hella Graber retrieving a filed negative at the Karsh Studio in Ottawa (detail), February 26, 1958, photograph by The Blade/Tom O'Reilly, Library and Archives Canada, Ottawa.

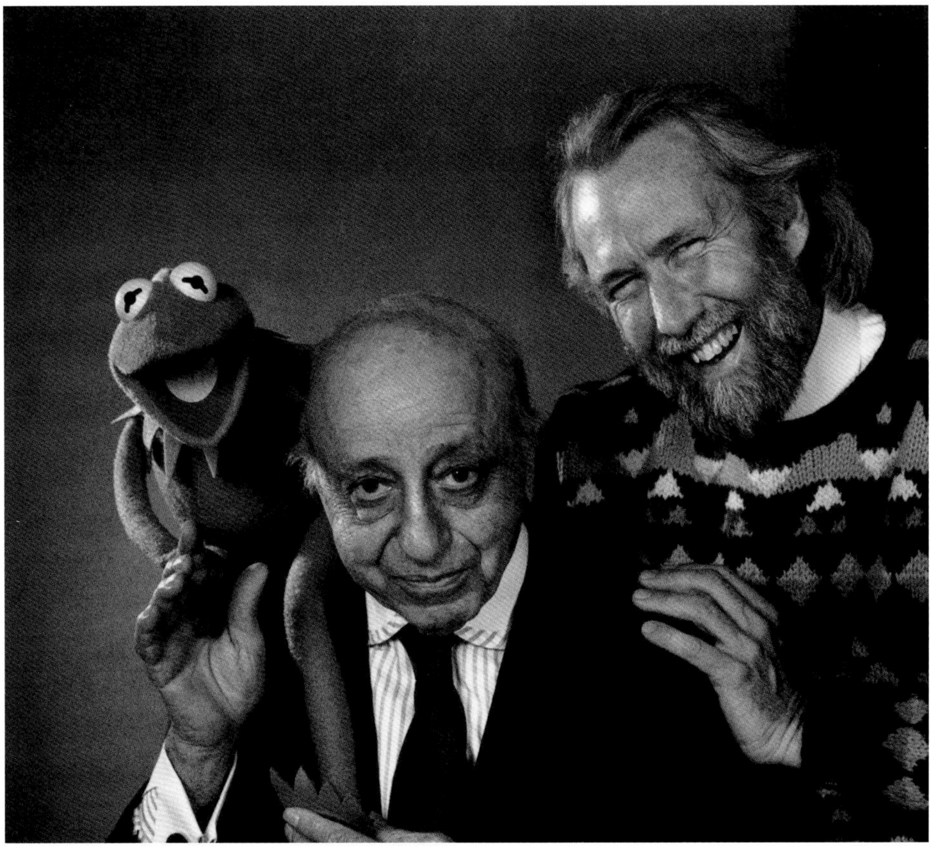

Yousuf Karsh, *Self-Portrait with Jim Henson and Kermit the Frog*, 1990, Estate of Yousuf Karsh.

1958

Portraits by Karsh, Expo 58, Brussels

1959

Karsh Photographs, National Gallery of Canada, Ottawa

1967

Men Who Make Our World, Expo 67, Montreal

Faces of Our Time, Museum of Fine Arts, Boston

1983

Karsh: A Fifty-Year Retrospective, International Center of Photography, New York

1988

Karsh: A Birthday Celebration, Barbican Centre of London

1989

Karsh: The Art of the Portrait, National Gallery of Canada, Ottawa

1991

British Personalities—A Tribute Exhibition, National Portrait Gallery, London

1992

American Legends, International Center of Photography, New York

1998

Karsh in London, Canada House, London

1999

Karsh: Faces of the Twentieth Century, National Portrait Gallery of Australia, Canberra

2000

Yousuf Karsh: Heroes of Light and Shadow, Deutsches Historisches Museum, Berlin
Karsh, Nagoya / Boston Museum of Fine Arts, Nagoya

Posthumous Exhibitions

2003

Karsh Portraits: Legends, Naples Museum of Art, Florida
Yousuf Karsh: Through the Lens, Whyte Museum of the Canadian Rockies, Banff

2004

Yousuf Karsh: Industrial Images, Art Gallery of Windsor, Ontario

2006

Yousuf Karsh: Portraits, Théâtre de la Photographie et de l'Image, Nice

2007

Yousuf Karsh Photographs, Kresge Art Museum, Michigan State University, East Lansing
Yousuf Karsh: Portraits, Canadian Cultural Centre, Paris

2008

Tribute to Karsh's 100th Birthday, National Portrait Gallery, London
In the Public Eye: Photography and Fame, Nelson-Atkins Museum of Art, Kansas City, Missouri
Karsh, Leonard, and Bagert: A Photographic Legacy, Polk Museum of Art, Lakeland, Florida

2009

Karsh: Image Maker, Canada Science and Technology Museum with the Portrait Gallery of Canada, Ottawa
Karsh Centenary Exhibition, The Camera Press Gallery, London
Karsh at 100: Portraits of Artists, Embassy of Canada, Washington, D.C.
In the Company of Artists, Detroit Institute of Arts
Behind the Words: Literary Portraits by Yousuf Karsh, Boston Public Library
Karsh 100: A Biography in Images, Museum of Fine Arts, Boston
Karsh 100: Faces of Our Time, Seoul Art Center
'Karshed': Yousuf Karsh Selected Portraits, McMichael Canadian Art Collection, Kleinburg
Yousuf Karsh: Industrial Images, McMichael Canadian Art Collection, Kleinburg
Yousuf Karsh: Regarding Heroes, Art Institute of Chicago

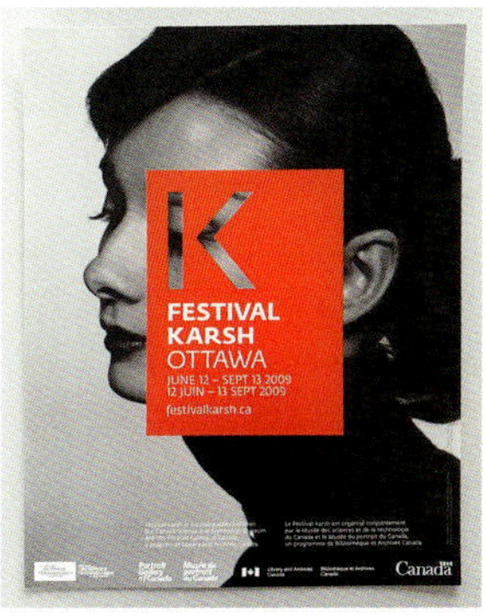

Poster for Festival Karsh, organized by the Portrait Gallery of Canada (as part of Library and Archives Canada, Ottawa) and the Canada Science and Technology Museum, Ottawa, June 12 to September 13, 2009.

2010

A Retrospective Look at the Career of Yousuf Karsh, Monterey Museum of Art, California
Karsh 100: A Biography in Images, Los Angeles Public Library
Yousuf Karsh: Regarding Heroes, USC Fisher Museum of Art, Los Angeles; Winnipeg Art Gallery
Karsh: Image Maker, Art Gallery of Alberta, Edmonton

2011

Karsh: Celebrating Humanity, Armenian Museum of America, Watertown, Massachusetts
Portrait Maestro KARSH, Sejong Center, Seoul
Yousuf Karsh and Edward Steichen: The Art of the Celebrity Portrait, McCord Museum, Montreal
Karsh: Regarding Heroes, Kalamazoo Institute of Arts, Michigan; Glenbow Museum, Calgary

2014

Yousuf Karsh: American Portraits, National Portrait Gallery, Washington, D.C.
Yousuf Karsh: Icons of the 20th Century, Mona Bismarck American Center for Art and Culture, Paris

2015

Karsh Goes Hollywood, Museum of Fine Arts, Boston

2016

Yousuf Karsh: Icons of the 20th Century, Bellagio Gallery of Fine Arts, Las Vegas

2018

Yousuf Karsh: American Portraits, Lowe Art Museum, Coral Gables;
Dayton Art Institute; Jimmy Carter Presidential Library and Museum, Atlanta

2019

Yousuf Karsh: American Portraits, The Rockwell Museum, Corning, New York

2021

The World of Yousuf Karsh: A Private Essence, Montreal Museum of Fine Arts

2022

The World of Yousuf Karsh: A Private Essence, Canadian Museum of Immigration at Pier 21, Halifax

2023

Influence and Identity [group exhibition], Irish Museum of Modern Art, Dublin

2024

Royal Portraits: A Century of Photography [group exhibition], Royal Collection Trust, King's Gallery, London

---

Archival Collections

Library and Archives Canada, Yousuf Karsh Fonds. Acquired between 1987 and 1998, the Fonds consists of over 350,000 negatives, photographic prints, and transparencies representing Karsh's creative output between 1932 and 1993. It also includes business papers, publishing projects, magazine tearsheets, personal correspondence, scrapbooks, awards and honours, and recorded interviews.

Canada Science and Technology Museum, Karsh of Ottawa Collection. At the close of the Karsh Studio, more than 385 pieces of Yousuf Karsh's photographic equipment, including lights, cameras, darkroom equipment, and retouching accessories, were transferred to the national collection.

Estate of Yousuf Karsh (Karsh.org). This is a comprehensive online resource with a complete digitized inventory of more than fifteen thousand portrait sittings and biographical notes about Karsh's sitters.

Museum Collections

Amon Carter Museum, Fort Worth
Art Institute of Chicago
Bibliothèque nationale de France, Paris
Detroit Institute of Fine Arts
Deutsches Historisches Museum, Berlin
George Eastman House, Rochester
Glenbow Museum, Calgary
Huntington Library, San Marino, California
International Center of Photography, New York
Metropolitan Museum of Art, New York
Montreal Museum of Fine Arts
Museum of Fine Arts, Boston
Museum of Modern Art, New York
National Gallery of Australia, Canberra
National Gallery of Canada, Ottawa
National Museum of Modern Art, Tokyo
National Portrait Gallery, London
National Portrait Gallery, Washington, D.C.
Philadelphia Museum of Art
Royal Library and Royal Archives, Windsor, England
Scottish National Portrait Gallery, Edinburgh

Selected Publications by Yousuf Karsh

Karsh, Yousuf. *Faces of Destiny: Portraits by Karsh.* Chicago: Ziff-Davis Publishing Company, 1946.
———. *Portraits of Greatness.* Toronto: University of Toronto Press, 1959.
———. *In Search of Greatness: Reflections of Yousuf Karsh.* Toronto: University of Toronto Press, 1962.
———. *Karsh Portfolio.* Toronto: University of Toronto Press, 1967.
———. *Faces of Our Time.* Toronto and Buffalo: University of Toronto Press, 1971.
———. *Karsh Portraits.* Toronto: University of Toronto Press, 1976.
———. *Karsh Canadians.* Toronto: University of Toronto Press, 1978.
———. *Karsh: A Fifty-Year Retrospective.* Boston and Toronto: Little, Brown and Company, 1986.
———. *Karsh: American Legends.* Boston: Bulfinch Press, 1992.
———. *Karsh: A Sixty-Year Retrospective.* Boston and Toronto: Little, Brown and Company, 1996.
Karsh, Yousuf, and John Fisher. *Karsh and Fisher See Canada.* Toronto: Thomas Allen Limited, 1960.

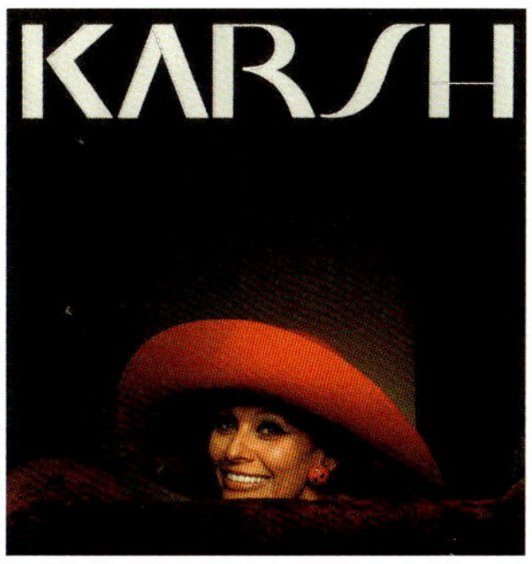

Cover of *Karsh: A Sixty-Year Retrospective*, by Yousuf Karsh (Boston and Toronto: Little, Brown and Company, 1996).

Selected Writings on Yousuf Karsh

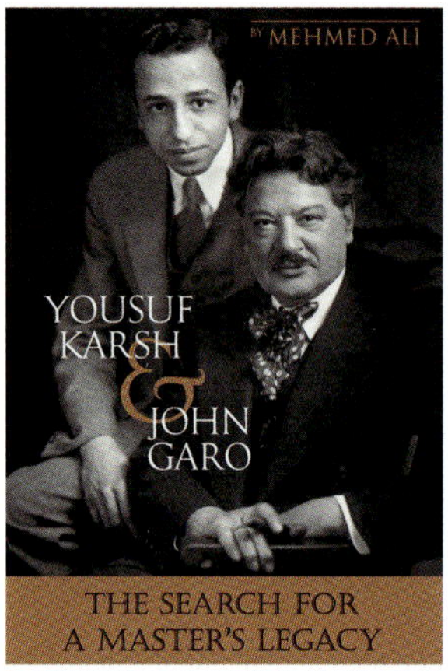

Cover of *Yousuf Karsh & John Garo: The Search for a Master's Legacy*, by Mehmed Ali (Mansfield, MA: Benna Books, 2016).

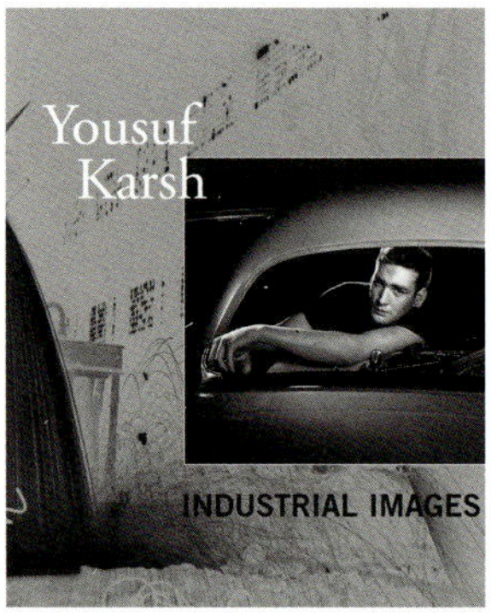

Cover of *Yousuf Karsh: Industrial Images*, by Cassandra Getty and Jerry Fielder (Windsor, ON: Art Gallery of Windsor, 2007).

Ali, Mehmed. *Yousuf Karsh & John Garo: The Search for a Master's Legacy*. Mansfield, MA: Benna Books, 2016.

Borcoman, James, ed. *Karsh: The Art of the Portrait*. Ottawa: National Gallery of Canada, 1989.

"Camera Notes; PSA Honors Four from New York—Contests." *New York Times*, October 5, 1947.

Danziger, James, and Barnaby Conrad III. *Interviews with Master Photographers: Minor White, Imogen Cunningham, Cornell Capa, Elliott Erwitt, Yousuf Karsh, Arnold Newman, Lord Snowdon, Brett Weston*. New York: Paddington Press, 1977.

Delaney, Jill. "Karsh and the Face of Canada." In *Yousuf Karsh: Heroes of Light and Shadow*, edited by Dieter Vorsteher and Janet Yates, 187–94. Toronto: Stoddart Publishing Company Ltd., 2001.

Deschin, Jacob. "Musicians Viewed by Six Photographers." *New York Times*, December 21, 1947.

Donegan, Rosemary. "Karsh's Working Man: Industrial Tensions and Cold War Anxieties." In *Yousuf Karsh: Heroes of Light and Shadow*, edited by Dieter Vorsteher and Janet Yates, 153–61. Toronto: Stoddart Publishing Company Ltd., 2001.

Fielder, Jerry. "John Buchan and Yousuf Karsh." *The John Buchan Journal* 50 (2017): 9–19. https://johnbuchansociety.co.uk/wp-content/uploads/2023/03/JBS-Journal-050-Inside-Contents.pdf.

Getty, Cassandra, and Jerry Fielder. *Yousuf Karsh: Industrial Images*. Windsor, ON: Art Gallery of Windsor, 2007.

Koltun, Lilly. "Framing a New Light: Karsh Addresses the Audience of the Theater and the Press." In *Yousuf Karsh: Heroes of Light and Shadow*, edited by Dieter Vorsteher and Janet Yates, 123–36. Toronto: Stoddart Publishing Company Ltd., 2001.

———. "'In Your Own Drama, You Are the Star': Portraiture Subjects Drawn from Cultural Life in Canadian Photography, circa 1895–1955." PhD diss., University of St. Andrews, 1996.

———. "The Karsh Collection." In *Karsh: The Art of the Portrait*, edited by James Borcoman, 141–50. Ottawa: National Gallery of Canada, 1989.

———. "Yousuf Karsh: Frame, Focus, Fame." In *Yousuf Karsh Portraits*. Nice: Musée des Beaux-Arts Nice, 2006.

Kramer, Hilton. "'Portrait Photographs'—A Historic Collision." *New York Times*, September 14, 1969.

Lesser, Rebecca. "By the Side of the 'Roaring Lion': Yousuf Karsh's Portrait of Winston Churchill and British/Canadian Wartime Relations." MA thesis, University of Calgary, 2010.

Museum of Fine Arts, Boston. *Karsh: A Biography in Images*. Boston: MFA Publications, 2003.

Newton, Gael. "Curatorial Essay: The Vision of Yousuf Karsh and His Photographs of the Illustrious Greats of Japan." *The Good, the Great & the Gifted: Camera Portraits by Yousuf Karsh and Athol Shmith of Melbourne*, National Gallery Exhibition History, National Gallery of Australia, accessed October 23, 2024, https://nga.gov.au/exhibitions/the-good-the-great-the-gifted.

Opp, James. "Picturing Communism: Yousuf Karsh, Canadair, and Cold War Advertising." *Queen's Quarterly* 118, no. 4 (Winter 2011): 584–97.

———. "Still Photographs, Publicity, and the Making of Cecil B. DeMille's *Ten Commandments* (1956)." *Film History* 34, no. 4 (January 2022): 1–29.
Rombout, Melissa. "Approaching the Legends of Yousuf Karsh." *Queen's Quarterly* 105 (Winter 1998): 586–99.
———. *Karsh: Faces of the Twentieth Century*. Canberra: National Portrait Gallery of Australia, 1998.
———. "Karsh in London." *Archivist* 116 (1998): 15–19.
Teodorescu, Ioana. "Karsh: Image Maker / Créateur d'images." *Material Culture Review* 70 (Fall 2009): 82–87.
Tippett, Maria. *The Life of Yousuf Karsh: Portrait in Light and Shadow*. Toronto: House of Anansi Press Inc., 2007.
Travis, David, ed. *Karsh: Beyond the Camera*. Boston: David R. Godine, 2012.
———. *Yousuf Karsh: Regarding Heroes*. Boston: David R. Godine, 2009

Audio and Video about the Artist

A Conversation with Estrellita Karsh. Museum of Fine Arts, Boston, 2021, 17 min. 50 sec. https://www.youtube.com/watch?v=FGlkOoyQ8h4.
Hillel, Joseph, dir. *Karsh Is History*. 2009, 52 min.
Rasky, Harry, dir. *The Searching Eye*. 1986, 1 hr. 22 min.
60 Minutes with Morley Safer: Hero Worship. CBS Inc., 1977, 10 min. Library and Archives Canada 314077.
Ten Minutes with Yousuf Karsh. Canadian Broadcasting Corporation, 1962, video, 9 min. 25 sec. Library and Archives Canada 314061.
"Yousuf Karsh: Pursuing Greatness." Podcast interview with Dr. Robert Evans (photohistorian) and Dr. Jill Delaney (photo-archivist). Episode 23, Library and Archives Canada, July 28, 2015, 50 min. 54 sec. https://library-archives.canada.ca/eng/collection/engage-learn/podcast/Pages/yousuf-karsh-pursuing-greatness.aspx.

Further Reading

Bassnett, Sarah, and Sarah Parsons. *Photography in Canada, 1839–1989: An Illustrated History*. Toronto: Art Canada Institute, 2023.
Loengard, John. *Celebrating the Negative*. New York: Arcade Publishing, 1994.
Lutz, Catherine, and Jane Collins. "The Photograph as an Intersection of Gazes: The Example of *National Geographic*," *Journal for the Society of Visual Anthropology* 7, no. 1 (March 1991): 134–49.
Lyons, Nathan, ed. *Contemporary Photographers: Toward a Social Landscape*, New York: Horizon Press, 1966.
Marien, Mary Warner. *Photography: A Cultural History*. New Jersey: Prentice-Hall, 2011.
Schwartz, Joan M. "Salon Crescendo / 1930–1940." In *Private Realms of Light: Amateur Photography in Canada, 1839–1940*, edited by Lilly Koltun, 88–113. Toronto: Fitzhenry & Whiteside, 1984.
Sekula, Allan. "The Body and the Archive." In *The Contest of Meaning: Critical Histories of Photography*, edited by Richard Bolton, 343–89. Cambridge, MA: MIT Press, 1989

Next page: Yousuf Karsh, *Peter Lorre* (detail), February 3, 1946, gelatin silver print, 47.2 × 40.2 cm (image), 71.3 x 56 cm (mount), Estate of Yousuf Karsh.

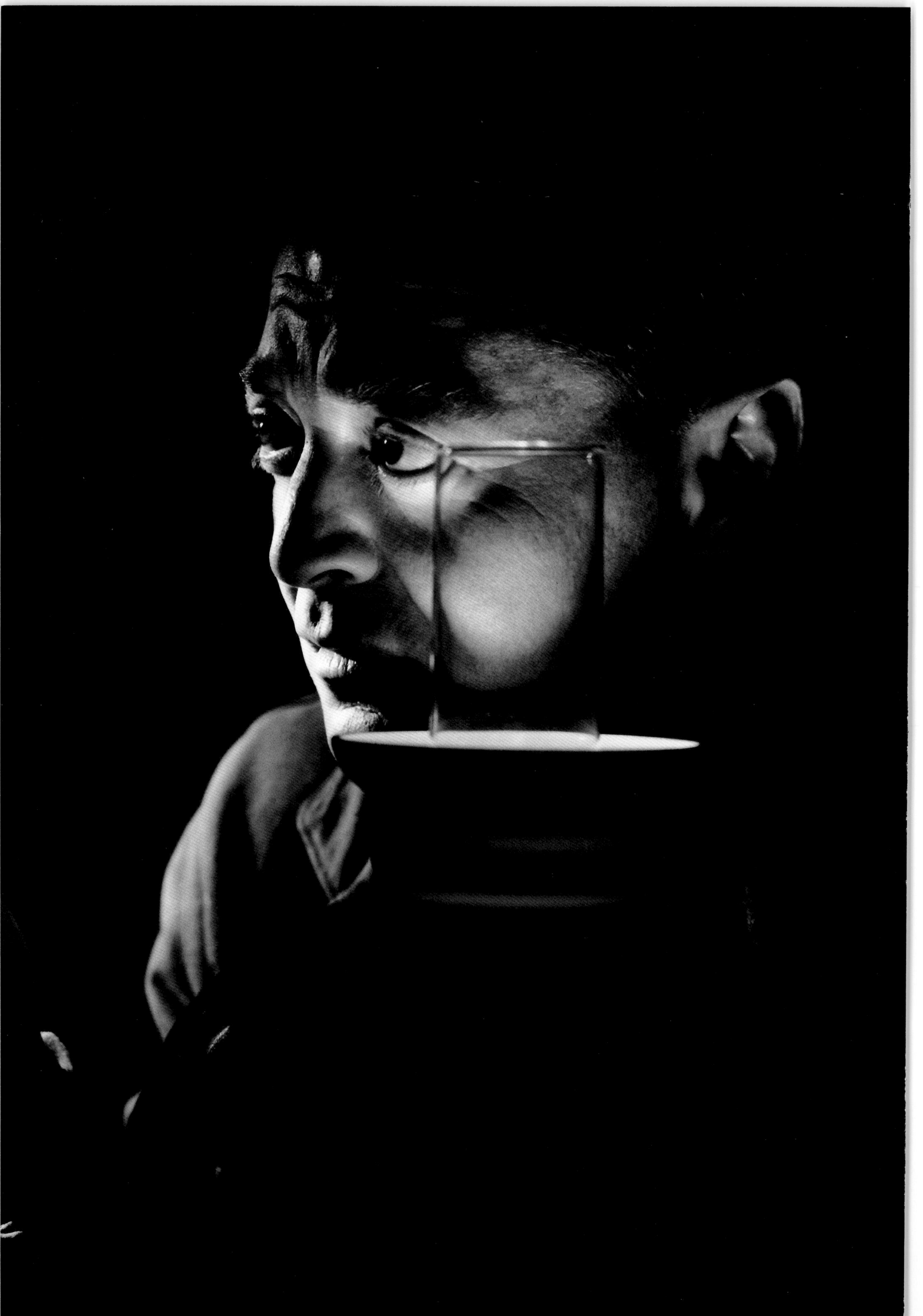

Where to See

The works of Yousuf Karsh are held in public and private collections in Canada and internationally. Although the following institutions hold the works listed below, they may not always be on view.

Art Gallery of Alberta

2 Sir Winston Churchill Square
Edmonton, Alberta, Canada
780-422-6223
youraga.ca

Yousuf Karsh, *Winston Churchill*,
December 30, 1941, printed before 1972
Gelatin silver print, 50 x 39.7 cm

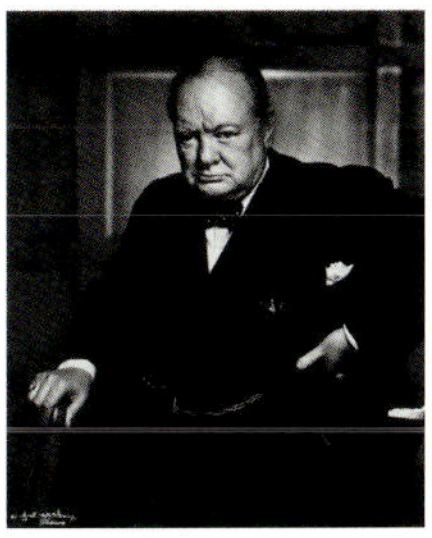

Art Windsor-Essex

401 Riverside Drive West
Windsor, Ontario, Canada
519-977-0013
artwindsoressex.ca

Yousuf Karsh, *Unidentified, Foundry*, 1951
Gelatin silver print
50.5 cm x 40.1 cm

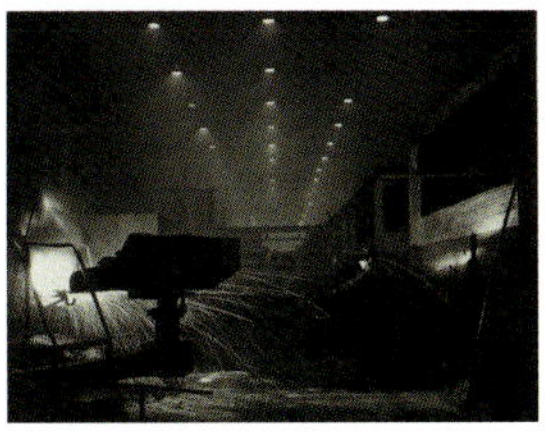

Library and Archives Canada

395 Wellington Street
Ottawa, Ontario, Canada
613-996-5115
canada.ca/en/library-archives.html

1. Yousuf Karsh, *Akira Kurosawa*,
   November 1, 1969
   Gelatin silver print
   34.1 x 27.2 cm
2. Yousuf Karsh, *Ambassador Vijaya Lakshmi Pandit*, October 2, 1949
   Gelatin silver print
   24 x 19.2 cm (image), 35.3 x 28 cm (sheet)
3. Yousuf Karsh, *Anita Ekberg*,
   March 28, 1956
   Colour transparency
   25.4 x 30.3 cm
4. Yousuf Karsh, *Beatrice Lillie*,
   March 18, 1948
   Gelatin silver print
   23.9 x 29.2 cm (image), 25.2 x 20.3 cm (sheet)

1. 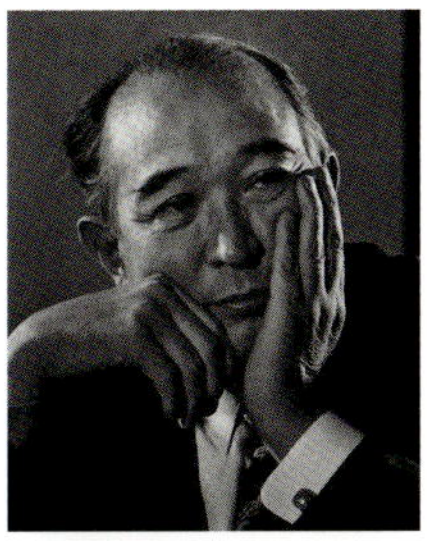

2. 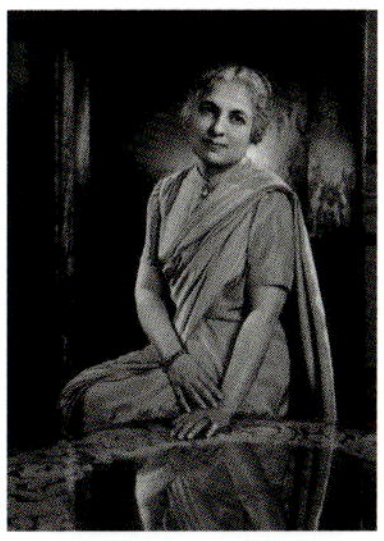

3. 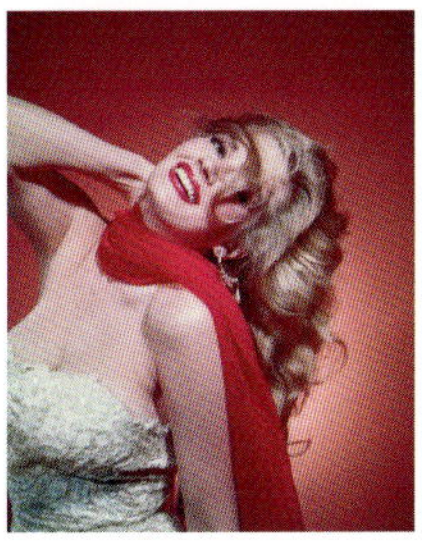

4. 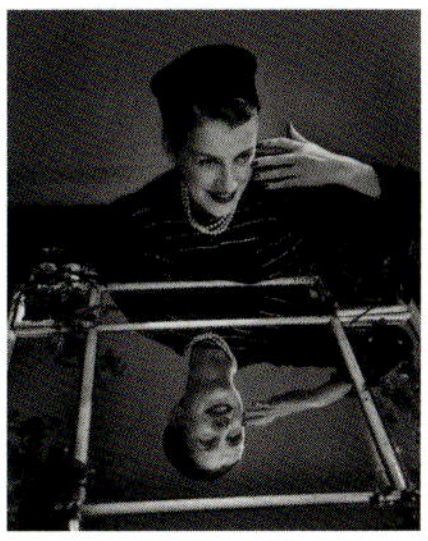

Library and Archives Canada

Continued

5. Yousuf Karsh, *Christl Thalhammer*, May 1965
   Interpositive made from the original negative
   25.2 x 20.1 cm
6. Yousuf Karsh, *Christopher Plummer*, April 13, 1959
   Gelatin silver print
   34.2 x 23.2 cm
7. Yousuf Karsh, *Douglas Cardinal*, April 7, 1989
   Gelatin silver print
   28 x 21.5 cm (image),
   35.5 x 27.7 cm (sheet)
8. Yousuf Karsh, *[Early Landscape]*, 1926
   Gelatin silver print
   24 x 18.3 cm
9. Yousuf Karsh, *Elixir*, September 1938
   Chlorobromide print
   44 x 31.7 cm
10. Yousuf Karsh, *Governor General Lord Tweedsmuir, John Buchan, Posed in His Honorary Chief Eagle Head Regalia*, May 5, 1937
    Gelatin silver print
    21.8 x 16.9 cm (image),
    24.2 x 18.4 cm (sheet)
11. Yousuf Karsh, *Lady Clark, with dog Angus*, August 9, 1934
    Gelatin silver print
    23.5 x 18.8 cm
12. Yousuf Karsh, *Lester B. Pearson*, November 23, 1957
    Gelatin silver print
    50.4 x 40.5 cm (image),
    50.4 x 40.5 cm (support)
13. Yousuf Karsh, *Lilly Koltun*, August 10, 1987
    Gelatin silver print
    25.4 x 19.1 cm
14. Yousuf Karsh, *Man Eating Lunch [Lawrence Heppler], Great Lakes Paper Company, Thunder Bay*, c.1953
    Gelatin silver print
    12.2 x 9.6 cm (image),
    12.6 x 9.8 cm (support)
15. Yousuf Karsh, *Margaret Atwood*, November 5, 1977
    Gelatin silver print
    23.8 x 17.4 cm (image),
    27.4 x 17.4 cm (sheet)
16. Yousuf Karsh, *Martin Luther King, Jr.*, August 18, 1962
    Gelatin silver print
    49.7 x 39.7 cm (image),
    49.5 x 39.7 cm (support)

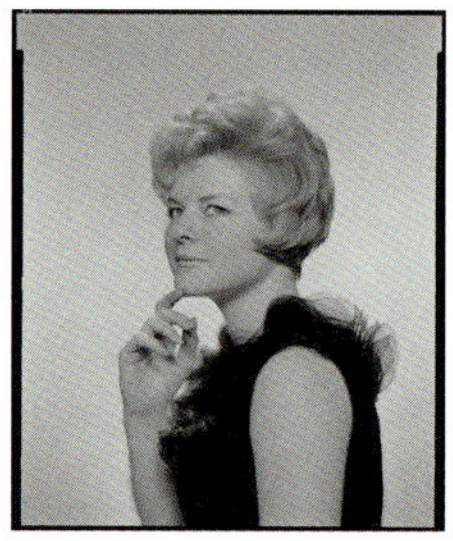
5.

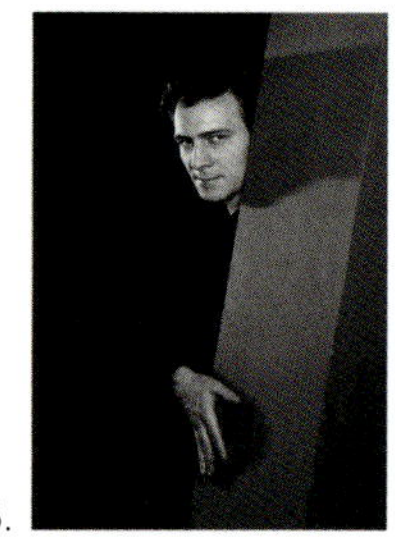
6.

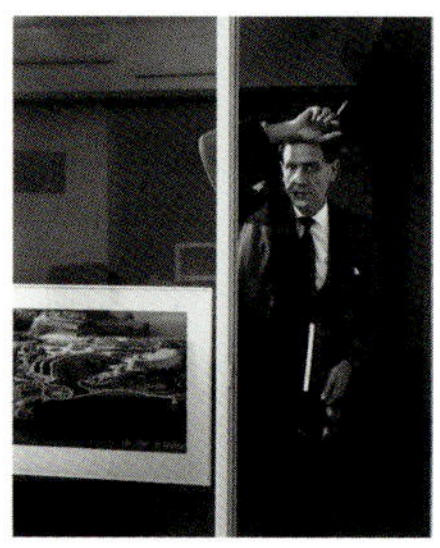
7.

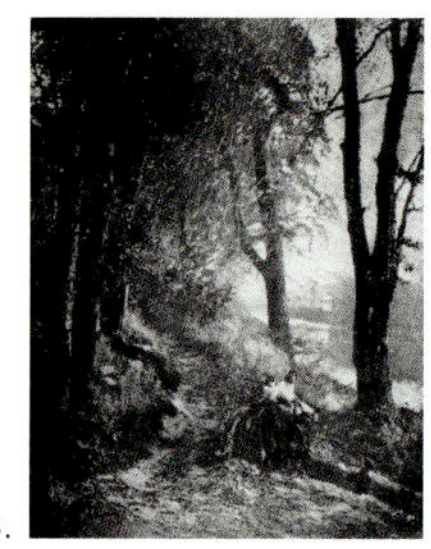
8.

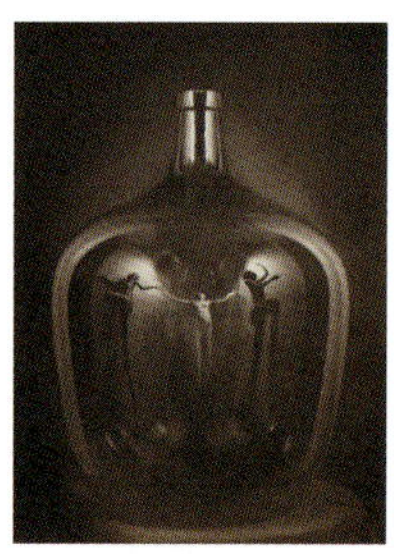
9.

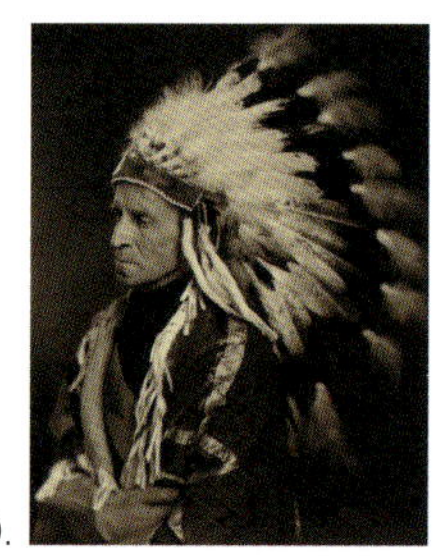
10.

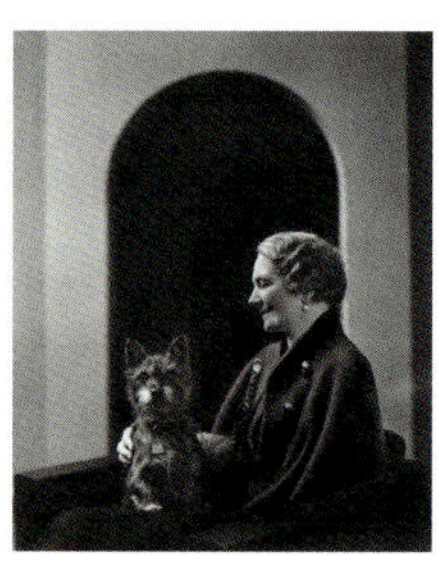
11.

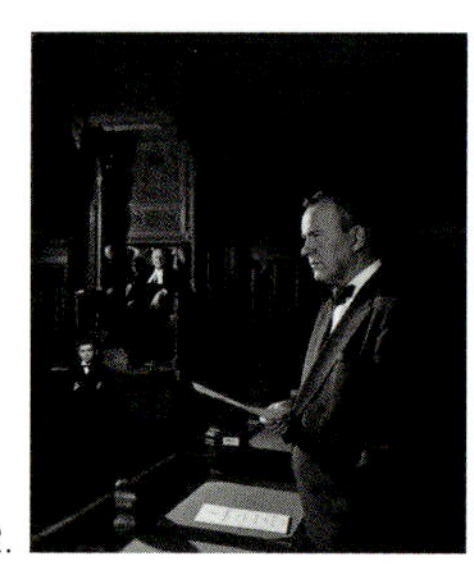
12.

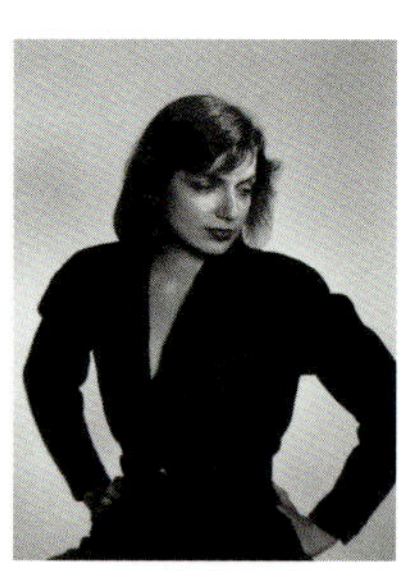
13.

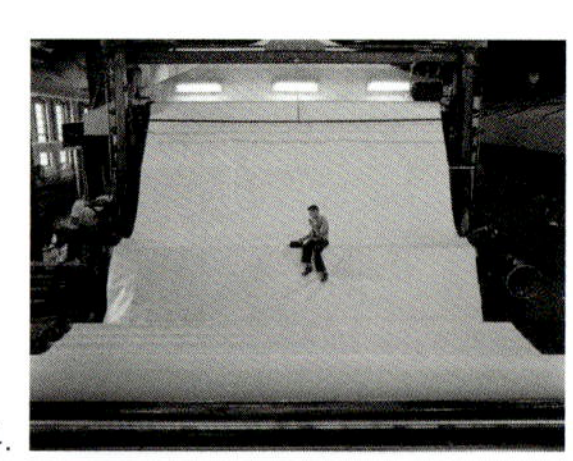
14.

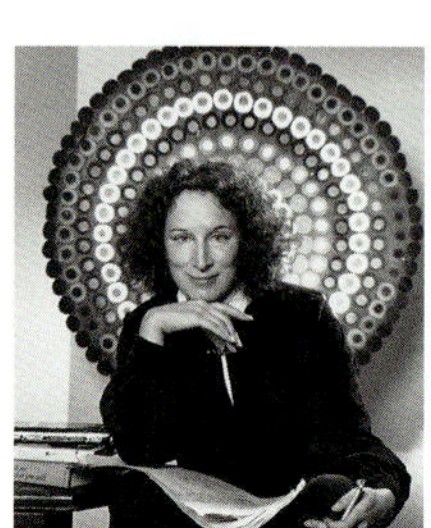
15.

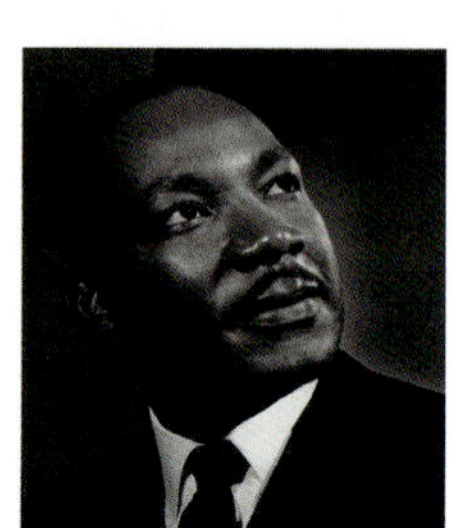
16.

Library and Archives Canada

Continued

17. Yousuf Karsh, *Master Michel Pharand*, March 19, 1937
    Interpositive made from original 25 x 19.9 cm nitrate negative
18. Yousuf Karsh, *Mrs. Norman Armour*, March 18, 1937
    Interpositive made from original nitrate negative
    25 x 19.9 cm
19. Yousuf Karsh, *Official Portrait of Sir Vere Brabazon Ponsonby, Ninth Earl of Bessborough, Governor General of Canada from 1931 to 1935 and His Wife Roberte Ponsonby (Born Neuflize), Countess Bessborough*, March 19, 1935
    Gelatin silver print
    24.1 x 17 cm (image), 29.2 x 22.9 cm (mount)
20. Yousuf Karsh, *Pope Pius XII*, June 16, 1949
    Positive paper colour dye transfer
    51.4 x 41 cm
21. Yousuf Karsh, *President Dwight Eisenhower*, July 20, 1966
    Gelatin silver print
    24.1 x 19.1 cm
22. Yousuf Karsh, *Prince Rainier III and Princess Grace of Monaco*, September 22, 1956
    Gelatin silver print
    14.9 x 13.5 cm
23. Yousuf Karsh, *Princess Elizabeth*, November 1, 1943
    Kodachrome print
    34.1 x.27.1 cm (image), 35.4 x 28.2 cm (support)
24. Yousuf Karsh, *Self-Portrait*, September 1938
    Gelatin silver print
    15.3 x 10.5 (image), 20.7 x 12.8 cm (sheet)
25. Yousuf Karsh, *Self-Portrait*, 1939
    Gelatin silver print
    23.4 x 15.7 cm (image), 25.1 x 16.8 cm (support)
26. Yousuf Karsh, *Self-Portrait*, 1956
    Gelatin silver print
    22.2 x 19 cm
27. Yousuf Karsh, *Shirley Lake*, June 5, 1937
    Gelatin silver print
    24.1 x 19 cm (image), 35 x 27.7 (sheet)
28. Yousuf Karsh, *Solange Gauthier posing with a stuffed dog in preparation for a portrait sitting with Lady Anne Elizabeth Clark*, About August 9, 1934
    Interpositive made from original cellulose nitrate negative

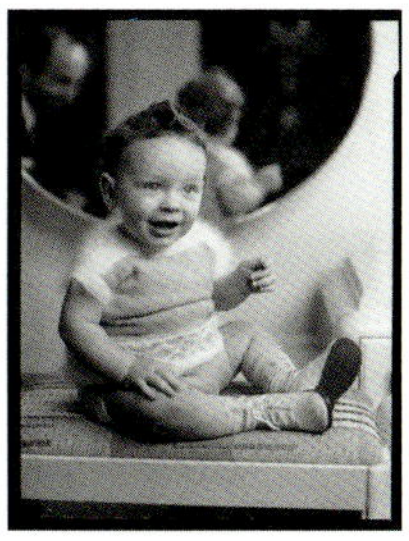
17.

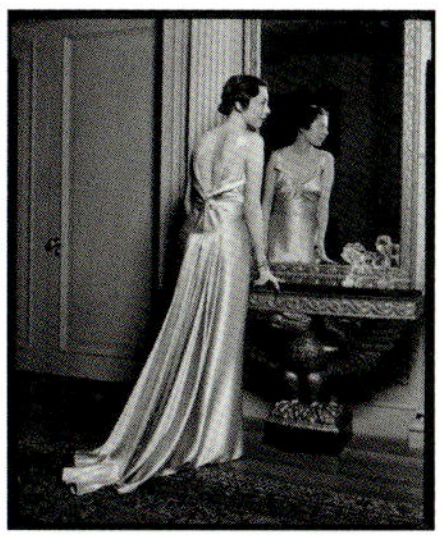
18.

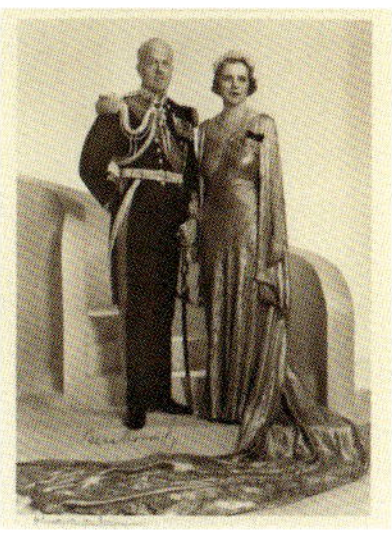
19.

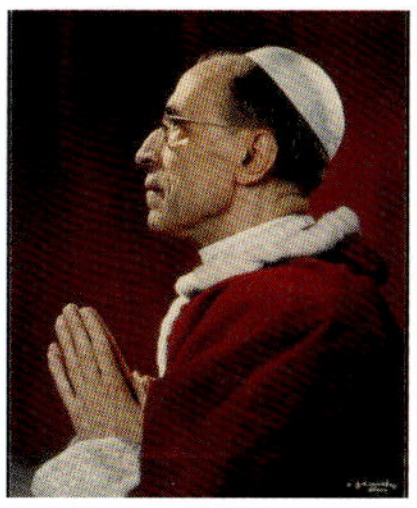
20.

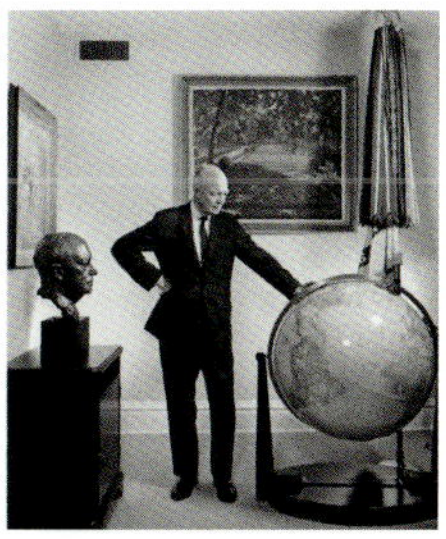
21.

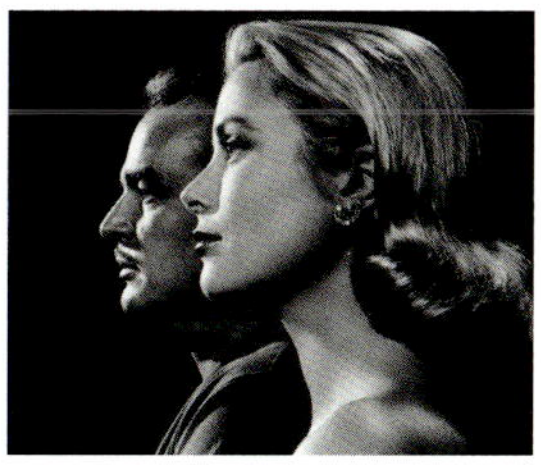
22.

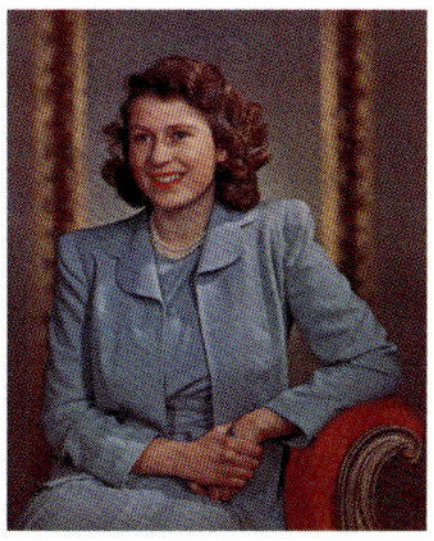
23.

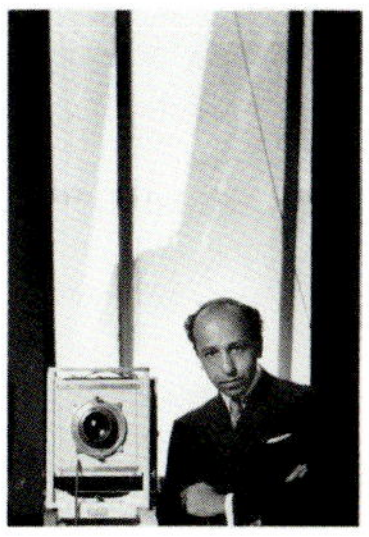
24.

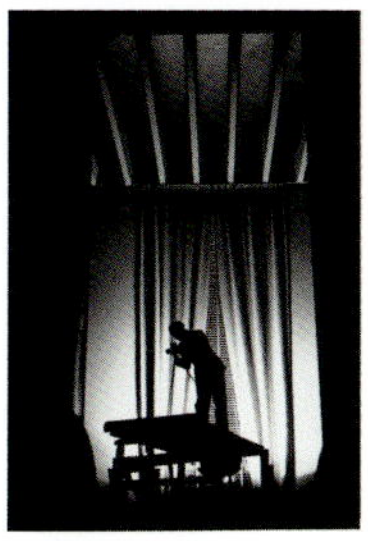
25.

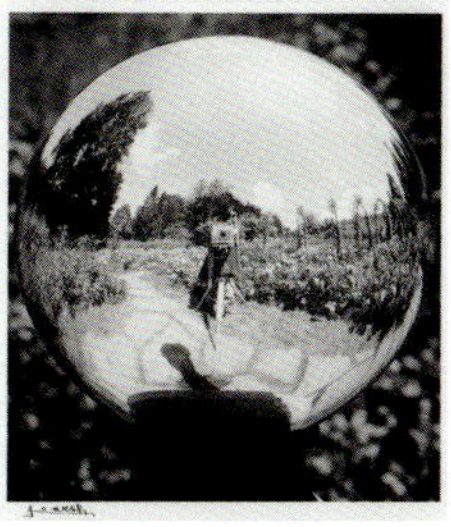
26.

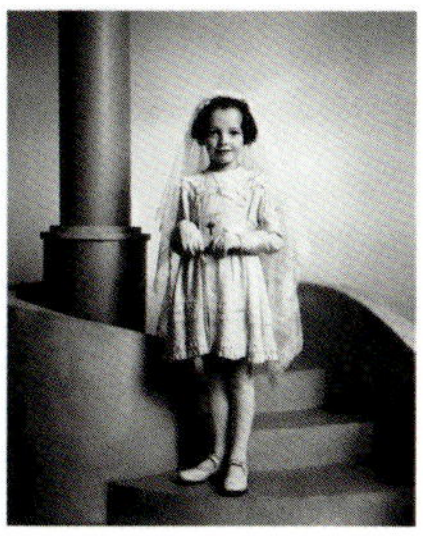
27.

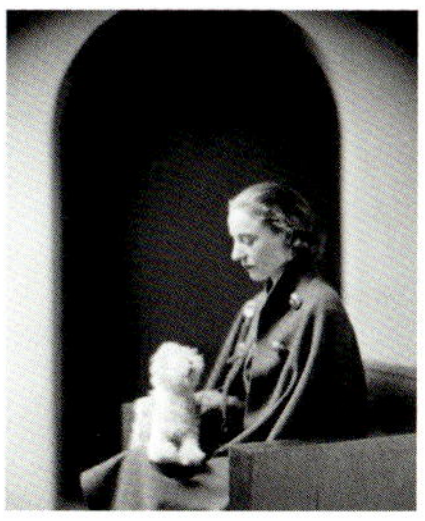
28.

Montreal Museum of Fine Arts

1380 Sherbrooke Street West
Montreal, Quebec, Canada
514-285-2000
mbam.qc.ca

1. Yousuf Karsh, *Albert Einstein*, February 11, 1948
   Gelatin silver print
   48.9 x 53.1 cm
2. Yousuf Karsh, *Andy Warhol*, November 21, 1979
   Gelatin silver print
   59.4 x 49.3 cm
3. Yousuf Karsh, *Anna Magnani*, May 1, 1958
   Gelatin silver print
   59.6 x 48.1 cm
4. Yousuf Karsh, *Brigitte Bardot*, May 1, 1958
   Gelatin silver print
   40.3 x 42.7 cm
5. Yousuf Karsh, *City of Straws*, 1940
   Gelatin silver print
   59.9 x 49.2 cm
6. Yousuf Karsh, *Ernest Hemingway*, March 15, 1957
   Gelatin silver print
   60.3 x 50.5 cm
7. Yousuf Karsh, *Estrellita Karsh*, January 1, 1963
   Gelatin silver print
   60.3 x 49 cm
8. Yousuf Karsh, *George Bernard Shaw*, September 12, 1943
   Gelatin silver print
   60 x 50.5 cm
9. Yousuf Karsh, *Georgia O'Keeffe*, March 18, 1956
   Gelatin silver print
   59.7 x 47.9 cm
10. Yousuf Karsh, *Hands of Gratien Gélinas*, March 29, 1945
    Gelatin silver print
    61 x 50.5 cm
11. Yousuf Karsh, *Helen Keller*, March 8, 1948
    Gelatin silver print
    43.1 x 35.4 cm
12. Yousuf Karsh, *Johan Helders*, August 12, 1936
    Gelatin silver print
    44.6 x 36.8 cm

1.
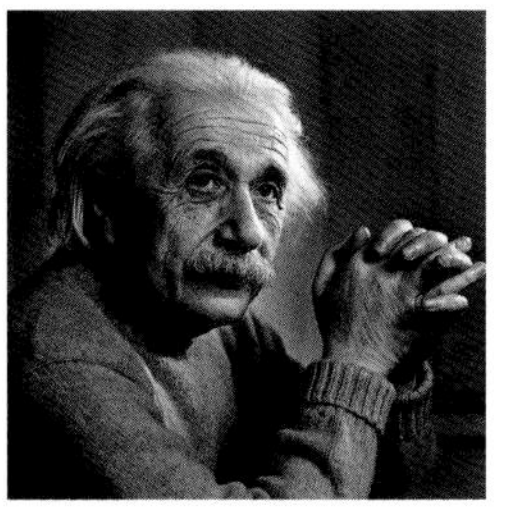

2.
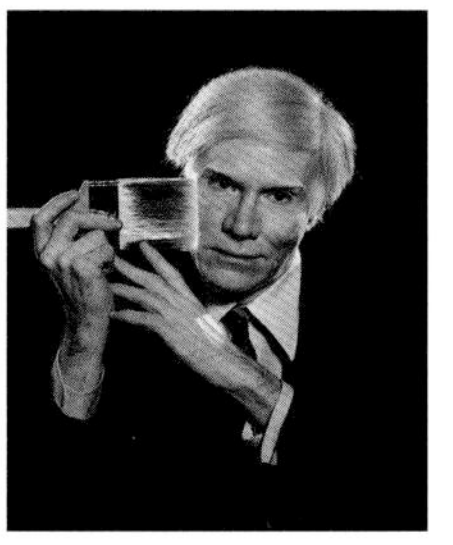

3.
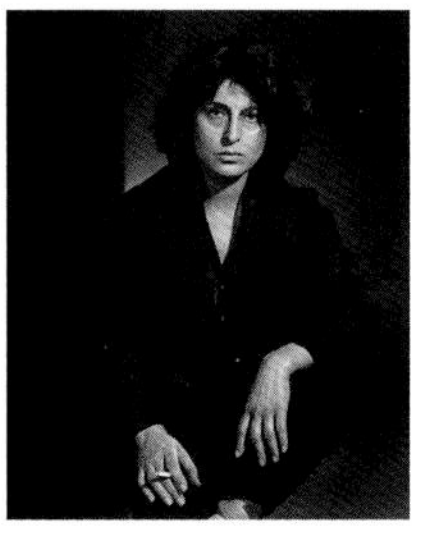

4.
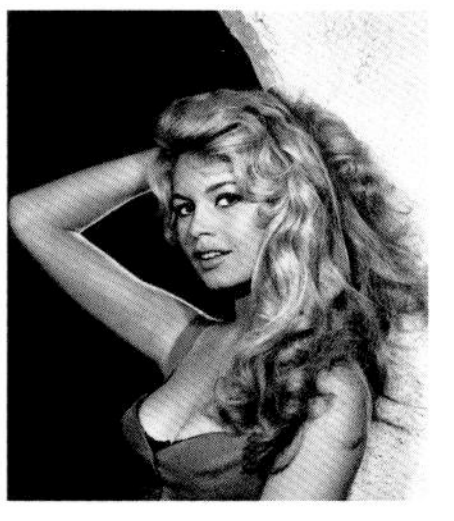

5.
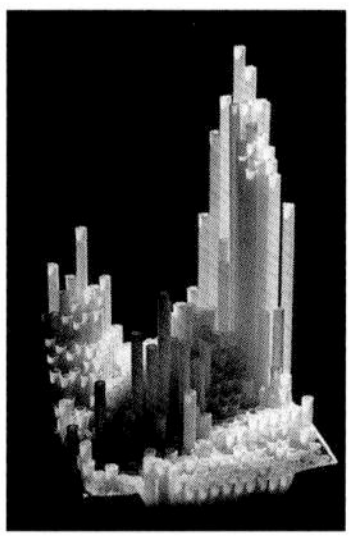

6.
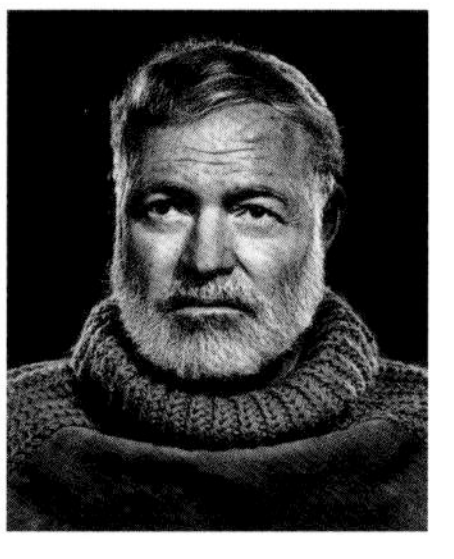

7.
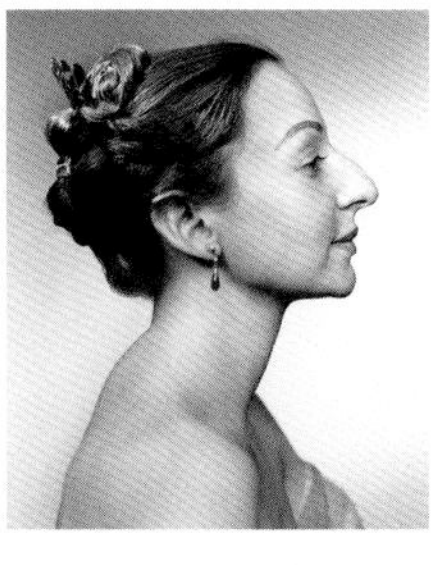

8.
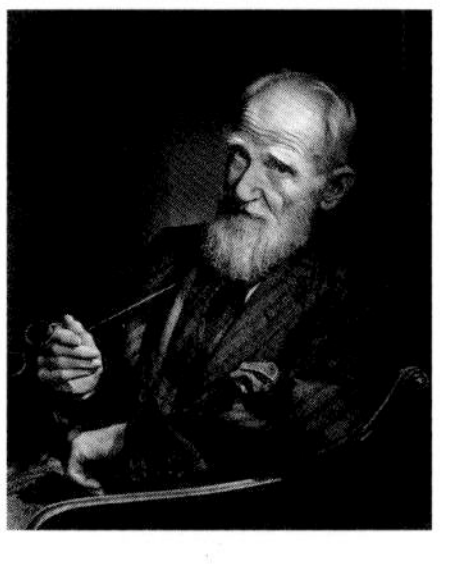

9.
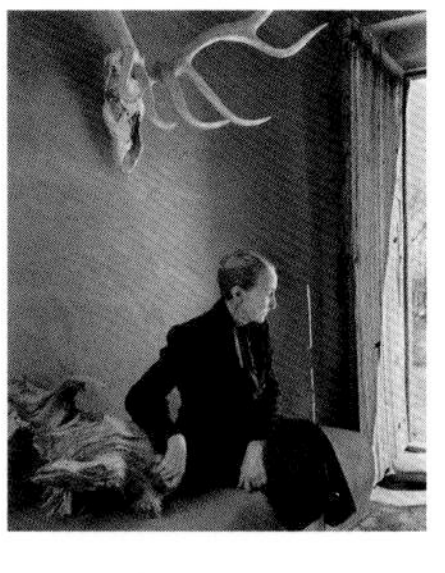

10.
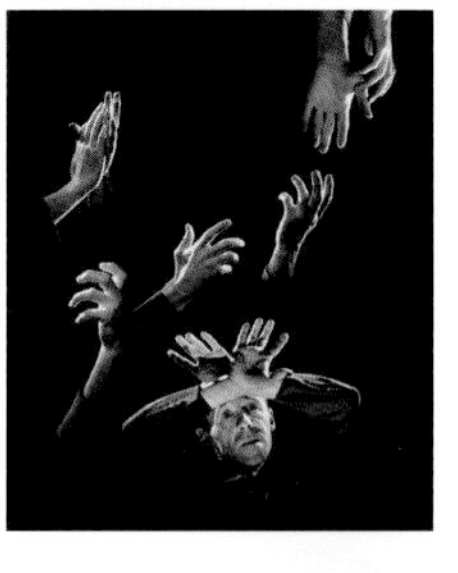

11.
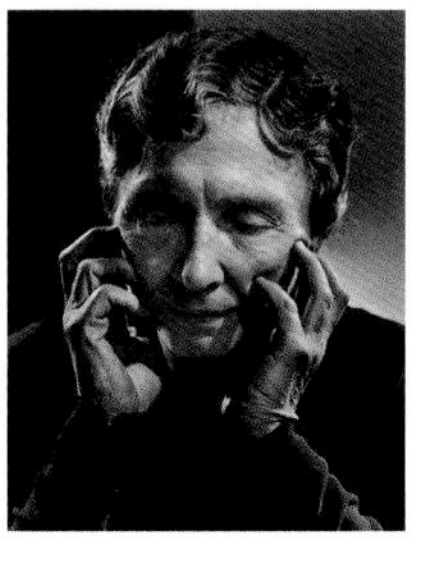

12.
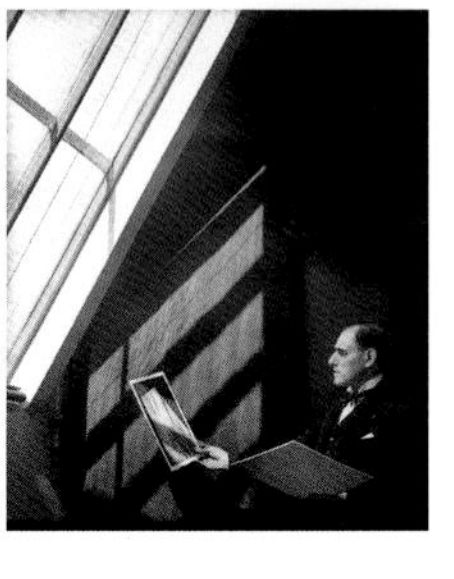

Montreal Museum of Fine Arts

Continued

13. Yousuf Karsh, *Ingrid Bergman*, February 24, 1946
    Gelatin silver print
    26 x 20 cm
14. Yousuf Karsh, *Jacques Cousteau*, January 22, 1972
    Gelatin silver print
    60.3 x 50.4 cm
15. Yousuf Karsh, *Karen Kain*, July 1, 1977
    Gelatin silver print
    50.1 x 40.3 cm
16. Yousuf Karsh, *Kenojuak Ashevak*, April 8, 1976
    Gelatin silver print
    25.3 x 20.3 cm
17. Yousuf Karsh, *Muhammad Ali*, March 27, 1970
    Gelatin silver print
    50.6 x 60.1 cm
18. Yousuf Karsh, *Pablo Casals*, June 30, 1954
    Gelatin silver print
    60.3 x 49.1 cm
19. Yousuf Karsh, *Pablo Picasso*, July 2, 1954
    Gelatin silver print
    60.1 x 50 cm
20. Yousuf Karsh, *Pierre Elliott Trudeau*, November 4, 1968
    Gelatin silver print
    43 x 35.5 cm

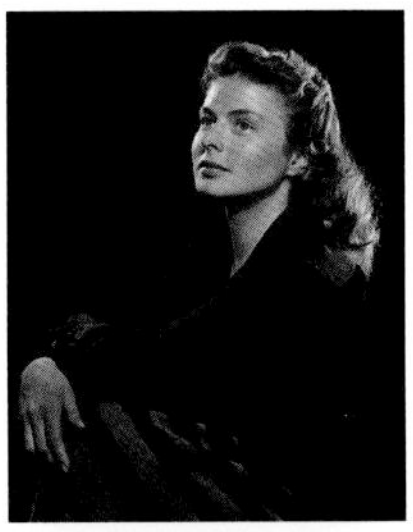
13.
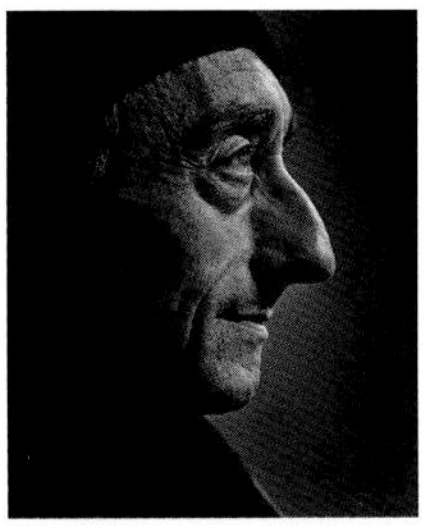
14.
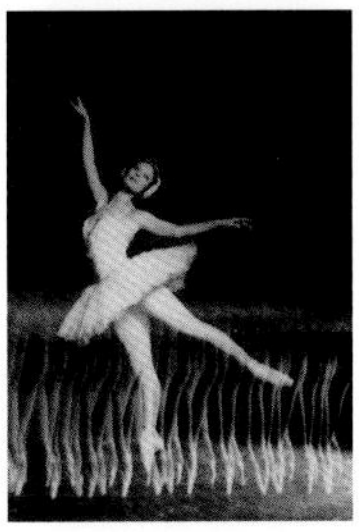
15.
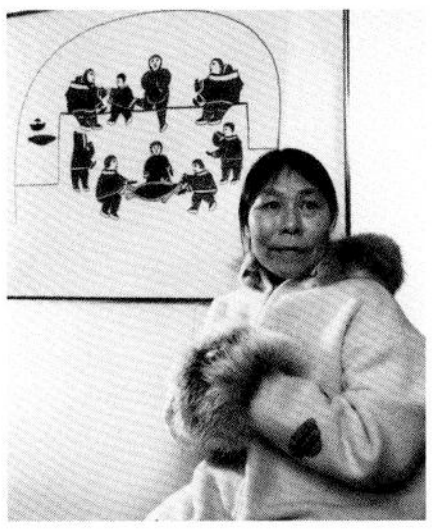
16.
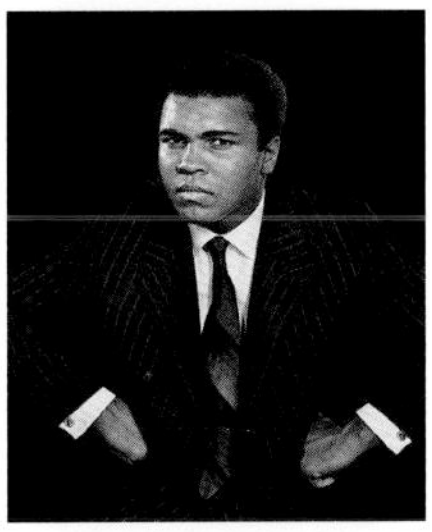
17.
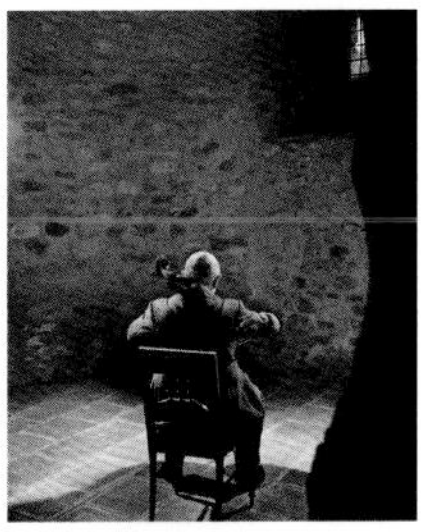
18.
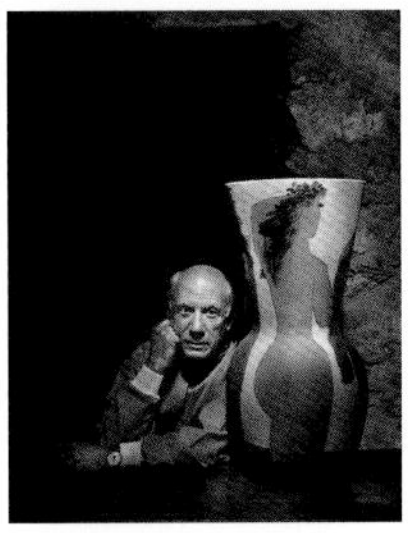
19.
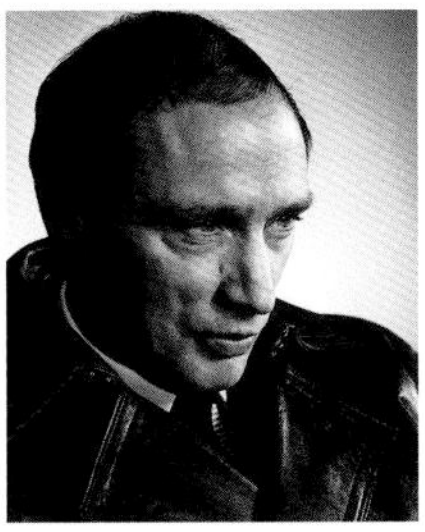
20.

National Gallery of Canada

380 Sussex Drive
Ottawa, Ontario, Canada
1-800-319-2787
gallery.ca

1. Yousuf Karsh, *Daniel Makokis, Edmonton*, 1952
   Gelatin silver print
   31.3 x 26.7 cm (image), 50.7 x 40.6 cm (sheet)
2. Yousuf Karsh, *Jean-Paul Riopelle, Photographed in His Paris Atelier*, April 7, 1965, printed 1987
   Gelatin silver print
   33.2 x 40.9 cm (image), 60.6 x 50.9 cm (sheet)
3. Yousuf Karsh, *Ruth Draper*, November 25, 1936, printed 1989
   Gelatin silver print, 48.6 x 37 cm
4. Yousuf Karsh, *Saint John, New Brunswick*, 1952, printed 1989
   Gelatin silver print, 40.9 x 39.8 cm

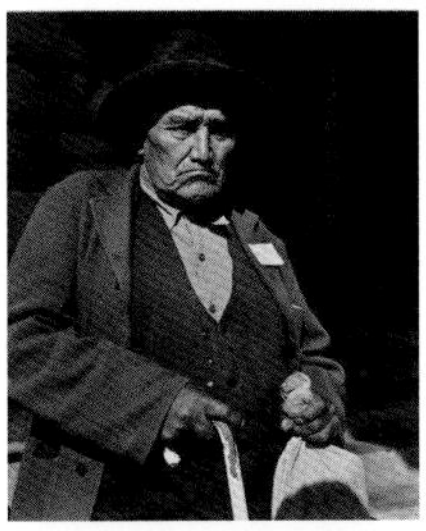
1.
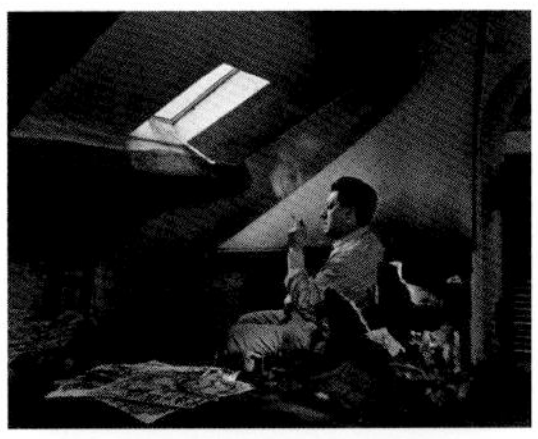
2.
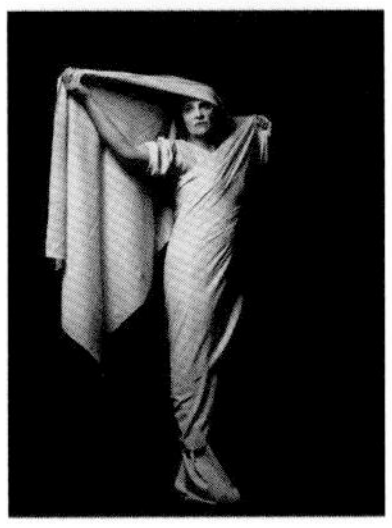
3.
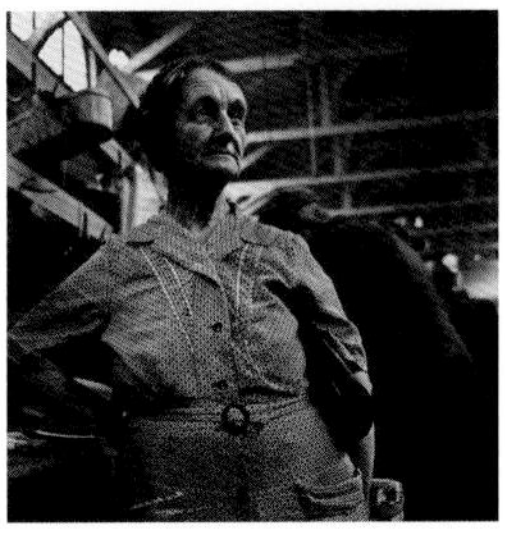
4.

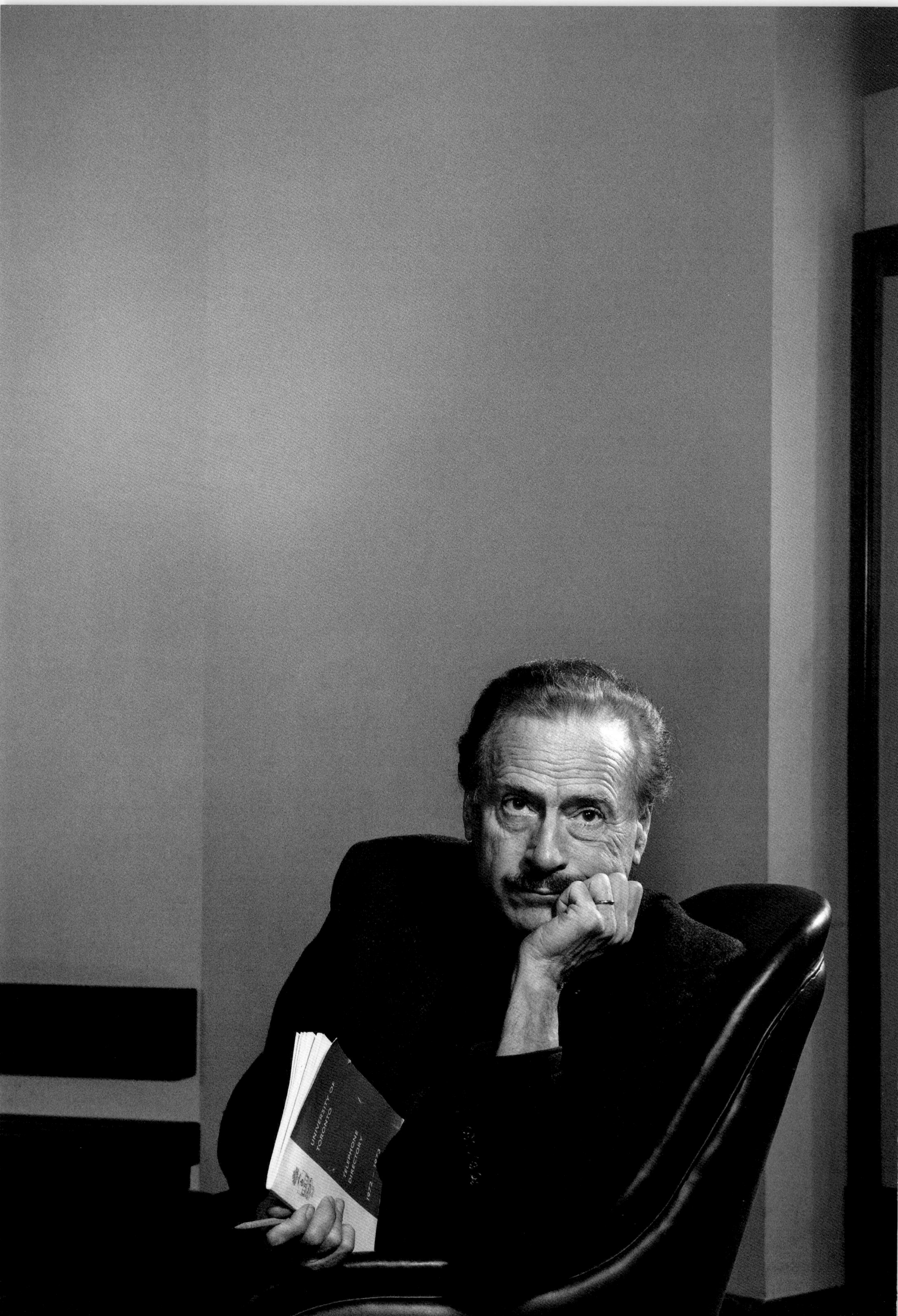
UNIVERSITY OF TORONTO
TELEPHONE DIRECTORY

Notes

BIOGRAPHY PAGES, 25–65

1 Maria Tippett, *The Life of Yousuf Karsh: Portrait in Light and Shadow* (Toronto: House of Anansi Press Inc., 2007), 16.

2 Tippett, *The Life of Yousuf Karsh*, 12.

3 Karsh recounted this harrowing narrative on several occasions during his lifetime, notably in his 1962 autobiography, *In Search of Greatness*. Author Maria Tippett extensively researched the complex intersection of cultural, religious, and linguistic components of Karsh's early life while writing *The Life of Yousuf Karsh* (2007).

4 Mehmed Ali, *Yousuf Karsh & John Garo: The Search for a Master's Legacy* (Mansfield, MA: Benna Books, 2016), 4.

5 Yousuf Karsh, *Karsh: A Fifty-Year Retrospective* (Boston and Toronto: Little, Brown and Company, 1986), 7

6 Yousuf Karsh, *In Search of Greatness: Reflections of Yousuf Karsh* (Toronto: University of Toronto Press, 1962), 19.

7 Karsh may have already become acquainted with the work of the prestigious New York–based Photo-Secession group, as his landscape study bears striking resemblance to Edward Steichen's moody landscapes of around 1903 and 1904.

8 Yousuf Karsh, *Karsh Canadians* (Toronto: University of Toronto Press, 1978), 13.

9 Ali, *Yousuf Karsh & John Garo*, 64. Ali, in collaboration with Estate of Yousuf Karsh Director and Curator Jerry Fielder, painstakingly traces the details of this period.

10 Garo photographed or knew many of the great figures of his age, including President Calvin Coolidge, Edward S. Curtis, Billy Burke, Edward Weston, Enrico Caruso, Arthur Fiedler, Ethel Barrymore, Edward Steichen, Alfred Stieglitz, and George Eastman. Ali, *Yousuf Karsh & John Garo*, 23.

11 Karsh learned to mix cocktails, illegal to consume during the American Prohibition period, concealing the ingredients as chemical solutions used in photographic development. "As mixer of the 'hypo' and the 'nitric acid' concoctions on those late afternoon sessions in Garo's salon, I was able to share in wonderful conversations and study some of the great personalities in the world of music, letters, the theatre, and the opera of the 1920s." Karsh, *In Search of Greatness*, 30.

12 "A Brief Biography," Karsh.org, https://karsh.org/a-brief-biography.

13 Karsh, *In Search of Greatness*, 30.

14 Karsh, *In Search of Greatness*, 48.

15 Ali, *Yousuf Karsh & John Garo*, 12. See Lilly Koltun's essay about Karsh's approach to lighting, which was formed during this period: "Framing a New Light: Karsh Addresses the Audience of the Theater and the Press," in *Yousuf Karsh: Heroes of Light and Shadow*, eds. Dieter Vorsteher and Janet Yates (Toronto: Stoddart Publishing Company Ltd., 2001), 123–36.

16 Yousuf Karsh, *Karsh: A Fifty-Year Retrospective* (Boston and Toronto: Little, Brown and Company, 1986), 12. See also Tippett, *The Life of Yousuf Karsh*, 63–67.

17 Quoted by Tippett, *The Life of Yousuf Karsh*, 110, from an interview Solange Karsh gave to the *Canadian Home Journal* in 1951.

18 Karsh, *In Search of Greatness*, 64.

19 These portraits, largely commissioned by the *Montreal Standard*, and their textual counterparts were later published in book form: see Corolyn Cox, *Canadian Strength* (Toronto: The Ryerson Press, 1946).

Yousuf Karsh, *Marshall McLuhan,* April 6, 1974, Estate of Yousuf Karsh.

20 The final print was an intricate montage made from four negatives carefully sandwiched together.

21 Karsh, *Karsh Canadians*, 14.

22 David Travis, ed., *Yousuf Karsh: Regarding Heroes* (Boston: David R. Godine, 2009), 28–29.

23 Yousuf Karsh, *Portraits of Greatness* (Toronto: University of Toronto Press, 1959), 13.

24 Regarding Karsh's advertising and promotional work, see Cassandra Getty and Jerry Fielder, *Yousuf Karsh: Industrial Images* (Windsor, ON: Art Gallery of Windsor, 2007); and James Opp, "Picturing Communism: Yousuf Karsh, Canadair, and Cold War Advertising," *Queen's Quarterly* 118, no. 4 (Winter 2011): 584–97.

25 This series has been extensively examined within the context of art and labour history. See Rosemary Donegan, "Karsh's Working Man: Industrial Tensions and Cold War Anxieties," in *Yousuf Karsh: Heroes of Light and Shadow*, eds. Vorsteher and Yates, 153–161; and Getty and Fielder, *Yousuf Karsh*.

26 Yousuf Karsh, quoted in Getty and Fielder, *Yousuf Karsh*, 100. See also the text accompanying the Atlas Steel photo essay "The Dignity of Labor," published in *Saturday Night* 66, no. 3 (October 24, 1950): 8–9.

27 Karsh's directorial mode, creating publicity film stills featuring lead actors, is discussed in James Opp, "Still Photographs, Publicity, and the Making of Cecil B. DeMille's *Ten Commandments* (1956)," *Film History* 34, no. 4 (January 2022): 1–29.

28 Lilly Koltun, "The Karsh Collection," in *Karsh: The Art of the Portrait*, ed. James Borcoman (Ottawa: National Gallery of Canada, 1989), 141–50.

29 See Jill Delaney's analysis "Karsh and the Face of Canada," in *Yousuf Karsh: Heroes of Light and Shadow*, eds. Vorsteher and Yates, 187–94.

30 Karsh had arranged to bring his brother to Canada in 1937. Malak also showed potential as a photographer, and in June 1939, he trained at the prestigious Clarence White School of Photography in New York. Malak's photographs of cheering crowds in Ottawa during the 1939 Royal Tour were published in *Saturday Night*, and by 1941, Malak had established his own commercial photography and photojournalism practice.

31 This creative freedom also included combining negatives to make optimal compositions, such as conflating foreground figures from one image to picturesque backgrounds from another, to create a seamless and credible scene.

32 Thanks to archivist Lisandra Cortina de la Noval, Library and Archives Canada, for sharing her research into the Canadian Cities series in the Karsh Fonds.

33 The documentary value of Karsh's assignment photographs continues to resonate: his photographs of Bell Island, a mining community in Conception Bay, Newfoundland and Labrador, for instance, have been selected to support an oral history display in the Bell Island Museum. Mike Rossiter, "Portraits of an Island," CBC News, September 2, 2024, https://www.cbc.ca/newsinteractives/features/portrait-of-an-island.

34 These portrayals, expressive of Karsh's own experience as an immigrant to Canada, provoked a negative reaction regarding the country's contemporary ethnic diversity from the generally conservative readership of *Maclean's*. See Tippett, *The Life of Yousuf Karsh*, 249–63.

35 A selection of these images was later reproduced in book form as *Karsh and Fisher See Canada* (1960).

36 See Tippett, *The Life of Yousuf Karsh*, 249–63.

37 Karsh personally supervised the printing by prestigious Dutch printing house Enchedé of Haarlem, which reproduced the look and feel of the velvety finish of Karsh's preferred photo-printing paper, Opal V.

38 Karsh, *Portraits of Greatness*, 13.

39 "Mrs. Karsh, Wife of Photographer; Business Manager of the Portraitist Is Dead—Did Research for His Work," *New York Times*, January 25, 1961, https://www.nytimes.com/1961/01/26/archives/mrs-karsh-wife-of-photographer-3usiness-manager-of-the-portraitist.html.

40 "Picture Bride," *Newsweek*, September 10, 1962, 64.

41 Yousuf Karsh and Montreal Museum of Fine Arts, *Men Who Make Our World: An Exhibition of Photographs at the Montreal Museum of Fine Arts, January 26 to March 3, 1968* (Montreal: Montreal Museum of Fine Arts, 1968).

42 Yousuf Karsh, *Karsh Portraits* (Toronto: University of Toronto Press, 1976), 86.

43 Karsh, *Karsh Canadians*, frontispiece.

44 Karsh, *Karsh Canadians*, 164.

45 Nathan Lyons curated the 1966 George Eastman House exhibition and accompanying catalogue *Toward a Social Landscape*, featuring the work of Bruce Davidson, Lee Friedlander, Garry Winogrand, Danny Lyon, and Duane Michals.

46 Kevin J. Holland, *Château Laurier—A Splendid Century: The Life and Times of Ottawa's Grand Railway Hotel* (Calgary: Canadian National Railways Historical Association, 2017), 99.

47 Vorsteher and Yates, eds., *Yousuf Karsh: Heroes of Light and Shadow*, 226.

48 "Estrellita Karsh Obituary," *New York Times*, March 30, 2025, https://www.legacy.com/us/obituaries/nytimes/name/estrellita-karsh-obituary?id=58016347.

KEY WORKS, PAGES 66–97

WOMAN IN A TURBAN (BETTY LOW)

1 The specific character embodied in her dramatic pose remains to be identified; it may be that Draper was performing stock emotional states popularized in the late eighteenth century as a performance of attitudes, or tableau vivant.

SIR WINSTON CHURCHILL

1 Maria Tippett, *The Life of Yousuf Karsh: Portrait in Light and Shadow* (Toronto: House of Anansi Press Inc., 2007), 139.

2 Yousuf Karsh, *In Search of Greatness: Reflections of Yousuf Karsh* (Toronto: University of Toronto Press, 1962), 66–67.

3 Karsh made minor retouching adjustments to the negative and cropped the edges when printing. See Tippett, *The Life of Yousuf Karsh*, 137–51; and John Loengard, *Celebrating the Negative* (New York: Arcade Publishing, 1994), 60–61.

4 Letter from Solange Karsh to B.K. Sandwell, 31 December 1941, R613, volume 5, file 20, Yousuf Karsh Fonds, Library and Archives Canada.

5 "Winston Churchill: A Great Champion of Freedom Faces the Disasters of War," *LIFE*, February 2, 1942, 27, and *The Illustrated London News*, February 28, 1942, cover.

6 Rebecca Lesser addresses the political performativity of the Churchill portrait in "By the Side of the 'Roaring Lion': Yousuf Karsh's Portrait of Winston Churchill and British/Canadian Wartime Relations" (MA thesis, University of Calgary, 2010), 23.

PRINCESS ELIZABETH

1 Graham Iddon, "Queen of the Bank Notes," *The Museum Blog*, Bank of Canada Museum, February 3, 2022, https://www.bankofcanadamuseum.ca/2022/02/queen-of-the-bank-notes.

2 Both portraits were among the works featured in the exhibition *Royal Portraits: A Century of Photography*, organized by the Royal Collection Trust, King's Gallery, in 2024.

DANIEL MAKOKIS

1 Of the 837 images taken by Karsh during this Edmonton trip, 159 depict Indigenous men, women, and children—all of which were photographed at Camsell. I am indebted to archivist Lisandra Cortina de la Noval, Library and Archives Canada, for sharing her ongoing research of the *Maclean's* Canadian Cities series, as well as to Jim Burant for finding Makokis listed in the 1931 Canada Census as a trapper and hunter born in 1874 and a member of the United Church of Canada.

2 Yousuf Karsh, *Karsh Canadians* (Toronto: University of Toronto Press, 1978), 112.

3 Yousuf Karsh, *Karsh: A Fifty-Year Retrospective* (Boston and Toronto: Little, Brown and Company, 1986), 103.

4 See critical essays about the migration of documentary photography into museums: Douglas Crimp, "The Museum's Old, the Library's New Subject," in *On the Museum's Ruins* (Cambridge, MA: The MIT Press, 1993), 66–83; and Abigail Solomon-Godeau, "Winning the Game When the Rules Have Been Changed: Art Photography and Postmodernism," *Screen* 25, no. 6 (November–December 1984): 88–102. By 1993, the date of the ICP retrospective, the Makokis image had been acquired by multiple fine art institutions, including the Museum of Fine Arts, Boston; the Montreal Museum of Fine Arts; and the National Portrait Gallery, Canberra, where they have been and may continue to be displayed in retrospective exhibitions of Karsh's work.

JAWAHARLAL NEHRU

1 According to the *Report on the Seventh Census of Canada*, 1931, people of British or French origin made up 80 per cent of the total population. Beginning around 1900, the greatest increase in population of other origins consisted of immigrants from Central and Eastern Europe, whereas Canadians of Chinese and Japanese origin totalled a mere 0.67 per cent; African, 0.19 per cent; and Indigenous, 1.24 per cent. See *Report on the Seventh Census of Canada*, 1931, vol. 1 (Ottawa: Dominion Bureau of Statistics Canada, 1936), https://publications.gc.ca/collections/collection_2017/statcan/CS98-1931-1-eng.pdf.

ANNA MAGNANI

1 Yousuf Karsh, *Karsh Canadians* (Toronto: University of Toronto Press, 1978), 18.

JEAN-PAUL RIOPELLE, PHOTOGRAPHED IN HIS PARIS ATELIER

1 Yousuf Karsh, *Karsh Canadians* (Toronto: University of Toronto Press, 1978), 136.

2 Karsh, *Karsh Canadians*, 136.

ROPPEITA KITA, WITH GRANDSON NAGAYO KITA

1 Yousuf Karsh, *Karsh Portraits* (Toronto: University of Toronto Press, 1976), 86.

2 Yousuf Karsh, *Faces of Our Time* (Toronto and Buffalo: University of Toronto Press, 1971), 102.

ANDY WARHOL

1 Andy Warhol's published diary does not include an entry for the date of the Karsh portrait sitting, and there is no record that Warhol reciprocated by photographing Karsh on that day. Andy Warhol and Pat Hackett, *The Andy Warhol Diaries* (New York: Warner Books, 1989).

2 On June 3, 1968, Valerie Solanas walked into Andy Warhol's studio and shot him and art critic Mario Amaya. Both survived. Solanas was the author of the *SCUM Manifesto*, a revolutionary call to arms against the male sex, and her story was depicted in Mary Harron's 1996 film, *I Shot Andy Warhol*. See Bonnie Wertheim, "Overlooked No More: Valerie Solanas, Radical Feminist Who Shot Andy Warhol," *New York Times*, June 26, 2020, https://www.nytimes.com/2020/06/26/obituaries/valerie-solanas-overlooked.html.

LILLY KOLTUN

1 Lilly Koltun, personal statement contributed to the My Karsh initiative during the 2009 Festival Karsh in Ottawa, a project led by Koltun, then in her role as director of the Portrait Gallery of Canada, in collaboration with the Canada Science and Technology Museum, and featuring the major travelling exhibition *Karsh: Image Maker*. Karsh's portrait accompanied an obituary written by Koltun's lifelong friend and colleague Joan M. Schwartz, "Lilly A. Koltun: 1951–2021," *Archivaria* 93 (Spring 2022): 184–89.

2 Susan Sontag, *On Photography* (New York: Anchor Books, Doubleday, 1977), 28.

3 Jerry Fielder, "Introduction," in Mehmed Ali, *Yousuf Karsh & John Garo: The Search for a Master's Legacy* (Mansfield, MA: Benna Books, 2016), 21–22.

JESSYE NORMAN

1 Jessye Norman quoted in "By the Book," *New York Times*, June 5, 2014.

2 Helen Molesworth, ed., *Face to Face: Portraits of Artists by Tacita Dean, Brigitte Lacombe and Catherine Opie* (New York and London: The International Center for Photography / MACK, 2023).

3 Molesworth, *Face to Face*, 116–17.

SIGNIFICANCE & CRITICAL ISSUES, PAGES 99–121

1 Yousuf Karsh, *In Search of Greatness: Reflections of Yousuf Karsh* (Toronto: University of Toronto Press, 1962), vii–viii.

2 This deep interconnection between image and narrative may have been the reason that Karsh's work was not included in Edward Steichen's 1955 monumental exhibition, *The Family of Man*, an awkward omission for Karsh as the exhibition travelled extensively, including to the National Gallery of Canada in 1957. Karsh deflected the snub by characterizing this project by his admired colleague as a "highly successful record of interpretations of human emotions," rather than a collection of portraits per se. See Karsh, *In Search of Greatness*, 94.

3 Yousuf Karsh, *Karsh Canadians* (Toronto: University of Toronto Press, 1978), 66.

4 Karsh's strategy can also be linked to *ekphrasis*, a narrative device that employs a verbal description of a visual representation.

5 Walter Benjamin, "The Storyteller: Reflections on the Work of Nikolai Leskov," in *Illuminations: Essays and Reflections*, ed. Hannah Arendt, trans. Harry Zohn (New York: Schocken Books, 1969), 83–110.

6 Karsh's use of text in his published portfolios is discussed by James Borcoman, *Karsh: The Art of the Portrait* (Ottawa: National Gallery of Canada, 1989), 77–79.

7 I am indebted to Jerry Fielder (Karsh's long-time assistant and the director of his estate) for his insightful account of the relationship between Karsh and the governor general: "John Buchan and Yousuf Karsh," *The John Buchan Journal* 50 (2017): 9–19, https://johnbuchansociety.co.uk/wp-content/uploads/2023/03/JBS-Journal-050-Inside-Contents.pdf. John Buchan is more popularly known as the author of the 1915 adventure novel *The Thirty-Nine Steps*, which has been adapted into film several times.

8 Excerpt from Karsh's commentary accompanying a black-and-white version of the portrait reproduced in Yousuf Karsh, *Faces of Destiny: Portraits by Karsh* (Ziff-Davis Publishing Company, 1946), 64.

9 Allan Sekula, "The Body and the Archive," in *The Contest of Meaning: Critical Histories of Photography*, ed. Richard Bolton (Cambridge, MA: The MIT Press, 1989), 343–89.

10 Karsh, *In Search of Greatness*, 101.

11 Yousuf Karsh, *Karsh Portfolio* (Toronto: University of Toronto Press, 1967), 42.

12 Karsh, *In Search of Greatness*, 127. Karsh's approach here accords with German sociologist philosopher Georg Simmel's concept of exterior appearance as a veiling (and unveiling) of the soul. Georg Simmel, "The Aesthetic Significance of the Face," in *Georg Simmel*, 1858–1918, ed. Kurt H. Wolff (Columbus: Ohio State University Press, 1959), 276–81.

13 Craig Owens, "The Allegorical Impulse: Toward a Theory of Postmodernism," in *Art After Modernism: Rethinking Representation*, ed. Brian Wallis (New York and Boston: The New Museum of Contemporary Art / David R. Godine, 1984), 203–35.

14 Discussions of the hero in Karsh's work are found in *Yousuf Karsh: Regarding Heroes*, ed. David Travis (Boston: David R. Godine, 2009); and in essays printed in the exhibition catalogue *Yousuf Karsh: Heroes of Light and Shadow*, eds. Dieter Vorsteher and Janet Yates (Toronto: Stoddart Publishing Company Ltd., 2001).

15 Norgay's role in the ascent was only properly recognized years later, and he was not photographed by Karsh.

16 Karsh's portrait of Hillary as inspirational hero was reproduced as an inset on Post's Grape-Nuts cereal packaging.

17 Karsh, *In Search of Greatness*, 155.

18 Karsh, *In Search of Greatness*, 63.

19 Karsh's mentor, John H. Garo, knew Edward S. Curtis (1868–1952), creator of the extensive photography project later published in limited editions as *The North American Indian* (1907–30). Karsh would have been aware of Curtis's influential Pictorialist-based documentary portraits.

20 Of the 837 images taken by Karsh in Edmonton, 159 depict Indigenous men, women, and children, all photographed at Camsell. I am indebted to archivist Lisandra Cortina de la Norval, Library and Archives Canada, for sharing her ongoing research on the *Maclean's* Canadian Cities series.

21 "Karsh's Edmonton: The Threshold of the Frontier," *Maclean's*, December 15, 1952, 12.

22 These portraits, like others in Karsh's body of work, such as his 1953 photographs of Inuit residents of Herschel Island for *TIME* magazine, require closer examination. Allan Sekula conceptualizes the judgmental "look down" in his seminal essay "The Body and the Archive," *October* 39 (Winter 1986): 3–64, republished in *The Contest of Meaning: Critical Histories of Photography*, ed. Richard Bolton (Cambridge, MA: The MIT Press, 1989), 343–89. See also Catherine Lutz and Jane Collins, "The Photograph as an Intersection of Gazes: The Example of *National Geographic*," in *The Photography Reader*, ed. Liz Wells (London and New York: Routledge, 2003), 354–79.

23 Karsh included this portrait in his portfolio *Karsh Canadians* (1978).

24 This project launched prior to a national conversation about and legal action pertaining to the role played by the Catholic Church in the horrors of the residential school system.

25 On assignment in 1953 for *TIME* magazine, Karsh, accompanied by Solange, visited the communities of Herschel Island, Yukon, and Tuktoyaktuk and Aklavik, Northwest Territories. He and his second wife, Estrellita, were avid collectors of Inuit art: their important collection, including works by Kenojuak, was showcased in the 2017 exhibition *Follow the North Star*, organized by the Museum of Fine Arts, Boston.

26 Yousuf Karsh, *Portraits of Greatness* (Toronto: University of Toronto Press, 1959), 68.

27 Museum of Fine Arts, Boston, *A Biography in Images* (Boston: MFA Publications, 2003), 179.

28 Karsh, *In Search of Greatness*, 94.

29 Lilly Koltun, "Yousuf Karsh: Frame, Focus, Fame," in *Yousuf Karsh Portraits* (Nice: Musée des Beaux-Arts Nice, 2006).

30 My thanks to Kate Laing, an early reviewer of this manuscript, for making this observation.

31 The viewer's moral role in contemplation has been both criticized as passive entrapment within a capitalist system of spectacle (Guy Debord, *The Society of the Spectacle* [1967]) and advanced as activation of the viewer's awareness of, and agency in, political space (Mieke Bal, *Double Exposures: The Subject of Cultural Analysis* [1996] and Ariella Azoulay, *The Civil Contract of Photography* [2012]).

STYLE & TECHNIQUE, PAGES 123–151

1 Steichen's fashion and celebrity photography during his tenure as chief photographer for *Vogue* and *Vanity Fair* was closely studied by Karsh, as can be seen in some of his compositional choices. See William A. Ewing, Todd Brandow, and Tobia Bezzola, *Edward Steichen in High Fashion: The Condé Nast Years 1923–1937* (London: Thames & Hudson, 2008).

2 In 1956, Karsh replaced his two Ansco models with a pair of Calumet cameras that he would use until his retirement in 1992. His studio equipment, including cameras, lights, lenses, and enlarger, is preserved by Ingenium Canada. See Anna Adamek, "Lights! Camera! Personality! The Karsh of Ottawa Collection Profile," Ingenium Channel, May 24, 2018, https://ingeniumcanada.org/channel/articles/lights-camera-personality-the-karsh-of-ottawa-collection-profile.

3 Lilly Koltun, "Framing a New Light: Karsh Addresses the Audience of the Theater and the Press," in *Yousuf Karsh: Heroes of Light and Shadow*, eds. Dieter Vorsteher and Janet Yates (Toronto: Stoddart Publishing Company Ltd., 2001), 123–36. Koltun argues that Karsh would have been familiar with artificial light during the period he spent with Nakash prior to opening his Ottawa studio in 1933, and that it may have been a feature of the Powis Studio, where Karsh worked when he first came to Ottawa in 1932. See also James Opp's excellent analysis of Karsh's directorial approach in the context of cinema: "Still Photographs, Publicity, and the Making of Cecil B. DeMille's *Ten Commandments* (1956)," *Film History* 34, no. 4 (January 2022): 1–29.

4 I credit my understanding of Karsh's studio equipment to my colleague Bryan deWalt (retired), who was my co-curator on the major 2009 travelling exhibition *Karsh: Image Maker*, organized by the Portrait Gallery of Canada and the Canada Science and Technology Museum. Bryan's thorough knowledge of Karsh's technical methods supported the section "In the Studio," where visitors could examine Karsh's aesthetic and technical decisions in sequence. See also Ioana Teodorescu, "Karsh: Image Maker / Créateur d'images," *Material Culture Review* 70 (Fall 2009): 82–87.

5 See "Introduction" by Jerry Fielder, Karsh's long-time colleague, assistant, and now director of the Karsh estate, in Mehmed Ali, *Yousuf Karsh & John Garo: The Search for a Master's Legacy* (Mansfield, MA: Benna Books, 2016).

6 Quote submitted by Hope Haire (née Wattsford) for inclusion in the 2009 major travelling exhibition *Karsh: Image Maker*, organized by the Portrait Gallery of Canada in collaboration with the Canada Science and Technology Museum.

7 Yousuf Karsh, *In Search of Greatness: Reflections of Yousuf Karsh* (Toronto: University of Toronto Press, 1962), 114.

8 William Lyon Mackenzie King, typescript entry from his diary, March 15, 1947, MG 26 J13, vol. 193, binder 76, William Lyon Mackenzie King Fonds, Library and Archives Canada, 217–18.

9 Maria Tippett, *The Life of Yousuf Karsh: Portrait in Light and Shadow* (Toronto: House of Anansi Press Inc., 2007), 234.

10 Karsh, *In Search of Greatness*, 103.

11 An excerpt of promotional text for Artvy, an AI art platform, states: "By using the Karsh style provided in the AI Art Style Library, Artvy will analyze your chosen photograph and apply the lighting techniques, composition principles, and emotional depth characteristic of Yousuf Karsh portraits."

Credits

Every effort has been made to secure permissions for all copyrighted material. The Art Canada Institute will gladly correct any errors or omissions.

The Art Canada Institute would like to thank the following for their assistance:

CREDITS FOR WORKS BY YOUSUF KARSH

Akira Kurosawa, November 1, 1969. Yousuf Karsh Fonds, Collection of Library and Archives Canada, Ottawa (R613-552-0-E, Box KAR 437, Item 3912344). Courtesy of Library and Archives Canada. © Museum of Fine Arts, Boston.

Albert Einstein, February 11, 1948. Collection of the Montreal Museum of Fine Arts, Gift of Estrellita Karsh in memory of Yousuf Karsh (2021.179). Courtesy of the Montreal Museum of Fine Arts. © Museum of Fine Arts, Boston.

Alfred Hitchcock, December 14, 1950. Courtesy of the Estate of Yousuf Karsh. © Museum of Fine Arts, Boston.

Ambassador Vijaya Lakshmi Pandit, October 2, 1949. Yousuf Karsh Fonds, Collection of Library and Archives Canada, Ottawa (R613-541-6-E, Box KAR 106, Item 3854738). Courtesy of Library and Archives Canada. © Museum of Fine Arts, Boston.

Andy Warhol, November 21, 1979. Collection of the Montreal Museum of Fine Arts, Gift of Estrellita Karsh in memory of Yousuf Karsh (2021.201). Courtesy of the Montreal Museum of Fine Arts. © Museum of Fine Arts, Boston.

Andy Warhol, November 21, 1979. Courtesy of the Estate of Yousuf Karsh. © Museum of Fine Arts, Boston.

Anita Ekberg, March 28, 1956. Yousuf Karsh Fonds, Collection of Library and Archives Canada, Ottawa (1987-054 NPC, e011916832). Courtesy of Library and Archives Canada. © Museum of Fine Arts, Boston.

Anna Magnani, May 1, 1958. Collection of the Montreal Museum of Fine Arts, Gift of Estrellita Karsh in memory of Yousuf Karsh (2021.194). Courtesy of the Montreal Museum of Fine Arts. © Museum of Fine Arts, Boston.

Ansel Adams, July 20, 1977. Courtesy of the Estate of Yousuf Karsh. © Museum of Fine Arts, Boston.

Apollo XI Crew, September 11, 1969. Courtesy of the Estate of Yousuf Karsh. © Museum of Fine Arts, Boston.

Audrey Hepburn, March 23, 1956. Courtesy of the Estate of Yousuf Karsh. © Museum of Fine Arts, Boston.

Barbara Ann Scott, November 26, 1946. Courtesy of the Estate of Yousuf Karsh. © Museum of Fine Arts, Boston.

Beatrice Lillie, March 18, 1948. Yousuf Karsh Fonds, Collection of Library and Archives Canada, Ottawa (R613-646-9-E, Box KAR 420, Item 3924878). Courtesy of Library and Archives Canada. © Museum of Fine Arts, Boston.

Bernard Madoff, October 3, 1988. Courtesy of the Estate of Yousuf Karsh. © Museum of Fine Arts, Boston.

Brigitte Bardot, May 1, 1958. Collection of the Montreal Museum of Fine Arts, Gift of Estrellita Karsh in memory of Yousuf Karsh (2021.207). Courtesy of the Montreal Museum of Fine Arts. © Museum of Fine Arts, Boston.

Bryan Adams, April 3, 1989. Courtesy of the Estate of Yousuf Karsh. © Museum of Fine Arts, Boston.

Canada's Governor General Lord Tweedsmuir and Prime Minister William Lyon Mackenzie King with American President Franklin Roosevelt and his son, James Roosevelt, August 14, 1936. Courtesy of the Estate of Yousuf Karsh. © Museum of Fine Arts, Boston.

Cecil B. DeMille, March 21, 1956. Courtesy of the Estate of Yousuf Karsh. © Museum of Fine Arts, Boston.

Christl Thalhammer, May 1965 (interpositive made from the original negative). Yousuf Karsh Fonds, Collection of Library and Archives Canada, Ottawa (R613-748-6-E, Box 196, 3991530). Courtesy of Library and Archives Canada. © Museum of Fine Arts, Boston.

Christl Thalhammer, May 1965 (red proof). Yousuf Karsh Fonds, Collection of Library and Archives Canada, Ottawa (R613-750-4- E, Box 196, Item 3991538). Courtesy of Library and Archives Canada. © Museum of Fine Arts, Boston.

Christopher Plummer, April 13, 1959. Yousuf Karsh Fonds, Collection of Library and Archives Canada, Ottawa (R613-546-5-E, Box KAR 451, Item 3855289). Courtesy of Library and Archives Canada. © Museum of Fine Arts, Boston.

City of Straws, 1940. Collection of the Montreal Museum of Fine Arts, Gift of Estrellita Karsh in memory of Yousuf Karsh (2021.266). Courtesy of the Montreal Museum of Fine Arts. © Museum of Fine Arts, Boston.

Daniel Makokis, Edmonton, 1952. CMCP Collection, Collection of the National Gallery of Canada, Ottawa, Purchased 1965 (65-8777). Courtesy of the National Gallery of Canada. © Museum of Fine Arts, Boston.
Douglas Cardinal, April 7, 1989. Courtesy of the Estate of Yousuf Karsh. © Museum of Fine Arts, Boston.
Douglas Cardinal, April 7, 1989. Yousuf Karsh Fonds, Collection of Library and Archives Canada, Ottawa (R613-445-X-E, Vol. 487, Item 3912452). Courtesy of Library and Archives Canada. © Museum of Fine Arts, Boston.
Duke and Duchess of Windsor, June 7, 1971. Courtesy of the Estate of Yousuf Karsh. © Museum of Fine Arts, Boston.
Early Landscape, 1926. Yousuf Karsh Fonds, Collection of Library and Archives Canada, Ottawa (1987-054 NPC, Item 3233044). Courtesy of Library and Archives Canada. © Museum of Fine Arts, Boston.
Early Portrait, 1929. Courtesy of the Estate of Yousuf Karsh. © Museum of Fine Arts, Boston.
Elixir, September 1938. Yousuf Karsh Fonds, Collection of Library and Archives Canada, Ottawa (R613-549-0- E, Box KAR 544, Item 3912309). Courtesy of Library and Archives Canada. © Museum of Fine Arts, Boston.
Elizabeth Taylor, February 14, 1946. Courtesy of the Estate of Yousuf Karsh. © Museum of Fine Arts, Boston.
Ernest Hemingway, March 15, 1957. Collection of the Montreal Museum of Fine Arts, Gift of Estrellita Karsh in memory of Yousuf Karsh (2021.181). Courtesy of the Montreal Museum of Fine Arts. © Museum of Fine Arts, Boston.
Estrellita Karsh, January 1, 1963. Collection of the Montreal Museum of Fine Arts, Gift of Estrellita Karsh in memory of Yousuf Karsh (2021.238). Courtesy of the Montreal Museum of Fine Arts. © Museum of Fine Arts, Boston.
Exterior view of 130 Sparks Street, renovated in 1936 into the Hardy Arcade, featuring Karsh's studio on the upper level, Ottawa, December 11, 1936. Yousuf Karsh Fonds, Collection of Library and Archives Canada, Ottawa (R613-529-5-E, Box 4/X1, Item 3845193). Courtesy of Library and Archives Canada. © Museum of Fine Arts, Boston.
Fidel Castro, August 1, 1971. Courtesy of the Estate of Yousuf Karsh. © Museum of Fine Arts, Boston.
George Bernard Shaw, September 12, 1943. Collection of the Montreal Museum of Fine Arts, Gift of Estrellita Karsh in memory of Yousuf Karsh (2021.187). Courtesy of the Montreal Museum of Fine Arts. © Museum of Fine Arts, Boston.
Georgia O'Keeffe, March 18, 1956. Collection of the Montreal Museum of Fine Arts, Gift of Estrellita Karsh in memory of Yousuf Karsh (2021.184). Courtesy of the Montreal Museum of Fine Arts. © Museum of Fine Arts, Boston.
Glenn Gould, February 21, 1957. Courtesy of the Estate of Yousuf Karsh. © Museum of Fine Arts, Boston.
Governor General Lord Tweedsmuir, John Buchan, Posed in His Honorary Chief Eagle Head Regalia, May 5, 1937. Yousuf Karsh Fonds, Collection of Library and Archives Canada, Ottawa (R613-590-8-E, Box KAR 646, Item 3916500). Courtesy of Library and Archives Canada. © Museum of Fine Arts, Boston.
Grey Owl (Archibald Belaney), February 27, 1936. Courtesy of the Estate of Yousuf Karsh. © Museum of Fine Arts, Boston.
Hands of Gratien Gélinas, March 29, 1945. Collection of the Montreal Museum of Fine Arts, Gift of Estrellita Karsh in memory of Yousuf Karsh (2021.229). Courtesy of the Montreal Museum of Fine Arts. © Museum of Fine Arts, Boston.
Helen Keller, March 8, 1948. Collection of the Montreal Museum of Fine Arts, Gift of Estrellita Karsh in memory of Yousuf Karsh (2021.241). Courtesy of the Montreal Museum of Fine Arts. © Museum of Fine Arts, Boston.
Hideki Yukawa, November 1, 1969. Courtesy of the Estate of Yousuf Karsh. © Museum of Fine Arts, Boston.
HRH Ibn Abdul Aziz (later King Faisal of Saudi Arabia), May 7, 1945. Courtesy of the Estate of Yousuf Karsh. © Museum of Fine Arts, Boston.
Igor Stravinsky, March 20, 1956. Courtesy of the Estate of Yousuf Karsh. © Museum of Fine Arts, Boston.
Ingrid Bergman, February 24, 1946. Collection of the Montreal Museum of Fine Arts, Gift of Estrellita Karsh in memory of Yousuf Karsh (2021.208). Courtesy of the Montreal Museum of Fine Arts. © Museum of Fine Arts, Boston.
Jacqueline Kennedy, June 14, 1957. Courtesy of the Estate of Yousuf Karsh. © Museum of Fine Arts, Boston.
Jacques Cousteau, January 22, 1972. Collection of the Montreal Museum of Fine Arts, Gift of Estrellita Karsh in memory of Yousuf Karsh (2021.178). Courtesy of the Montreal Museum of Fine Arts. © Museum of Fine Arts, Boston.

Jasper Johns, December 7, 1990. Courtesy of the Estate of Yousuf Karsh. © Museum of Fine Arts, Boston.
Jawaharlal Nehru, December 22, 1956. Courtesy of the Estate of Yousuf Karsh. © Museum of Fine Arts, Boston.
Jean-Paul Riopelle, Photographed in His Paris Atelier, April 7, 1965, printed 1987. Collection of the National Gallery of Canada, Ottawa, Gift of the artist, Ottawa, 1989 (30272). Courtesy of the National Gallery of Canada. © Museum of Fine Arts, Boston.
Jessye Norman, April 4, 1990. Courtesy of the Estate of Yousuf Karsh. Courtesy of the Museum of Fine Arts, Boston. © Museum of Fine Arts, Boston.
Jessye Norman, April 4, 1990. Courtesy of the Estate of Yousuf Karsh. Courtesy of the Museum of Fine Arts, Boston. © Museum of Fine Arts, Boston.
Johan Helders, August 12, 1936. Collection of the Montreal Museum of Fine Arts, Gift of Estrellita Karsh in memory of Yousuf Karsh (2021.233). Courtesy of the Montreal Museum of Fine Arts. © Museum of Fine Arts, Boston.
Karen Kain, July 1, 1977. Collection of the Montreal Museum of Fine Arts, Gift of Estrellita Karsh in memory of Yousuf Karsh (2021.237). Courtesy of the Montreal Museum of Fine Arts. © Museum of Fine Arts, Boston.
Kenojuak Ashevak, April 8, 1976. Collection of the Montreal Museum of Fine Arts, Gift of Estrellita Karsh in memory of Yousuf Karsh (2021.244). Courtesy of the Montreal Museum of Fine Arts. © Museum of Fine Arts, Boston.
King George VI, September 12, 1943. Courtesy of the Estate of Yousuf Karsh. © Museum of Fine Arts, Boston.
Lady Clark, with dog Angus, August 9, 1934. Yousuf Karsh Fonds, Collection of Library and Archives Canada, Ottawa (Box 1/X1, INT 010/X1, KAR 743, RV2 007, File 532, 3842242). Courtesy of Library and Archives Canada. © Museum of Fine Arts, Boston.
Lauren Bacall, March 27, 1957. Courtesy of the Estate of Yousuf Karsh. © Museum of Fine Arts, Boston.
Lenore Tawney, November 14, 1959. Courtesy of the Estate of Yousuf Karsh. © Museum of Fine Arts, Boston.
The Lesson, January 1, 1935. Courtesy of the Estate of Yousuf Karsh. © Museum of Fine Arts, Boston.
Lester B. Pearson, November 23, 1957. Yousuf Karsh Fonds, Collection of Library and Archives Canada, Ottawa (R613-453-9-E, Vol. 614, Item 3915639). Courtesy of Library and Archives Canada. © Museum of Fine Arts, Boston.
Lilly Koltun, August 10, 1987. Yousuf Karsh Fonds, Collection of Library and Archives Canada, Ottawa (R613-933-1-E, Item 5688232). Courtesy of Library and Archives Canada. © Museum of Fine Arts, Boston.
Lord Beaverbrook, September 12, 1943. Courtesy of the Estate of Yousuf Karsh. © Museum of Fine Arts, Boston.
Madame Chiang Kai-Shek, June 15, 1943. Courtesy of the Estate of Yousuf Karsh. © Museum of Fine Arts, Boston.
Madge Macbeth, August 3, 1936. Courtesy of the Estate of Yousuf Karsh. © Museum of Fine Arts, Boston.
Man Eating Lunch [Lawrence Heppler], Great Lakes Paper Company, Thunder Bay, c.1953. Yousuf Karsh Fonds, Collection of Library and Archives Canada, Ottawa (R613-883-1-E, Box KAR 663, 4193348). Courtesy of Library and Archives Canada. © Museum of Fine Arts, Boston.
Margaret Atwood, November 5, 1977. Yousuf Karsh Fonds, Collection of Library and Archives Canada, Ottawa (Box KAR 422, Item 4332282). Courtesy of Library and Archives Canada. © Museum of Fine Arts, Boston.
Marian Anderson, December 9, 1945. Courtesy of the Estate of Yousuf Karsh. © Museum of Fine Arts, Boston.
Marshall McLuhan, April 6, 1974. Courtesy of the Estate of Yousuf Karsh. © Museum of Fine Arts, Boston.
Martha Graham, February 13, 1948. Courtesy of the Estate of Yousuf Karsh. © Museum of Fine Arts, Boston.
Martin Luther King, Jr., August 18, 1962. Yousuf Karsh Fonds, Collection of Library and Archives Canada, Ottawa (R613-418-7-E, Vol. 613, Item 3845172). Courtesy of Library and Archives Canada. © Museum of Fine Arts, Boston.
Master Michel Pharand, March 19, 1937. Yousuf Karsh Fonds, Collection of Library and Archives Canada, Ottawa (R613-556-8-E, Box RV2 123, Item 3912418). Courtesy of Library and Archives Canada. © Museum of Fine Arts, Boston.
Mrs. Norman Armour, March 18, 1937. Yousuf Karsh Fonds, Collection of Library and Archives Canada, Ottawa (Box RV2 123, Item 4332211). Courtesy of Library and Archives Canada. © Museum of Fine Arts, Boston.
Muhammad Ali, March 27, 1970. Collection of the Montreal Museum of Fine Arts, Gift of Estrellita Karsh in memory of Yousuf Karsh (2021.174). Courtesy of the Montreal Museum of Fine Arts. © Museum of Fine Arts, Boston.
Nelson Mandela, June 17, 1990. Courtesy of the Estate of Yousuf Karsh. © Museum of Fine Arts, Boston.

Official Portrait of Sir Vere Brabazon Ponsonby, Ninth Earl of Bessborough, Governor General of Canada from 1931 to 1935 and His Wife Roberte Ponsonby (Born Neuflize), Countess Bessborough, March 19, 1935. Yousuf Karsh Fonds, Collection of Library and Archives Canada, Ottawa (R3884-10-0-E, Box C 0494, Item 3194977). Courtesy of Library and Archives Canada. © Museum of Fine Arts, Boston.
Pablo Casals, June 30, 1954. Collection of the Montreal Museum of Fine Arts, Gift of Estrellita Karsh in memory of Yousuf Karsh (2021.175). Courtesy of the Montreal Museum of Fine Arts. © Museum of Fine Arts, Boston.
Pablo Picasso, July 2, 1954. Collection of the Montreal Museum of Fine Arts, Gift of Estrellita Karsh in memory of Yousuf Karsh (2021.185). Courtesy of the Montreal Museum of Fine Arts. © Museum of Fine Arts, Boston.
Paul Robeson, October 30, 1941. Courtesy of the Estate of Yousuf Karsh. © Museum of Fine Arts, Boston.
Peter Lorre, February 3, 1946. Courtesy of the Estate of Yousuf Karsh. © Museum of Fine Arts, Boston.
Pierre Elliott Trudeau, November 4, 1968. Collection of the Montreal Museum of Fine Arts, Gift of Estrellita Karsh in memory of Yousuf Karsh (2021.277). Courtesy of the Montreal Museum of Fine Arts. © Museum of Fine Arts, Boston.
Pope Pius XII, June 16, 1949. Yousuf Karsh Fonds, Collection of Library and Archives Canada, Ottawa (3195224). Courtesy of Library and Archives Canada. © Museum of Fine Arts, Boston.
President Dwight Eisenhower, July 20, 1966. Yousuf Karsh Fonds, Collection of Library and Archives Canada, Ottawa (3222431). Courtesy of Library and Archives Canada. © Museum of Fine Arts, Boston.
Prince Rainier III and Princess Grace of Monaco, September 22, 1956. Yousuf Karsh Fonds, Collection of Library and Archives Canada, Ottawa (PA-212509). Courtesy of the Estate of Yousuf Karsh. © Museum of Fine Arts, Boston.
Princess Elizabeth, November 1, 1943. Yousuf Karsh Fonds, Collection of Library and Archives Canada, Ottawa (R613-740-1-E, Vol. 652, Item 3988607). Courtesy of Library and Archives Canada. © Museum of Fine Arts, Boston.
Princess Elizabeth, July 30, 1951. Courtesy of the Estate of Yousuf Karsh. © Museum of Fine Arts, Boston.
Production image from *Submerged*, Dominion Drama Festival, Ottawa, April 27, 1934. Yousuf Karsh Fonds, Collection of Library and Archives Canada, Ottawa (R613-739-5-E, Box: 1/X1, INT 010/X1, KAR 743, RV2 003, File 401, Item 3836745). Courtesy of Library and Archives Canada.
Queen Elizabeth and Prince Philip, August 2, 1966. Courtesy of the Estate of Yousuf Karsh. © Museum of Fine Arts, Boston.
Robert Oppenheimer, February 9, 1956. Collection of the Museum of Fine Arts, Boston, Gift of Estrellita and Yousuf Karsh, September 1998 (1998.373). Courtesy of the Museum of Fine Arts, Boston. © Museum of Fine Arts, Boston.
Roppeita Kita, with Grandson Nagayo Kita, November 1, 1969. Courtesy of the Estate of Yousuf Karsh. © Museum of Fine Arts, Boston.
Ruth Draper, November 25, 1936, printed 1989. Collection of the National Gallery of Canada, Ottawa, Gift of the artist, Ottawa, 1997 (38508). Courtesy of the National Gallery of Canada. © Museum of Fine Arts, Boston.
Saint John, New Brunswick, 1952, printed 1989. Collection of the National Gallery of Canada, Ottawa, Gift of the artist, Ottawa, 1997 (38510). Courtesy of the National Gallery of Canada. © Museum of Fine Arts, Boston.
Self-Portrait, September 1938. Yousuf Karsh Fonds, Collection of Library and Archives Canada, Ottawa (R613- 718-8-E, Vol. 6, Item 3821081). Courtesy of Library and Archives Canada. © Museum of Fine Arts, Boston.
Self-Portrait, 1939. Yousuf Karsh Fonds, Collection of Library and Archives Canada, Ottawa (R613-543-X-E, Box 7/X1, Item 3854753). Courtesy of Library and Archives Canada. © Museum of Fine Arts, Boston.
Self-Portrait, 1956. Yousuf Karsh Fonds, Collection of Library and Archives Canada, Ottawa (3198648). Courtesy of Library and Archives Canada. © Museum of Fine Arts, Boston.
Self-Portrait with Jim Henson and Kermit the Frog, 1990. Courtesy of the Estate of Yousuf Karsh. © Museum of Fine Arts, Boston.
Shirley Lake, June 5, 1937. Yousuf Karsh Fonds, Collection of Library and Archives Canada, Ottawa (R613-433-3-E, Vol. 467, Item 3852557). Courtesy of Library and Archives Canada. © Museum of Fine Arts, Boston.

Sikh Workers at Logging Camp, British Columbia, 1953. Courtesy of the Estate of Yousuf Karsh. © Museum of Fine Arts, Boston.
Sir Edmund Hillary, January 30, 1960. Courtesy of the Estate of Yousuf Karsh. Courtesy of the Estate of Yousuf Karsh. © Museum of Fine Arts, Boston.
Sir Winston Churchill, December 30, 1941, printed before 1972. Collection of the Art Gallery of Alberta, Edmonton, Gift of Nancy Tousley Cameron in memory of Duncan F. Cameron (2016.15). Courtesy of the Art Gallery of Alberta. © Museum of Fine Arts, Boston.
Sir Winston Churchill, December 30, 1941. Courtesy of the Estate of Yousuf Karsh. © Museum of Fine Arts, Boston.
Solange Gauthier, June 14, 1935. Courtesy of the Estate of Yousuf Karsh. © Museum of Fine Arts, Boston.
Solange Gauthier posing with a stuffed dog in preparation for a portrait sitting with Lady Anne Elizabeth Clark, about August 9, 1934. Yousuf Karsh Fonds, Collection of Library and Archives Canada, Ottawa (Box 1/X1, INT 010/X1, KAR 743, RV2 007, File 532, 3842242). Courtesy of Library and Archives Canada. © Museum of Fine Arts, Boston.
Sophia Loren, March 12, 1981. Courtesy of the Estate of Yousuf Karsh. © Museum of Fine Arts, Boston.
Thomas J. Watson, January 28, 1948. Courtesy of the Estate of Yousuf Karsh. © Museum of Fine Arts, Boston.
Unidentified, Foundry, 1951. Collection of Art Windsor-Essex, Windsor, Ontario, Gift of the Ford Motor Company of Canada, Limited, 2013 (2013.019). Courtesy of Art Windsor-Essex. © Museum of Fine Arts, Boston.
Walt Disney, March 20, 1954. Courtesy of the Estate of Yousuf Karsh. © Museum of Fine Arts, Boston.
William Lyon Mackenzie King and Winston Churchill, December 30, 1941. Courtesy of the Estate of Yousuf Karsh. © Museum of Fine Arts, Boston.
Woman in a Turban (Betty Low), 1936. Courtesy of the Estate of Yousuf Karsh. © Museum of Fine Arts, Boston.

CREDITS FOR PHOTOGRAPHS AND WORKS BY OTHER ARTISTS:

The 8 x 10 bellows Calumet, Yousuf Karsh's main camera, draped with a focusing cloth made for Karsh by his assistant and librarian, Hella Graber. Ingenium—Canada's Museums of Science and Innovation, Collection of the Canada Science and Technology Museum, Ottawa (1997.0319, 1997.0351). Courtesy of Ingenium, Ottawa. Photo credit: Ingenium.
48 Views of Yousuf Karsh, 1981–83, by Arnaud Maggs. Courtesy of Stephen Bulger Gallery. © Arnaud Maggs, The Estate of Arnaud Maggs.
Cover of *Faces of Destiny*, by Yousuf Karsh (Chicago: Ziff-Davis Publishing, 1946).
Cover of *Faces of Our Time*, by Yousuf Karsh (Toronto: University of Toronto Press, 1971).
Cover of *In Search of Greatness: Reflections of Yousuf Karsh*, by Yousuf Karsh (Toronto: University of Toronto Press, 1962).
Cover of *Karsh: American Legends*, by Yousuf Karsh (Boston: Bulfinch Press, 1992).
Cover of *Karsh: A Sixty-Year Retrospective*, by Yousuf Karsh (Boston and Toronto: Little, Brown and Company, 1996).
Cover of *Karsh Canadians*, by Yousuf Karsh (Toronto: University of Toronto Press, 1978). Private collection. Courtesy of Cowley Abbott, Toronto.
Cover of *Karsh Portfolio*, by Yousuf Karsh (Toronto: University of Toronto Press, 1967).
Cover of *Karsh Portraits*, by Yousuf Karsh (Toronto: University of Toronto Press, 1976).
Cover of *LIFE*, May 21, 1945. Courtesy of the Estate of Yousuf Karsh.
Cover of *Portraits of Greatness*, by Yousuf Karsh (Toronto: University of Toronto Press, 1959).
Cover of *Saturday Night*, January 10, 1942. Collection of the University of Wisconsin–Madison Libraries. Courtesy of the University of Wisconsin–Madison Libraries. Photo credit: University of Wisconsin–Madison Libraries.
Cover of *Saturday Night*, November 25, 1944. Collection of the University of Wisconsin–Madison Libraries. Courtesy of the University of Wisconsin–Madison Libraries. Photo credit: University of Wisconsin–Madison Libraries.
Cover of *This Is Newfoundland*, edited by Ewart Young with portraits by Yousuf Karsh (Toronto, Halifax, and Vancouver: The Ryerson Press, 1949).

Cover of *Yousuf Karsh & John Fisher See Canada*, written by John Fisher, illustrated by Yousuf Karsh (Toronto: Thomas Allen, 1960).

Cover of *Yousuf Karsh & John Garo: The Search for a Master's Legacy*, by Mehmed Ali (Mansfield, MA: Benna Books, 2016).

Cover of *Yousuf Karsh: Industrial Images*, by Cassandra Getty and Jerry Fielder (Windsor, ON: Art Gallery of Windsor, 2007). Courtesy of Art Windsor-Essex, Windsor, Ontario.

Declaration of Passenger to Canada, December 31, 1924. Department of Employment and Immigration fonds, Library and Archives Canada, Ottawa (Ocean Arrivals, Form 30A, 1919-1924, Reel T-15085, Page 267). Courtesy of Library and Archives Canada. © Government of Canada. Reproduced with the permission of Library and Archives Canada (2025).

Delphic Sibyl (detail from the Sistine Chapel ceiling), 1508–12, by Michelangelo. Collection of the Vatican Museums, Vatican City. Courtesy of Wikimedia Commons.

Donald Sutherland, 1983, by Robert Mapplethorpe. Private collection. Courtesy of Olga Korper Gallery, Toronto. © Robert Mapplethorpe Foundation. Used by permission.

Eastman Kodak Company's No. 2 Brownie Model D camera with Brownie character box, 1914. Collection of the George Eastman Museum, Rochester, New York, Gift of Frederick W. Randall (1988.0583.0001). Courtesy of the George Eastman Museum.

Estrellita and Yousuf Karsh at the pre–Carnation Ball event held at the Waldorf-Astoria Hotel, New York, April 26, 1972. Photographer unknown. Getty Images, Fairchild Archive / WWD / Penske Media (1469099373). Courtesy of Getty Images.

Estrellita and Yousuf Karsh during a portrait session with Thomas Hoving, April 17, 1967. Photograph by Ivan Dmitri. Yousuf Karsh Fonds, Collection of Library and Archives Canada, Ottawa (R613-567-2-E, Box KAR 653, 3916009). Courtesy of Library and Archives Canada. © Estate of Dmitri Ivan.

Fidel Castro, 2001, by Hiroshi Sugimoto. Courtesy of Fraenkel Gallery, San Francisco. © Hiroshi Sugimoto, courtesy Fraenkel Gallery, San Francisco and Lisson Gallery.

First-day cover of the Canadian postage stamps featuring Yousuf Karsh's *Princess Elizabeth*, July 30, 1951; May 1, 1953. Elizabeth Hutchinson Collection, Collection of the Library and Archives Canada, Ottawa (2261146). Courtesy of Library and Archives Canada. Postage stamps © Canada Post Corporation, 1951. Reproduced with permission. © Museum of Fine Arts, Boston.

Horace Silver, Newport Jazz Festival, Rhode Island, c.1954–57, by Lisette Model. Collection of the National Gallery of Canada, Ottawa, Gift of the Estate of Lisette Model, 1990, by direction of Joseph G. Blum, New York, through the American Friends of Canada (35315). Courtesy of the National Gallery of Canada. © Lisette Model Foundation, Inc.

James Stanley, Lord Strange, Later Seventh Earl of Derby, with His Wife, Charlotte, and Their Daughter, c.1636, by Anthony van Dyck. The Frick Collection, New York, Henry Clay Frick Bequest (1913.1.40). Courtesy of The Frick Collection.

Karsh's Finishing Pencils, 2024, by Christine Fitzgerald. Courtesy of Christine Fitzgerald. © Christine Fitzgerald.

Laurente Torno, 1927, by John H. Garo. Collection of the Harvard Art Museums / Fogg Museum, Cambridge, Massachusetts, Transfer from the Carpenter Center for the Visual Arts (2.2002.830). Courtesy of the Harvard Art Museums / Fogg Museum. Photo credit: © President and Fellows of Harvard College.

Page from Yousuf Karsh's photo essay "Karsh's Edmonton: The Threshold of the Frontier," featured in the December 15, 1952, issue of *Maclean's* magazine.

Paul Revere, 1768, by John Singleton Copley. Collection of the Museum of Fine Arts, Boston, Gift of Joseph W. Revere, William B. Revere, and Edward H.R. Revere, December 4, 1930 (30.781). Courtesy of the Museum of Fine Arts, Boston.

Pier 2, the Deep Water Terminals, Halifax, c.1928. Photograph by W.R. MacAskill. Nova Scotia Archives, Halifax (1987-453 number 2625). Courtesy of the Nova Scotia Archives.

Portrait of Fräulein Lieser, c.1917, by Gustav Klimt. Private collection. Courtesy of im Kinsky, Vienna.

Portrait of members of Alexander First Nation (including Chief Alexis Arcand and Councillor Mark Bruno) standing in front of Ration House, Calgary, c.1918. Photographer unknown. Department of Indian Affairs and Northern Development Fonds, Collection of Library and Archives Canada, Ottawa (R216, RG10, Box 3678, Item 5316241). Courtesy of Library and Archives Canada. © Government of Canada.

Portrait of Yousuf Karsh at age twenty-two with John Garo, 1930. Photographer unknown. Courtesy of the Estate of Yousuf Karsh.

Poster for Festival Karsh, organized by the Portrait Gallery of Canada (as part of Library and Archives Canada, Ottawa) and the Canada Science and Technology Museum, Ottawa, June 12 to September 13, 2009. Courtesy of Collection of Things, Ottawa.

Queen Elizabeth II of the United Kingdom, from the series Reigning Queens, 1985, by Andy Warhol, printed by Rupert Jasen Smith, New York, published by George C.P. Mulder, Amsterdam. Private collection. Courtesy of Cowley Abbott, Toronto. © 2025 The Andy Warhol Foundation for the Visual Arts, Inc. / Licensed by Artists Rights Society (ARS), NY / CARCC Ottawa.

Solange Karsh interviewing French architect Le Corbusier during a Yousuf Karsh portrait shoot in Europe, 1954. Photograph by Peter Miller. Getty Images, Michael Ochs Archives (1178098433). Courtesy of Getty Images. © Peter Miller.

Thelma, 2017, by Catherine Opie. Courtesy of Lehmann Maupin, New York, Seoul, and London. © Catherine Opie.

Yousuf and Estrellita Karsh with Jerry Fielder, Santa Barbara, 1985. Photographer unknown. Courtesy of the Estate of Yousuf Karsh.

Yousuf Karsh and his long-time master printer, Ignas Gabalis, inspecting a print of Anita Ekberg, 1957. Photograph by Chris Lund. National Film Board of Canada Fonds, Collection of Library and Archives Canada, Ottawa (1971-271 NPC, Box 75, Item 4949270). Courtesy of Library and Archives Canada.

Yousuf Karsh and Joyce Large at the Karsh Studio, 1957. Photograph by Chris Lund. National Film Board of Canada Fonds, Collection of Library and Archives Canada, Ottawa (4949269). Courtesy of Library and Archives Canada.

Yousuf Karsh and librarian/technician Hella Graber retrieving a filed negative at the Karsh Studio in Ottawa, February 26, 1958. Photograph by The Blade/Tom O'Reilly. Yousuf Karsh Fonds, Collection of Library and Archives Canada, Ottawa (R613-580-5-E, Box KAR 654, Item 3916430). Courtesy of Library and Archives Canada. © The Blade.

Yousuf Karsh at age eighteen in a family portrait, c.1926. Photograph by George Nakash. Senator Raymond Setlakwe Collection, Collection of Library and Archives Canada, Ottawa (R12521-1-2-E, Vol. 1, Box 2003- 0284, Item 3608293). Courtesy of Library and Archives Canada.

Yousuf Karsh at Expo 67, Montreal, 1967. Photograph by Sam Tata. Sam Tata Fonds, Collection of Library and Archives Canada, Ottawa (3602958). Courtesy of Library and Archives Canada. © Sam Tata.

Yousuf Karsh at the University of British Columbia's new gym, taken for *Maclean's* magazine, Vancouver, May 24, 1952. Photograph by Solange Karsh. Yousuf Karsh Fonds, Collection of Library and Archives Canada, Ottawa (R613-843-0-E, Box number: KAR 658, Item 3994721). Courtesy of Library and Archives Canada. © Estate of Solange Karsh.

Yousuf Karsh in-studio with sitter Leonard Brockington, January 12, 1945. Photograph by Eric Schaal. Yousuf Karsh Fonds, Collection of Library and Archives Canada, Ottawa (3613575). Courtesy of Library and Archives Canada.

Yousuf Karsh in the doorway of his studio at the Château Laurier, Ottawa, 1998. Photograph by George Pimentel. Getty Images, WireImage (529832). Courtesy of Getty Images. © George Pimentel.

Yousuf Karsh leaving Canada House, London, 1943. Photograph by Pictorial Press. Yousuf Karsh Fonds, Collection of Library and Archives Canada, Ottawa (R613-1013-8-E, Box 1B DAP-10A-3, Item 3574000). Courtesy of Library and Archives Canada.

Yousuf Karsh relaxing with Ansel Adams during the Yosemite Photo Workshop, Yosemite National Park, California, June 1977. Photograph attributed to Craig McFarland. Courtesy of the Estate of Yousuf Karsh.

Yousuf Karsh's appointment calendar noting Shirley Lake's eleven o'clock sitting on Saturday, June 5, 1937. Yousuf Karsh Fonds, Collection of Library and Archives Canada, Ottawa (R613-524-6-E, Vol. 150, Item 3948397). Courtesy of Library and Archives Canada. © Museum of Fine Arts, Boston.

Yousuf Karsh with his brother Malak Karsh, Ottawa, 1940s. Photographer unknown. Courtesy of the Estate of Yousuf Karsh.

Yousuf Karsh with his parents, Abel al-Massih and Bahiyah Karsh, c.1948. Photographer unknown. Yousuf Karsh Fonds, Collection of Library and Archives Canada, Ottawa (R613-828-4-E, Box KAR 657, Item 3994516). Courtesy of Library and Archives Canada.

Acknowledgements

Yousuf Karsh: Life & Work was made possible thanks to the generous sponsorship of Power Corporation of Canada, Season Sponsor, 2025–2026 Publications; Tim and Frances Price, Title Sponsor; David Binet, Gold Sponsor; Jason Donville, Bronze Sponsor; and The Karsh Center at the Museum of Fine Arts, Boston, Print Sponsor.

From the Author

Sparkling comet Yousuf Karsh zoomed past me as a child in 1968: he arrived in my hometown, Sackville, New Brunswick, to receive a doctorate from Mount Allison University. My father, Luke Rombout, then fine arts professor and curator of the Owens Art Gallery, was in attendance. Years later, as a photography specialist at Library and Archives Canada (LAC), I met Yousuf and his wife Estrellita Karsh on occasion to discuss his collection as they held court at the Château Laurier, an experience both thrilling and daunting.

I wish to extend my gratitude to my former director and mentor, the late Dr. Lilly Koltun, who entrusted to me deeper examination of LAC's massive Karsh Fonds. Her closest friend, also my friend and colleague, Dr. Joan M. Schwartz, encouraged me to write for the Art Canada Institute's (ACI) Canadian Online Art Book Project. At last, those boxes of long-preserved research notes found their purpose.

I am deeply appreciative to my dear Karsh colleague and friend, Jerry Fielder, curator and director of the Karsh Estate. Since Karsh's passing in 2002, Jerry and I have discussed how new forms of photography, the production of identity, and the ever-expanding circulation of images intersect with Karsh's own portrait practice. Across the years, spending time with keen-witted Estrellita Karsh was both scary and fun, and I am saddened by her passing just as this manuscript neared completion. Jerry's colleague, Julie Grahame, reviewed the manuscript and provided key images for publication.

LAC archivist Lisandra Cortina de la Noval located needles in the Karsh haystack and shared insights on cultural identity in Karsh's *Maclean's* Canadian Cities images. Several libraries made first editions of Karsh's publications available for study: Carleton, Concordia and Queen's universities and public libraries in Boston, Halifax, Hamilton and Kingston.

ACI's Executive Director, Sara Angel, lent her enthusiastic support, and Commissioning Editor Victoria Nolte steered the manuscript's development, taming instances of my beloved Long Sentence. ACI peer reviewers' thoughtful feedback also strengthened this work, and Stephen Gregory's elegant graphic design made it beautiful to read.

My friend Kate Laing's incisive comments on drafts sharpened my clarity, as did her trenchant marginalia: "Really, Karsh, ready to photograph Churchill, leader of the Allied command, anxious about meeting Margaret Atwood, feminist?" Along the way, I was bolstered by Dr. Joyce Harris, artist Catherine Feraday Miller (OCAD University), artist and Karsh Award laureate Christine Fitzgerald, Dr. Margaret Hanni, and my amazing partner, fellow displaced Maritimer and principal mirth-maker, Lorin Russell.

To everyone above, my heartfelt thanks. It has been a happy surprise to craft this contribution to the legacy of Yousuf Karsh. I would still be filling research boxes without your encouragement.

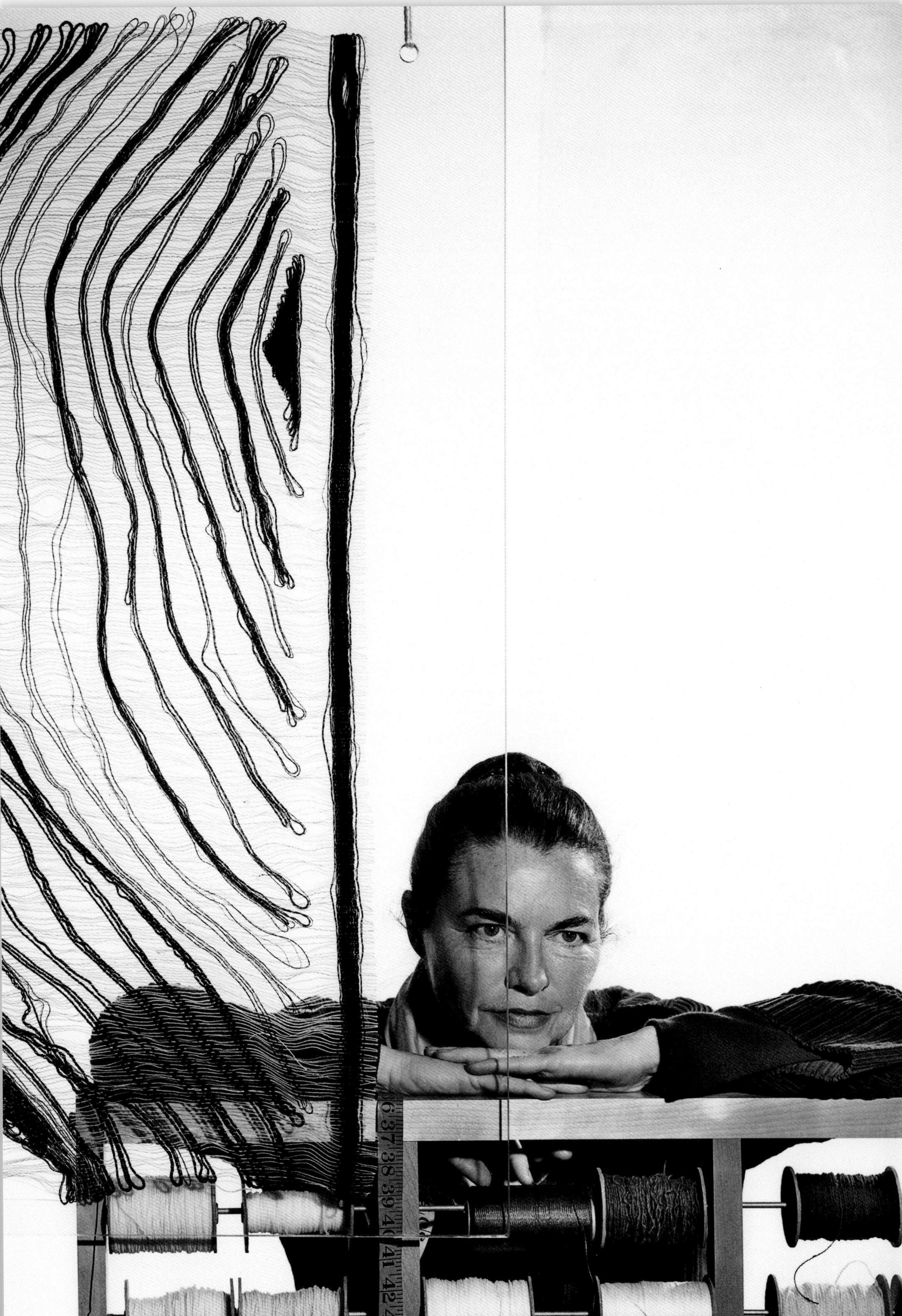

About the Author

"The world of Yousuf Karsh and the people he photographed belong now to history, their critical influence no longer familiar to emerging artmakers and art audiences; for me, it is an exciting moment to start new discussions about Karsh's artistic choices in the context of image making and image sharing, practices of our present time, and critically, the role of the portrait in the contemporary social space."

Melissa Rombout is an independent curator and lecturer on histories of photography. She received her PhD from the Amsterdam School for Cultural Analysis for considering the political performativity of historical and contemporary photographic collage. Active as an advisor for arts administration and museum planning projects, Rombout has had a prolific consulting career working with public agencies, museums, libraries, and archives in Canada and internationally, including the Department of Canadian Heritage, Royal Ontario Museum, Canadian War Museum, Global Affairs Canada Visual Art Collection, city of Ottawa, and U.S. National Park Service.

In her earlier role as photo-archivist at Library and Archives Canada, Rombout specialized in researching the vast Yousuf Karsh archive and has since curated several Karsh exhibitions organized in Ottawa, London, and Canberra, including the major 2009 travelling exhibition *Karsh: Image Maker*, organized by the Portrait Gallery of Canada in collaboration with the Canada Science and Technology Museum. Rombout's current research focuses on collaborative practices between artists and scientists in fostering environmental advocacy and the resurgence of "extinct" photographic technologies as medium and metaphor in addressing eco-anxiety. An avid "wild swimmer," Rombout divides her time between the waters of Lake Ontario near Kingston and the East Coast.

Opposite: Yousuf Karsh, *Lenore Tawney* (detail), November 14, 1959, gelatin silver print, 39.4 x 49.2 cm (image), 55.9 x 63.5 cm (mount), Estate of Yousuf Karsh.

Yousuf Karsh
Life & Work

This book is part of the Canadian Art Library Series, published by the Art Canada Institute.

Cover images: (clockwise from top right) Yousuf Karsh, *Self-Portrait*, September 1938, gelatin silver print, 23.4 x 15.7 cm (image), 25.1 x 16.8 cm (support), Yousuf Karsh Fonds, Library and Archives Canada, Ottawa; Yousuf Karsh, *Audrey Hepburn*, March 23, 1956, Estate of Yousuf Karsh; Yousuf Karsh, *Winston Churchill*, December 30, 1941, printed before 1972; gelatin silver print, 50 x 39.7 cm, Art Gallery of Alberta, Edmonton.
Half title image: Yousuf Karsh, *Self-Portrait* (detail), 1939, gelatin silver print, 15.3 x 10.5 (image), 20.7 x 12.8 cm (sheet), Yousuf Karsh Fonds, Library and Archives Canada, Ottawa.
Page 2 and 3: Yousuf Karsh, *Brigitte Bardot* (detail), May 1, 1958, Montreal Museum of Fine Arts; Yousuf Karsh, *Nelson Mandela* (detail), June 17, 1990, Estate of Yousuf Karsh.
Page 4 and 5: Yousuf Karsh, *Bryan Adams* (detail), April 3, 1989, gelatin silver print, 34.5 x 26.8 cm (image), 35.4 x 27.6 cm (support), Estate of Yousuf Karsh; Yousuf Karsh, *Helen Keller* (detail), March 8, 1948, gelatin silver print, 43.1 x 35.4 cm, Montreal Museum of Fine Arts.
Page 6 and 7: Yousuf Karsh, *Margaret Atwood* (detail), November 5, 1977, gelatin silver print, 23.8 x 17.4 cm (image), 27.4 x 17.4 cm (sheet), Yousuf Karsh Fonds, Library and Archives Canada, Ottawa; Yousuf Karsh, *Pablo Picasso* (detail), July 2, 1954, gelatin silver print, 60.1 x 50 cm, Montreal Museum of Fine Arts.
Page 8 and 9: Yousuf Karsh, *Walt Disney* (detail), March 20, 1954, gelatin silver print, 49.6 x 39.6 cm (image), 71.2 x 56 cm (mount), Estate of Yousuf Karsh; Yousuf Karsh, *Barbara Ann Scott* (detail), November 26, 1946, Estate of Yousuf Karsh.
Page 10 and 11: Yousuf Karsh, *Jacques Cousteau* (detail), January 22, 1972, gelatin silver print, 60.3 x 50.4 cm, Montreal Museum of Fine Arts; Yousuf Karsh, *Jessye Norman* (detail), April 4, 1990, gelatin silver print, 60 x 45 cm (image), 76.3 x 61 cm (mount), Estate of Yousuf Karsh.
Page 12 and 13: Yousuf Karsh, *Thomas J. Watson* (detail), January 28, 1948, gelatin silver print, Estate of Yousuf Karsh; Yousuf Karsh, *Martha Graham* (detail), 1948, gelatin silver print, 58.7 x 48.7 cm, Estate of Yousuf Karsh.
Title page: Yousuf Karsh, *Self-Portrait* (detail), 1939, gelatin silver print, 23.4 x 15.7 cm (image), 25.1 x 16.8 cm (support), Yousuf Karsh Fonds, Library and Archives Canada, Ottawa.
Page 17: Yousuf Karsh at the University of British Columbia's new gym, taken for *Maclean's* magazine, Vancouver, May 24, 1952, photograph by Solange Karsh, Yousuf Karsh Fonds, Library and Archives Canada, Ottawa.
Contents page: Arnaud Maggs, *48 Views of Yousuf Karsh* (detail), 1981–83, gelatin silver contact print, 40.6 x 50.8 cm, Stephen Bulger Gallery, Toronto.
Back cover images: (clockwise from top left) Yousuf Karsh, *Ernest Hemingway*, March 15, 1957, gelatin silver print, 60.3 x 50.5 cm, Montreal Museum of Fine Arts; Yousuf Karsh, *Jessye Norman*, April 4, 1990, chromogenic print, 101.6 x 76.2 cm (image), 121.9 x 90.5 cm (sheet), Estate of Yousuf Karsh; Yousuf Karsh, *Pierre Elliott Trudeau*, November 4, 1968, gelatin silver print, 43 x 35.5 cm, Montreal Museum of Fine Arts; Yousuf Karsh, *Margaret Atwood*, November 5, 1977, gelatin silver print, 23.8 x 17.4 cm (image), 27.4 x 17.4 cm (sheet), Yousuf Karsh Fonds, Library and Archives Canada, Ottawa.

Art Canada Institute
Massey College, University of Toronto
4 Devonshire Place
Toronto, ON M5S 2E1

Library and Archives Canada Cataloguing in Publication

Title: Yousuf Karsh : life & work / by Melissa Rombout. Names: Rombout, Melissa, author | Container of (work): Karsh, Yousuf, 1908-2002. Photographs. Selections. | Art Canada Institute, publisher.
Description: Includes bibliographical references.
Identifiers: Canadiana (print) 20250265060 | Canadiana (ebook) 20250163004 | ISBN 9781487103781 (hardcover) | ISBN 9781487103699 (HTML) | ISBN 9781487103712 (PDF)
Subjects: LCSH: Karsh, Yousuf, 1908-2002. | LCSH: Karsh, Yousuf, 1908-2002—Criticism and interpretation. | LCSH: Portrait photographers—Canada—Biography. | LCGFT: Biographies.
Classification: LCC TR140.K3 R66 2025 | DDC 779/.2092—dc23